尾田栄一郎

Puppies ♡ Birdies ♡ Piggies ♡
Isn't it cute when you call little things "-ies"?
Bunnies, kitties, horsies, koalies, Columbies,
teddies, zebries, Copernicies, Kobayashies...
Get ready, because adorable little volume 72
is about to startsies!!

-Eiichiro Oda, 2013

iichiro Oda began his manga career at the age of
17, when his one-shot cowboy manga **Wanted!**
won second place in the coveted Tezuka manga
awards. Oda went on to work as an assistant to
some of the biggest manga artists in the industry,
including Nobuhiro Watsuki, before winning the
Hop Step Award for new artists. His pirate
adventure **One Piece**, which debuted in
Weekly Shonen Jump in 1997, quickly became
one of the most popular manga in Japan.

ONE PIECE VOL. 72
NEW WORLD PART 12

SHONEN JUMP Manga Edition

STORY AND ART BY EIICHIRO ODA

Translation/Stephen Paul
Touch-up Art & Lettering/Vanessa Satone
Design/Fawn Lau
Editor/Alexis Kirsch

ONE PIECE © 1997 by Eiichiro Oda. All rights reserved.
First published in Japan in 1997 by SHUEISHA Inc., Tokyo.
English translation rights arranged by SHUEISHA Inc.

The stories, characters and incidents mentioned
in this publication are entirely fictional.

No portion of this book may be reproduced or
transmitted in any form or by any means without
written permission from the copyright holders.

Printed in the U.S.A.

Published by VIZ Media, LLC
P.O. Box 77010
San Francisco, CA 94107

10 9 8 7 6 5 4 3 2 1
First printing, September 2014

www.viz.com

RATED **T** FOR TEEN

PARENTAL ADVISORY
ONE PIECE is rated T for Teen and is recommended
for ages 13 and up. This volume contains fantasy
violence and tobacco usage.

ratings.viz.com

THE WORLD'S
MOST POPULAR MANGA
SHONEN JUMP
www.shonenjump.com

SHONEN JUMP MANGA

ONE PIECE

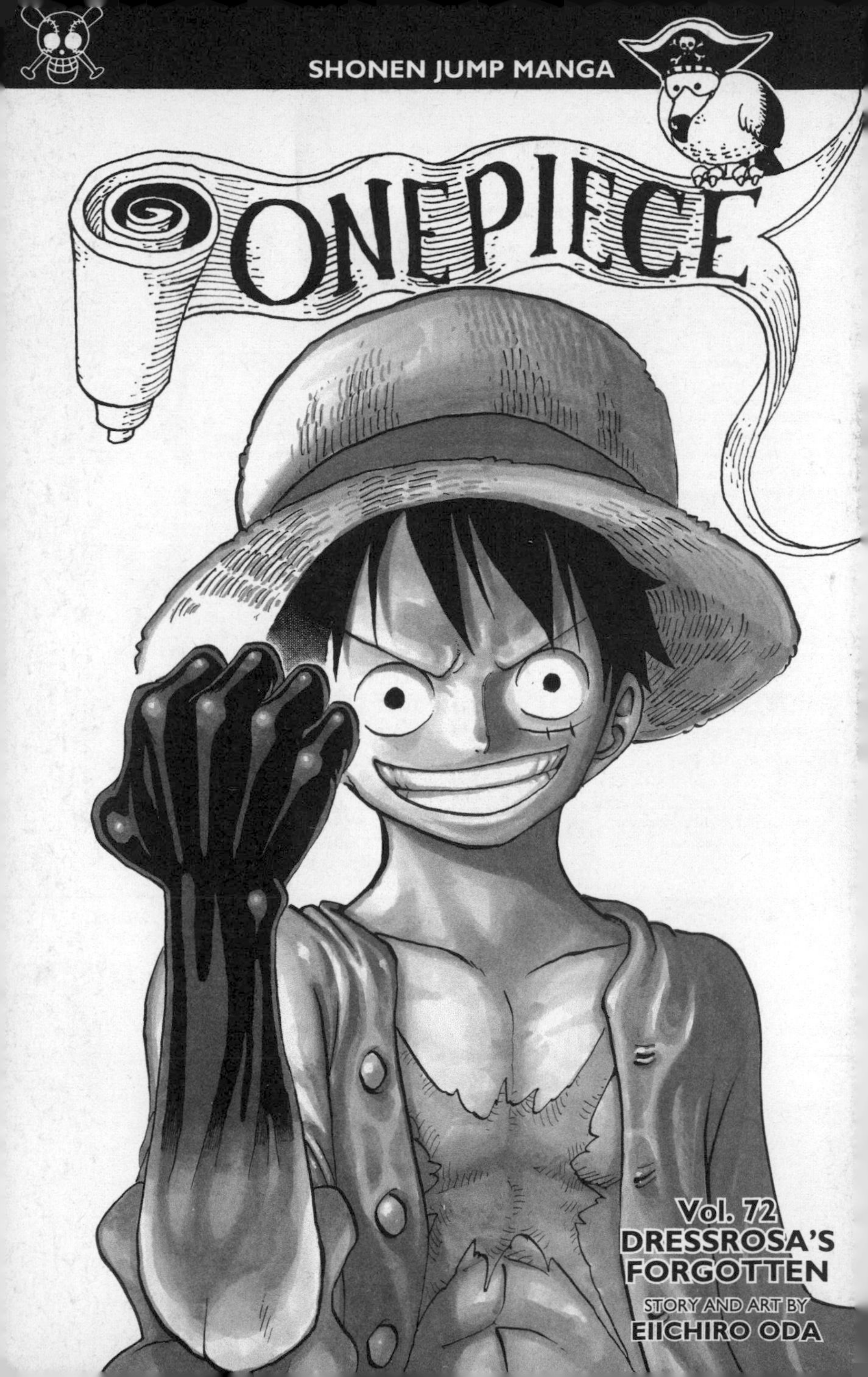

Vol. 72

DRESSROSA'S FORGOTTEN

STORY AND ART BY
EIICHIRO ODA

The Straw Hat Crew

Monkey D. Luffy

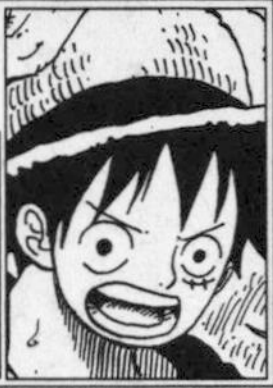

A young man who dreams of becoming the Pirate King. After training with Rayleigh, he and his crew head for the New World!

Captain, Bounty: 400 million berries

Roronoa Zolo

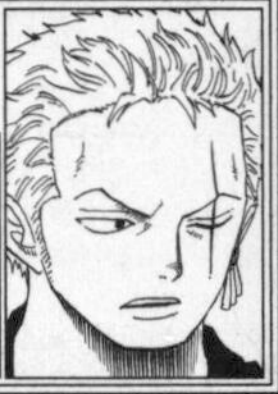

He swallowed his pride and asked to be trained by Mihawk on Gloom Island before reuniting with the rest of the crew.

Fighter, Bounty: 120 million berries

Tony Tony Chopper

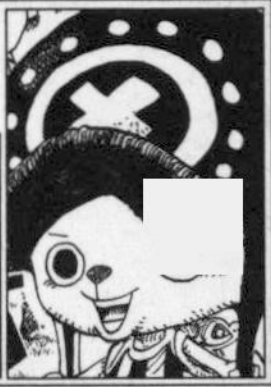

After researching powerful medicine in Birdie Kingdom, he reunites with the rest of the crew.

Ship's Doctor, Bounty: 50 berries

Nami

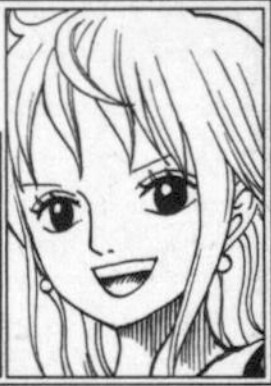

She studied the weather of the New World on the small Sky Island Weatheria, a place where weather is studied as a science.

Navigator, Bounty: 16 million berries

Nico Robin

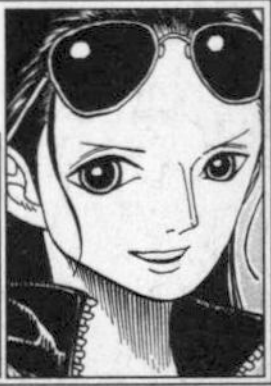

She spent her time in Baltigo with the leader of the Revolutionary Army: Luffy's father, Dragon.

Archeologist, Bounty: 80 million berries

Usopp

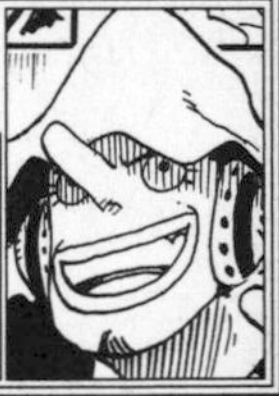

He trained under Heracles at the Bowin Islands to become the King of Snipers.

Sniper, Bounty: 30 million berries

Franky

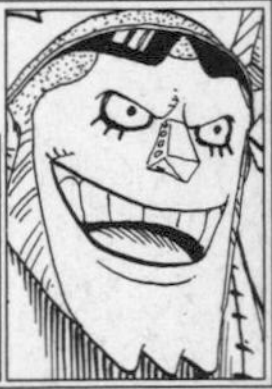

He modified himself in Future Land Baldimore and turned himself into Armored Franky before reuniting with the rest of the crew.

Shipwright, Bounty: 44 million berries

Sanji

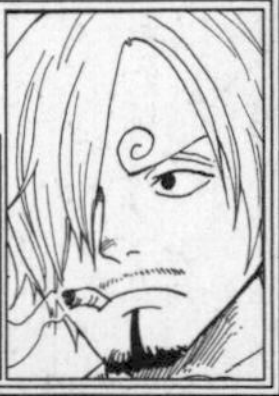

After fighting the New Kama Karate masters in the Kamabakka Kingdom, he returned to the crew.

Cook, Bounty: 77 million berries

Brook

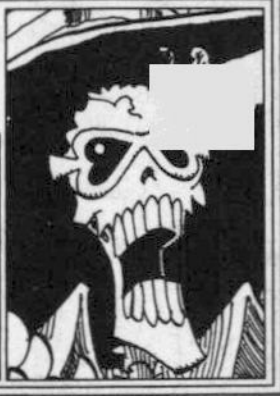

After being captured and used as a freak show by the Longarm Tribe, he became a famous rock star called "Soul King" Brook.

Musician, Bounty: 33 million berries

Doflamingo sells to the Emperor, Kaido. They force Doflamingo to swear to leave the Seven Warlords and infiltrate his kingdom, Dressrosa. The crew splits up into three teams: destroying the factory, handing over Caesar, and guarding the *Thousand Sunny*. Luffy's in the factory-destroying team, but he takes a detour to join a coliseum tournament offering Ace's Flame-Flame Fruit as a prize! Meanwhile, Law's team goes to hand over Caesar, but it was a trap! And now Usopp's team has been captured by little people?!

Shanks

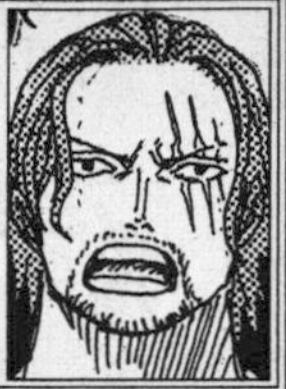

One of the Four Emperors. He continues to wait for Luffy in the second half of the Grand Line, called the New World.

Captain of the Red-Haired Pirates

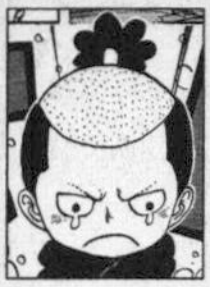

Momonosuke

Kin'emon's Son

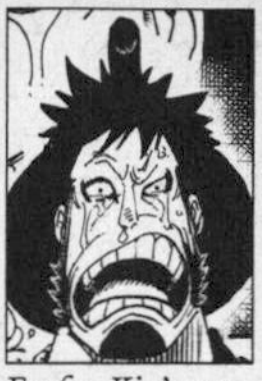

Foxfire Kin'emon

Samurai of Wano

Trafalgar Law

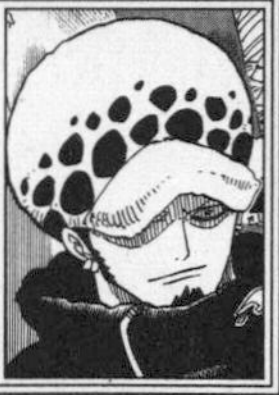

The Surgeon of Death, wielder of the Op-Op Fruit's powers. Currently allied with Luffy.

Pirate, Warlord

Master Caesar Clown

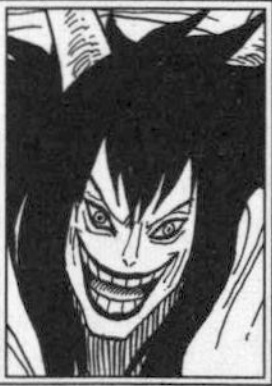

An authority on weapons of mass murder. Kidnapped by Law in an attempt to goad Doflamingo out of hiding.

Former government scientist

Fujitora (Issho)

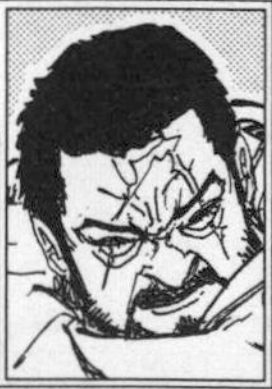

A blind swordsman. One of the Three Admirals after Aokiji's departure.

Naval HQ Admiral

Don Quixote Pirates

Don Quixote Doflamingo (Joker)

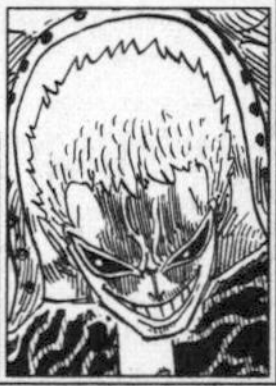

One of the Seven Warlords of the sea and a weapons broker. He works under the alias of "Joker."

Pirate, Warlord (former)

Tontatta Kingdom

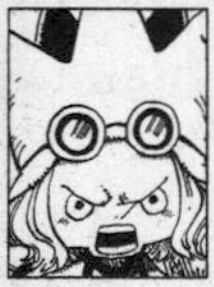

Leo

Warrior

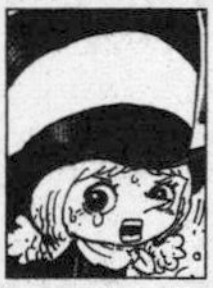

Wicka

Reconnaissance

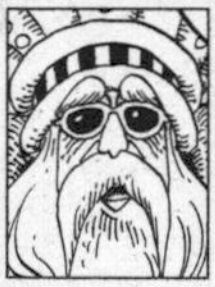

Gancho

King of the Tontattas

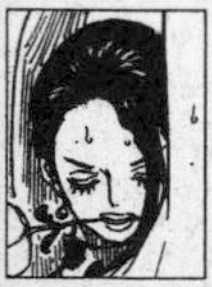

Violet

Dancer

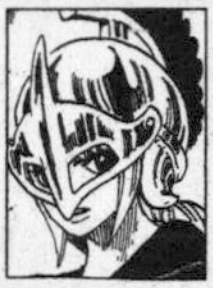

Rebecca

Gladiator

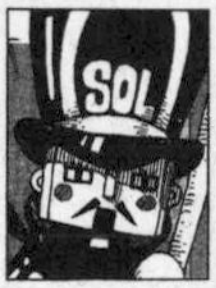
SOL

One-Legged Soldier

Toy

Story

After two years of hard training, the Straw Hat pirates are back together, first at the Sabaody Archipelago and then through Fish-Man Island to their next stage: the New World!!

The crew happens upon Trafalgar Law on the island of Punk Hazard, run by Caesar Clown. At his suggestion, they form a new pirate alliance that seeks to take down one of the Four Emperors. In order to draw Doflamingo's attention, they must first capture Caesar, who is producing the artificial Devil Fruit that

Vol. 72
Dressrosa's Forgotten

CONTENTS

Chapter 712:
VIOLET

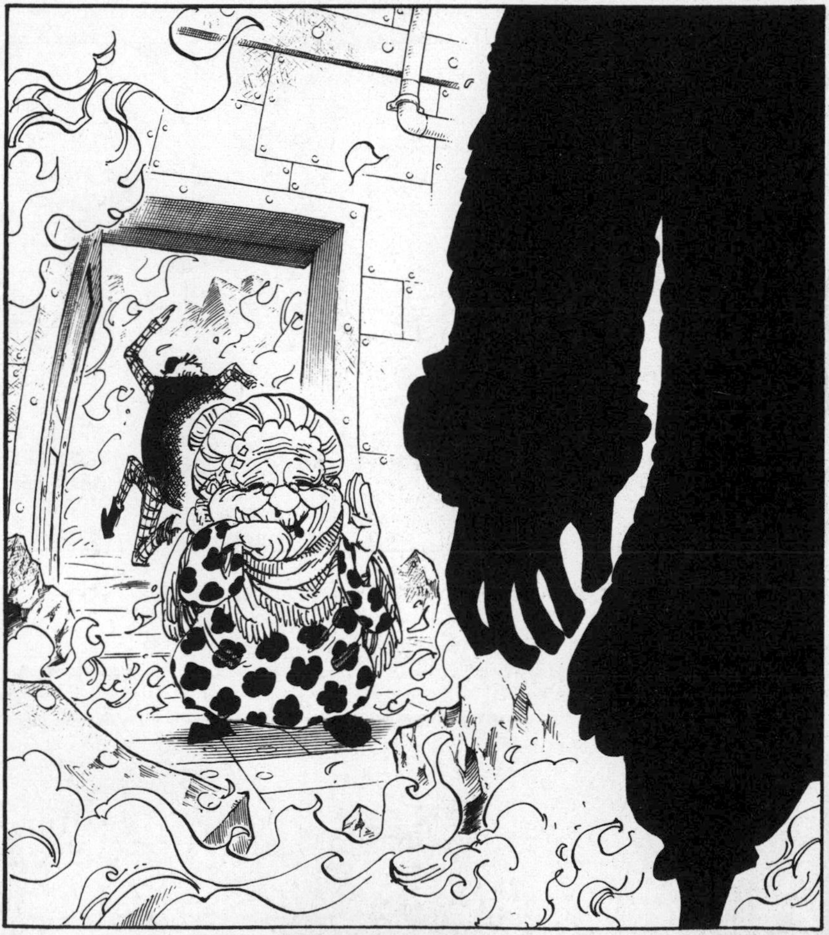

CARIBOU'S NEW WORLD KEE HEE HEE, VOL. 30:
"RUN, GABURU!" "IF YOU INSIST!!"

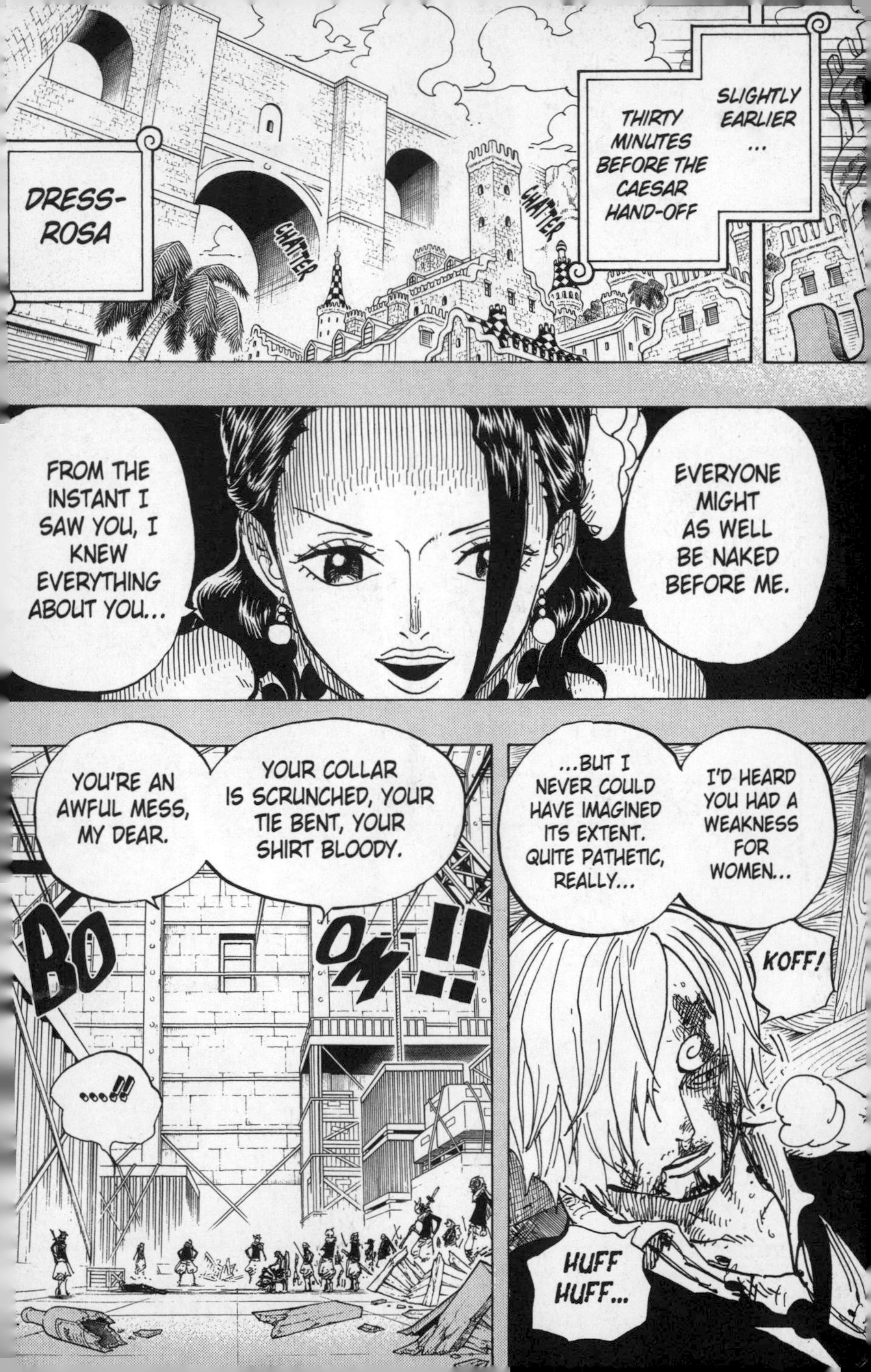
SLIGHTLY EARLIER...
THIRTY MINUTES BEFORE THE CAESAR HAND-OFF
CHATTER
CHATTER
DRESS-ROSA
EVERYONE MIGHT AS WELL BE NAKED BEFORE ME.
FROM THE INSTANT I SAW YOU, I KNEW EVERYTHING ABOUT YOU...
I'D HEARD YOU HAD A WEAKNESS FOR WOMEN...
...BUT I NEVER COULD HAVE IMAGINED ITS EXTENT. QUITE PATHETIC, REALLY...
KOFF!
HUFF HUFF...
YOUR COLLAR IS SCRUNCHED, YOUR TIE BENT, YOUR SHIRT BLOODY.
YOU'RE AN AWFUL MESS, MY DEAR.
BOOM!!
....!!

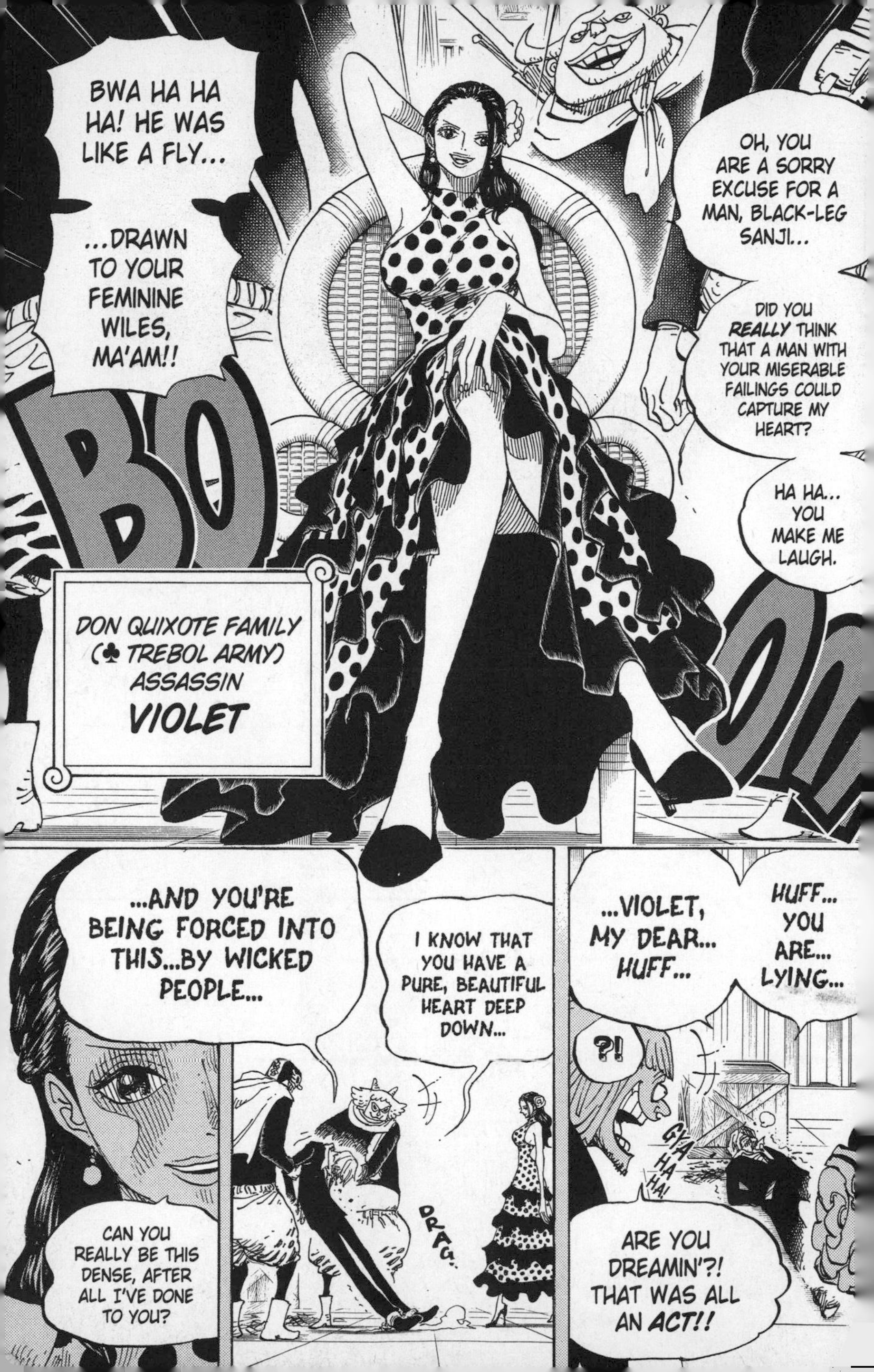

OH, YOU ARE A SORRY EXCUSE FOR A MAN, BLACK-LEG SANJI...
DID YOU *REALLY* THINK THAT A MAN WITH YOUR MISERABLE FAILINGS COULD CAPTURE MY HEART?
HA HA... YOU MAKE ME LAUGH.
BWA HA HA HA! HE WAS LIKE A FLY...
...DRAWN TO YOUR FEMININE WILES, MA'AM!!
OO
BO
DON QUIXOTE FAMILY (♣ TREBOL ARMY) ASSASSIN
VIOLET
...VIOLET, MY DEAR... HUFF...
HUFF... YOU ARE... LYING...
?!
GYA HA HA HA!
ARE YOU DREAMIN'?! THAT WAS ALL AN *ACT*!!
I KNOW THAT YOU HAVE A PURE, BEAUTIFUL HEART DEEP DOWN...
...AND YOU'RE BEING FORCED INTO THIS...BY WICKED PEOPLE...
DRAG.
CAN YOU REALLY BE THIS DENSE, AFTER ALL I'VE DONE TO YOU?

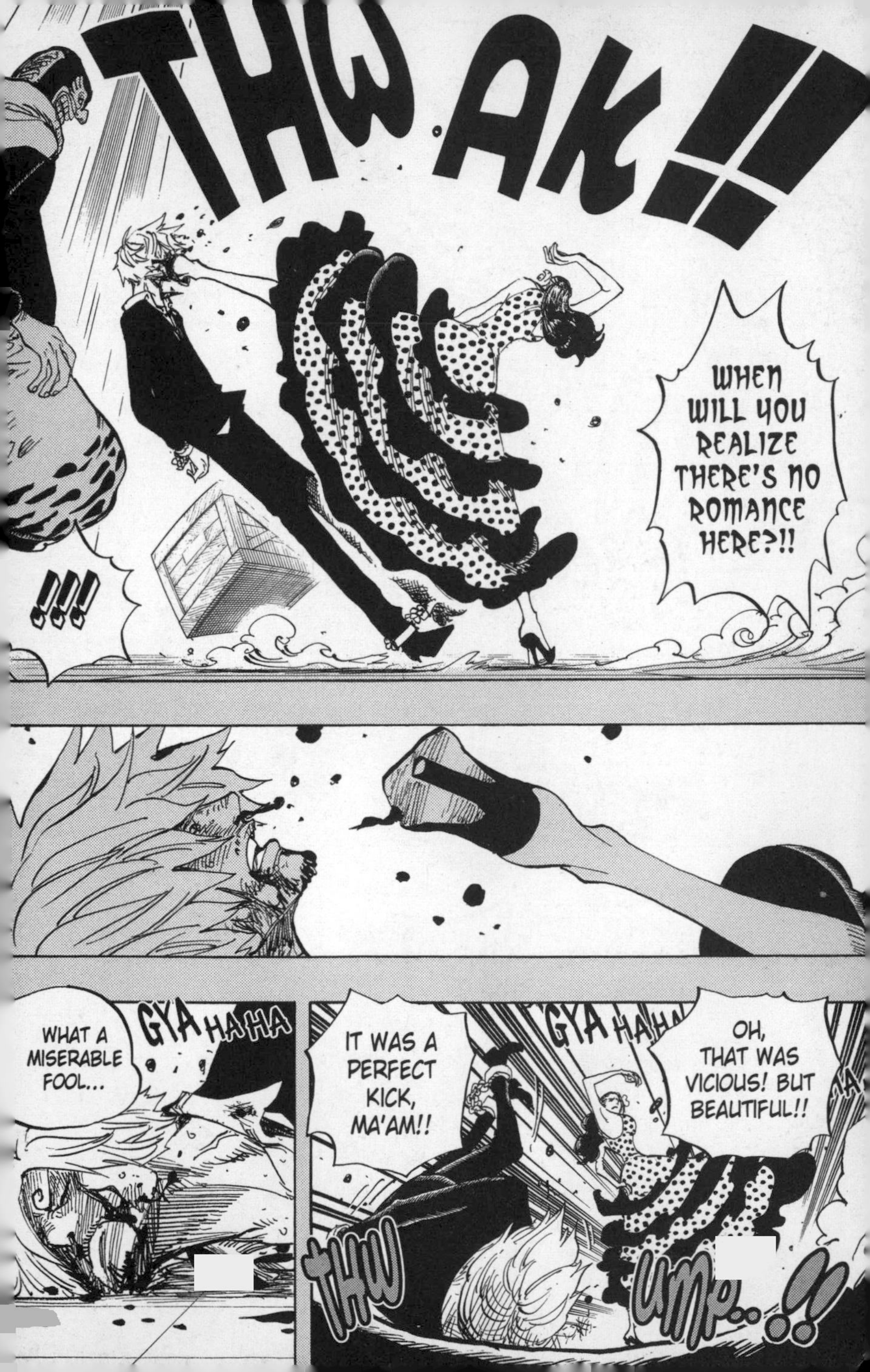
THWAK!!
WHEN WILL YOU REALIZE THERE'S NO ROMANCE HERE?!!
!!!
OH, THAT WAS VICIOUS! BUT BEAUTIFUL!!
GYA HAHA
IT WAS A PERFECT KICK, MA'AM!!
THWUMP..!!
GYA HAHA
WHAT A MISERABLE FOOL...

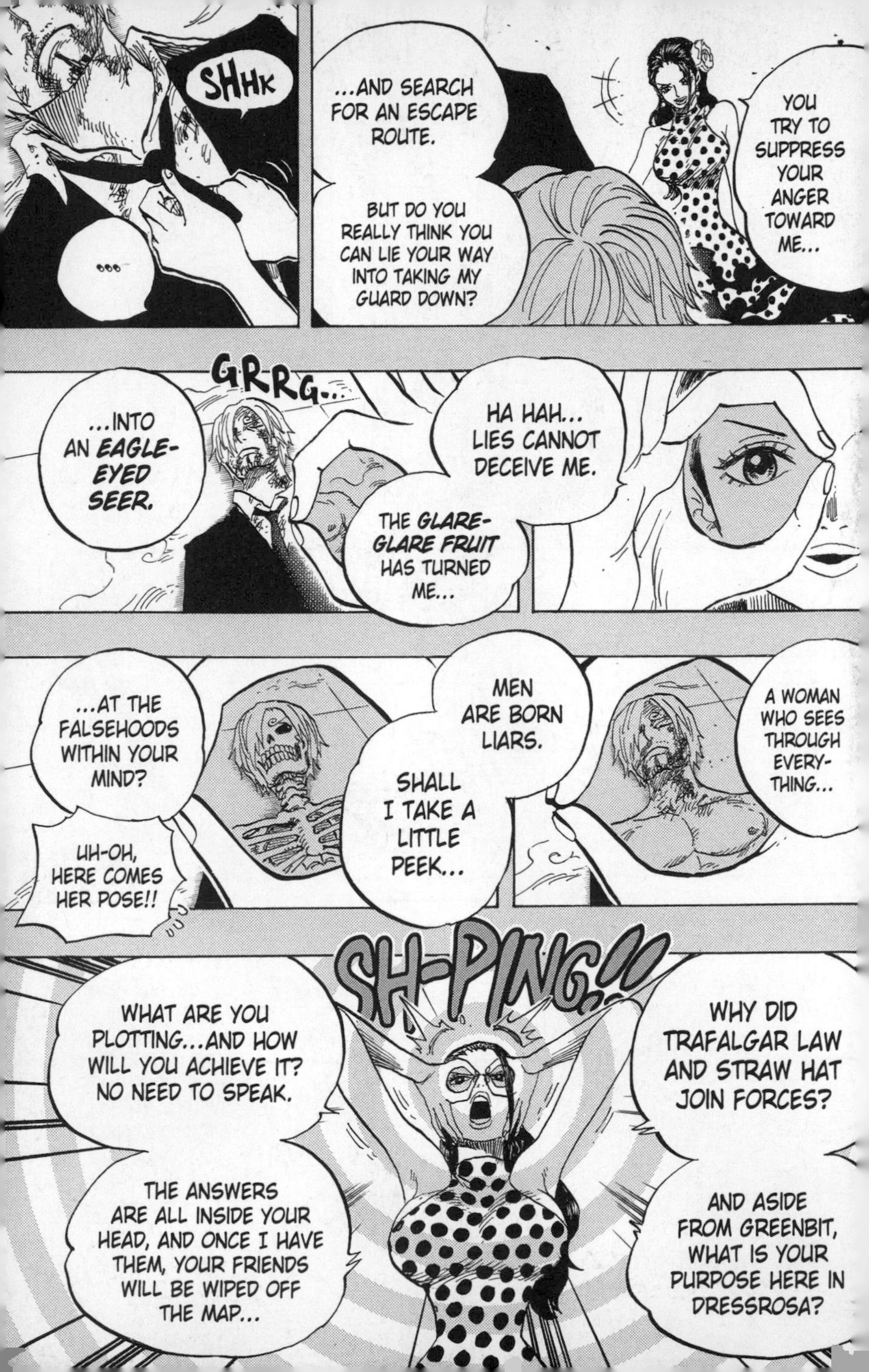
YOU TRY TO SUPPRESS YOUR ANGER TOWARD ME...
...AND SEARCH FOR AN ESCAPE ROUTE.
BUT DO YOU REALLY THINK YOU CAN LIE YOUR WAY INTO TAKING MY GUARD DOWN?
SHHK
...
HA HAH... LIES CANNOT DECEIVE ME.
THE *GLARE-GLARE FRUIT* HAS TURNED ME...
GRRG...
...INTO AN *EAGLE-EYED SEER.*
A WOMAN WHO SEES THROUGH EVERY-THING...
MEN ARE BORN LIARS.
SHALL I TAKE A LITTLE PEEK...
...AT THE FALSEHOODS WITHIN YOUR MIND?
UH-OH, HERE COMES HER POSE!!
SH-PING!!
WHY DID TRAFALGAR LAW AND STRAW HAT JOIN FORCES?
AND ASIDE FROM GREENBIT, WHAT IS YOUR PURPOSE HERE IN DRESSROSA?
WHAT ARE YOU PLOTTING...AND HOW WILL YOU ACHIEVE IT? NO NEED TO SPEAK.
THE ANSWERS ARE ALL INSIDE YOUR HEAD, AND ONCE I HAVE THEM, YOUR FRIENDS WILL BE WIPED OFF THE MAP...

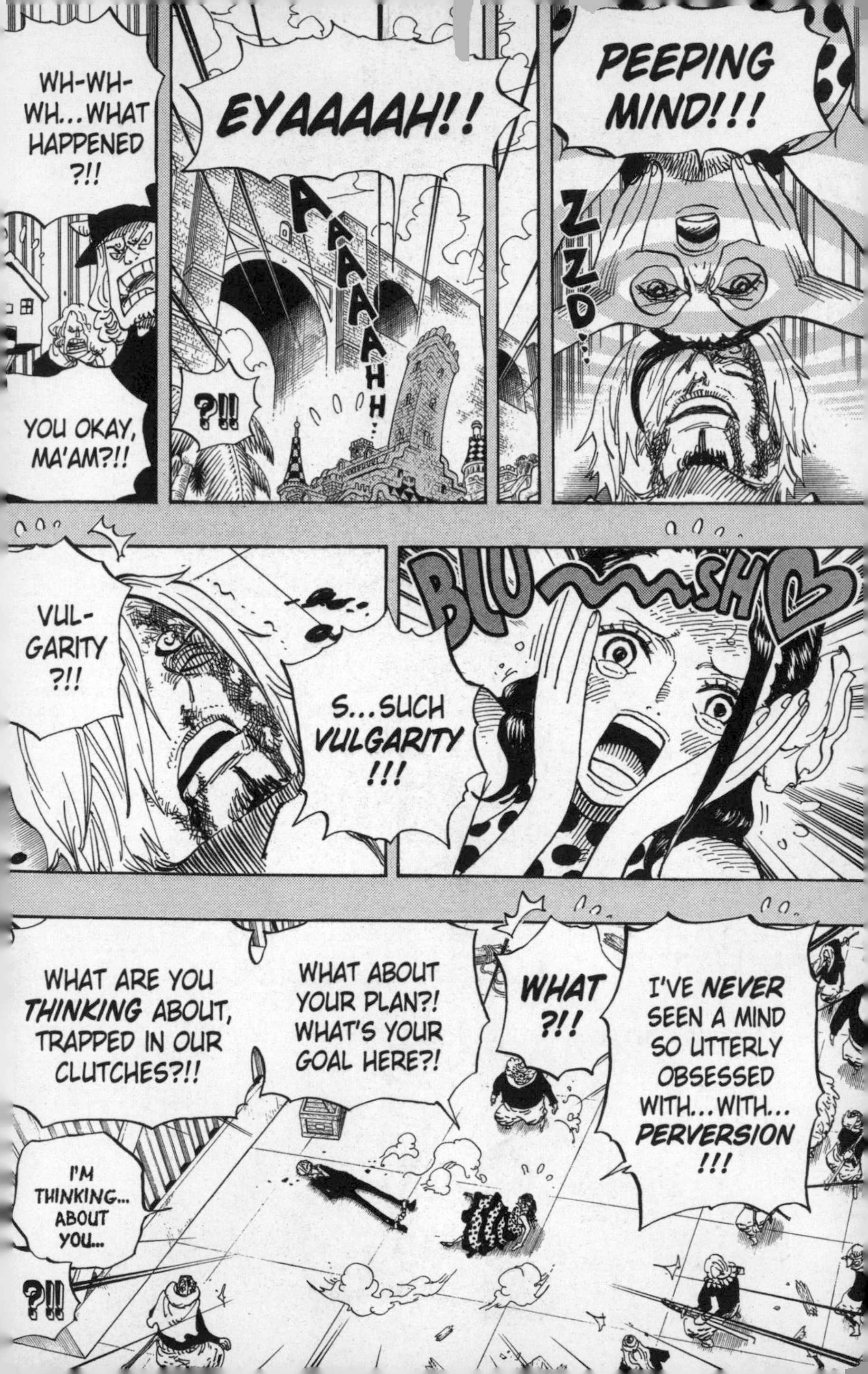
PEEPING MIND!!!
ZZZD
EYAAAAH!!
AAAAAHH...
?!!
WH-WH-WH...WHAT HAPPENED?!!
YOU OKAY, MA'AM?!!
BLUSH
S...SUCH VULGARITY!!!
VULGARITY?!!
I'VE NEVER SEEN A MIND SO UTTERLY OBSESSED WITH...WITH... PERVERSION!!!
WHAT?!!
WHAT ABOUT YOUR PLAN?! WHAT'S YOUR GOAL HERE?!
WHAT ARE YOU THINKING ABOUT, TRAPPED IN OUR CLUTCHES?!!
I'M THINKING... ABOUT YOU...
?!!

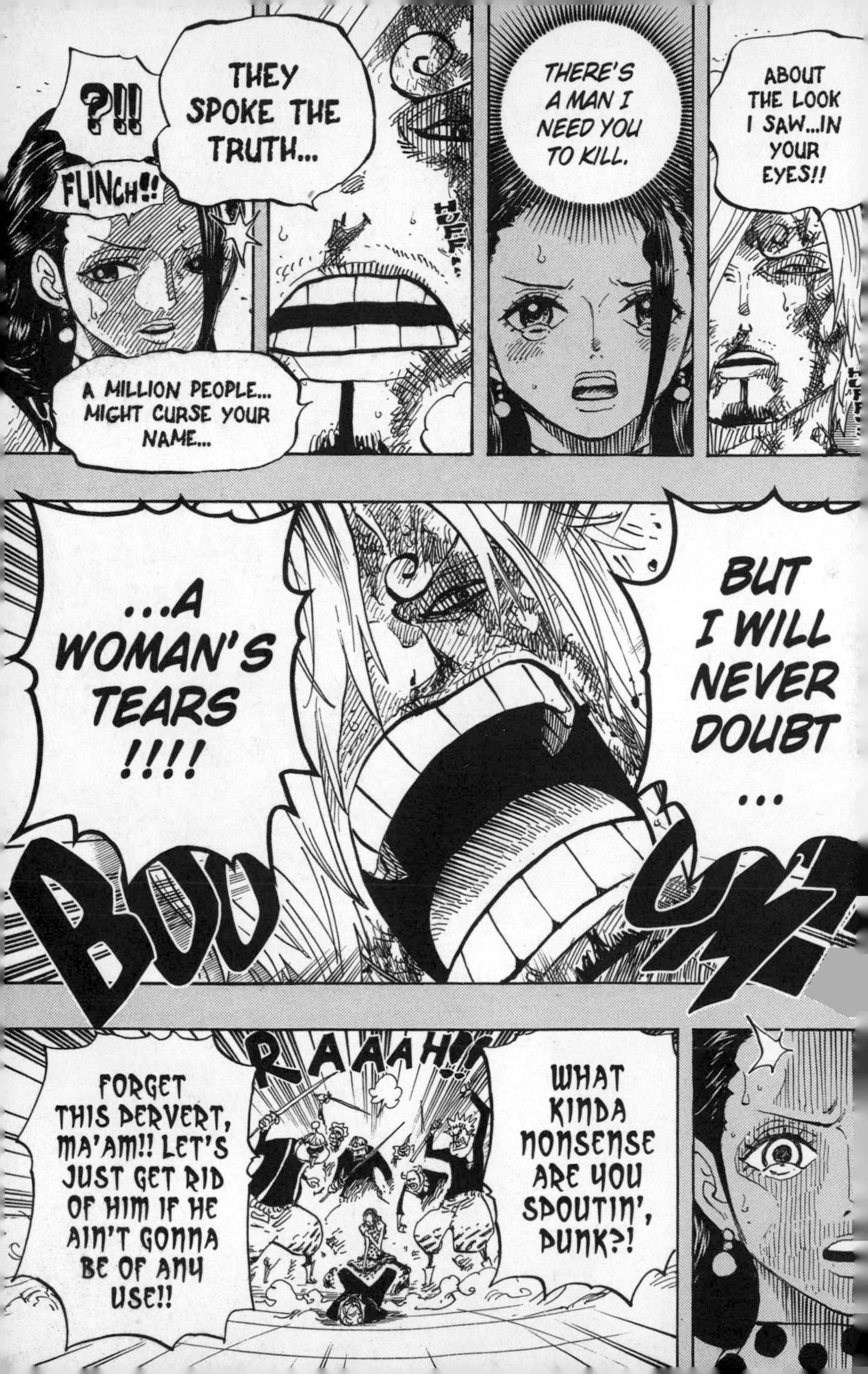
ABOUT THE LOOK I SAW...IN YOUR EYES!!
HUFF
THERE'S A MAN I NEED YOU TO KILL.
THEY SPOKE THE TRUTH...
HUFF
?!!
FLINCH!!
A MILLION PEOPLE... MIGHT CURSE YOUR NAME...
BUT I WILL NEVER DOUBT ...
...A WOMAN'S TEARS !!!!
WHAT KINDA NONSENSE ARE YOU SPOUTIN', PUNK?!
RAAAH!!
FORGET THIS PERVERT, MA'AM!! LET'S JUST GET RID OF HIM IF HE AIN'T GONNA BE OF ANY USE!!

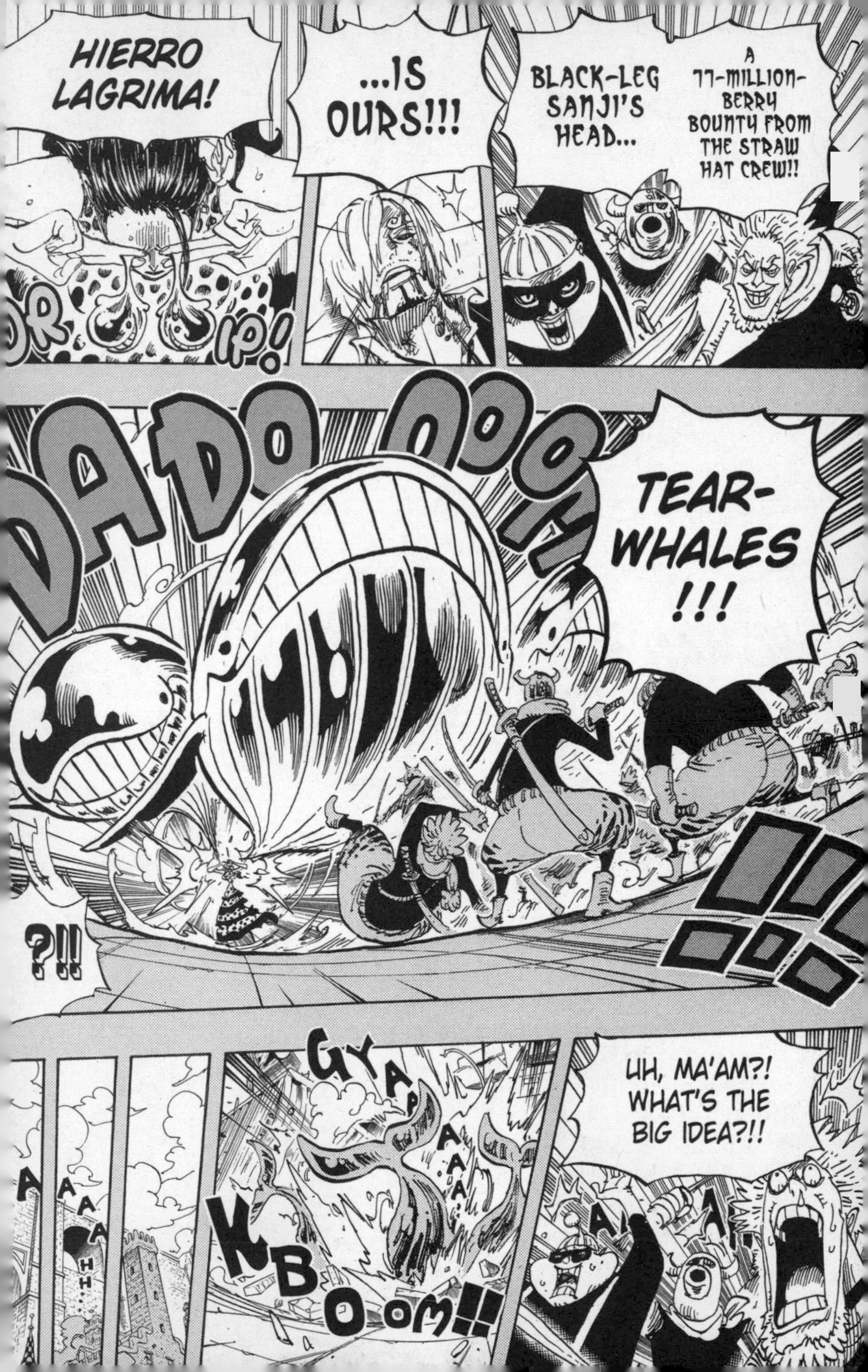
A 77-MILLION-BERRY BOUNTY FROM THE STRAW HAT CREW!!
BLACK-LEG SANJI'S HEAD...
...IS OURS!!!
HIERRO LAGRIMA!
DRIP!
TEAR-WHALES!!!
DADOOOM
!!
?!!
UH, MA'AM?! WHAT'S THE BIG IDEA?!!
AAA!
GYAAAAAA
KBOOOM!!
AAAAHH...

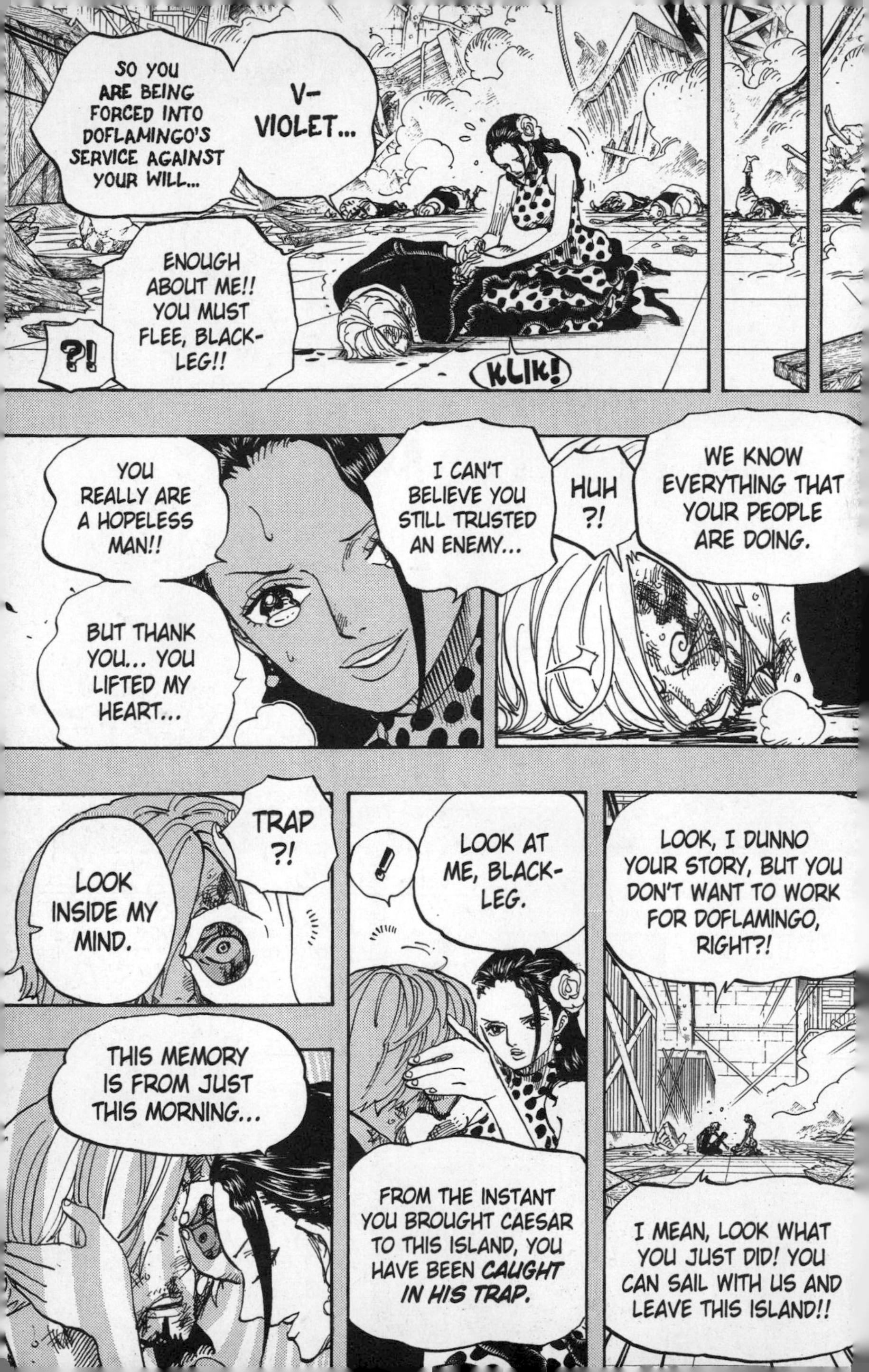

V- VIOLET...
SO YOU ARE BEING FORCED INTO DOFLAMINGO'S SERVICE AGAINST YOUR WILL...
ENOUGH ABOUT ME!! YOU MUST FLEE, BLACK-LEG!!
KLIK!
?!
WE KNOW EVERYTHING THAT YOUR PEOPLE ARE DOING.
HUH ?!
I CAN'T BELIEVE YOU STILL TRUSTED AN ENEMY...
YOU REALLY ARE A HOPELESS MAN!!
BUT THANK YOU... YOU LIFTED MY HEART...
LOOK, I DUNNO YOUR STORY, BUT YOU DON'T WANT TO WORK FOR DOFLAMINGO, RIGHT?!
I MEAN, LOOK WHAT YOU JUST DID! YOU CAN SAIL WITH US AND LEAVE THIS ISLAND!!
LOOK AT ME, BLACK-LEG.
!
FROM THE INSTANT YOU BROUGHT CAESAR TO THIS ISLAND, YOU HAVE BEEN *CAUGHT IN HIS TRAP.*
TRAP ?!
LOOK INSIDE MY MIND.
THIS MEMORY IS FROM JUST THIS MORNING...

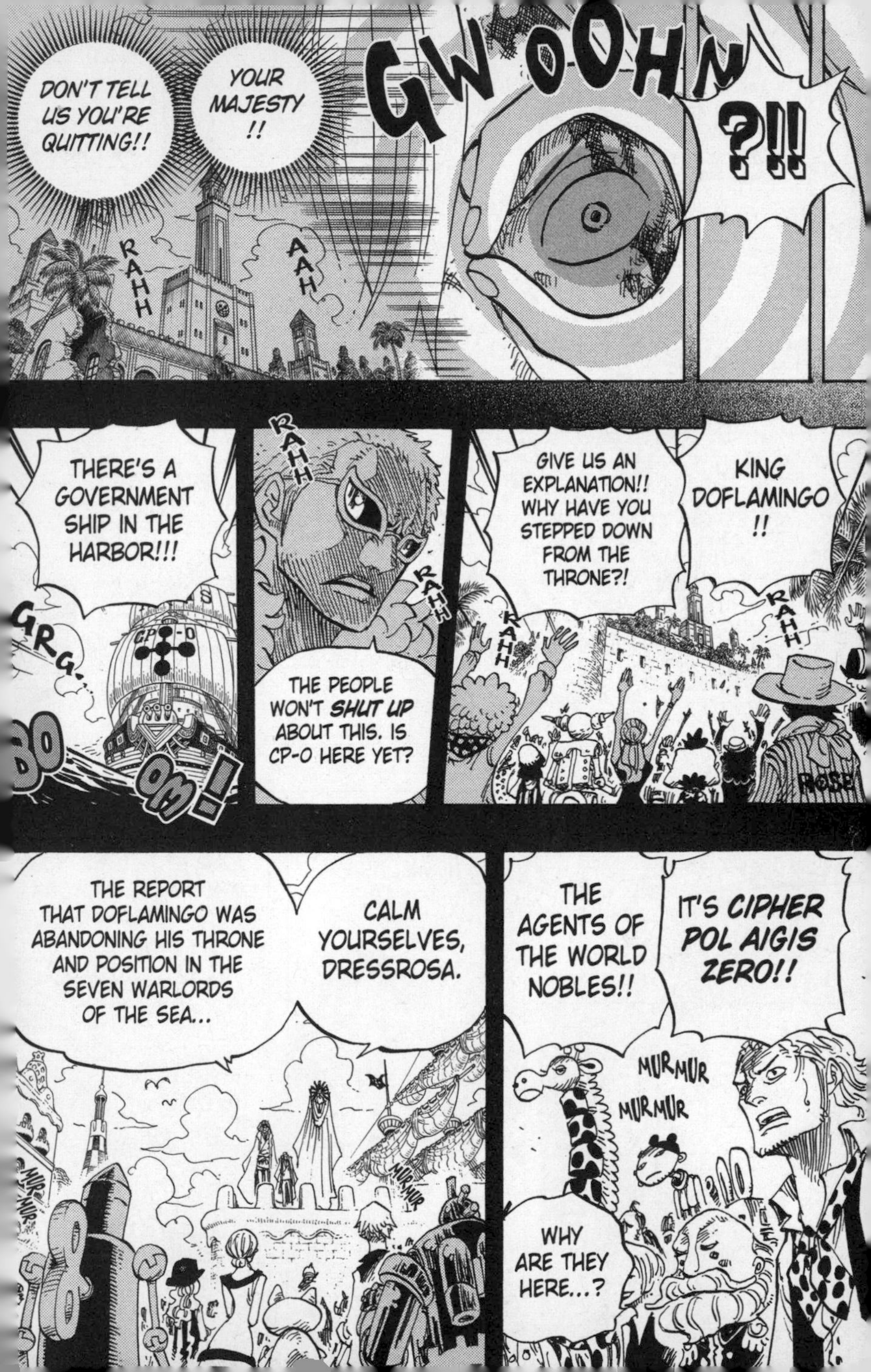
GWOOOHN
?!!
YOUR MAJESTY!!
DON'T TELL US YOU'RE QUITTING!!
AAH
RAHH
KING DOFLAMINGO!!
GIVE US AN EXPLANATION!! WHY HAVE YOU STEPPED DOWN FROM THE THRONE?!
RAHH
RAHH
ROSE
RAHH
RAHH
THE PEOPLE WON'T SHUT UP ABOUT THIS. IS CP-0 HERE YET?
THERE'S A GOVERNMENT SHIP IN THE HARBOR!!!
CP-0
GRG...
BOOM!
IT'S CIPHER POL AIGIS ZERO!!
THE AGENTS OF THE WORLD NOBLES!!
MURMUR
MURMUR
WHY ARE THEY HERE...?
CALM YOURSELVES, DRESSROSA.
THE REPORT THAT DOFLAMINGO WAS ABANDONING HIS THRONE AND POSITION IN THE SEVEN WARLORDS OF THE SEA...
MURMUR
MURMUR

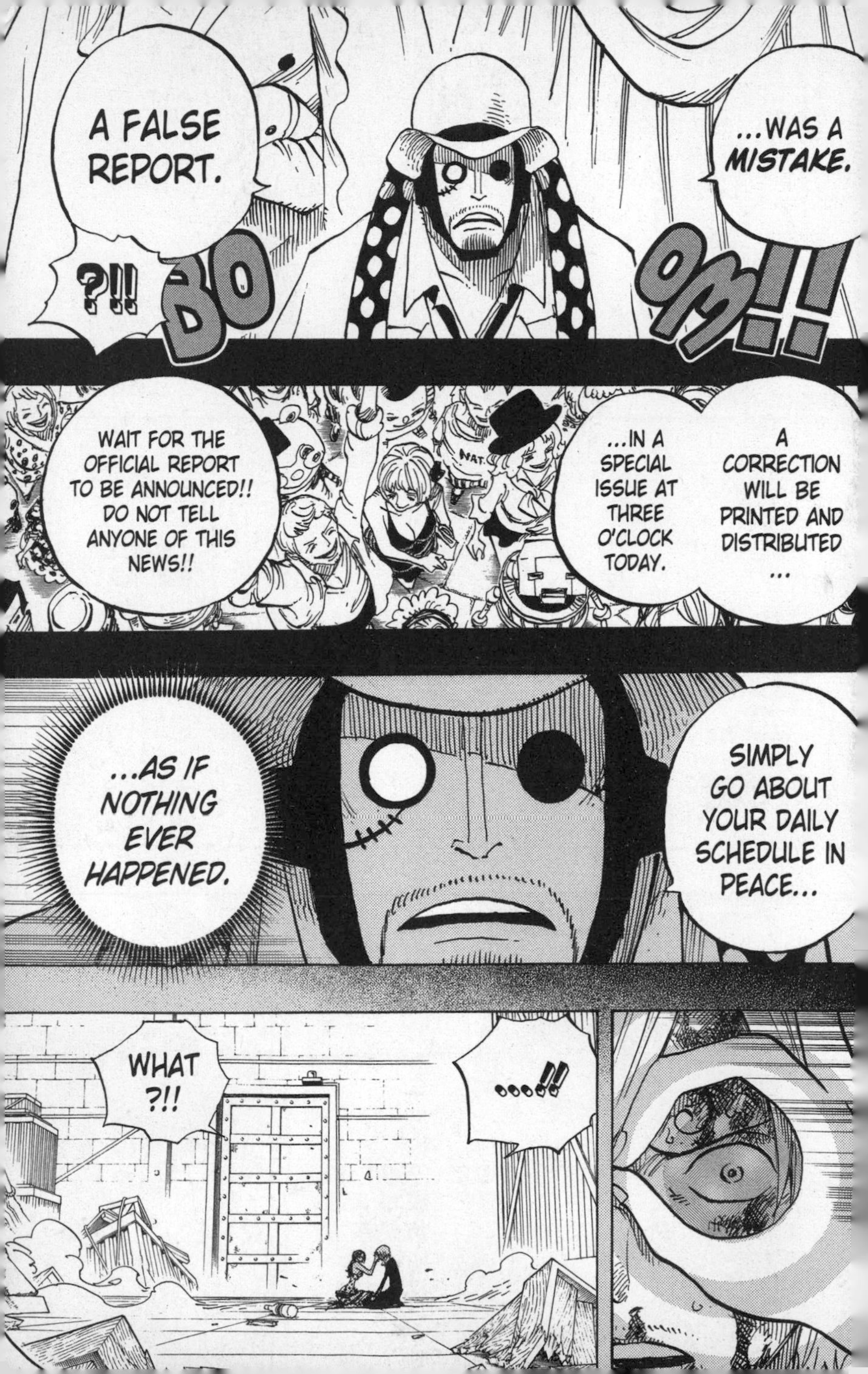
...WAS A MISTAKE.
A FALSE REPORT.
?!!
BOOM!!
A CORRECTION WILL BE PRINTED AND DISTRIBUTED ...
...IN A SPECIAL ISSUE AT THREE O'CLOCK TODAY.
WAIT FOR THE OFFICIAL REPORT TO BE ANNOUNCED!! DO NOT TELL ANYONE OF THIS NEWS!!
SIMPLY GO ABOUT YOUR DAILY SCHEDULE IN PEACE...
...AS IF NOTHING EVER HAPPENED.
....!!
WHAT ?!!

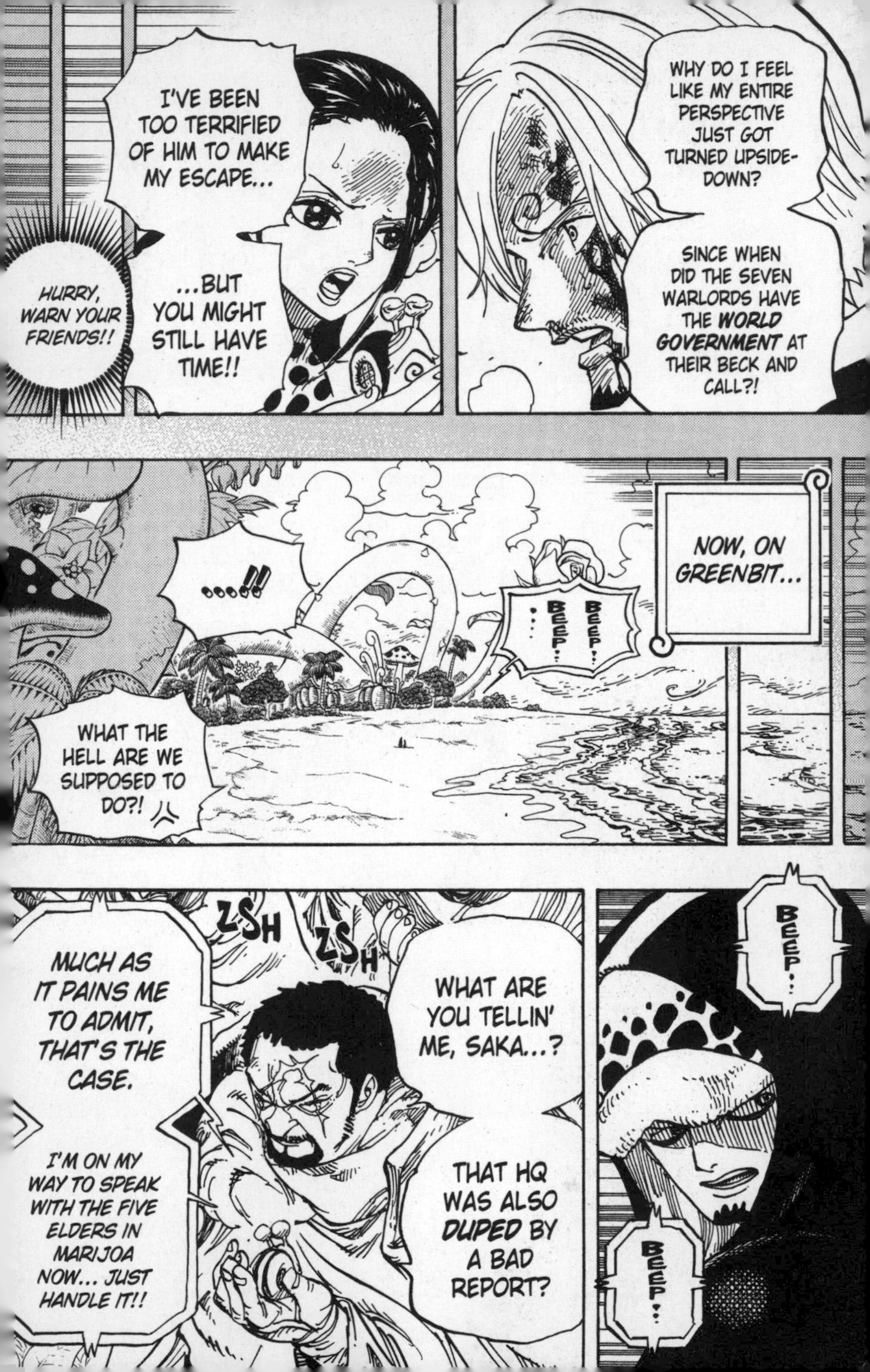
WHY DO I FEEL LIKE MY ENTIRE PERSPECTIVE JUST GOT TURNED UPSIDE-DOWN?
SINCE WHEN DID THE SEVEN WARLORDS HAVE THE WORLD GOVERNMENT AT THEIR BECK AND CALL?!
I'VE BEEN TOO TERRIFIED OF HIM TO MAKE MY ESCAPE...
...BUT YOU MIGHT STILL HAVE TIME!!
HURRY, WARN YOUR FRIENDS!!
NOW, ON GREENBIT...
BEEP... BEEP...
.....!!
WHAT THE HELL ARE WE SUPPOSED TO DO?!
BEEP...
BEEP...
ZSH ZSH
WHAT ARE YOU TELLIN' ME, SAKA...?
THAT HQ WAS ALSO DUPED BY A BAD REPORT?
MUCH AS IT PAINS ME TO ADMIT, THAT'S THE CASE.
I'M ON MY WAY TO SPEAK WITH THE FIVE ELDERS IN MARIJOA NOW... JUST HANDLE IT!!

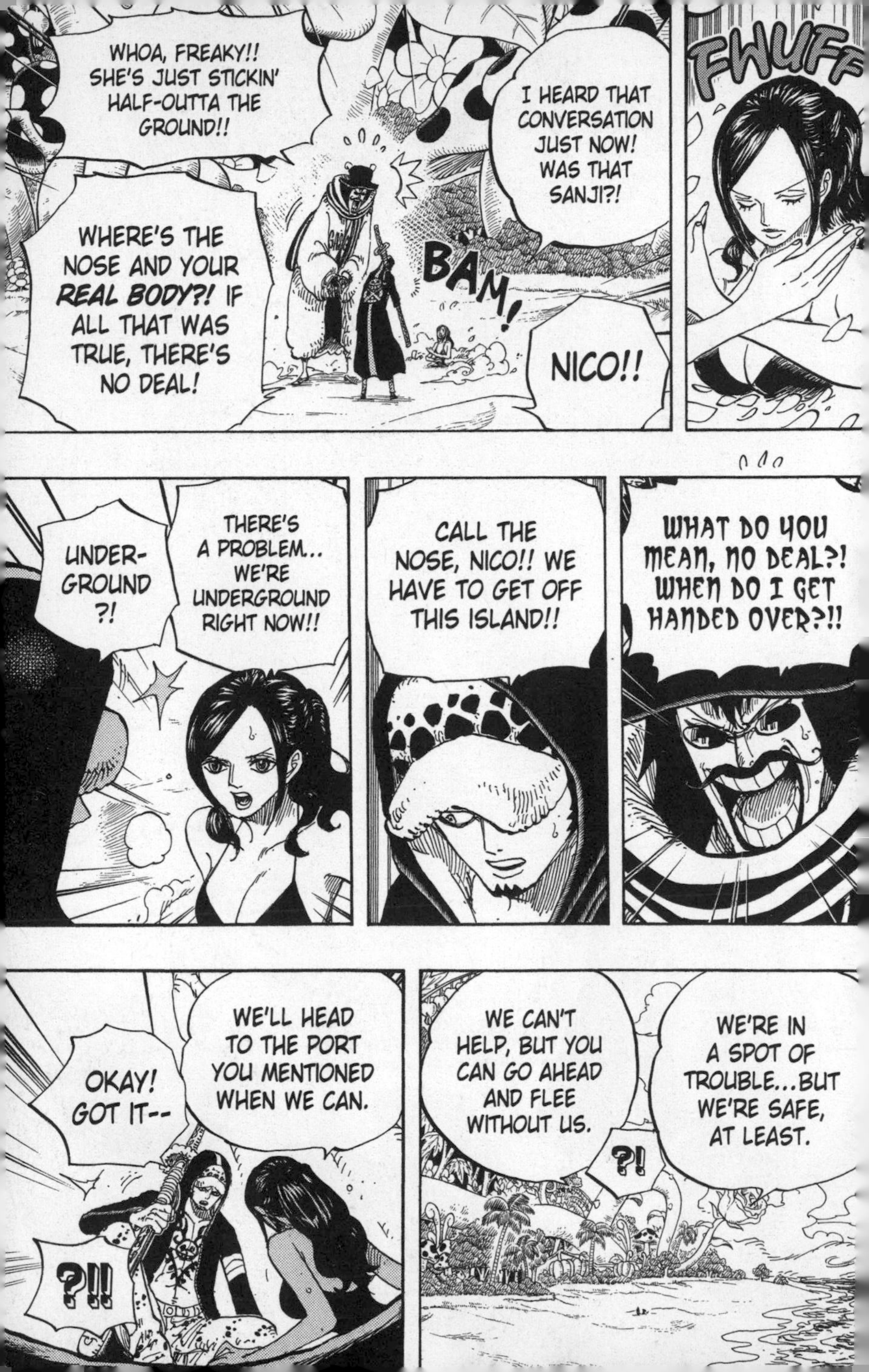
FWUFF
I HEARD THAT CONVERSATION JUST NOW! WAS THAT SANJI?!
BAM!
NICO!!
WHOA, FREAKY!! SHE'S JUST STICKIN' HALF-OUTTA THE GROUND!!
WHERE'S THE NOSE AND YOUR **REAL BODY?!** IF ALL THAT WAS TRUE, THERE'S NO DEAL!
WHAT DO YOU MEAN, NO DEAL?! WHEN DO I GET HANDED OVER?!!
CALL THE NOSE, NICO!! WE HAVE TO GET OFF THIS ISLAND!!
THERE'S A PROBLEM... WE'RE UNDERGROUND RIGHT NOW!!
UNDER-GROUND?!
WE'RE IN A SPOT OF TROUBLE...BUT WE'RE SAFE, AT LEAST.
WE CAN'T HELP, BUT YOU CAN GO AHEAD AND FLEE WITHOUT US.
?!
WE'LL HEAD TO THE PORT YOU MENTIONED WHEN WE CAN.
OKAY! GOT IT--
?!!

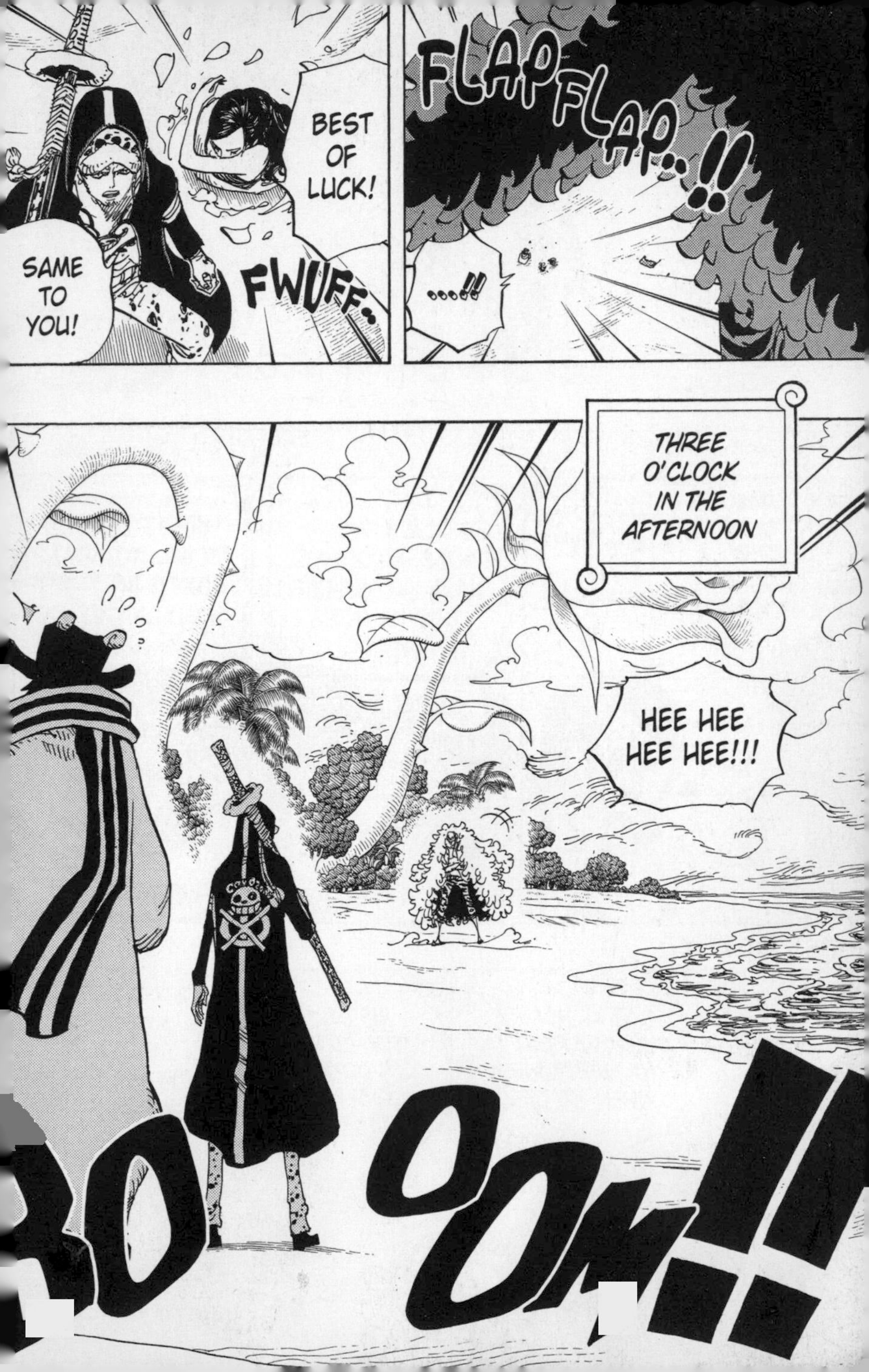
FLAP FLAP..!!
...!!
BEST OF LUCK!
SAME TO YOU!
FWUFF
THREE O'CLOCK IN THE AFTERNOON
HEE HEE HEE HEE!!!
BOOOM!!

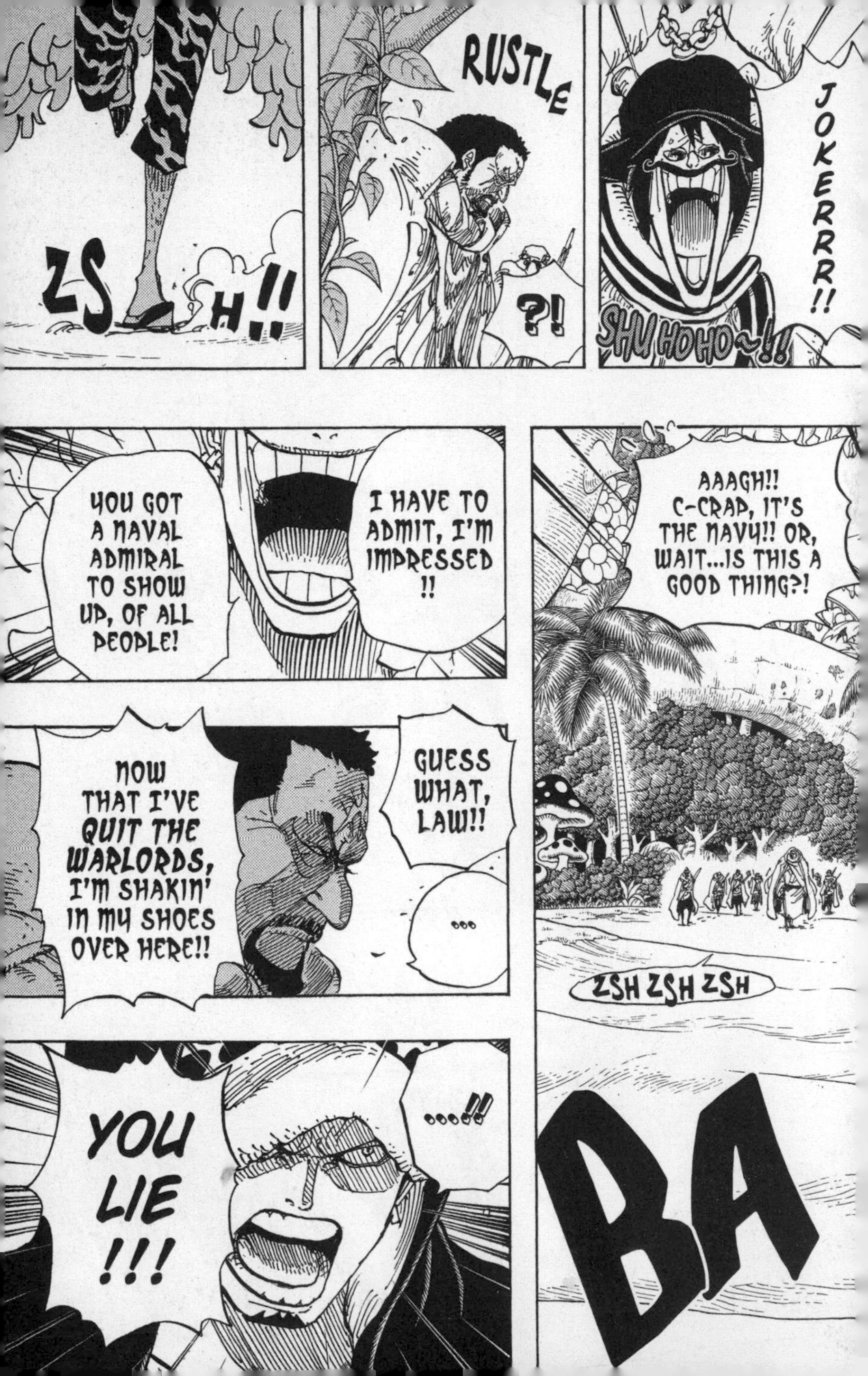
JOKERRR!!
SHU HO HO~!!
RUSTLE
?!
ZS H!!
AAAGH!! C-CRAP, IT'S THE NAVY!! OR, WAIT...IS THIS A GOOD THING?!
ZSH ZSH ZSH
BA
I HAVE TO ADMIT, I'M IMPRESSED!!
YOU GOT A NAVAL ADMIRAL TO SHOW UP, OF ALL PEOPLE!
GUESS WHAT, LAW!!
...
NOW THAT I'VE QUIT THE WARLORDS, I'M SHAKIN' IN MY SHOES OVER HERE!!
...!!
YOU LIE!!!

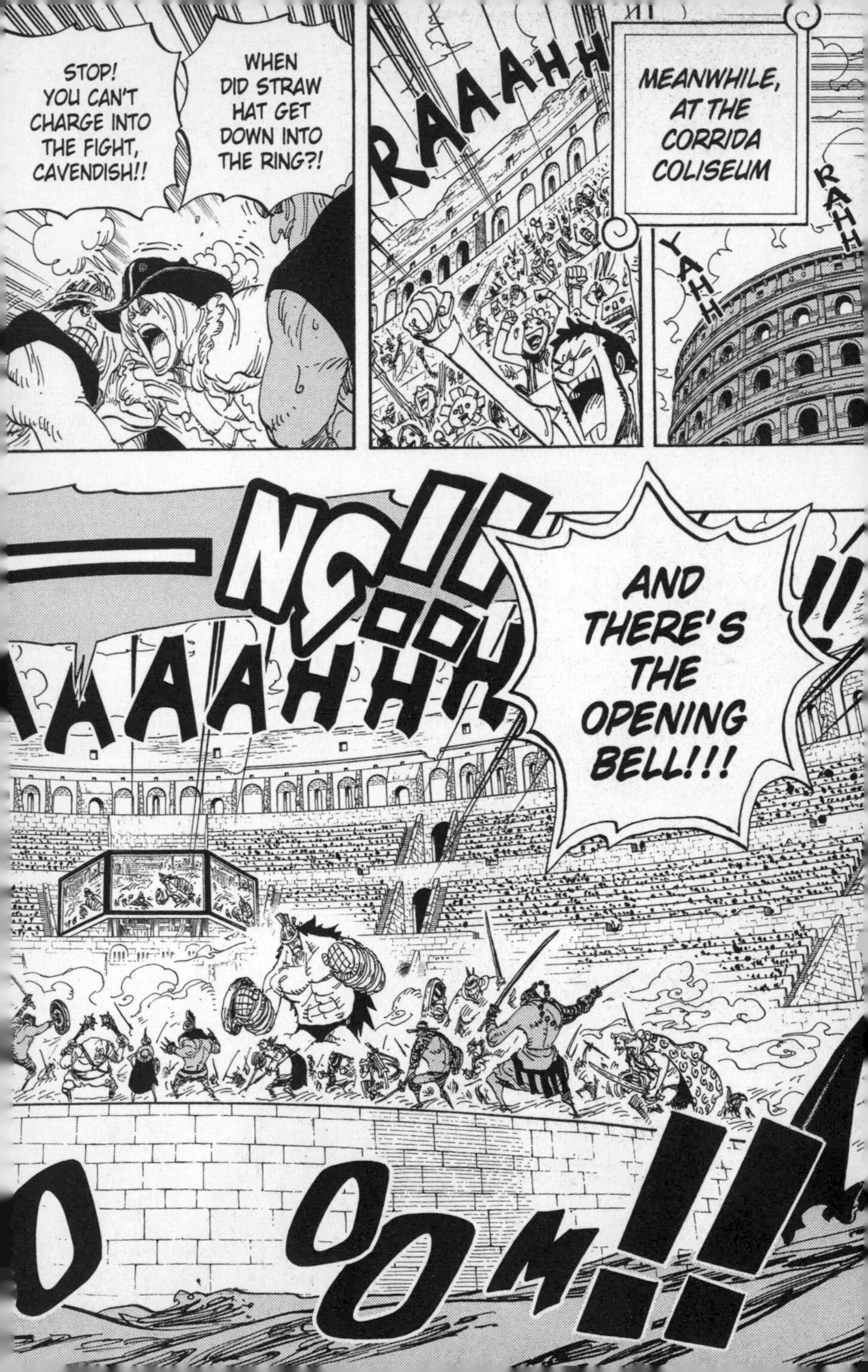
MEANWHILE, AT THE CORRIDA COLISEUM
YAHH
RAHH
RAAAHH
WHEN DID STRAW HAT GET DOWN INTO THE RING?!
STOP! YOU CAN'T CHARGE INTO THE FIGHT, CAVENDISH!!
AND THERE'S THE OPENING BELL!!!

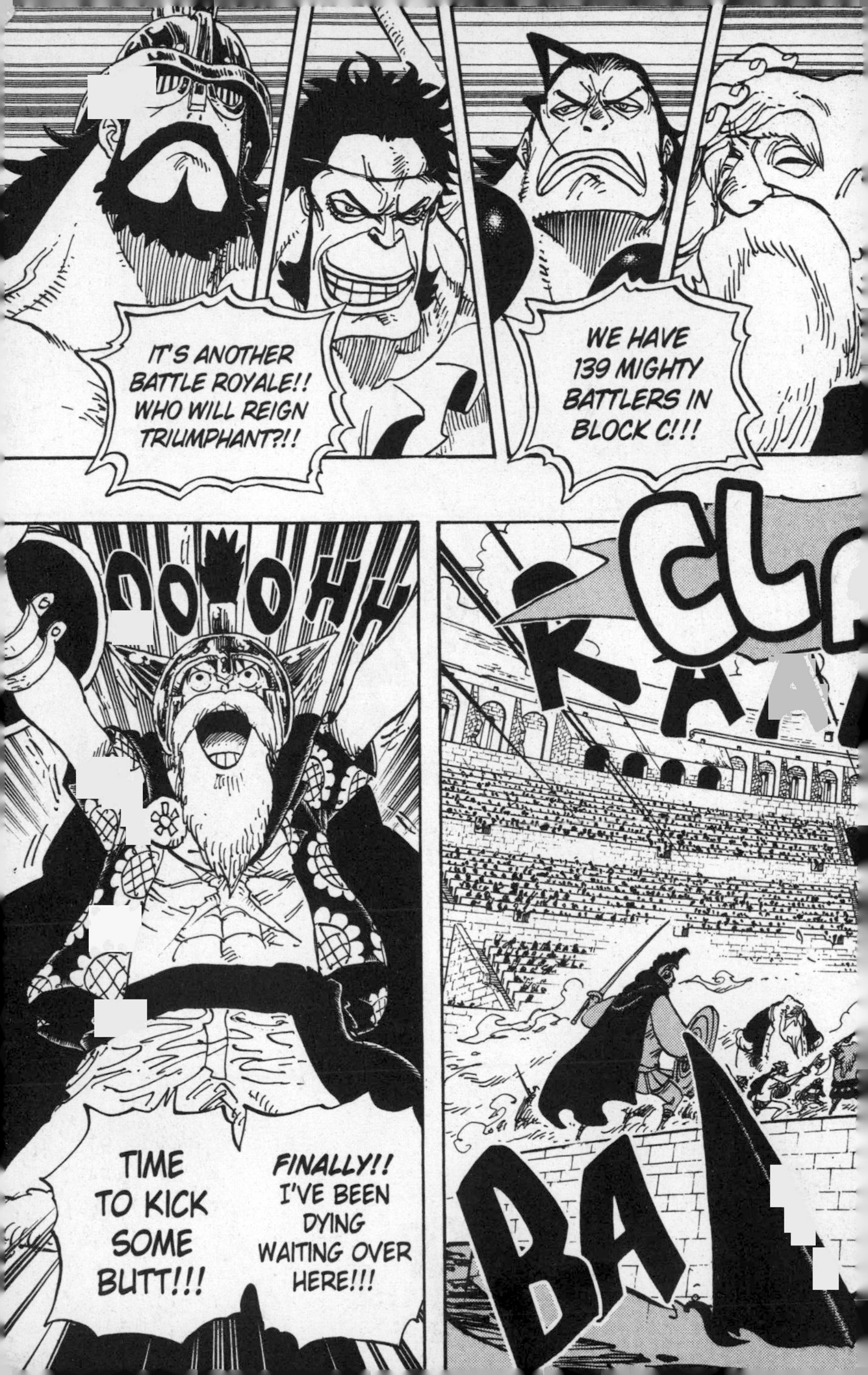
WE HAVE 139 MIGHTY BATTLERS IN BLOCK C!!!
IT'S ANOTHER BATTLE ROYALE!! WHO WILL REIGN TRIUMPHANT?!!
FINALLY!! I'VE BEEN DYING WAITING OVER HERE!!!
TIME TO KICK SOME BUTT!!!

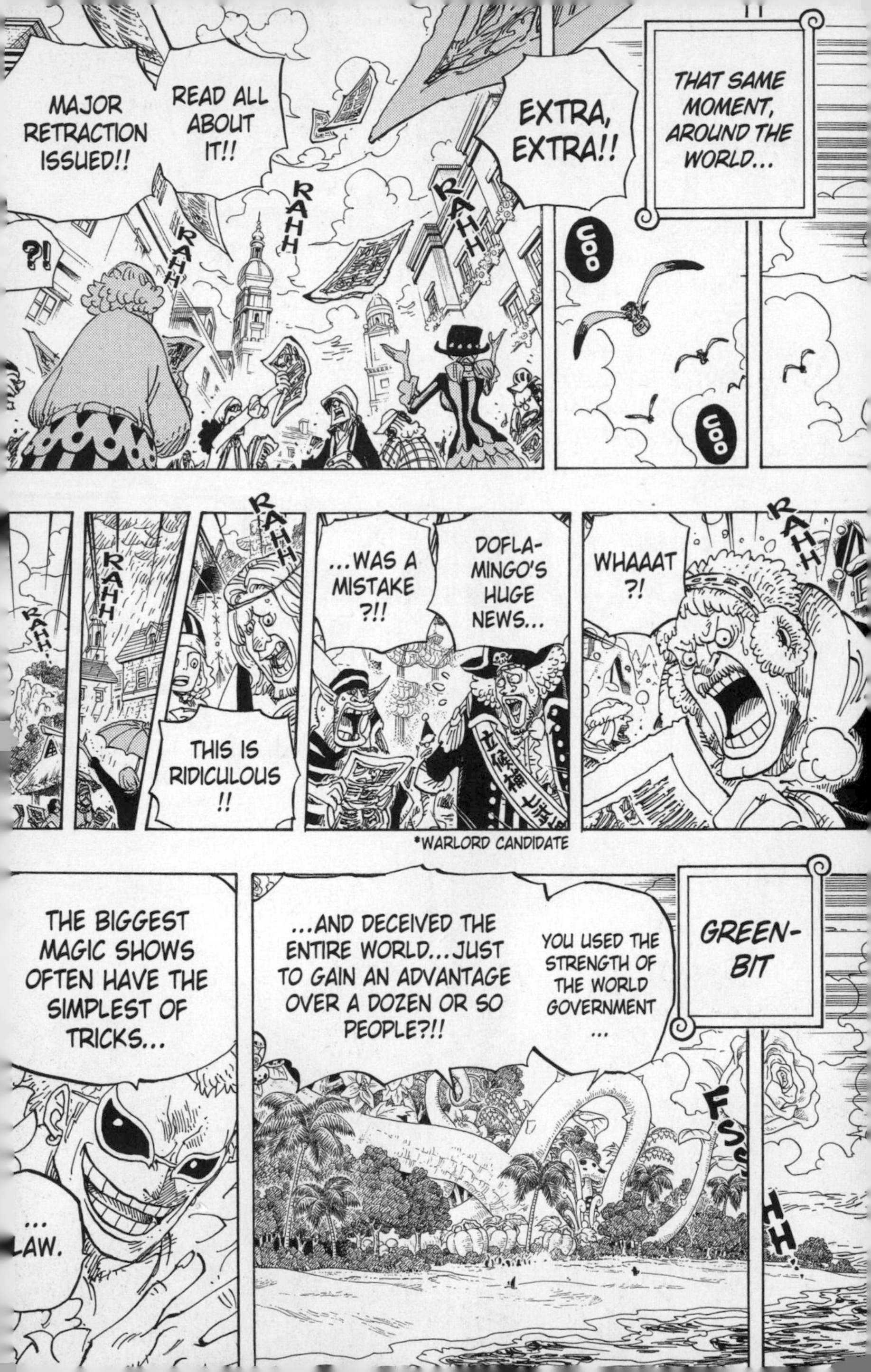
THAT SAME MOMENT, AROUND THE WORLD...
UOO
UOO
EXTRA, EXTRA!!
READ ALL ABOUT IT!!
MAJOR RETRACTION ISSUED!!
RAHH
RAHH
RAHH
?!
RAHH
WHAAAT?!
DOFLAMINGO'S HUGE NEWS...
...WAS A MISTAKE?!!
RAHH
THIS IS RIDICULOUS!!
RAHH
RAHH...
*WARLORD CANDIDATE
GREEN-BIT
FSSHH
YOU USED THE STRENGTH OF THE WORLD GOVERNMENT...
...AND DECEIVED THE ENTIRE WORLD...JUST TO GAIN AN ADVANTAGE OVER A DOZEN OR SO PEOPLE?!!
THE BIGGEST MAGIC SHOWS OFTEN HAVE THE SIMPLEST OF TRICKS...
...LAW.

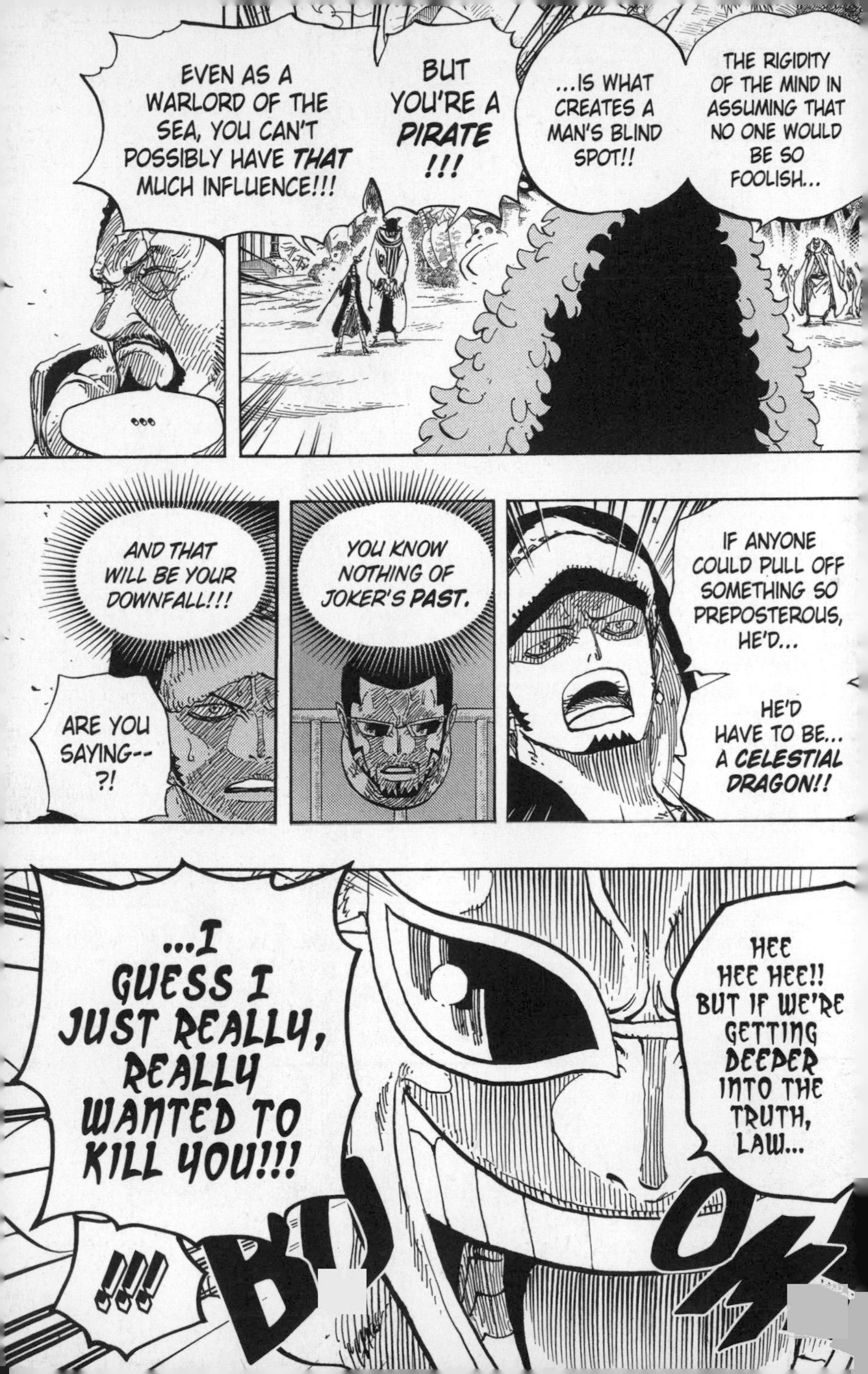
THE RIGIDITY OF THE MIND IN ASSUMING THAT NO ONE WOULD BE SO FOOLISH...
...IS WHAT CREATES A MAN'S BLIND SPOT!!
BUT YOU'RE A PIRATE!!!
EVEN AS A WARLORD OF THE SEA, YOU CAN'T POSSIBLY HAVE THAT MUCH INFLUENCE!!!
...
IF ANYONE COULD PULL OFF SOMETHING SO PREPOSTEROUS, HE'D...
HE'D HAVE TO BE... A CELESTIAL DRAGON!!
YOU KNOW NOTHING OF JOKER'S PAST.
AND THAT WILL BE YOUR DOWNFALL!!!
ARE YOU SAYING-- ?!
HEE HEE HEE!! BUT IF WE'RE GETTING DEEPER INTO THE TRUTH, LAW...
...I GUESS I JUST REALLY, REALLY WANTED TO KILL YOU!!!
BO
OM
!!!

SBS Question Corner

質問コーナー
エス
ビー
エス

(Hippo Iron, Saitama)

Q: Odacchi, Odacchi, Odacchi, good morning. By the way, let's begin the SBS. And now, my question. On page 128 of Volume 31, the kids are asking for a story about the land of the dwarves, right? Right? Right? Please explain.

--Uekenger

TELL US ABOUT THE COUNTRY OF DWARVES!

A: Geez, you've got the momentum of an avalanche, don't you? Starting the SBS, asking questions--I can't get a word in! I'm glad you found this, though. Perhaps you might find the answer to your question in Chapter 713, which starts right over there <--
Give it a read.

Q: When the crew left Punk Hazard, Franky's shirt said "JK" on it... But like, he makes such a gross JK (*joshi-kosei,* female high schooler)!!!

--Sanji Ikari

BF-
JK
LMNOPQ

A: Like OMG, I totally agree!! He's like, totally creepy!! But the more I see those braided pigtails, the more I think they look good on him...and that's like totally gross too!!

Q: Good day, Odacchi. Is this what you meant by the Ancient Weapon Pluton?

--Dobin

A: Those are croutons, right?!!
They're not ancient weapons named after gods in that soup...
They're just croutons, right?!! Σ(•□•)
Just crispy little pieces of bread, right?!

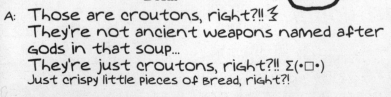

Chapter 713:
USOLAND

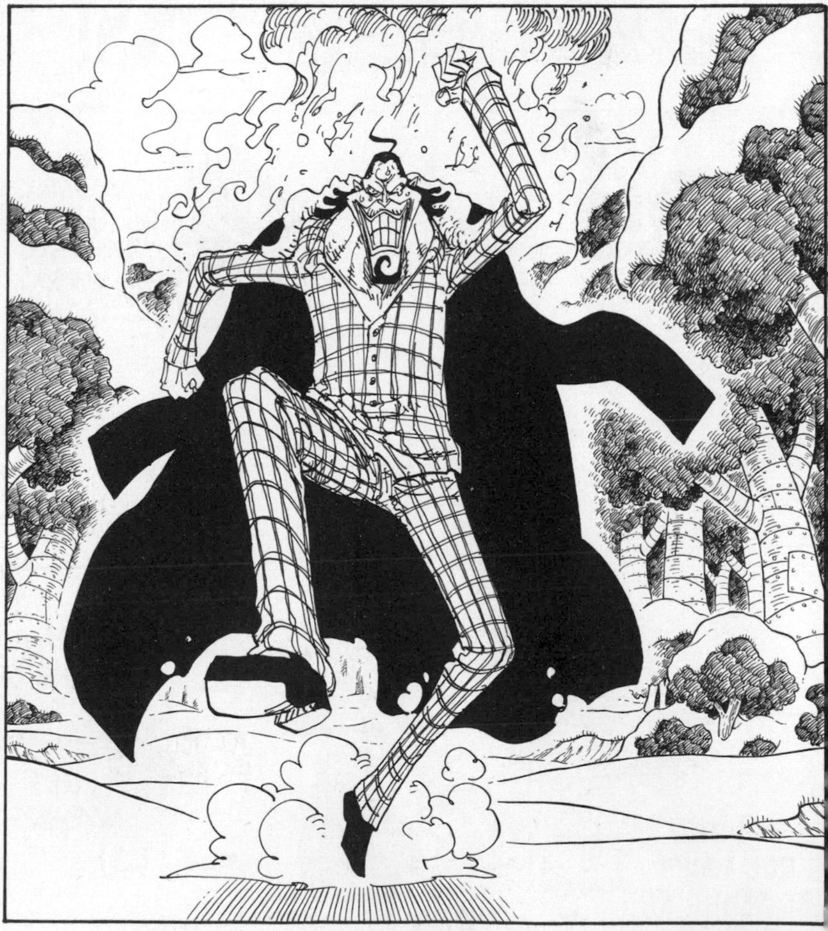

CARIBOU'S NEW WORLD KEE HEE HEE, VOL. 31:
"MAD DASH TO ESCAPE THE DEADLY PIRATE SCOTCH!!"

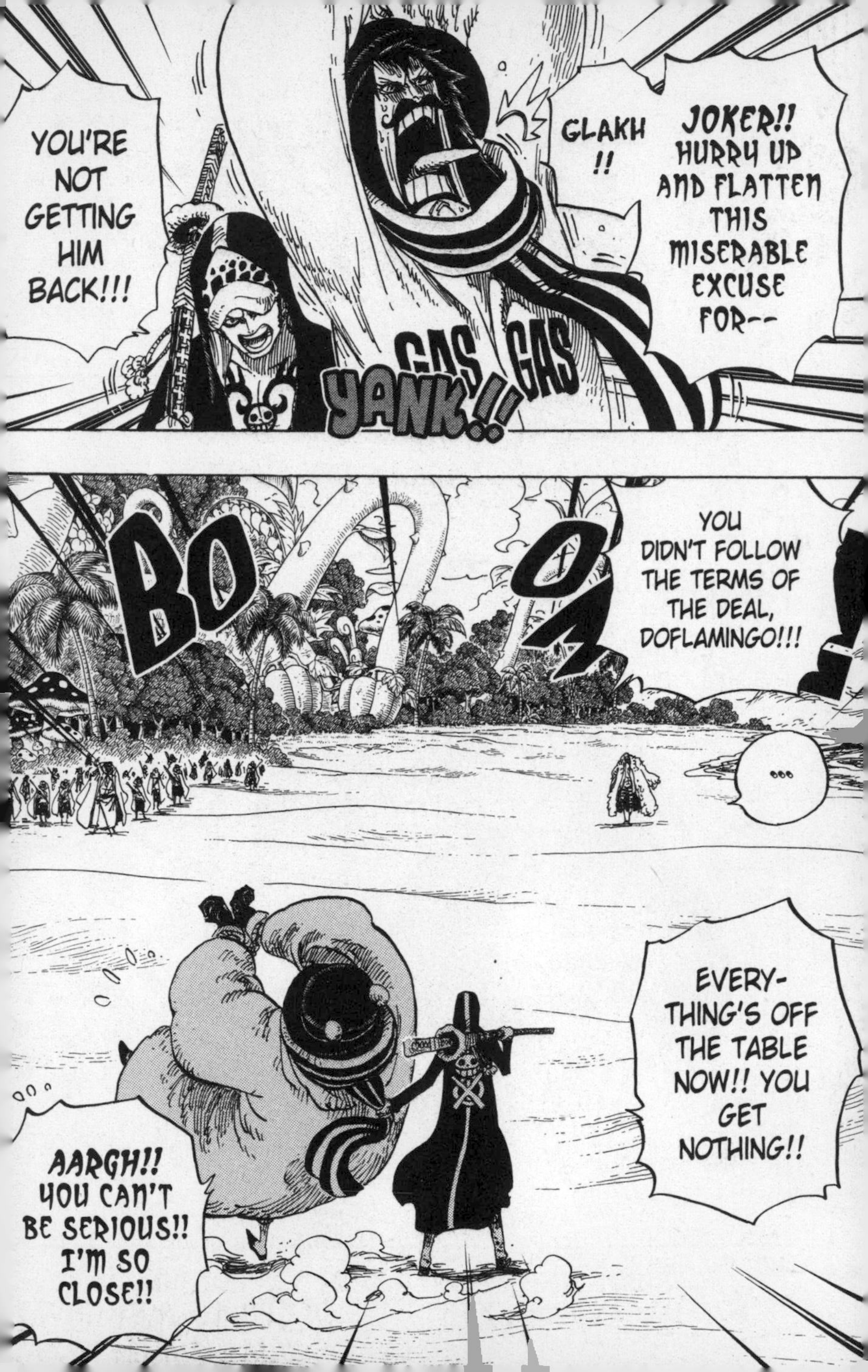
JOKER!! HURRY UP AND FLATTEN THIS MISERABLE EXCUSE FOR--
GLAKH !!
YOU'RE NOT GETTING HIM BACK!!!
GAS GAS
YANK!!
BOOM!
YOU DIDN'T FOLLOW THE TERMS OF THE DEAL, DOFLAMINGO!!!
...
EVERY-THING'S OFF THE TABLE NOW!! YOU GET NOTHING!!
AARGH!! YOU CAN'T BE SERIOUS!! I'M SO CLOSE!!

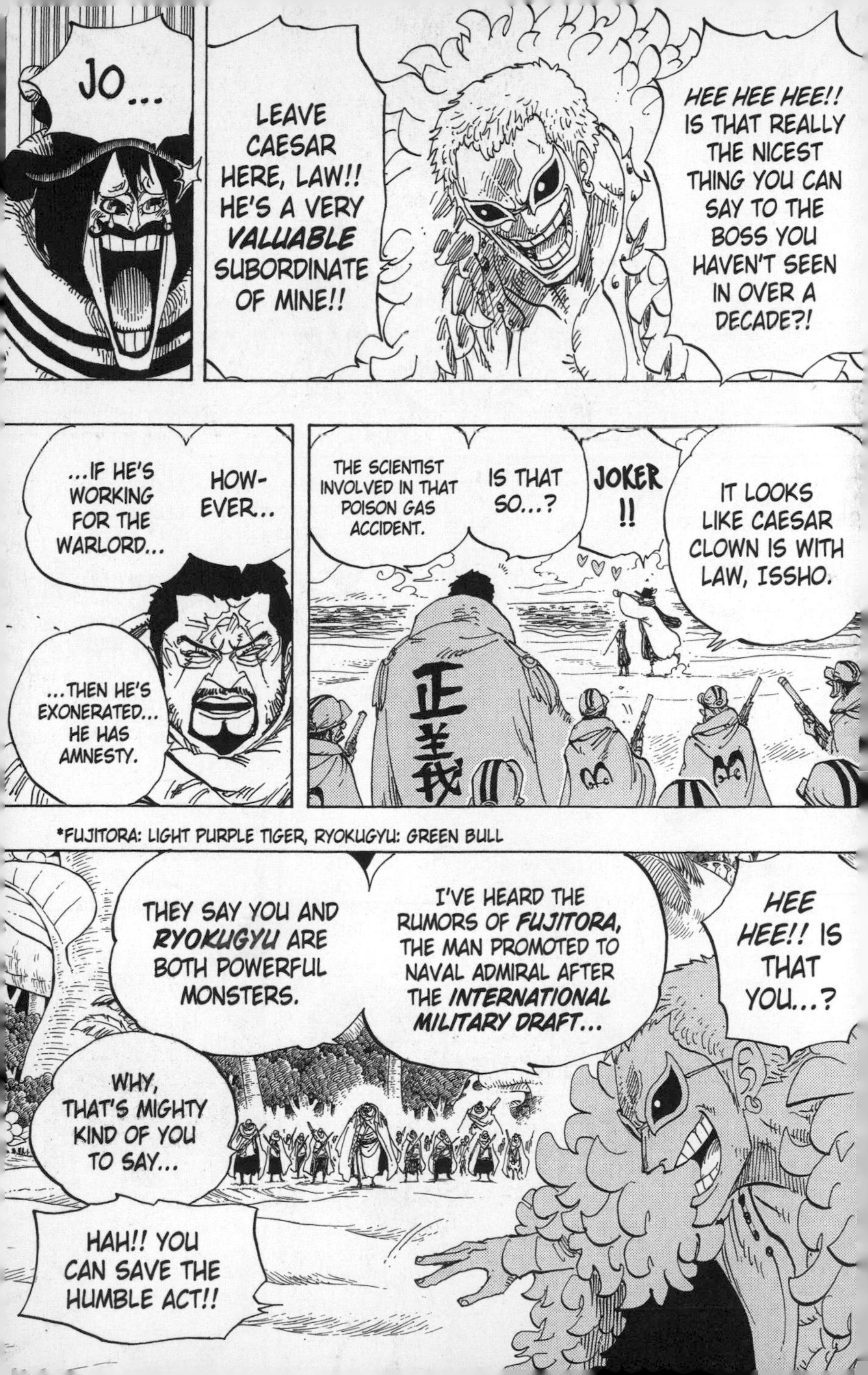
HEE HEE HEE!! IS THAT REALLY THE NICEST THING YOU CAN SAY TO THE BOSS YOU HAVEN'T SEEN IN OVER A DECADE?!
LEAVE CAESAR HERE, LAW!! HE'S A VERY VALUABLE SUBORDINATE OF MINE!!
JO...
IT LOOKS LIKE CAESAR CLOWN IS WITH LAW, ISSHO.
JOKER !!
IS THAT SO...?
THE SCIENTIST INVOLVED IN THAT POISON GAS ACCIDENT.
HOW-EVER...
...IF HE'S WORKING FOR THE WARLORD...
...THEN HE'S EXONERATED... HE HAS AMNESTY.
HEE HEE!! IS THAT YOU...?
I'VE HEARD THE RUMORS OF FUJITORA, THE MAN PROMOTED TO NAVAL ADMIRAL AFTER THE INTERNATIONAL MILITARY DRAFT...
THEY SAY YOU AND RYOKUGYU ARE BOTH POWERFUL MONSTERS.
WHY, THAT'S MIGHTY KIND OF YOU TO SAY...
HAH!! YOU CAN SAVE THE HUMBLE ACT!!

*FUJITORA: LIGHT PURPLE TIGER, RYOKUGYU: GREEN BULL

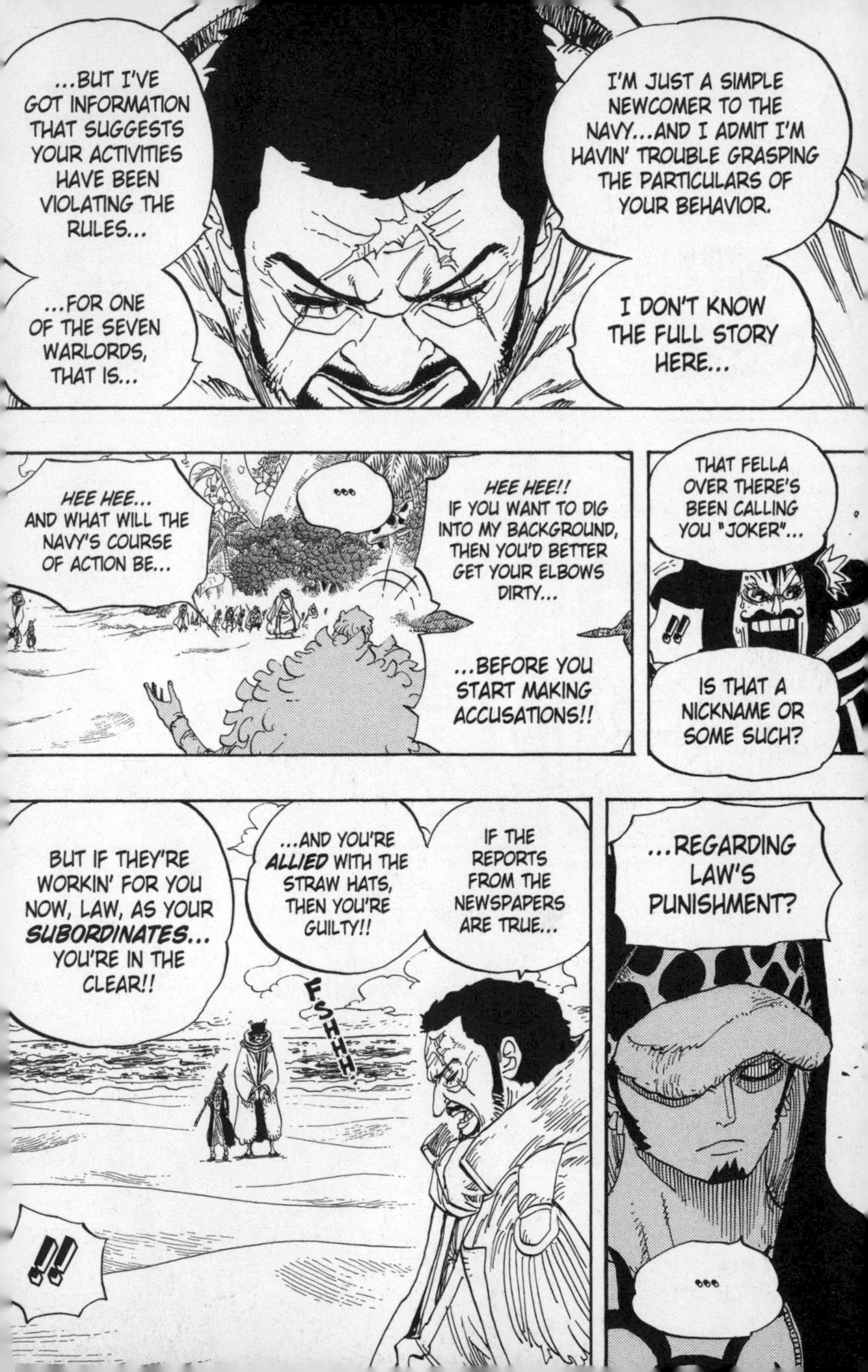
I'M JUST A SIMPLE NEWCOMER TO THE NAVY...AND I ADMIT I'M HAVIN' TROUBLE GRASPING THE PARTICULARS OF YOUR BEHAVIOR.
I DON'T KNOW THE FULL STORY HERE...
...BUT I'VE GOT INFORMATION THAT SUGGESTS YOUR ACTIVITIES HAVE BEEN VIOLATING THE RULES...
...FOR ONE OF THE SEVEN WARLORDS, THAT IS...
THAT FELLA OVER THERE'S BEEN CALLING YOU "JOKER"...
!!
IS THAT A NICKNAME OR SOME SUCH?
...
HEE HEE!! IF YOU WANT TO DIG INTO MY BACKGROUND, THEN YOU'D BETTER GET YOUR ELBOWS DIRTY...
...BEFORE YOU START MAKING ACCUSATIONS!!
HEE HEE... AND WHAT WILL THE NAVY'S COURSE OF ACTION BE...
...REGARDING LAW'S PUNISHMENT?
...
IF THE REPORTS FROM THE NEWSPAPERS ARE TRUE...
...AND YOU'RE ***ALLIED*** WITH THE STRAW HATS, THEN YOU'RE GUILTY!!
FSHHH
BUT IF THEY'RE WORKIN' FOR YOU NOW, LAW, AS YOUR ***SUBORDINATES...*** YOU'RE IN THE CLEAR!!
!!

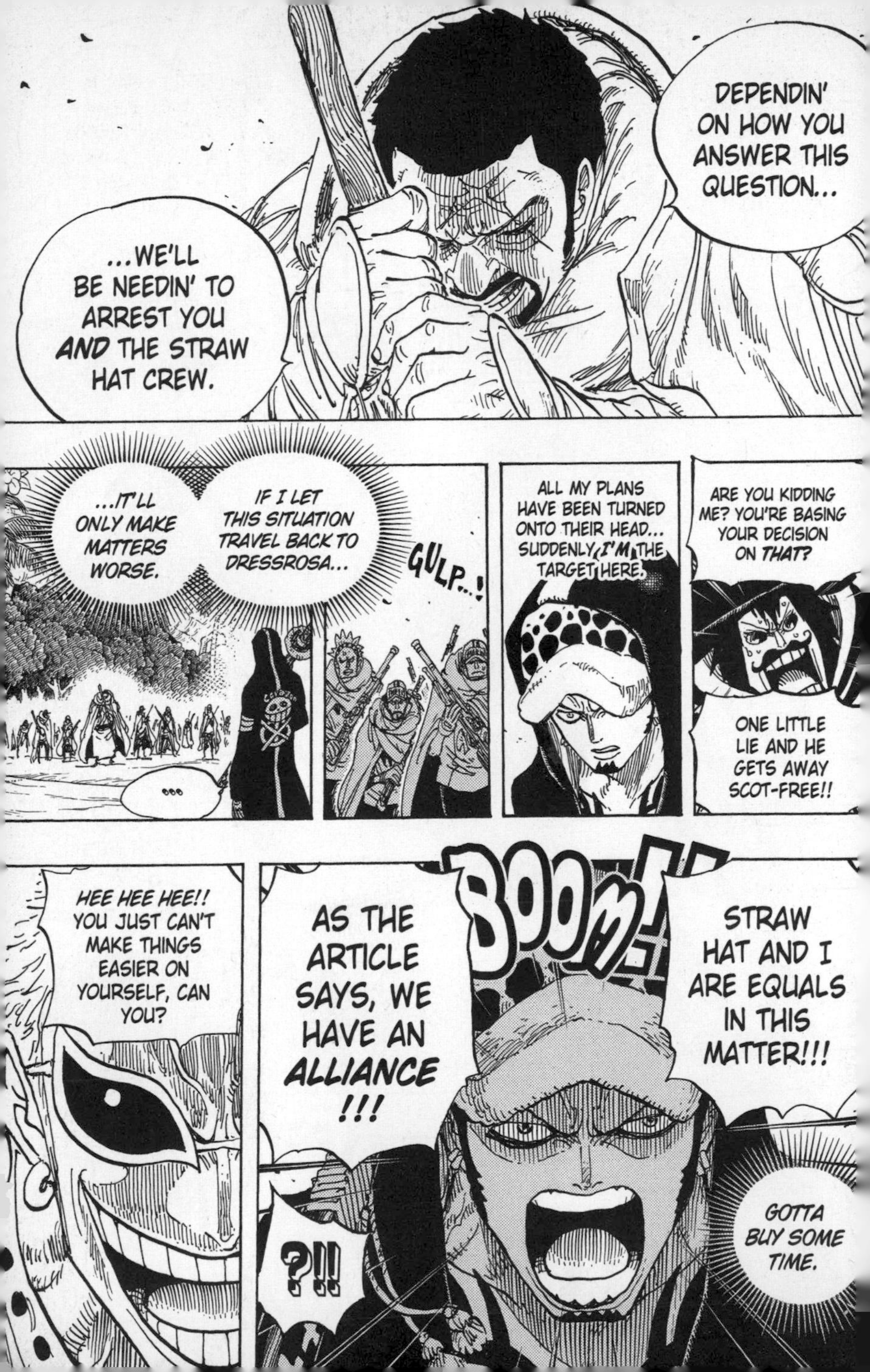
DEPENDIN' ON HOW YOU ANSWER THIS QUESTION...
...WE'LL BE NEEDIN' TO ARREST YOU AND THE STRAW HAT CREW.
ARE YOU KIDDING ME? YOU'RE BASING YOUR DECISION ON THAT?
ONE LITTLE LIE AND HE GETS AWAY SCOT-FREE!!
ALL MY PLANS HAVE BEEN TURNED ONTO THEIR HEAD... SUDDENLY I'M THE TARGET HERE.
GULP...!
IF I LET THIS SITUATION TRAVEL BACK TO DRESSROSA...
...IT'LL ONLY MAKE MATTERS WORSE.
...
BOOM!!
STRAW HAT AND I ARE EQUALS IN THIS MATTER!!!
AS THE ARTICLE SAYS, WE HAVE AN ALLIANCE!!!
GOTTA BUY SOME TIME.
?!!
HEE HEE HEE!! YOU JUST CAN'T MAKE THINGS EASIER ON YOURSELF, CAN YOU?

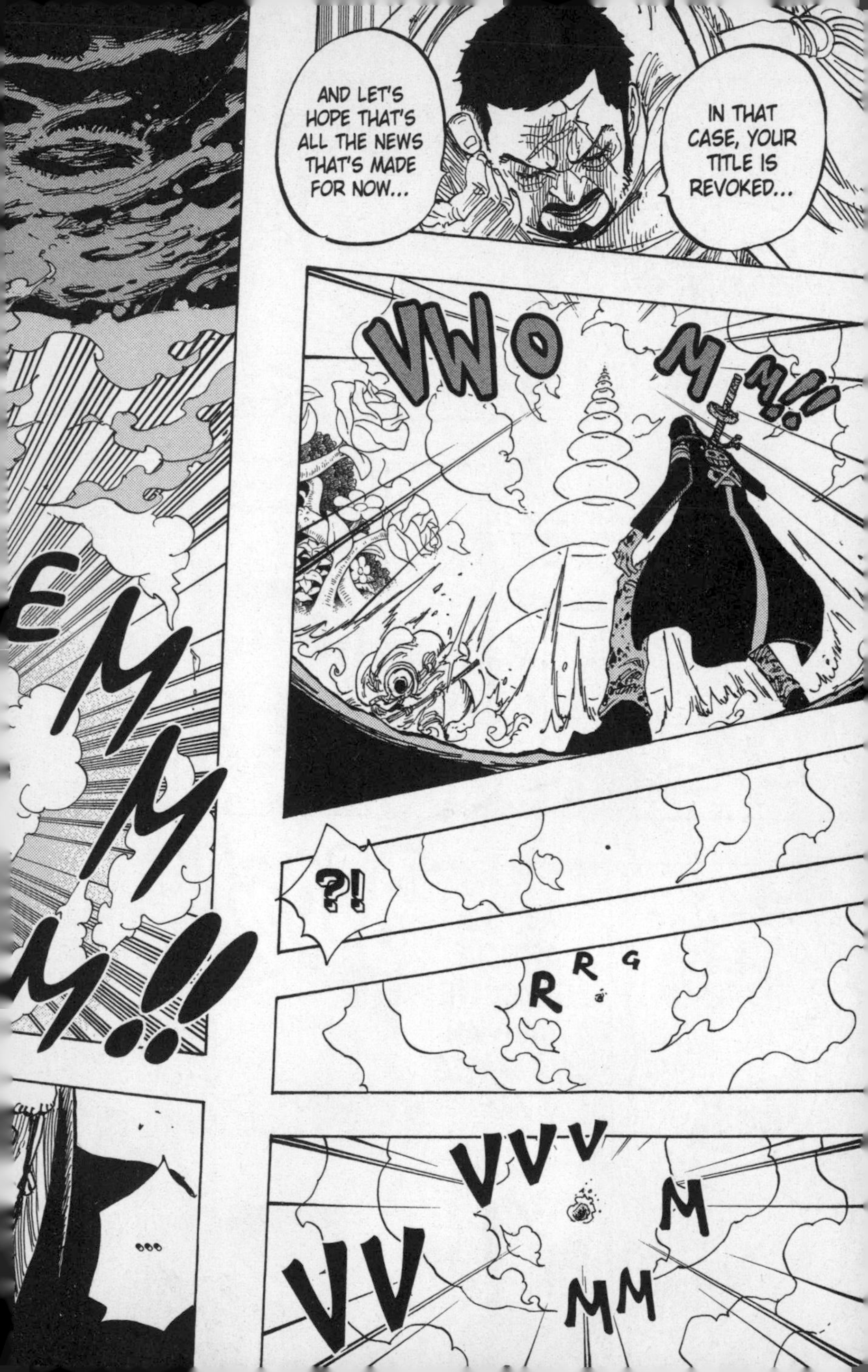
IN THAT CASE, YOUR TITLE IS REVOKED...
AND LET'S HOPE THAT'S ALL THE NEWS THAT'S MADE FOR NOW...
VWOMM!!
?!
RRG
VVVVVMMM
EMMM!!
...

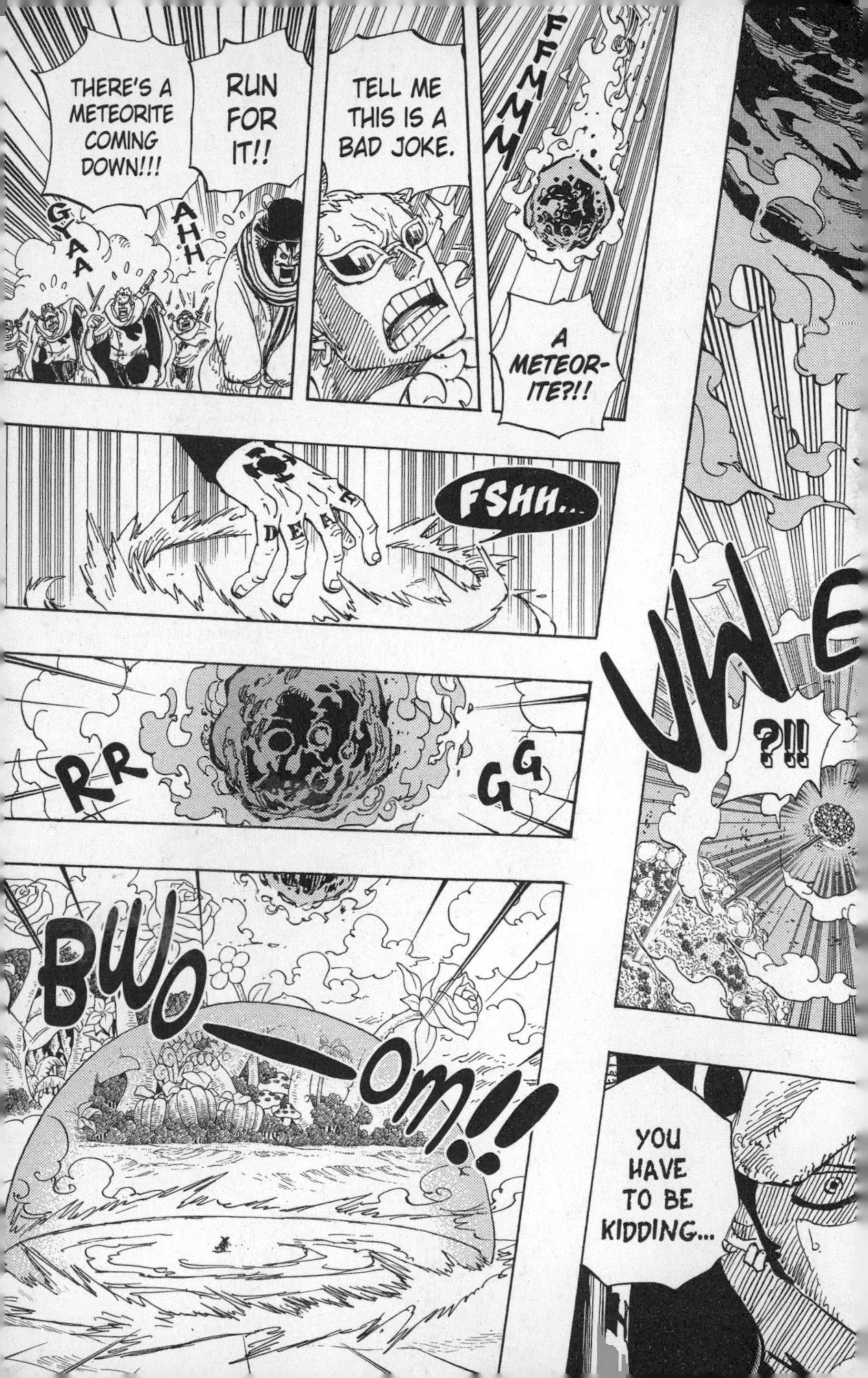
FFMMMM
A METEOR-ITE?!!
TELL ME THIS IS A BAD JOKE.
RUN FOR IT!!
THERE'S A METEORITE COMING DOWN!!!
AHH
GYAA
FSHH...
VWE
?!!
RR
GG
BUOO—OM!!
YOU HAVE TO BE KIDDING...

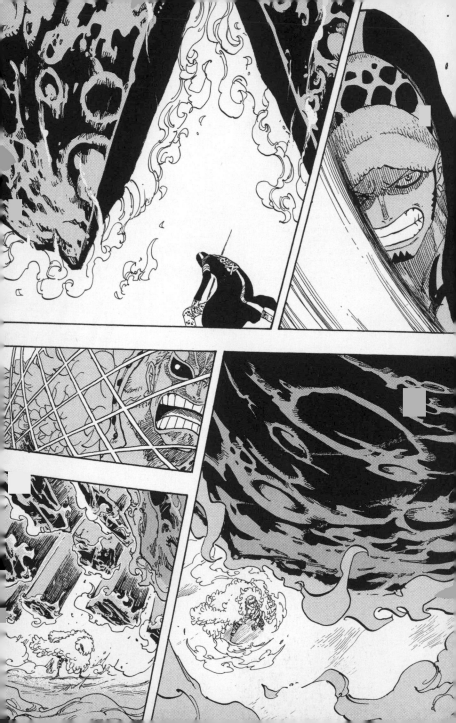

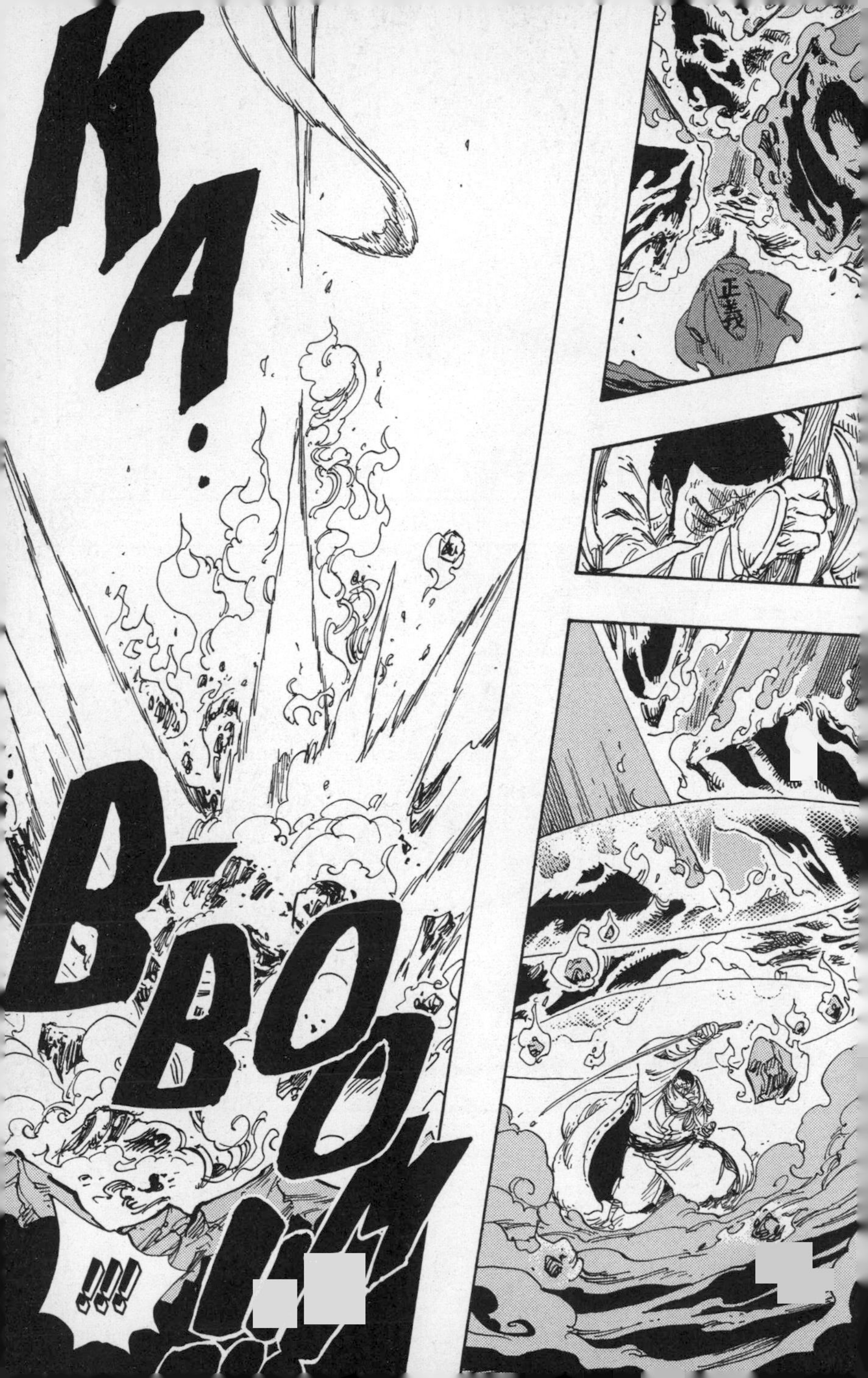
正義
KA-BOOM!!!

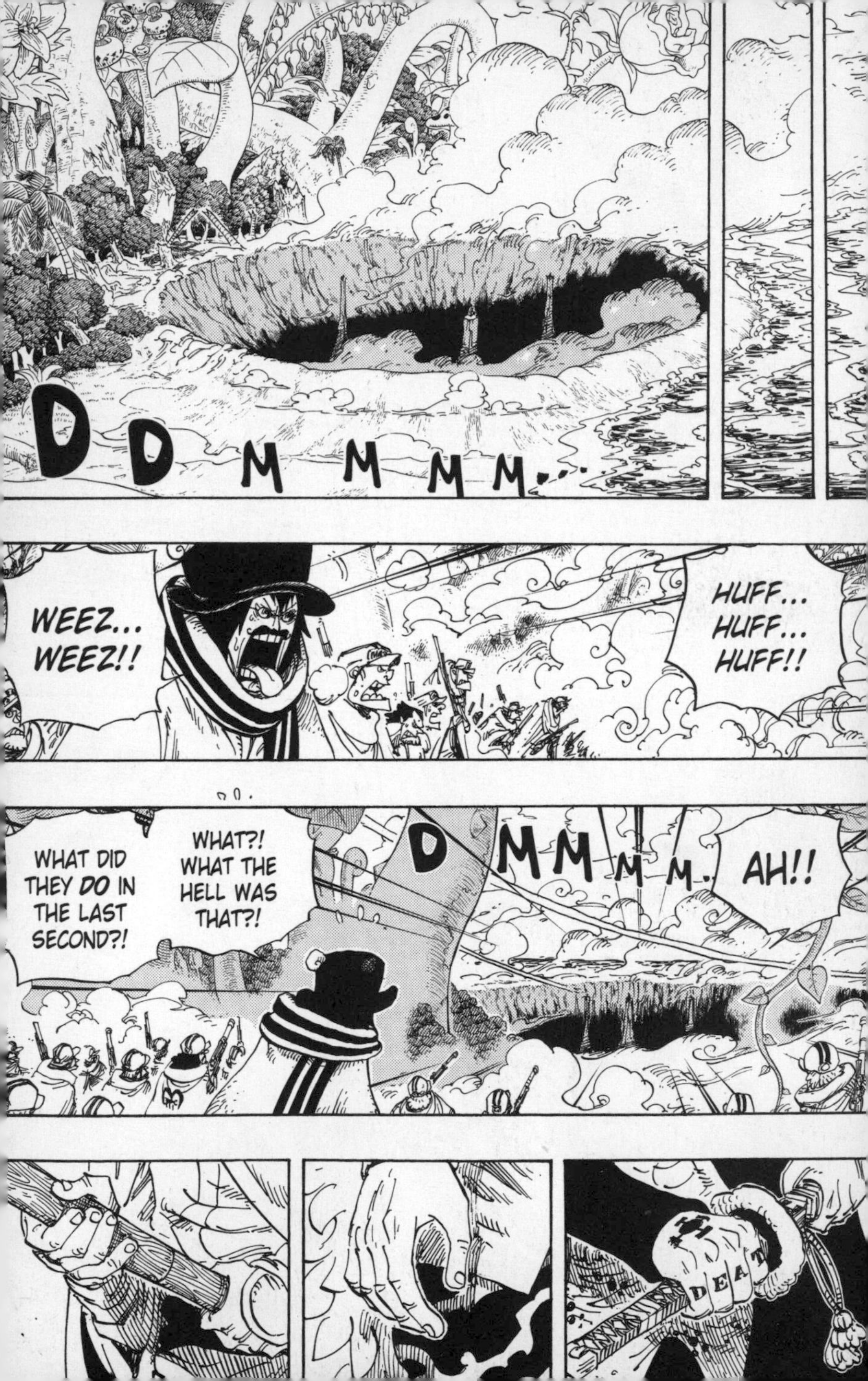
DDMMMM...
HUFF... HUFF... HUFF!!
WEEZ... WEEZ!!
AH!!
DMMMM...
WHAT?! WHAT THE HELL WAS THAT?!
WHAT DID THEY DO IN THE LAST SECOND?!
DEAT

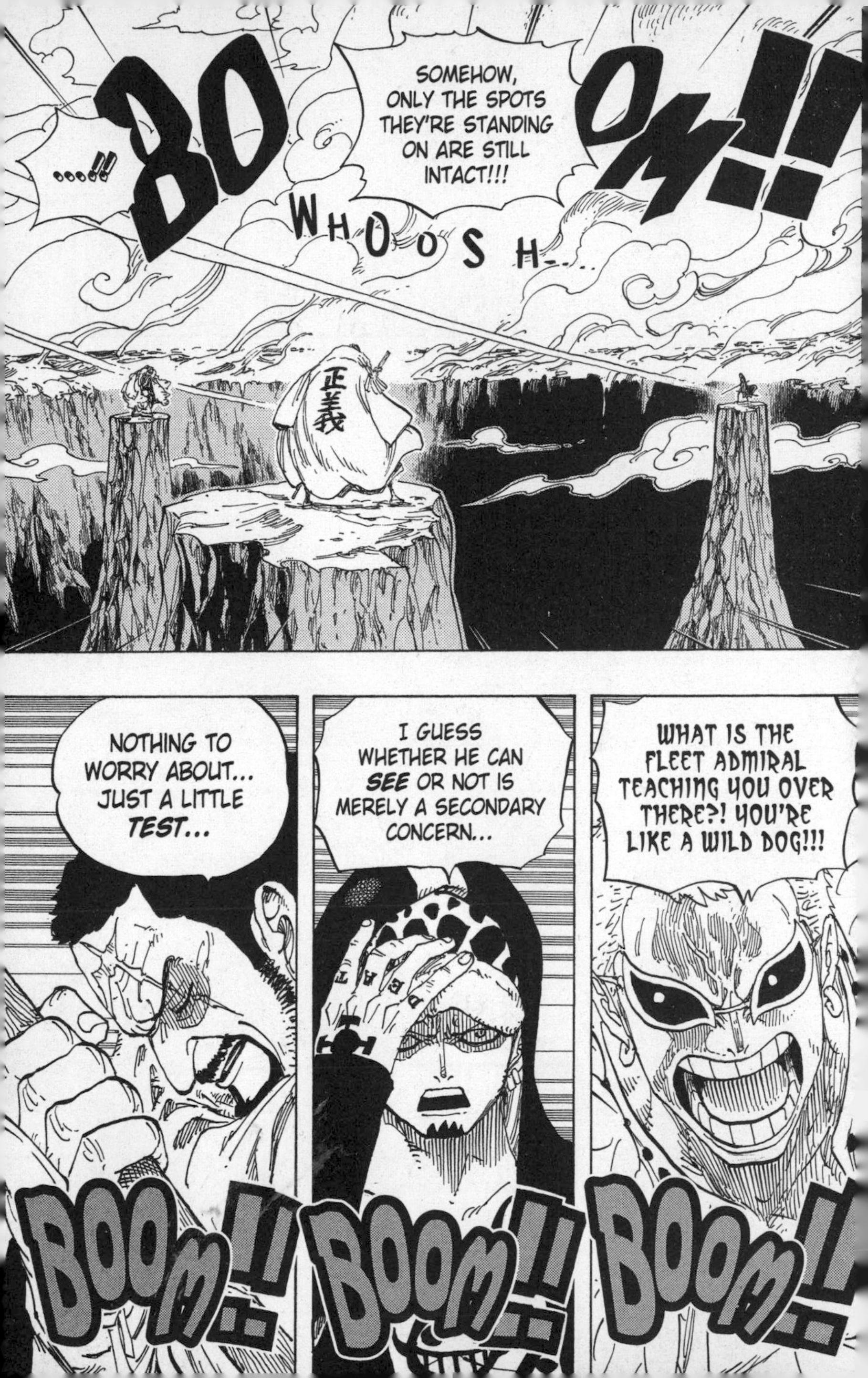
BOOM!!
SOMEHOW, ONLY THE SPOTS THEY'RE STANDING ON ARE STILL INTACT!!!
.....!!
WHOOSH...
正義
WHAT IS THE FLEET ADMIRAL TEACHING YOU OVER THERE?! YOU'RE LIKE A WILD DOG!!!
BOOM!!
I GUESS WHETHER HE CAN SEE OR NOT IS MERELY A SECONDARY CONCERN...
BOOM!!
NOTHING TO WORRY ABOUT... JUST A LITTLE TEST...
BOOM!!

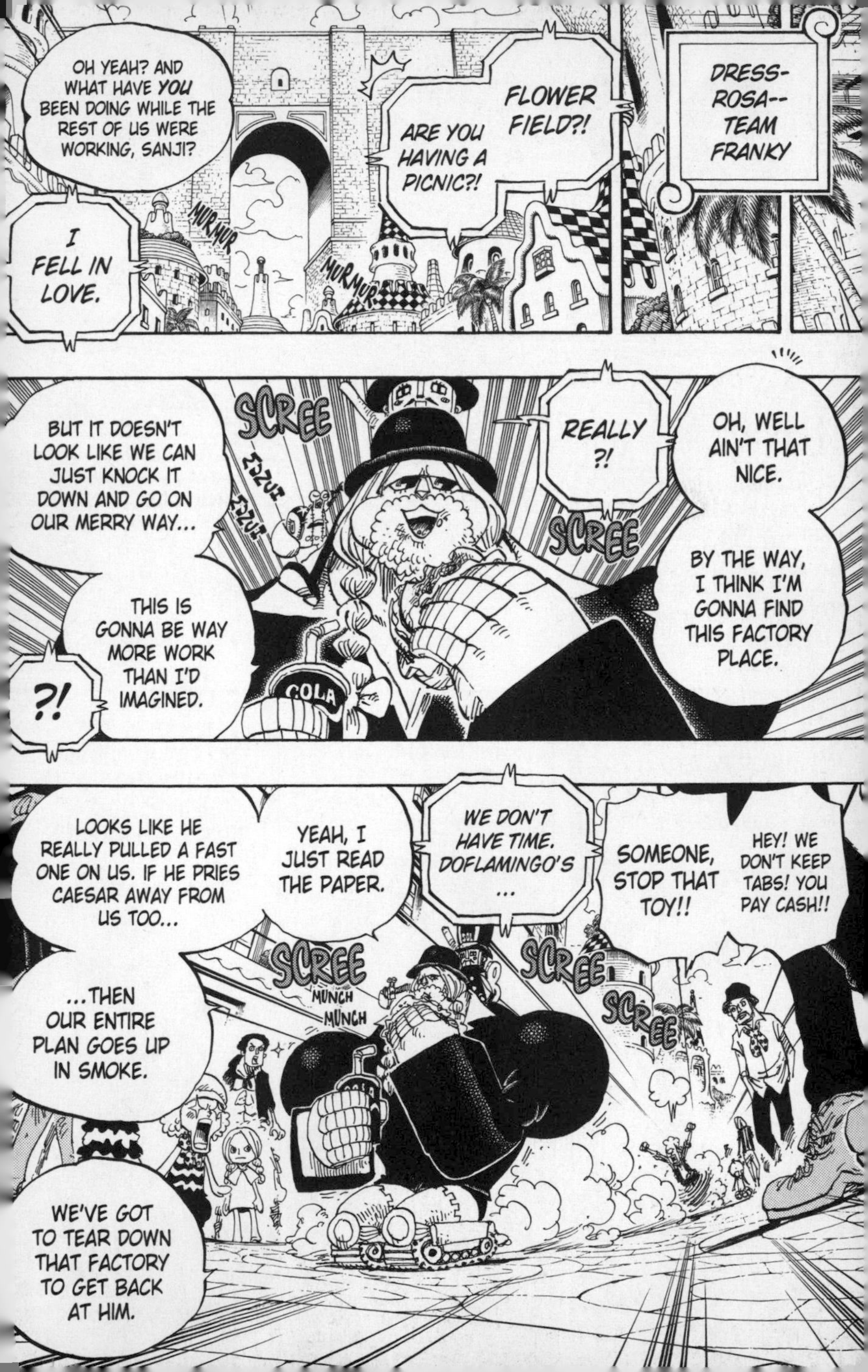
DRESS-ROSA--TEAM FRANKY
FLOWER FIELD?!
ARE YOU HAVING A PICNIC?!
MURMUR
MURMUR
OH YEAH? AND WHAT HAVE YOU BEEN DOING WHILE THE REST OF US WERE WORKING, SANJI?
I FELL IN LOVE.
OH, WELL AIN'T THAT NICE.
REALLY?!
SCREE
BY THE WAY, I THINK I'M GONNA FIND THIS FACTORY PLACE.
SCREE
BUT IT DOESN'T LOOK LIKE WE CAN JUST KNOCK IT DOWN AND GO ON OUR MERRY WAY...
THIS IS GONNA BE WAY MORE WORK THAN I'D IMAGINED.
?!
COLA
HEY! WE DON'T KEEP TABS! YOU PAY CASH!!
SOMEONE, STOP THAT TOY!!
WE DON'T HAVE TIME. DOFLAMINGO'S ...
SCREE
SCREE
YEAH, I JUST READ THE PAPER.
SCREE
MUNCH
MUNCH
LOOKS LIKE HE REALLY PULLED A FAST ONE ON US. IF HE PRIES CAESAR AWAY FROM US TOO...
...THEN OUR ENTIRE PLAN GOES UP IN SMOKE.
WE'VE GOT TO TEAR DOWN THAT FACTORY TO GET BACK AT HIM.

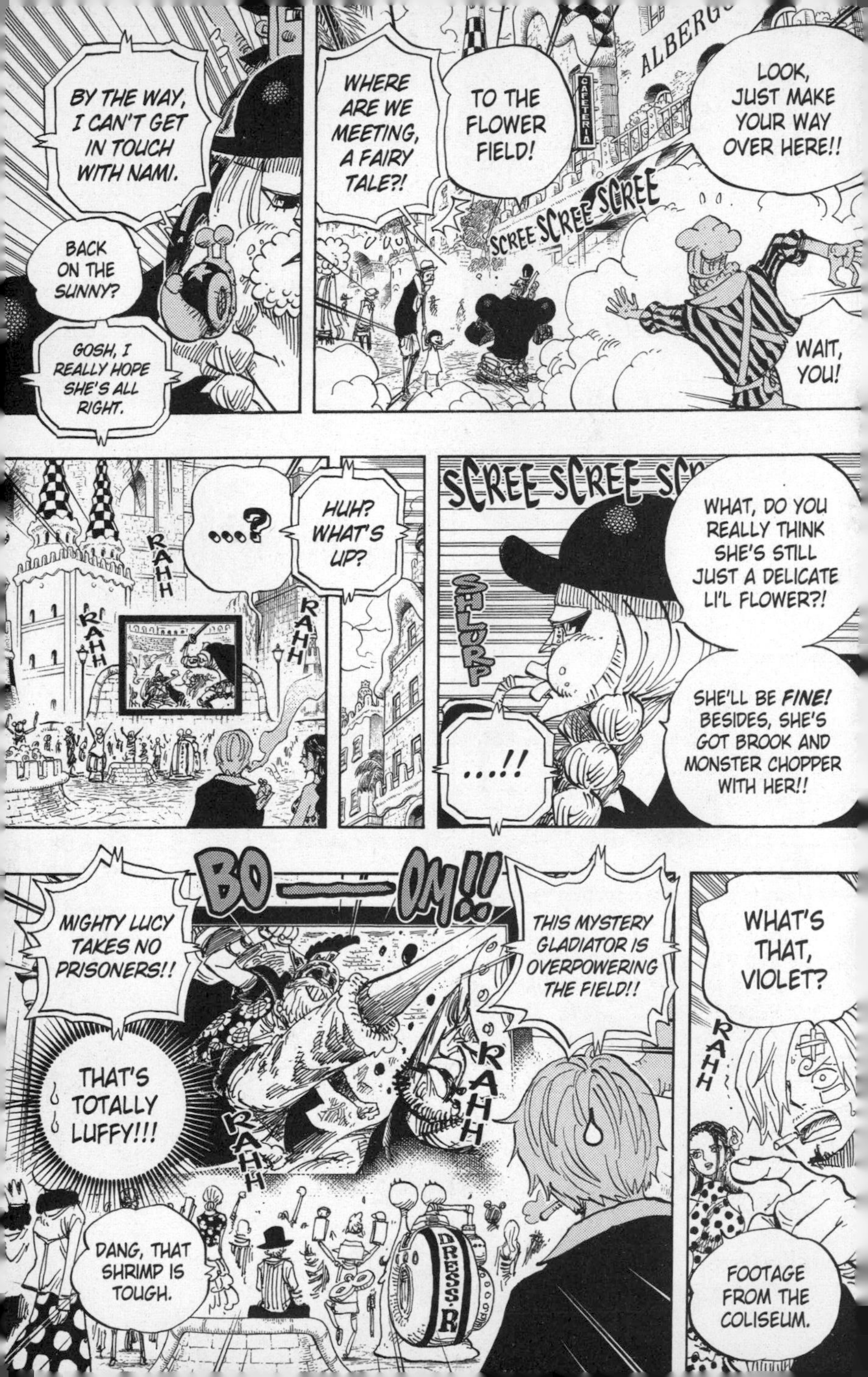
ALBERGO
CAFETERIA
LOOK, JUST MAKE YOUR WAY OVER HERE!!
TO THE FLOWER FIELD!
WHERE ARE WE MEETING, A FAIRY TALE?!
SCREE SCREE SCREE
WAIT, YOU!
BY THE WAY, I CAN'T GET IN TOUCH WITH NAMI.
BACK ON THE SUNNY?
GOSH, I REALLY HOPE SHE'S ALL RIGHT.
SCREE SCREE
WHAT, DO YOU REALLY THINK SHE'S STILL JUST A DELICATE LI'L FLOWER?!
SHLURP
SHE'LL BE *FINE!* BESIDES, SHE'S GOT BROOK AND MONSTER CHOPPER WITH HER!!
...!!
HUH? WHAT'S UP?
RAHH
RAHH
...?
RAHH
RAHH
WHAT'S THAT, VIOLET?
RAHH
FOOTAGE FROM THE COLISEUM.
BO—OM!!
THIS MYSTERY GLADIATOR IS OVERPOWERING THE FIELD!!
MIGHTY LUCY TAKES NO PRISONERS!!
RAHH
RAHH
THAT'S TOTALLY LUFFY!!!
DANG, THAT SHRIMP IS TOUGH.
DRESS R

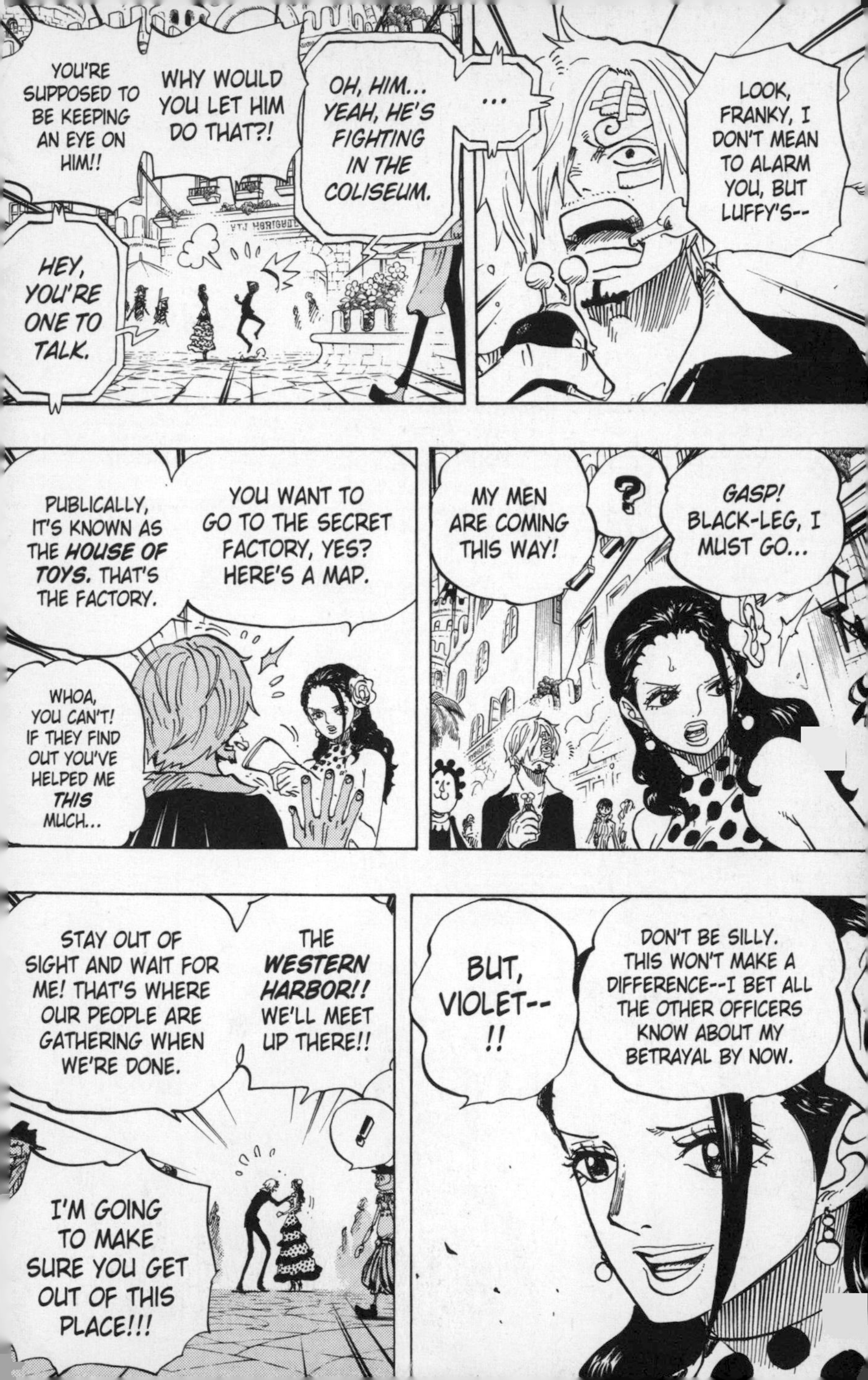
LOOK, FRANKY, I DON'T MEAN TO ALARM YOU, BUT LUFFY'S--
...
OH, HIM... YEAH, HE'S FIGHTING IN THE COLISEUM.
WHY WOULD YOU LET HIM DO THAT?!
YOU'RE SUPPOSED TO BE KEEPING AN EYE ON HIM!!
HEY, YOU'RE ONE TO TALK.
GASP! BLACK-LEG, I MUST GO...
?
MY MEN ARE COMING THIS WAY!
YOU WANT TO GO TO THE SECRET FACTORY, YES? HERE'S A MAP.
PUBLICALLY, IT'S KNOWN AS THE HOUSE OF TOYS. THAT'S THE FACTORY.
WHOA, YOU CAN'T! IF THEY FIND OUT YOU'VE HELPED ME THIS MUCH...
DON'T BE SILLY. THIS WON'T MAKE A DIFFERENCE--I BET ALL THE OTHER OFFICERS KNOW ABOUT MY BETRAYAL BY NOW.
BUT, VIOLET-- !!
THE WESTERN HARBOR!! WE'LL MEET UP THERE!!
STAY OUT OF SIGHT AND WAIT FOR ME! THAT'S WHERE OUR PEOPLE ARE GATHERING WHEN WE'RE DONE.
!
I'M GOING TO MAKE SURE YOU GET OUT OF THIS PLACE!!!

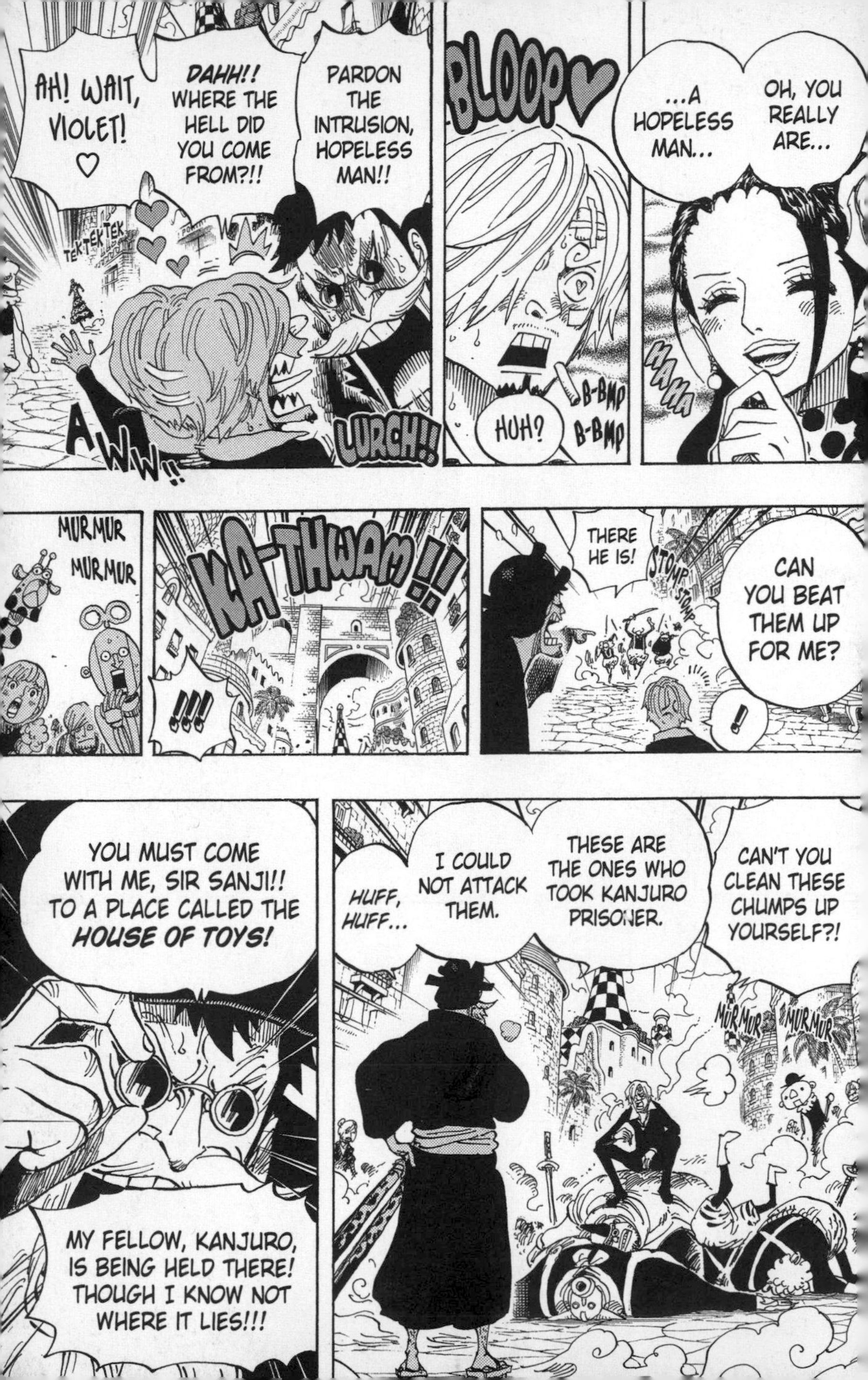
OH, YOU REALLY ARE...
...A HOPELESS MAN...
HAHA
BLOOP♡
HUH?
B-BMP
B-BMP
PARDON THE INTRUSION, HOPELESS MAN!!
DAHH!! WHERE THE HELL DID YOU COME FROM?!!
AH! WAIT, VIOLET! ♡
TEKTEKTEK
LURCH!!
AWWW!!
CAN YOU BEAT THEM UP FOR ME?
THERE HE IS!
STOMP STOMP
!
KA-THWAM!!
!!!
MURMUR
MURMUR
CAN'T YOU CLEAN THESE CHUMPS UP YOURSELF?!
THESE ARE THE ONES WHO TOOK KANJURO PRISONER.
I COULD NOT ATTACK THEM.
HUFF, HUFF...
MURMUR
MURMUR
YOU MUST COME WITH ME, SIR SANJI!! TO A PLACE CALLED THE HOUSE OF TOYS!
MY FELLOW, KANJURO, IS BEING HELD THERE! THOUGH I KNOW NOT WHERE IT LIES!!!

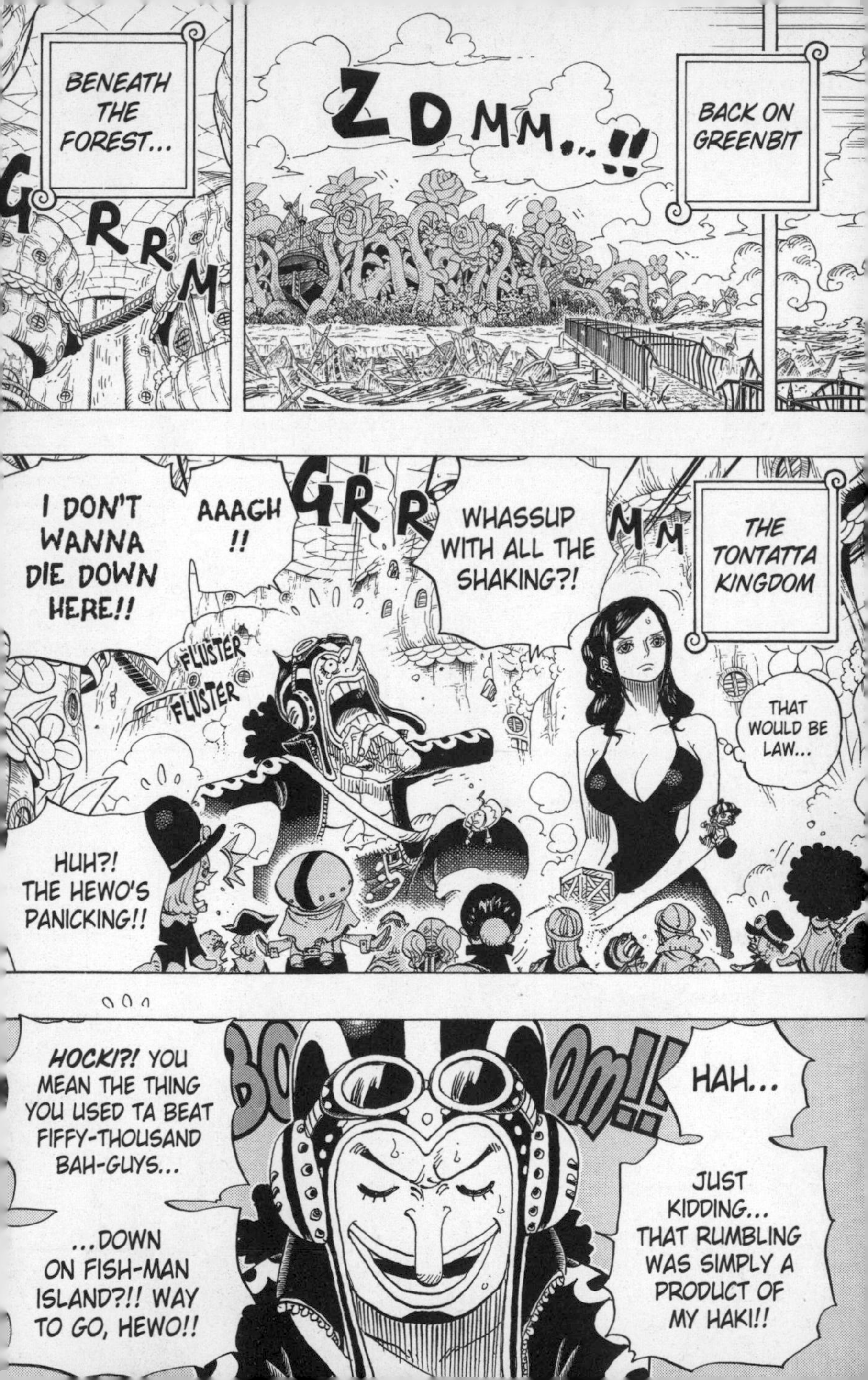
BACK ON GREENBIT
ZDMM...!!
BENEATH THE FOREST...
GRRRM
THE TONTATTA KINGDOM
GRR
MM
THAT WOULD BE LAW...
WHASSUP WITH ALL THE SHAKING?!
AAAGH !!
I DON'T WANNA DIE DOWN HERE!!
FLUSTER FLUSTER
HUH?! THE HEWO'S PANICKING!!
HAH...
BO
OM!!
JUST KIDDING... THAT RUMBLING WAS SIMPLY A PRODUCT OF MY HAKI!!
HOCKI?! YOU MEAN THE THING YOU USED TA BEAT FIFFY-THOUSAND BAH-GUYS...
...DOWN ON FISH-MAN ISLAND?!! WAY TO GO, HEWO!!

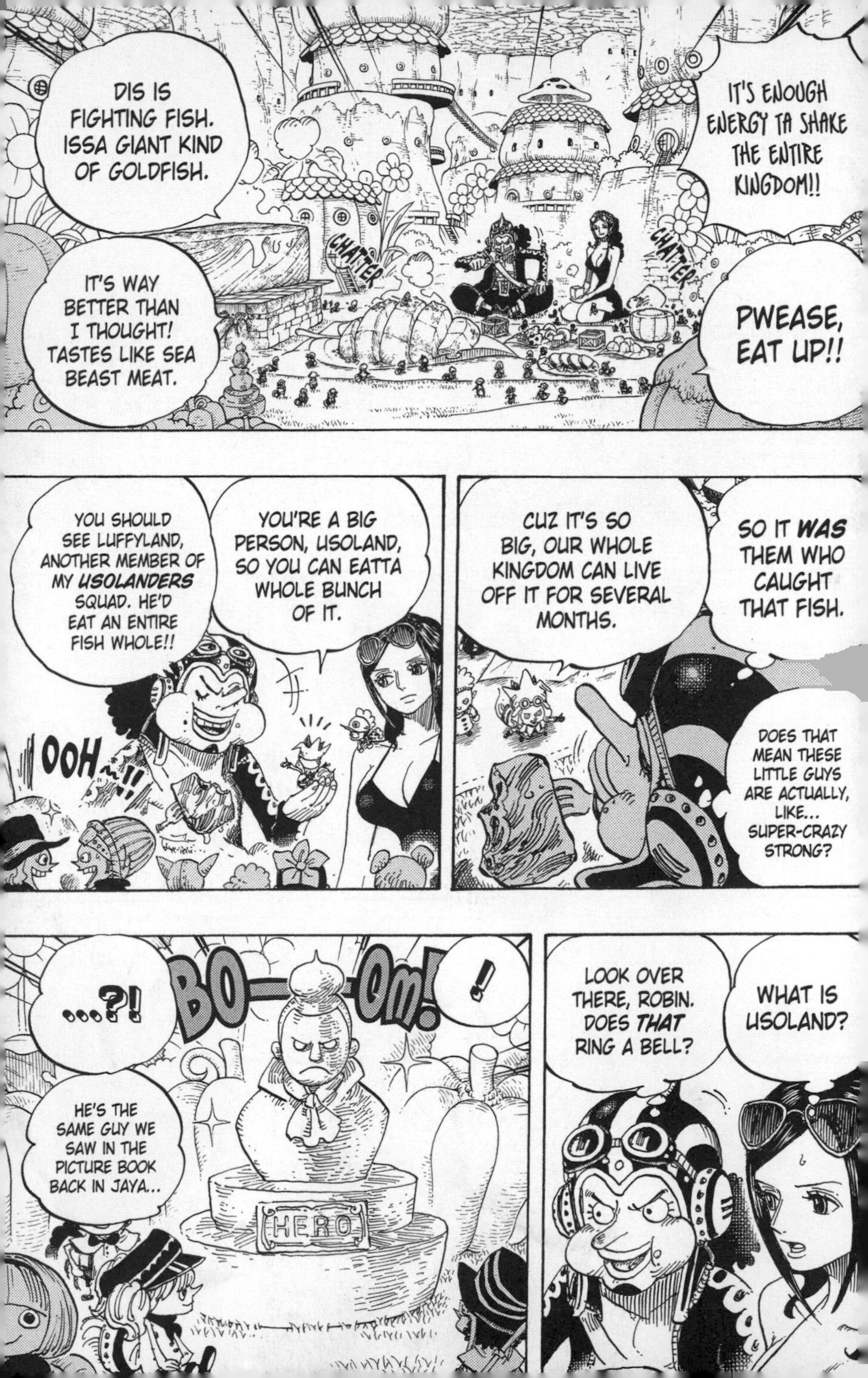

IT'S ENOUGH ENERGY TA SHAKE THE ENTIRE KINGDOM!!
PWEASE, EAT UP!!
DIS IS FIGHTING FISH. ISSA GIANT KIND OF GOLDFISH.
CHATTER
CHATTER
IT'S WAY BETTER THAN I THOUGHT! TASTES LIKE SEA BEAST MEAT.
SO IT **WAS** THEM WHO CAUGHT THAT FISH.
CUZ IT'S SO BIG, OUR WHOLE KINGDOM CAN LIVE OFF IT FOR SEVERAL MONTHS.
DOES THAT MEAN THESE LITTLE GUYS ARE ACTUALLY, LIKE... SUPER-CRAZY STRONG?
YOU'RE A BIG PERSON, USOLAND, SO YOU CAN EATTA WHOLE BUNCH OF IT.
YOU SHOULD SEE LUFFYLAND, ANOTHER MEMBER OF MY ***USOLANDERS*** SQUAD. HE'D EAT AN ENTIRE FISH WHOLE!!
OOH~!!
WHAT IS USOLAND?
LOOK OVER THERE, ROBIN. DOES ***THAT*** RING A BELL?
!
BO—OM!
...?!
HE'S THE SAME GUY WE SAW IN THE PICTURE BOOK BACK IN JAYA...
HERO

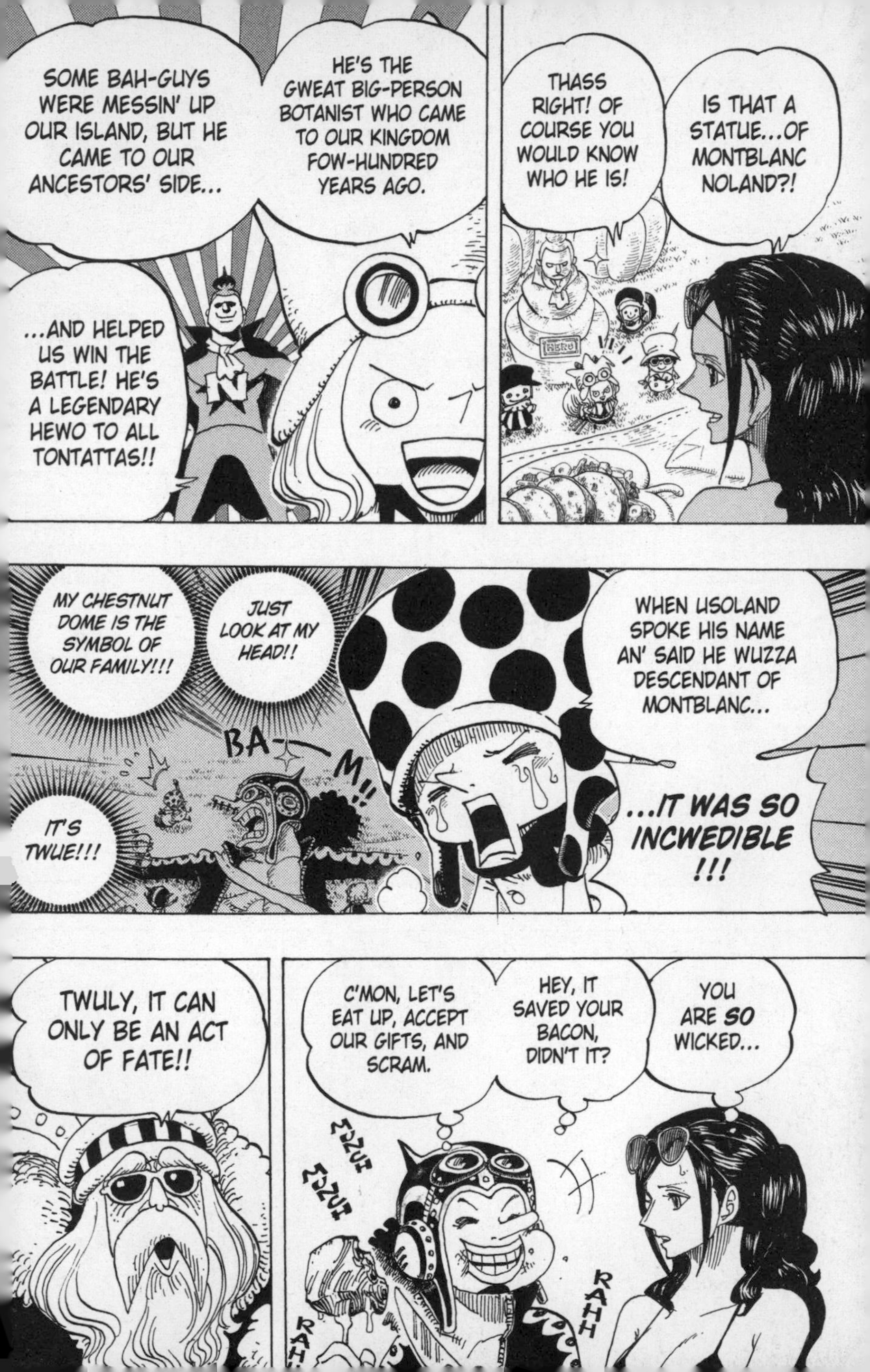
IS THAT A STATUE...OF MONTBLANC NOLAND?!
THASS RIGHT! OF COURSE YOU WOULD KNOW WHO HE IS!
HE'S THE GWEAT BIG-PERSON BOTANIST WHO CAME TO OUR KINGDOM FOW-HUNDRED YEARS AGO.
SOME BAH-GUYS WERE MESSIN' UP OUR ISLAND, BUT HE CAME TO OUR ANCESTORS' SIDE...
...AND HELPED US WIN THE BATTLE! HE'S A LEGENDARY HEWO TO ALL TONTATTAS!!
WHEN USOLAND SPOKE HIS NAME AN' SAID HE WUZZA DESCENDANT OF MONTBLANC...
...IT WAS SO INCWEDIBLE !!!
JUST LOOK AT MY HEAD!!
MY CHESTNUT DOME IS THE SYMBOL OF OUR FAMILY!!!
BA-M!!
IT'S TWUE!!!
YOU ARE SO WICKED...
HEY, IT SAVED YOUR BACON, DIDN'T IT?
C'MON, LET'S EAT UP, ACCEPT OUR GIFTS, AND SCRAM.
RAHH
RAHH
TWULY, IT CAN ONLY BE AN ACT OF FATE!!

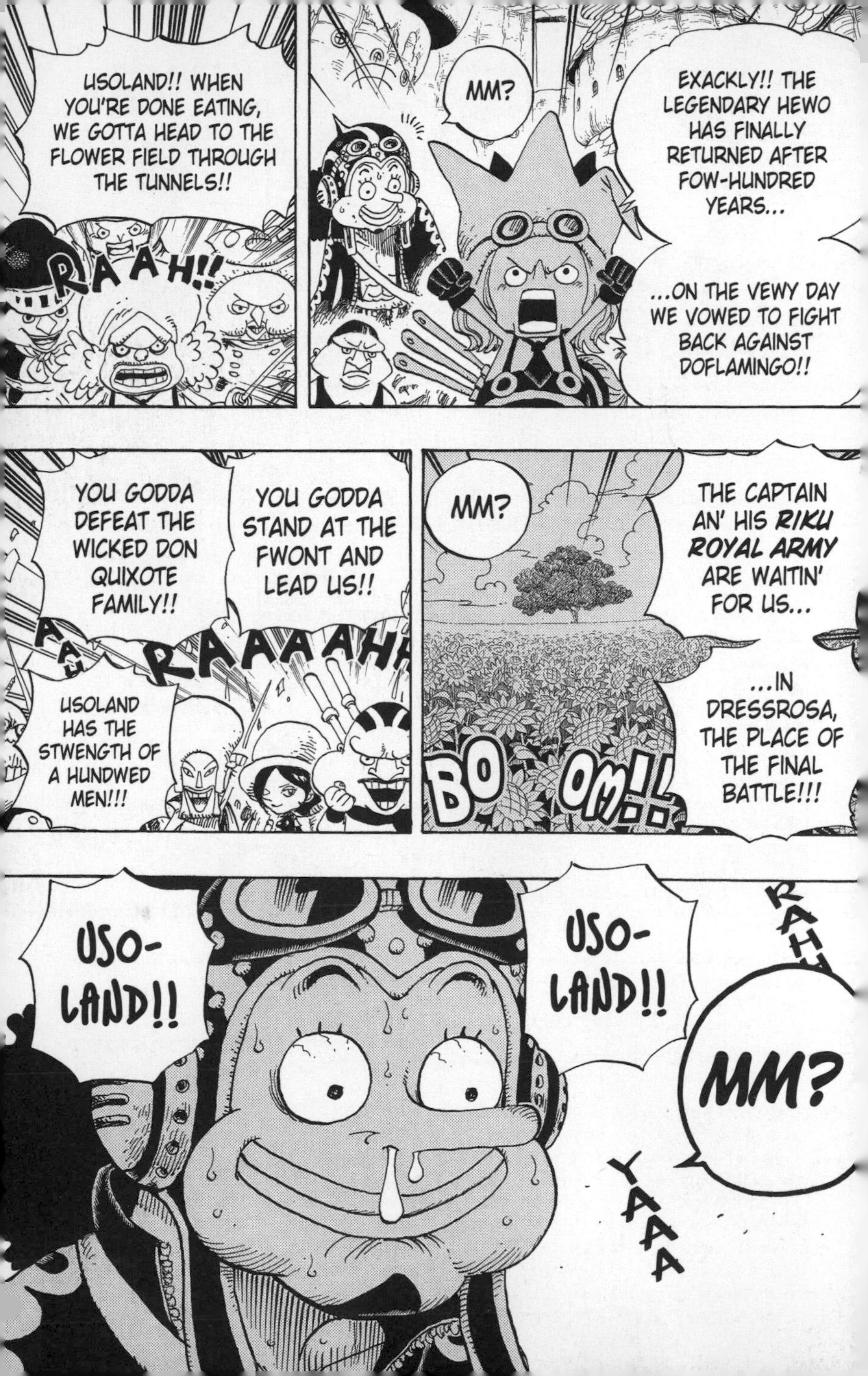

EXACKLY!! THE LEGENDARY HEWO HAS FINALLY RETURNED AFTER FOW-HUNDRED YEARS...
...ON THE VEWY DAY WE VOWED TO FIGHT BACK AGAINST DOFLAMINGO!!
MM?
USOLAND!! WHEN YOU'RE DONE EATING, WE GOTTA HEAD TO THE FLOWER FIELD THROUGH THE TUNNELS!!
RAAH!!
THE CAPTAIN AN' HIS *RIKU ROYAL ARMY* ARE WAITIN' FOR US...
MM?
...IN DRESSROSA, THE PLACE OF THE FINAL BATTLE!!!
BOOM!!
YOU GODDA STAND AT THE FWONT AND LEAD US!!
YOU GODDA DEFEAT THE WICKED DON QUIXOTE FAMILY!!
RAAAAAHH
USOLAND HAS THE STWENGTH OF A HUNDWED MEN!!!
MM?
USO-LAND!!
USO-LAND!!
YAAA

SBS Question Corner

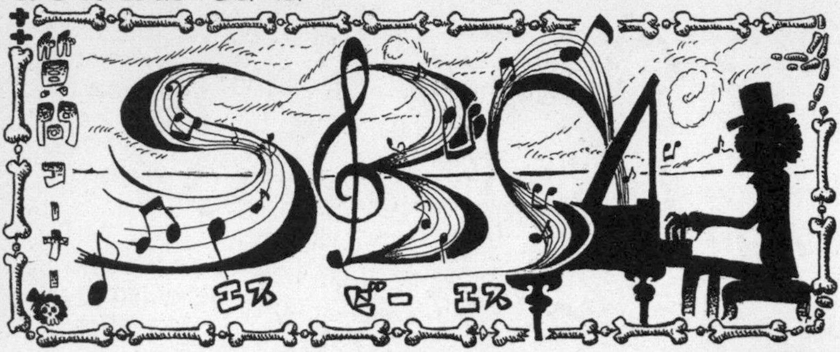

(Hiromitsu Shimojo, Gunma)

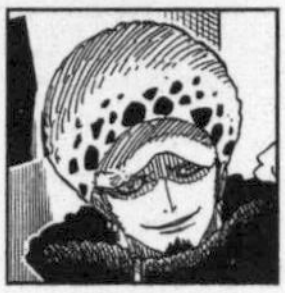

Q: It seems like Trafalgar Law, in the midst of his alliance with the Straw Hats, gives them some nicknames. What are all the things he calls the various members of the crew like Zoro and Franky?

--Edward Yacchi

Q: Mr. Oda, hello! If the Straw Hats were different prefectures of the Japan, what would they be? For example, would Nami be from Ehime? I'd love to hear from you!

--T. Rina

A: Tell you what, I'll answer these both at the same time.

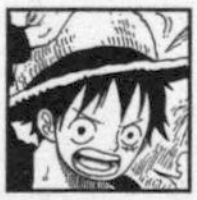

Luffy
Straw Hat
(Okinawa)

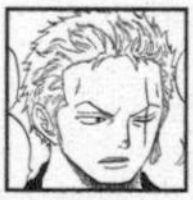

Zoro
Zoro
(Hokkaido)

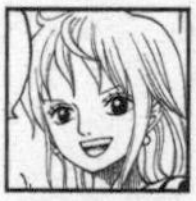

Nami
Nami
(Ehime)

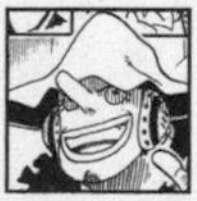

Usopp
The Nose
(Kanagawa)

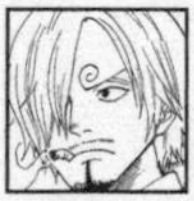

Sanji
Black-Leg
(Kyoto)

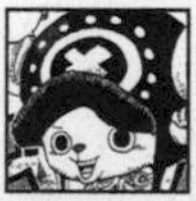

Chopper
Tony
(Toyama)

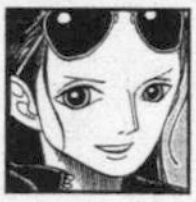

Robin
Nico
(Osaka)

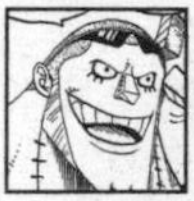

Franky
Robo
(Nagasaki)

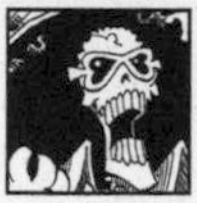

Brook
Boney
(Tottori)

A: I think that should do it. Some of those prefectures were probably influenced by the voice actors' hometowns (laughs).

Q: Odacchi, Odacchi!!! All I can see in the waves on p.154 of Volume 70 is bunnies!!! What have you done to me?!!!

--Law-Loving Y, Law-Loving A's Friend

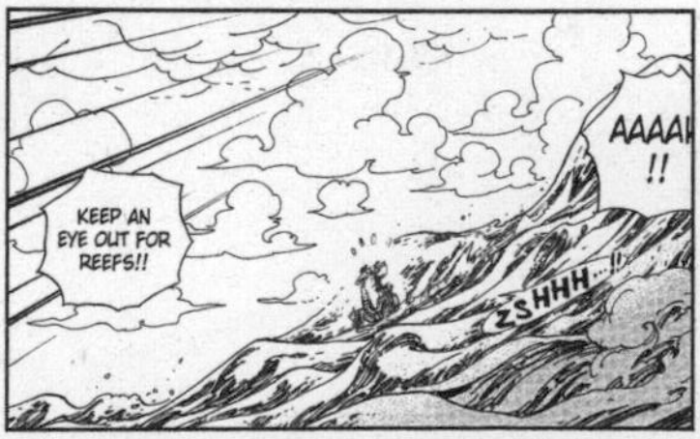
AAAA!
!!
KEEP AN EYE OUT FOR REEFS!!
ZSHHH...!!

A: Geez, that's a long pen name!! I'd like to tell you a story from Papua New Guinea. It is said that when the rabbits ran out of food to eat, they tricked the fish into lining up so they could cross the sea on the backs of the fish. Do you suppose they made up that folk tale when they noticed the dancing white waves looked like rabbits? They do look like that sometimes, don't they?

Chapter 714:
LUCY AND MOOCY

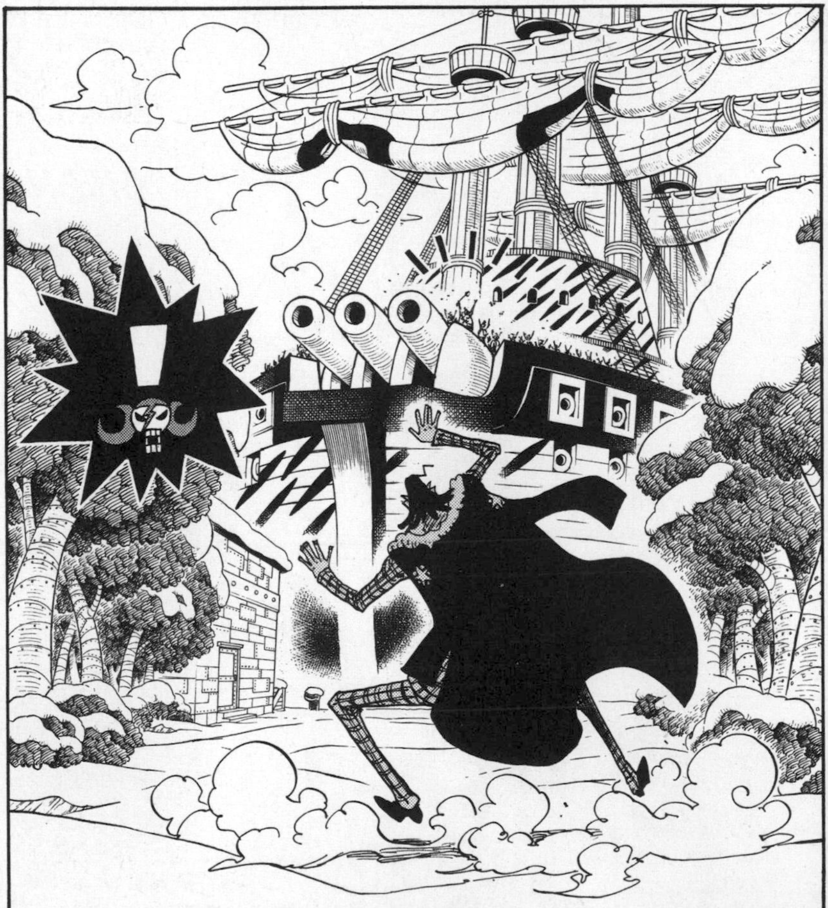

CARIBOU'S NEW WORLD KEE HEE HEE, VOL. 32:
"BACK AT THE PORT, MY ABANDONED LACKEYS"

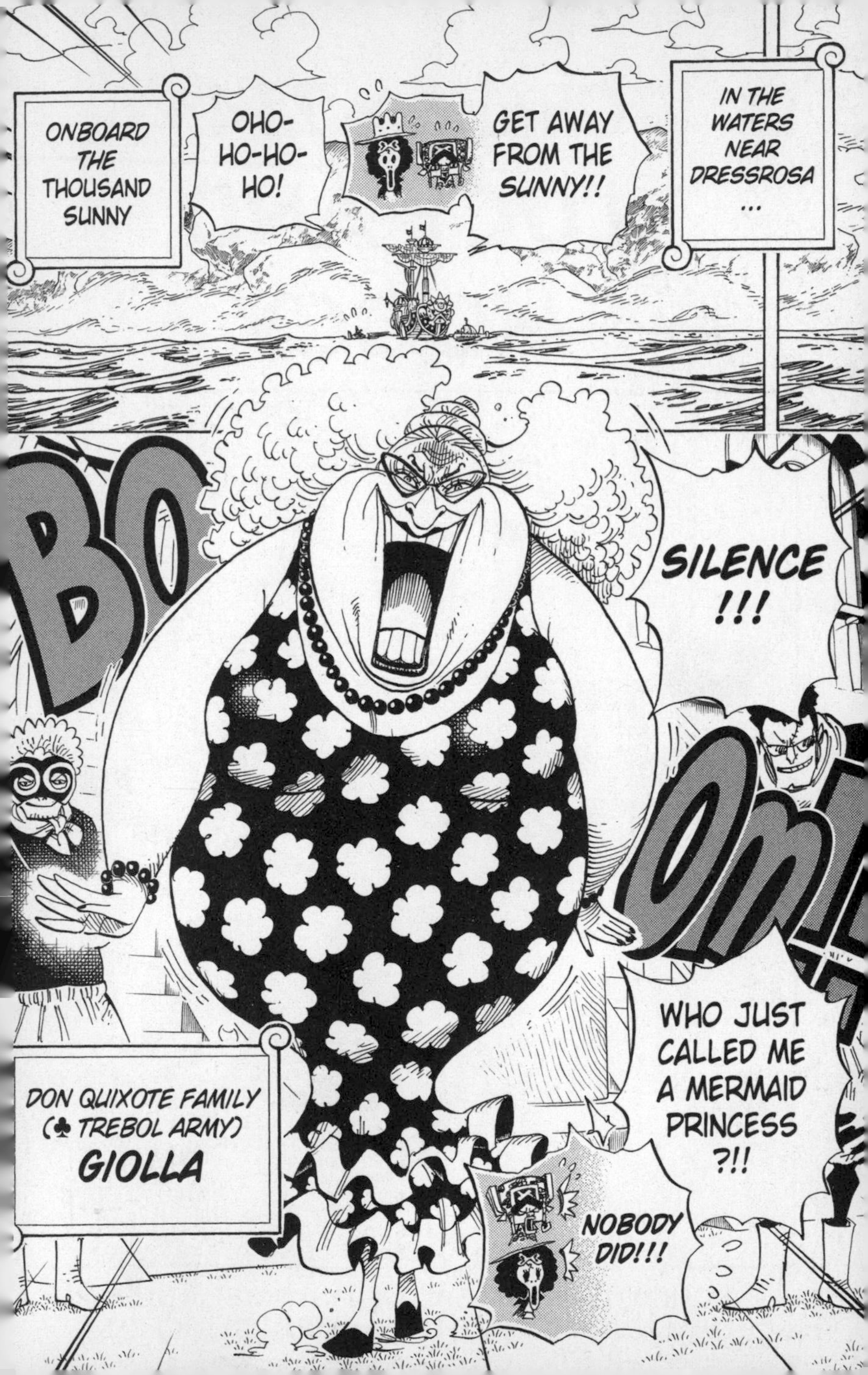
IN THE WATERS NEAR DRESSROSA ...
GET AWAY FROM THE SUNNY!!
OHO-HO-HO-HO!
ONBOARD THE THOUSAND SUNNY
SILENCE !!!
OM
BO
WHO JUST CALLED ME A MERMAID PRINCESS ?!!
NOBODY DID!!!
DON QUIXOTE FAMILY (♣ TREBOL ARMY)
GIOLLA

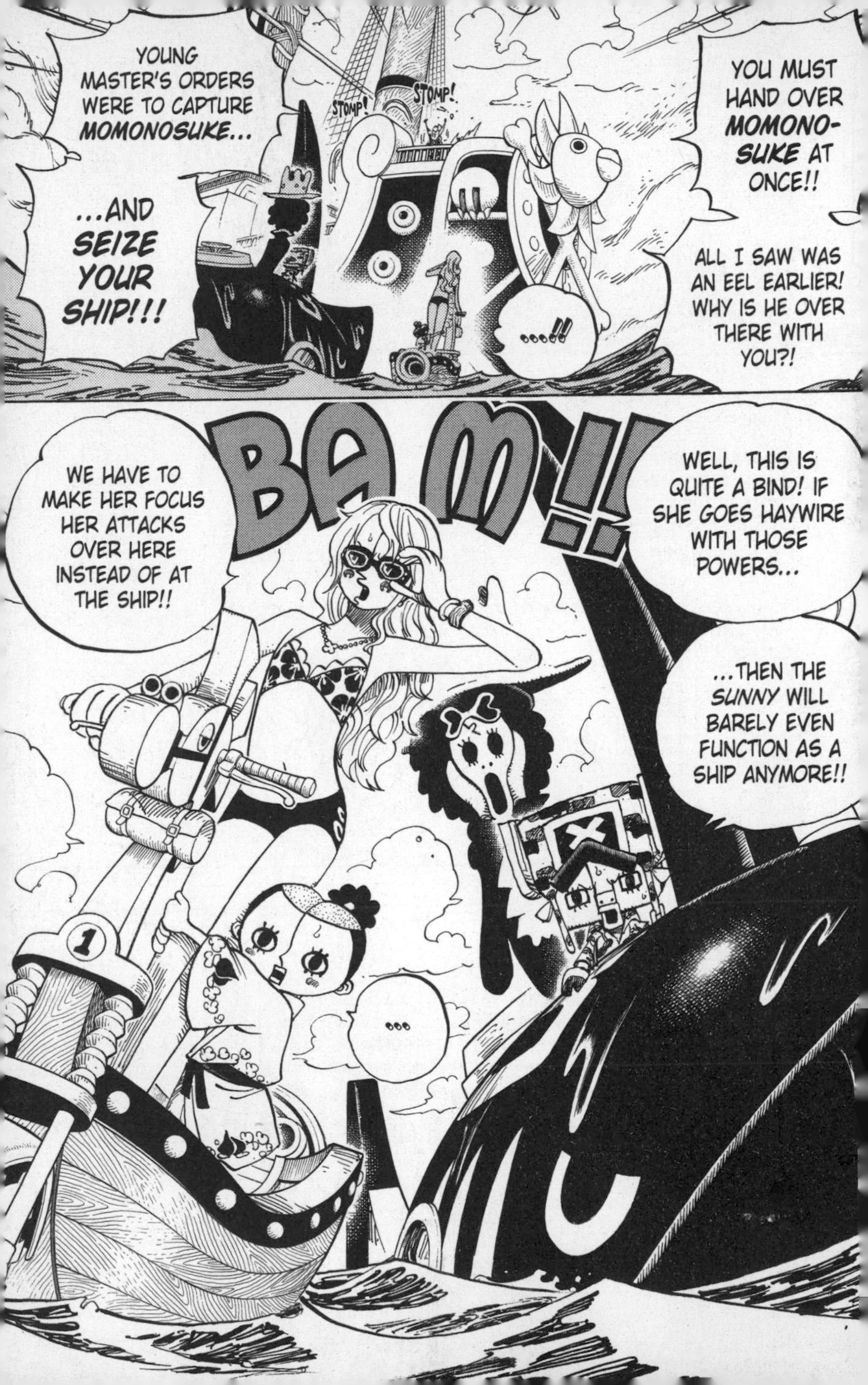
YOU MUST HAND OVER MOMONOSUKE AT ONCE!!
ALL I SAW WAS AN EEL EARLIER! WHY IS HE OVER THERE WITH YOU?!
STOMP!
STOMP!
....!!
YOUNG MASTER'S ORDERS WERE TO CAPTURE MOMONOSUKE...
...AND SEIZE YOUR SHIP!!!
WELL, THIS IS QUITE A BIND! IF SHE GOES HAYWIRE WITH THOSE POWERS...
...THEN THE SUNNY WILL BARELY EVEN FUNCTION AS A SHIP ANYMORE!!
BAM!!
WE HAVE TO MAKE HER FOCUS HER ATTACKS OVER HERE INSTEAD OF AT THE SHIP!!
...

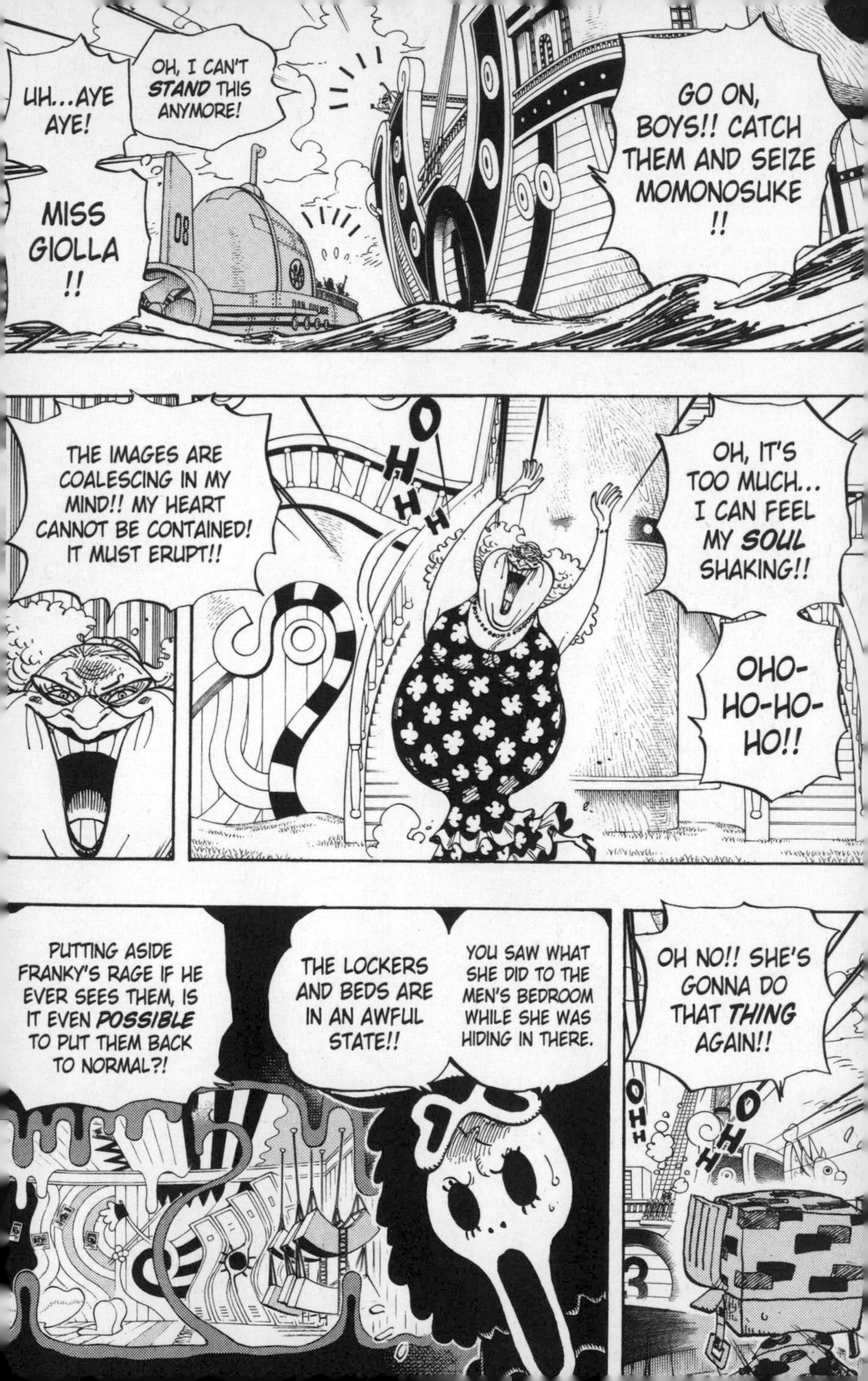
GO ON, BOYS!! CATCH THEM AND SEIZE MOMONOSUKE !!
OH, I CAN'T STAND THIS ANYMORE!
UH...AYE AYE!
MISS GIOLLA !!
OH, IT'S TOO MUCH... I CAN FEEL MY SOUL SHAKING!!
OHO-HO-HO-HO!!
OHHH
THE IMAGES ARE COALESCING IN MY MIND!! MY HEART CANNOT BE CONTAINED! IT MUST ERUPT!!
OH NO!! SHE'S GONNA DO THAT THING AGAIN!!
OHHH
OHHH
YOU SAW WHAT SHE DID TO THE MEN'S BEDROOM WHILE SHE WAS HIDING IN THERE.
THE LOCKERS AND BEDS ARE IN AN AWFUL STATE!!
PUTTING ASIDE FRANKY'S RAGE IF HE EVER SEES THEM, IS IT EVEN POSSIBLE TO PUT THEM BACK TO NORMAL?!

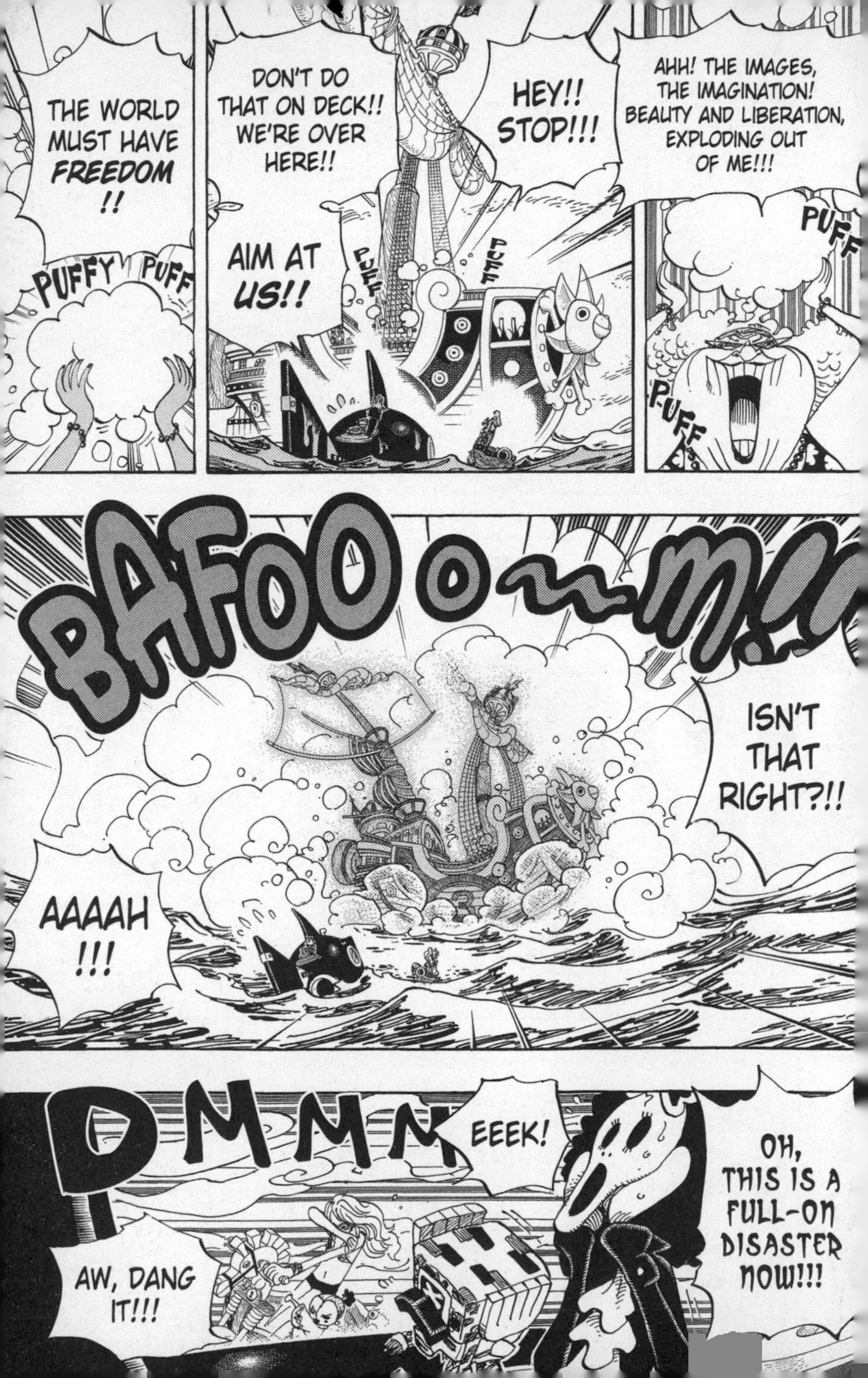
AHH! THE IMAGES, THE IMAGINATION! BEAUTY AND LIBERATION, EXPLODING OUT OF ME!!!
PUFF
P-UFF
HEY!! STOP!!!
DON'T DO THAT ON DECK!! WE'RE OVER HERE!!
PUFF
PUFF
AIM AT US!!
THE WORLD MUST HAVE FREEDOM!!
PUFF
PUFFY
BAFOOoom!!
ISN'T THAT RIGHT?!!
AAAAH!!!
OH, THIS IS A FULL-ON DISASTER NOW!!!
EEEK!
DMMM
AW, DANG IT!!!

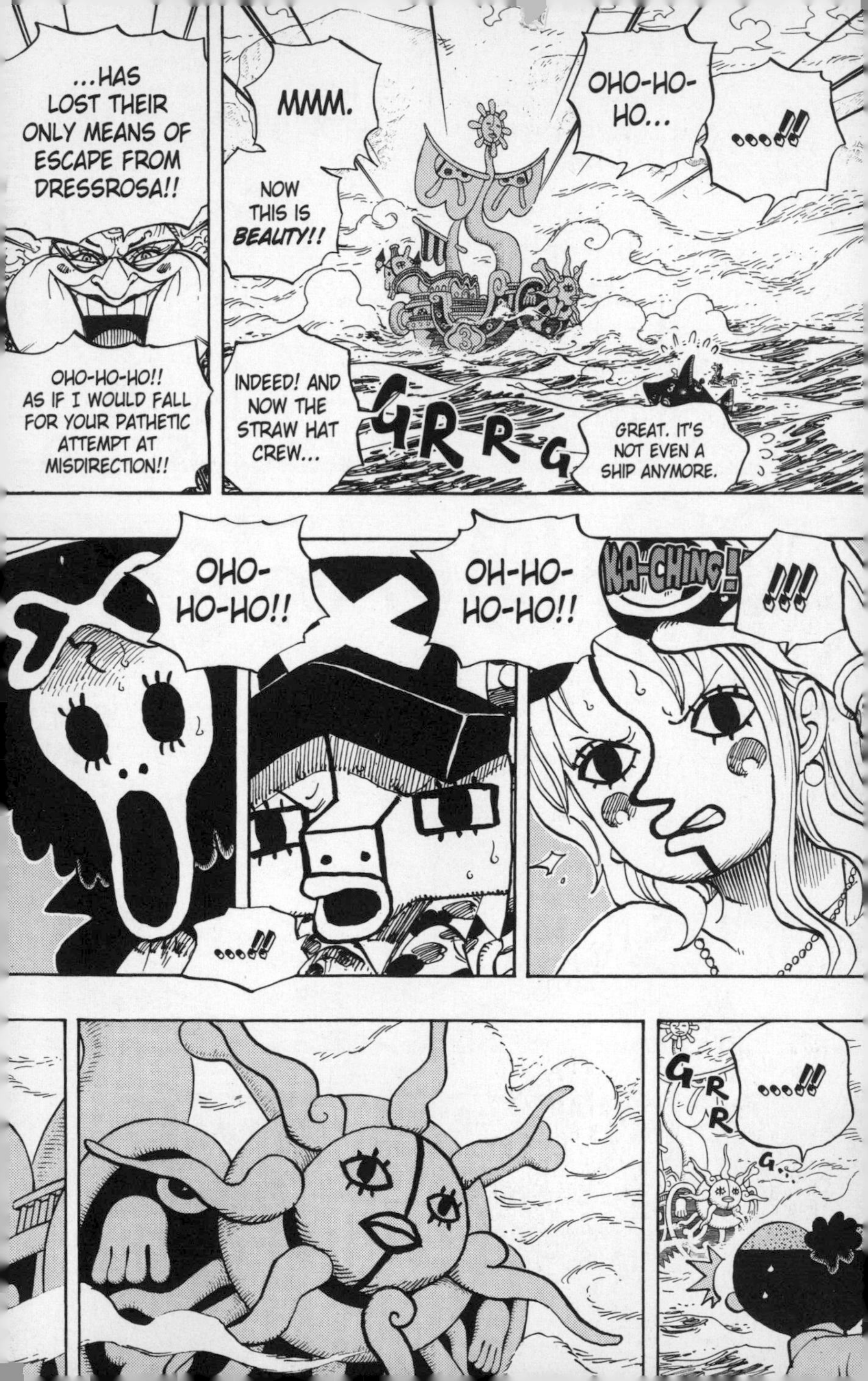

....!!
OHO-HO-HO...
MMM.
NOW THIS IS BEAUTY!!
GREAT. IT'S NOT EVEN A SHIP ANYMORE.
GRRG
INDEED! AND NOW THE STRAW HAT CREW...
...HAS LOST THEIR ONLY MEANS OF ESCAPE FROM DRESSROSA!!
OHO-HO-HO!! AS IF I WOULD FALL FOR YOUR PATHETIC ATTEMPT AT MISDIRECTION!!
!!!
KA-CHING!!
OH-HO-HO-HO!!
....!!
OHO-HO-HO!!
....!!
GRRG

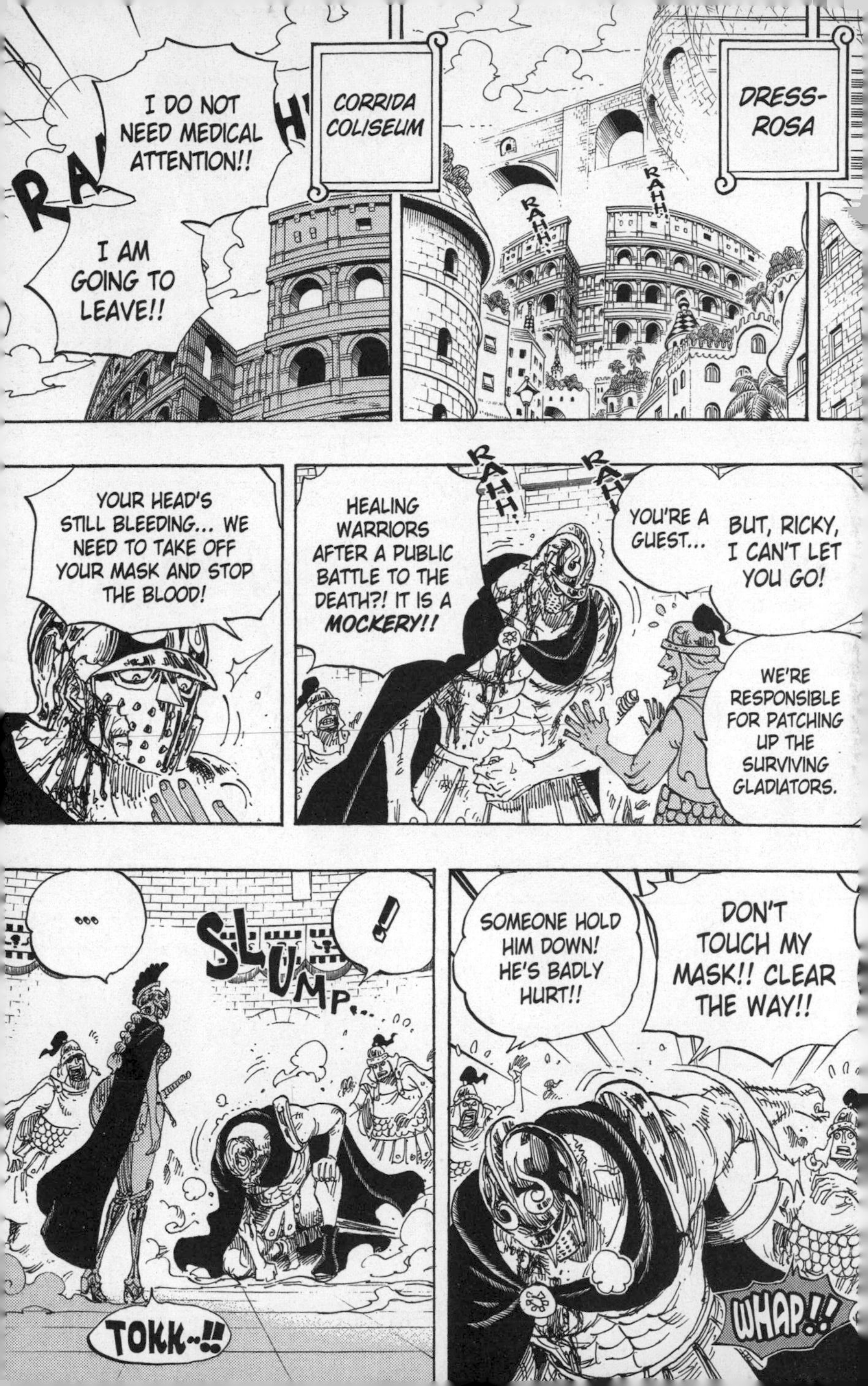
DRESS-ROSA
RAHH...
RAHH...
CORRIDA COLISEUM
I DO NOT NEED MEDICAL ATTENTION!!
I AM GOING TO LEAVE!!
RAHH
RAHH
BUT, RICKY, I CAN'T LET YOU GO!
YOU'RE A GUEST...
WE'RE RESPONSIBLE FOR PATCHING UP THE SURVIVING GLADIATORS.
HEALING WARRIORS AFTER A PUBLIC BATTLE TO THE DEATH?! IT IS A MOCKERY!!
YOUR HEAD'S STILL BLEEDING... WE NEED TO TAKE OFF YOUR MASK AND STOP THE BLOOD!
DON'T TOUCH MY MASK!! CLEAR THE WAY!!
SOMEONE HOLD HIM DOWN! HE'S BADLY HURT!!
WHAP!!
!
SLUMP...
...
TOKK-!!

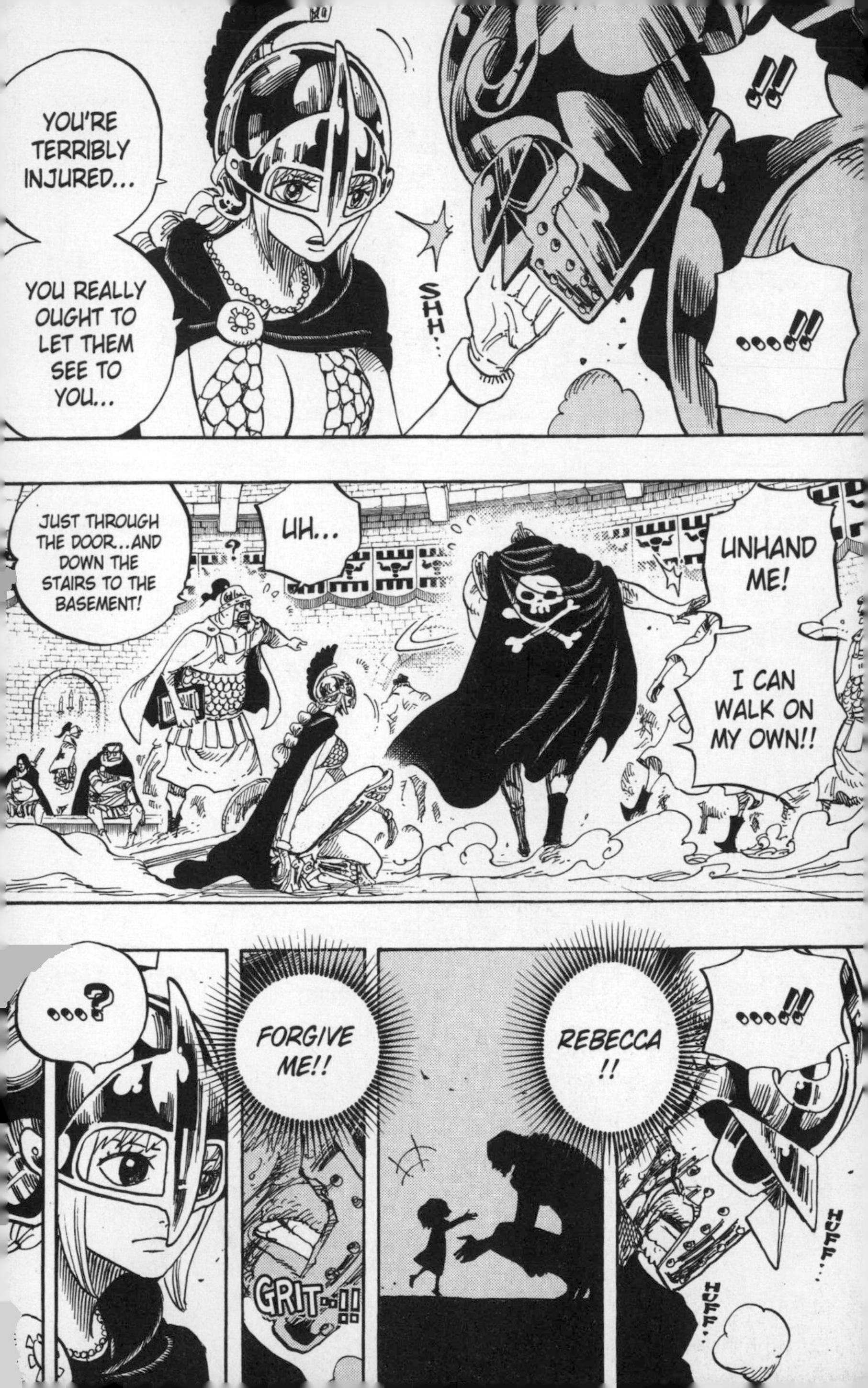
!!
YOU'RE TERRIBLY INJURED...
...!!
YOU REALLY OUGHT TO LET THEM SEE TO YOU...
SHH...
UNHAND ME!
I CAN WALK ON MY OWN!!
UH...
JUST THROUGH THE DOOR...AND DOWN THE STAIRS TO THE BASEMENT!
...!!
HUFF...
HUFF...
REBECCA!!
FORGIVE ME!!
GRIT..!!
...?

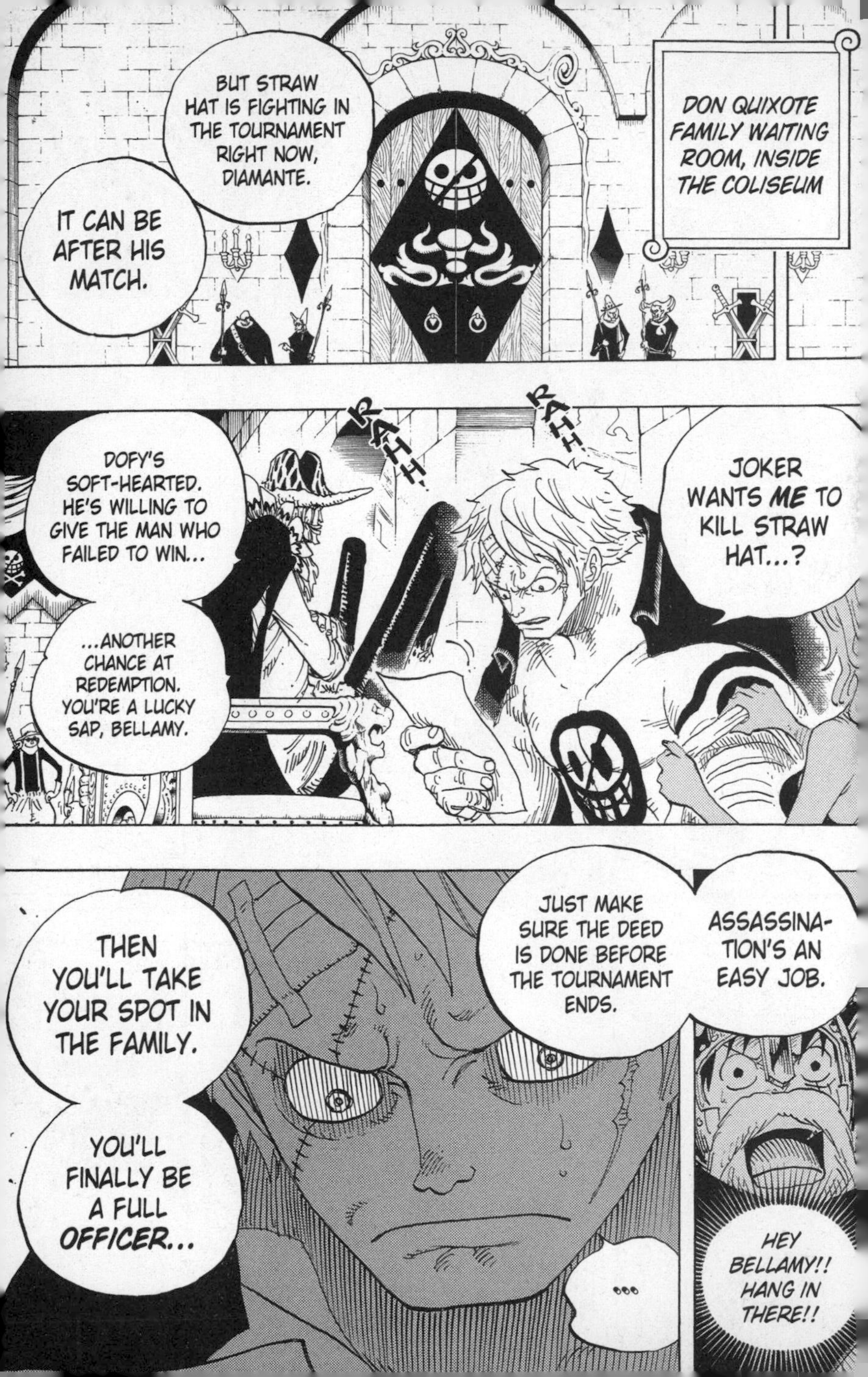
DON QUIXOTE FAMILY WAITING ROOM, INSIDE THE COLISEUM
BUT STRAW HAT IS FIGHTING IN THE TOURNAMENT RIGHT NOW, DIAMANTE.
IT CAN BE AFTER HIS MATCH.
JOKER WANTS *ME* TO KILL STRAW HAT...?
RAHH
RAHH
DOFY'S SOFT-HEARTED. HE'S WILLING TO GIVE THE MAN WHO FAILED TO WIN...
...ANOTHER CHANCE AT REDEMPTION. YOU'RE A LUCKY SAP, BELLAMY.
ASSASSINA-TION'S AN EASY JOB.
JUST MAKE SURE THE DEED IS DONE BEFORE THE TOURNAMENT ENDS.
THEN YOU'LL TAKE YOUR SPOT IN THE FAMILY.
YOU'LL FINALLY BE A FULL *OFFICER*...
HEY BELLAMY!! HANG IN THERE!!
...

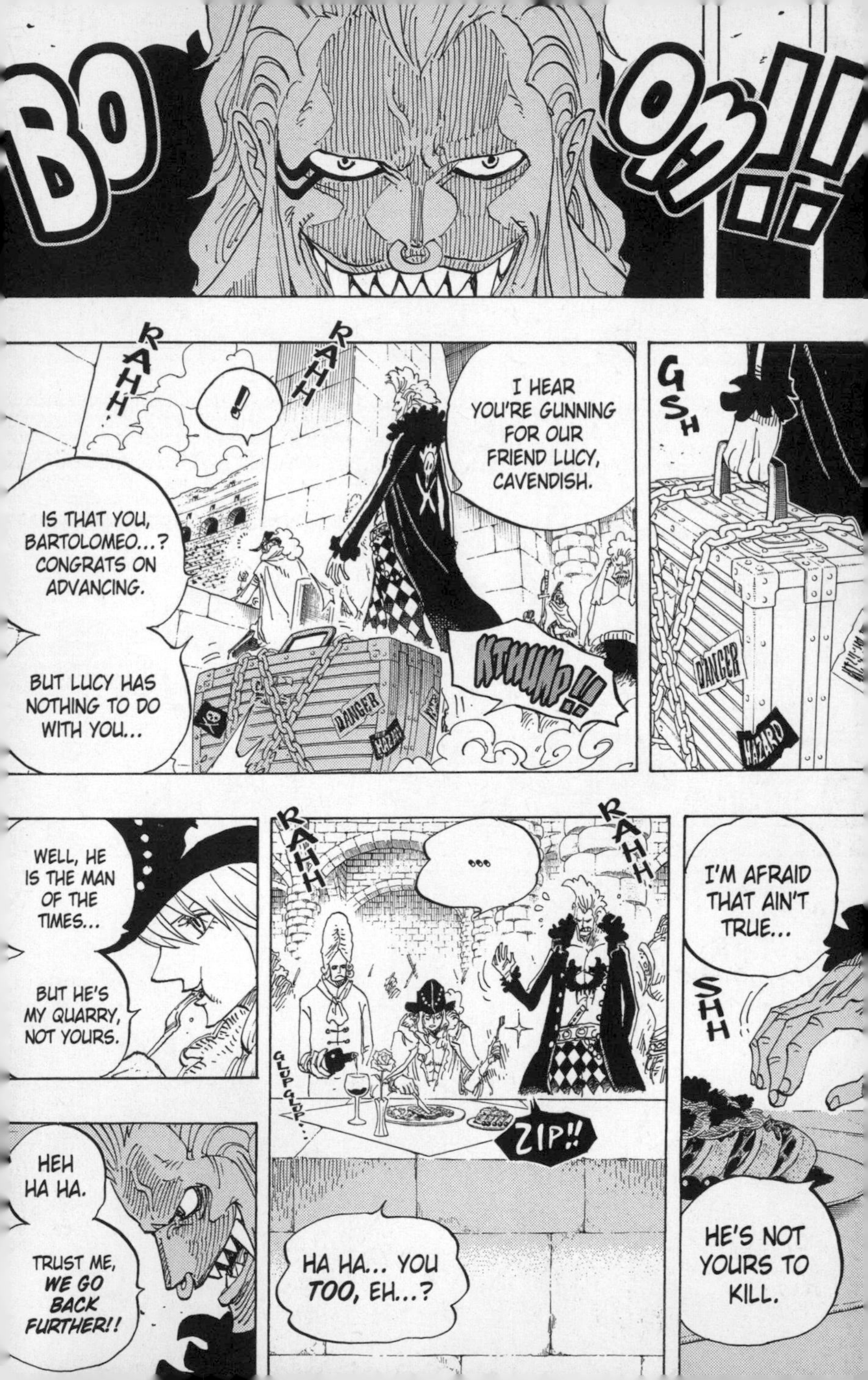
BOOOM!!
GSH
I HEAR YOU'RE GUNNING FOR OUR FRIEND LUCY, CAVENDISH.
RAHH
KTHUMP!!
!
RAHH
IS THAT YOU, BARTOLOMEO...? CONGRATS ON ADVANCING.
BUT LUCY HAS NOTHING TO DO WITH YOU...
I'M AFRAID THAT AIN'T TRUE...
SHH
HE'S NOT YOURS TO KILL.
RAHH
...
RAHH
ZIP!!
GLUP GLUP...
HA HA... YOU TOO, EH...?
WELL, HE IS THE MAN OF THE TIMES...
BUT HE'S MY QUARRY, NOT YOURS.
HEH HA HA.
TRUST ME, WE GO BACK FURTHER!!

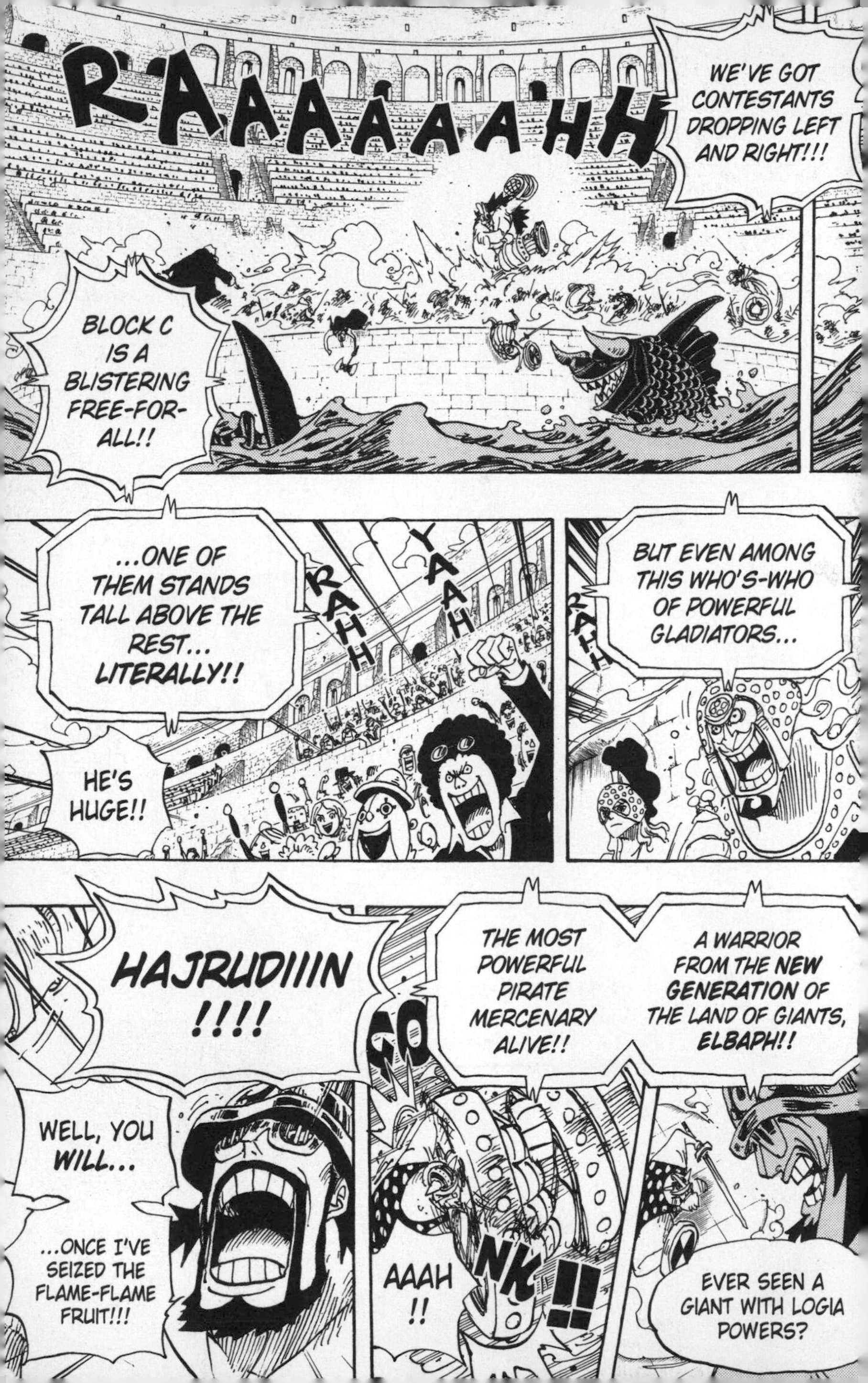
RAAAAAAHH
WE'VE GOT CONTESTANTS DROPPING LEFT AND RIGHT!!!
BLOCK C IS A BLISTERING FREE-FOR-ALL!!
BUT EVEN AMONG THIS WHO'S-WHO OF POWERFUL GLADIATORS...
RAHH
YAAAH
RAHH
...ONE OF THEM STANDS TALL ABOVE THE REST... LITERALLY!!
HE'S HUGE!!
A WARRIOR FROM THE NEW GENERATION OF THE LAND OF GIANTS, ELBAPH!!
THE MOST POWERFUL PIRATE MERCENARY ALIVE!!
HAJRUDIIIN !!!!
EVER SEEN A GIANT WITH LOGIA POWERS?
GO
NK!!
AAAH !!
WELL, YOU WILL...
...ONCE I'VE SEIZED THE FLAME-FLAME FRUIT!!!

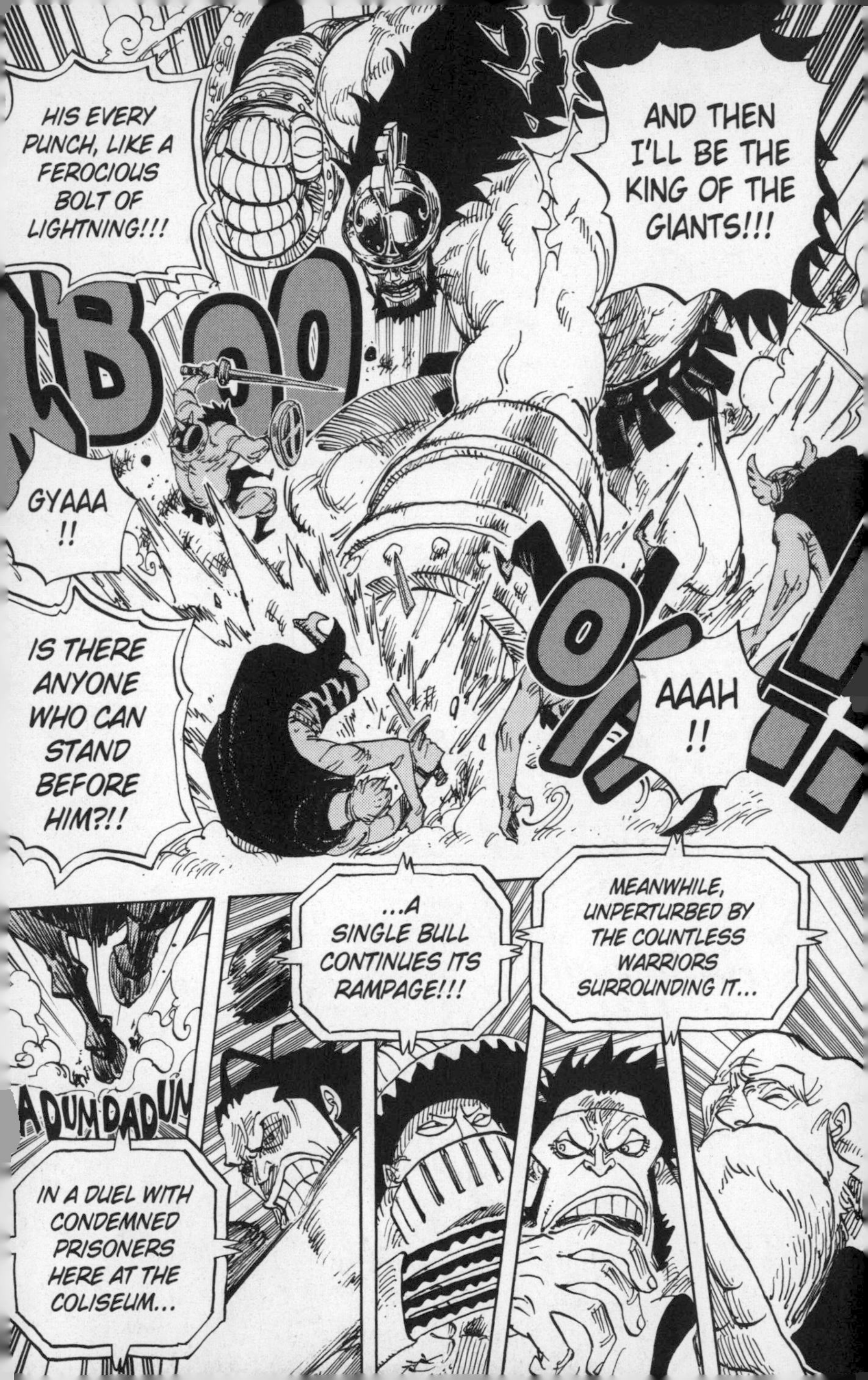
AND THEN I'LL BE THE KING OF THE GIANTS!!!
HIS EVERY PUNCH, LIKE A FEROCIOUS BOLT OF LIGHTNING!!!
BOO
AAAH !!
GYAAA !!
IS THERE ANYONE WHO CAN STAND BEFORE HIM?!!
MEANWHILE, UNPERTURBED BY THE COUNTLESS WARRIORS SURROUNDING IT...
...A SINGLE BULL CONTINUES ITS RAMPAGE!!!
ADUM DADUN
IN A DUEL WITH CONDEMNED PRISONERS HERE AT THE COLISEUM...

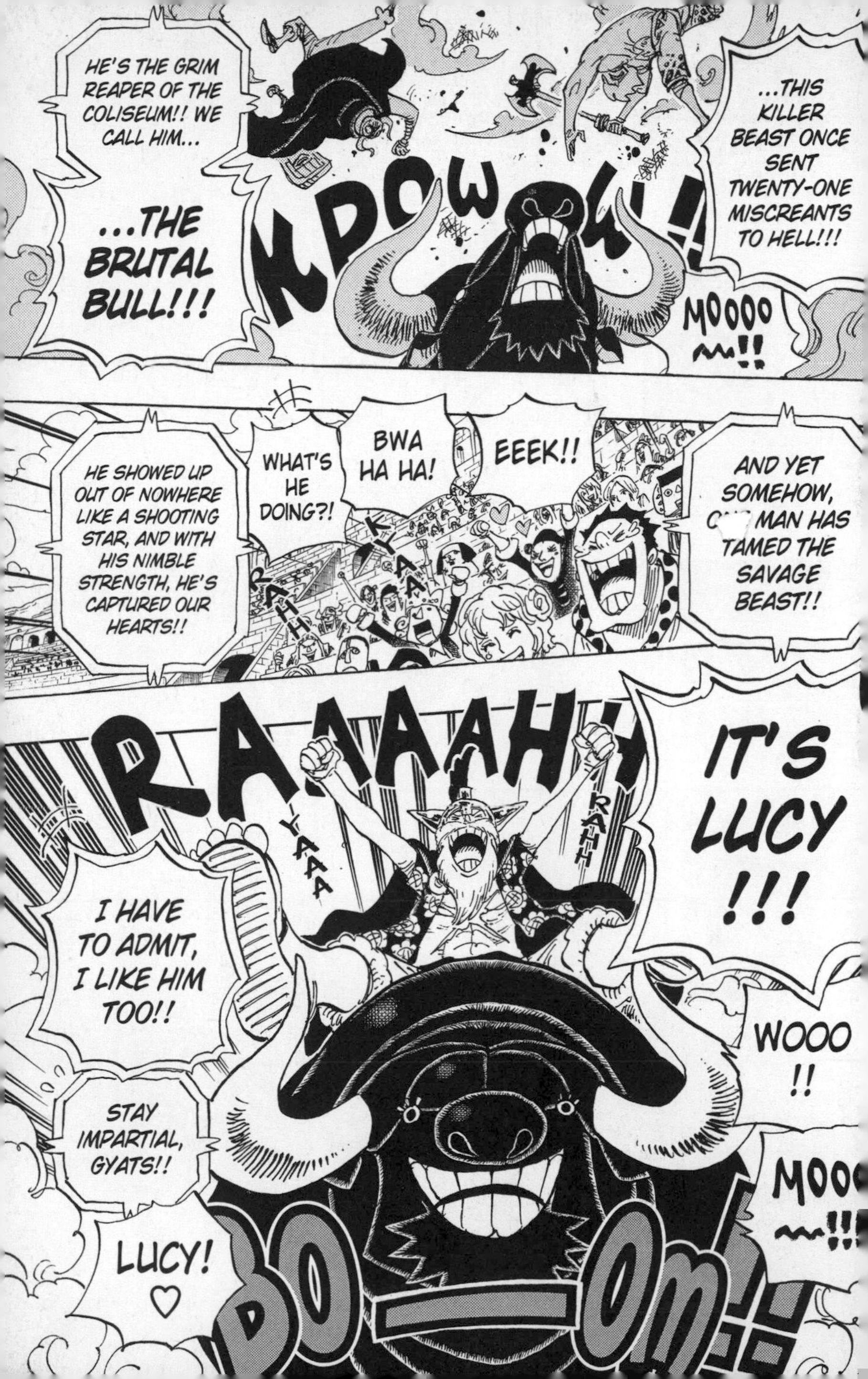
...THIS KILLER BEAST ONCE SENT TWENTY-ONE MISCREANTS TO HELL!!!
KPOW
MOOOO~~!!
HE'S THE GRIM REAPER OF THE COLISEUM!! WE CALL HIM...
...THE BRUTAL BULL!!!
AND YET SOMEHOW, MAN HAS TAMED THE SAVAGE BEAST!!
EEEK!!
BWA HA HA!
WHAT'S HE DOING?!
KYAA
RAHH
HE SHOWED UP OUT OF NOWHERE LIKE A SHOOTING STAR, AND WITH HIS NIMBLE STRENGTH, HE'S CAPTURED OUR HEARTS!!
IT'S LUCY!!!
RAAAAHH
RAHH
YAAA
WOOO!!
I HAVE TO ADMIT, I LIKE HIM TOO!!
MOOO~~!!!
BOOM!!
STAY IMPARTIAL, GYATS!!
LUCY! ♡

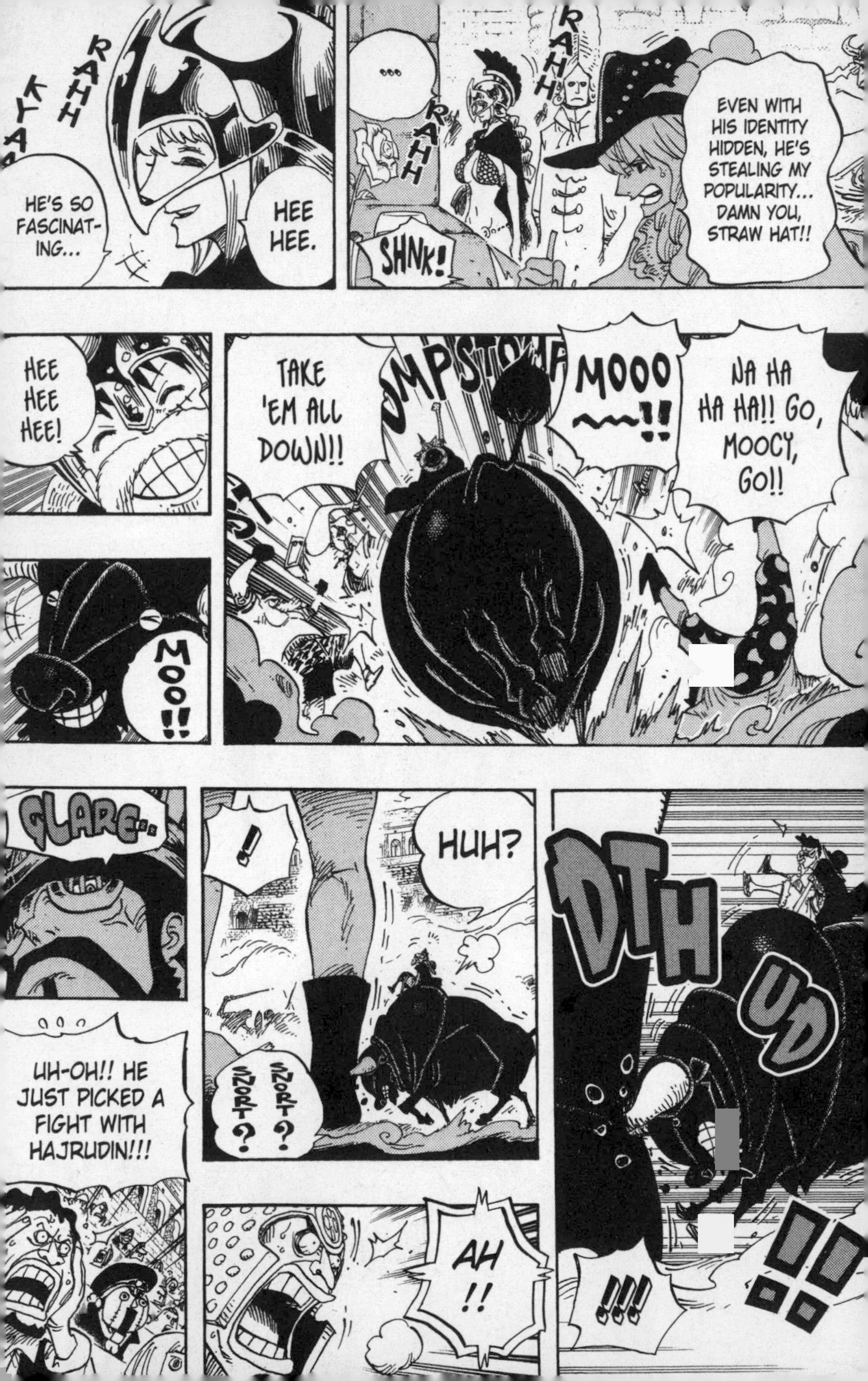
EVEN WITH HIS IDENTITY HIDDEN, HE'S STEALING MY POPULARITY... DAMN YOU, STRAW HAT!!
RAHH
RAHH
...
SHNK!
RAHH
KYAA
HEE HEE.
HE'S SO FASCINATING...
NA HA HA HA!! GO, MOOCY, GO!!
MOOO~~~!!
TAKE 'EM ALL DOWN!!
HEE HEE HEE!
MOO!!
DTHUD
!!
!!!
HUH?
!
SNORT?
SNORT?
GLARE..
UH-OH!! HE JUST PICKED A FIGHT WITH HAJRUDIN!!!
AH!!

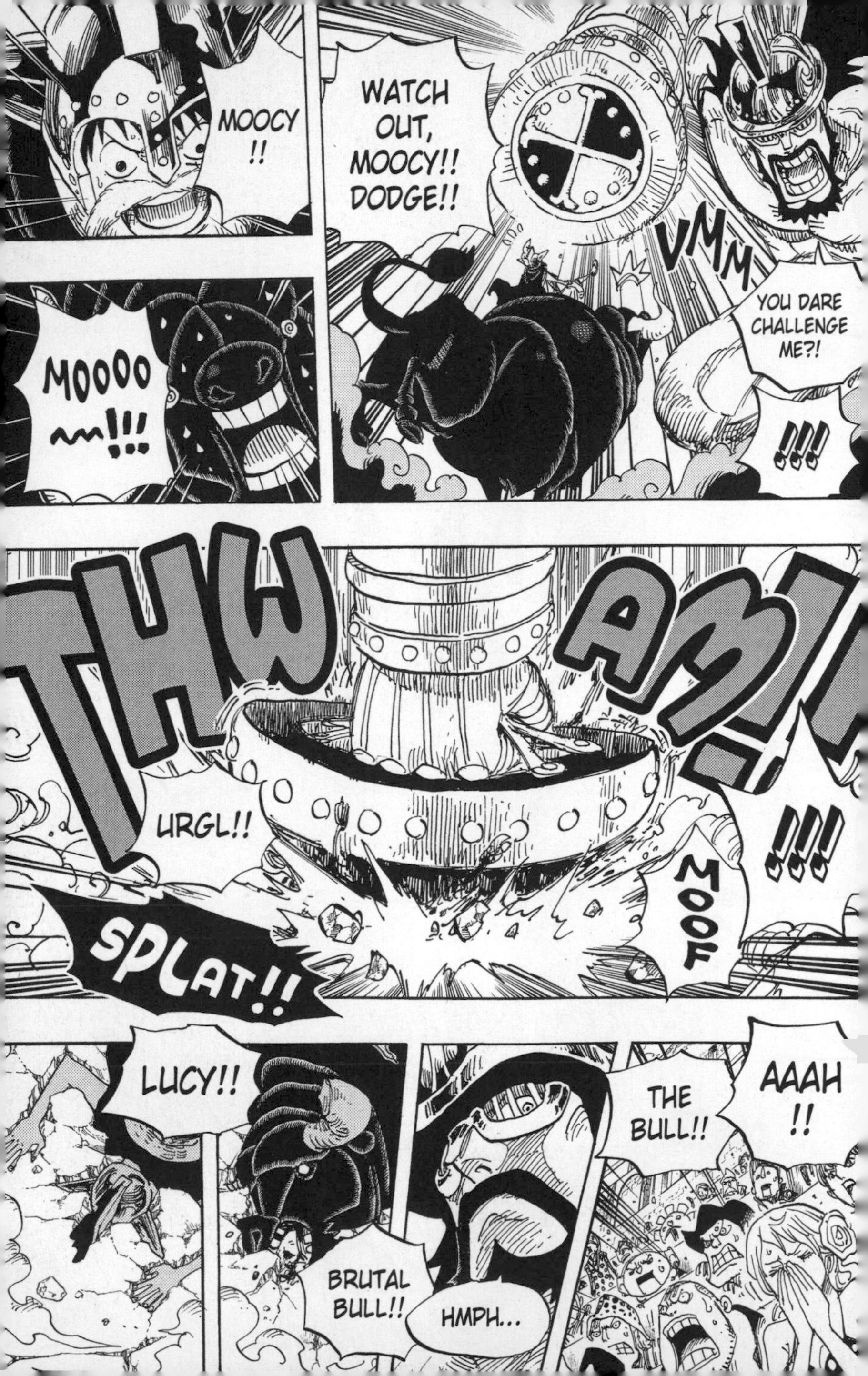

WATCH OUT, MOOCY!! DODGE!!
VMM
YOU DARE CHALLENGE ME?!
!!!
MOOCY !!
MOOOO ~!!!
THWAM!!!
MOOF
URGL!!
SPLAT!!
AAAH !!
THE BULL!!
HMPH...
BRUTAL BULL!!
LUCY!!

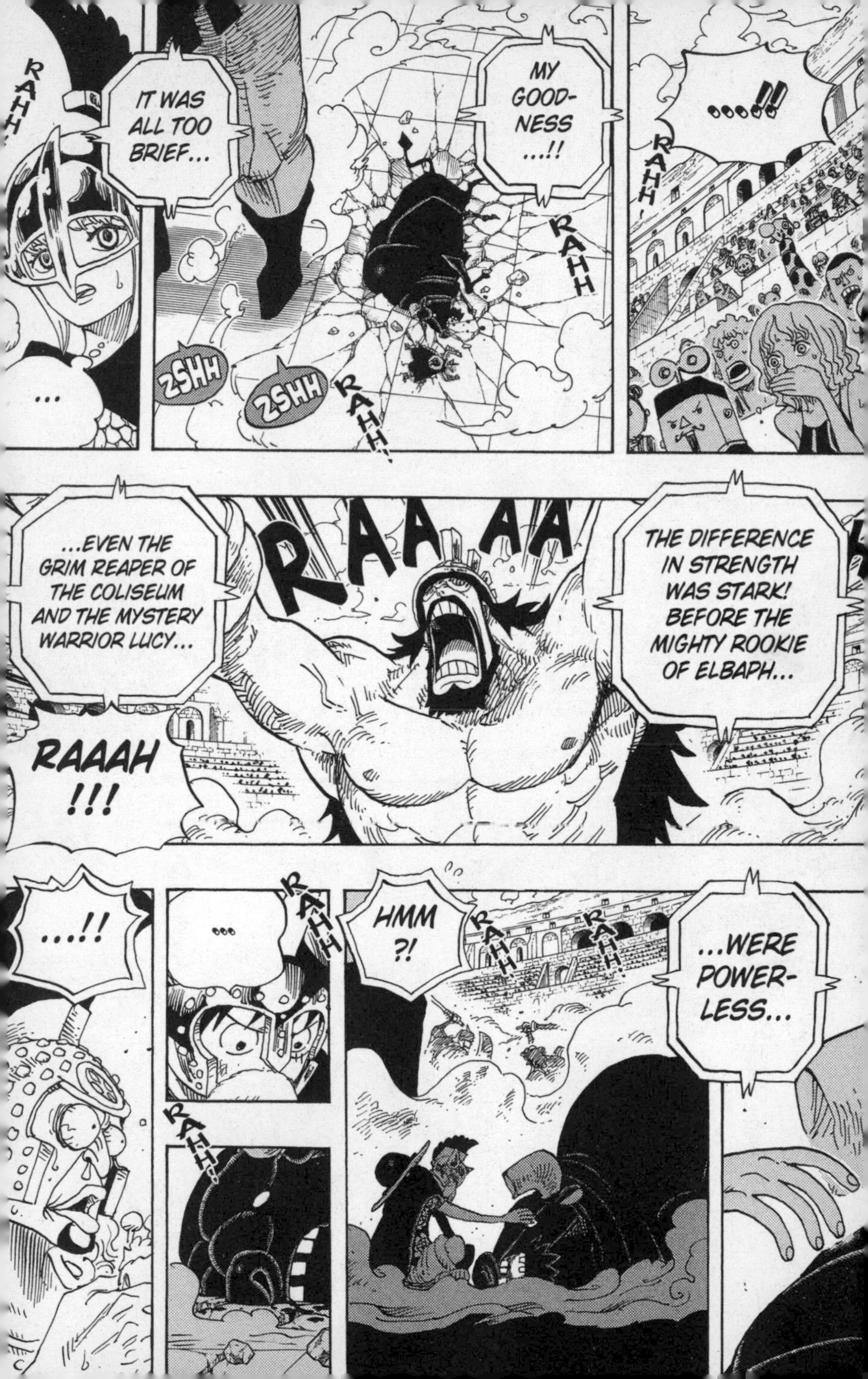
...!!
RAHH!
MY GOODNESS...!!
RAHH
ZSHH
ZSHH
RAHH!
IT WAS ALL TOO BRIEF...
RAHH
...
THE DIFFERENCE IN STRENGTH WAS STARK! BEFORE THE MIGHTY ROOKIE OF ELBAPH...
RAAAA
...EVEN THE GRIM REAPER OF THE COLISEUM AND THE MYSTERY WARRIOR LUCY...
RAAAH!!!
...WERE POWERLESS...
RAHH
RAHH
HMM?!
RAHH
...
RAHH
...!!

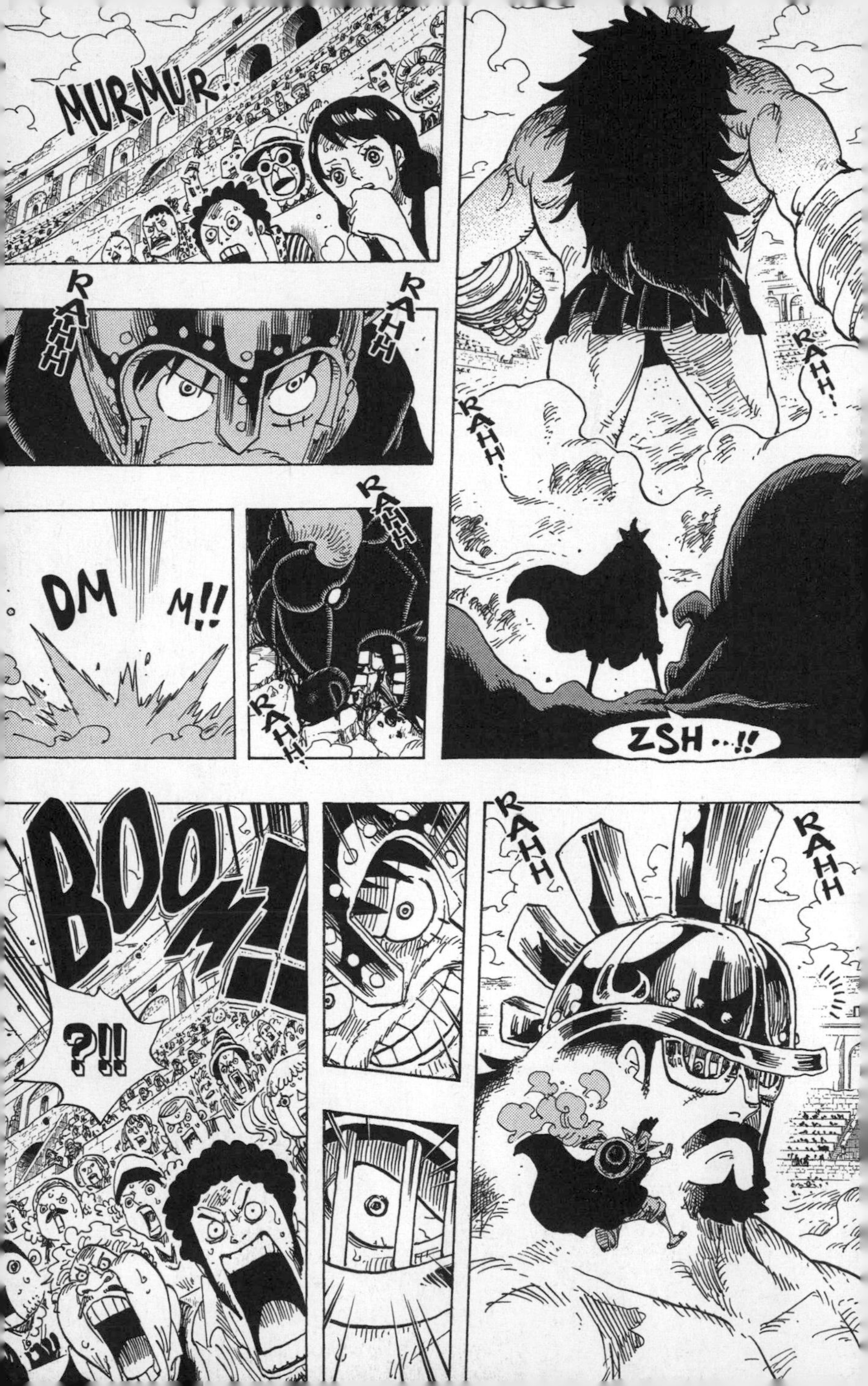
RAHH!
RAHH!
ZSH...!!
MURMUR
RAHH
RAHH
RAHH
RAHH!
DM M!!
RAHH
RAHH
BOOM!!
?!!

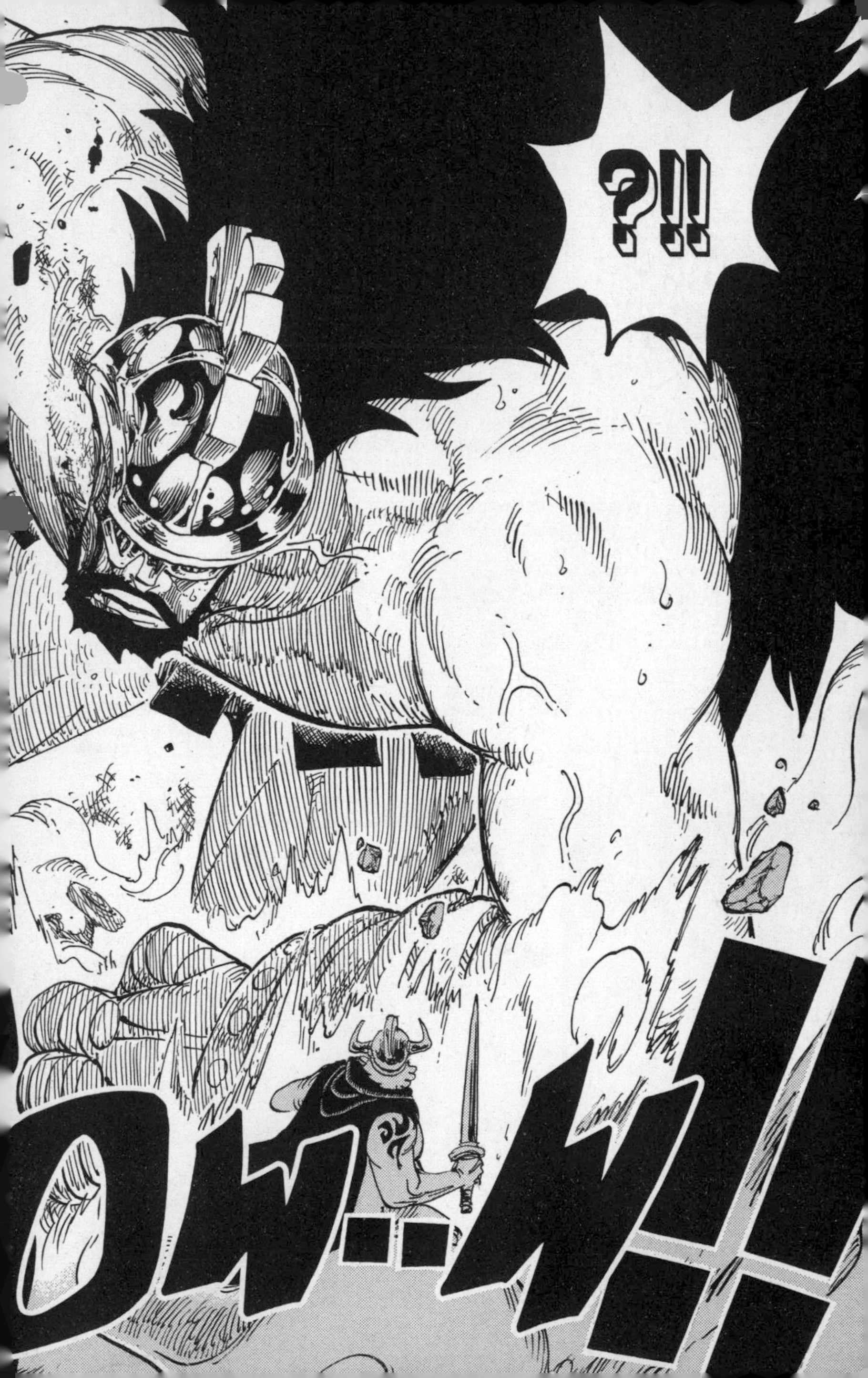
?!!

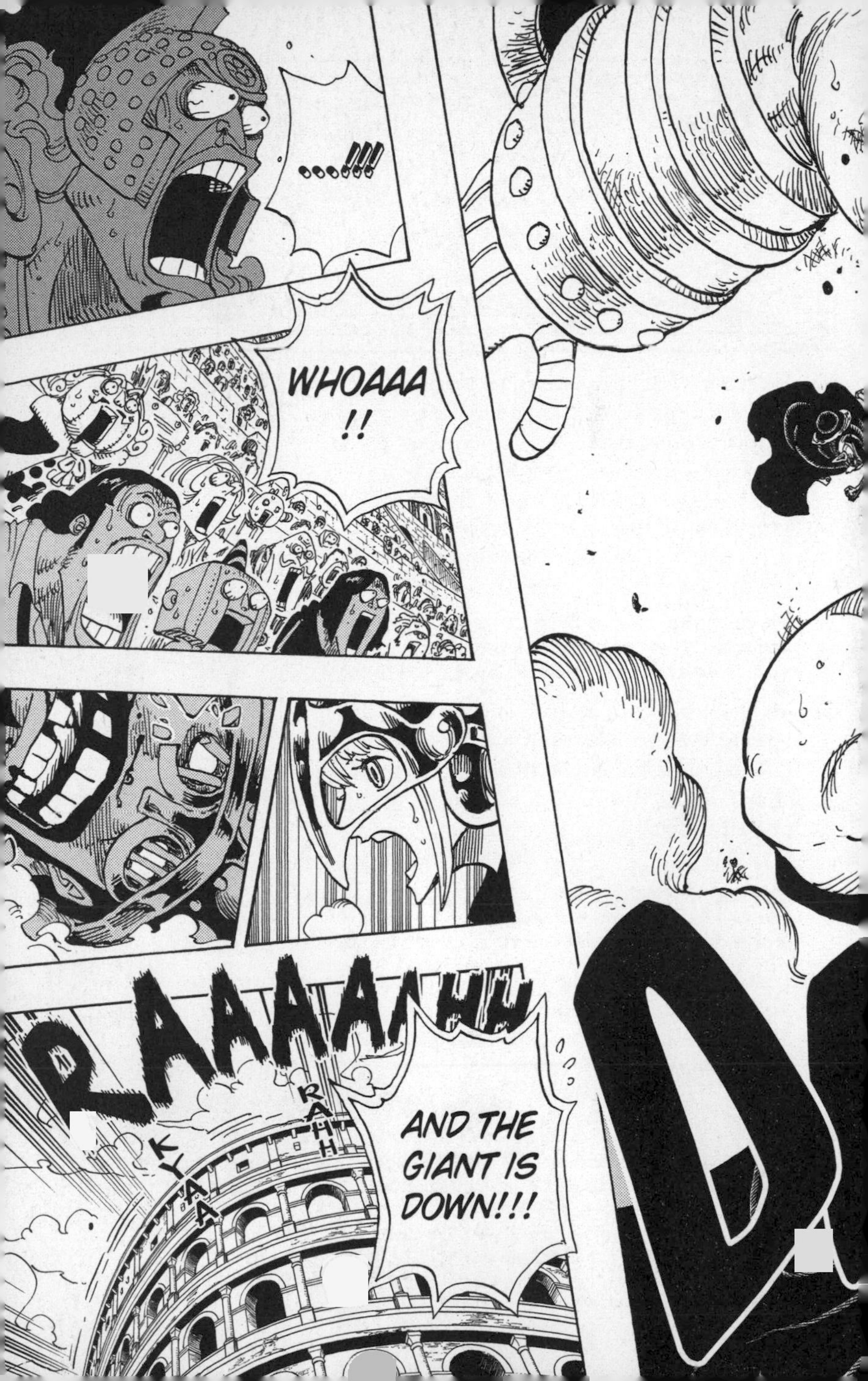
...!!!
WHOAAA!!
RAAAAAHH
KYAA
RAHH
AND THE GIANT IS DOWN!!!

SBS Question Corner

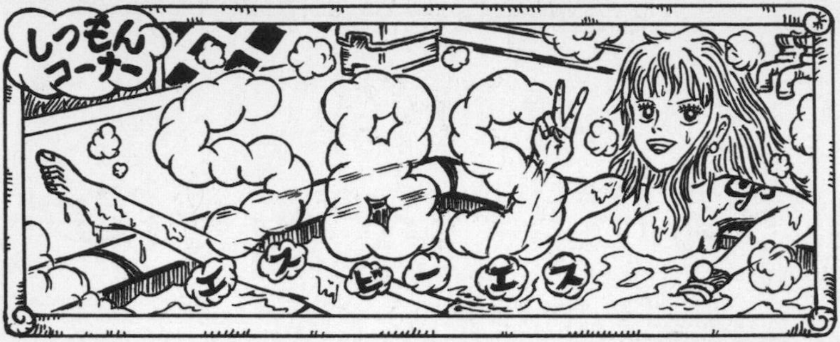
しつもんコーナー
エスビーエス

(Sashinji, Chiba)

Q: Hello, Mr. Oda! I have a question about Rebecca the gladiator. I couldn't help but notice that, perhaps due to your personal tastes, she is exposing quite a lot of skin. My question regards her bikini bottom. Is it possible that beneath that flap of cloth is a paradise of non-pantyness? I'm so curious about this, I can't even put on any underwear.

--Tanpopo

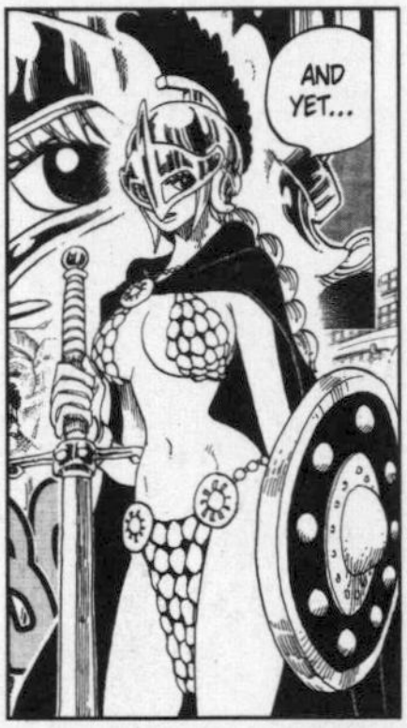
AND YET...

A: Hmm, I see. I have a feeling that I shouldn't answer this question. I know the answer, but I'll keep it to myself! Sweet dreams!!

Q: Mr. Odacchi, howdy!☆ Bartolomeo's so cool, right? So what if his birthday was October 6th? (Y'know, since "to" can be 10, and "lo" is short for "roku," or six!) Also, what are his height, age and place of birth details?!

--*One Piece* is my reason for living

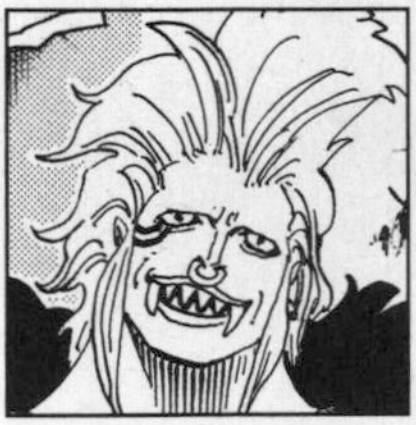

A: Birthday?! Hmm... I dunno, should I use that? Sure, I guess. His height is 7'3", he's 24 years old, and he's from the East Blue.

Q: I'm so jealous of Leo the Tontatta! …my dad says. Apparently he wants to explore in Robin's region B too. Can you help him explore her boo…er, region B without my mom finding out?

--Orika Kakyoin

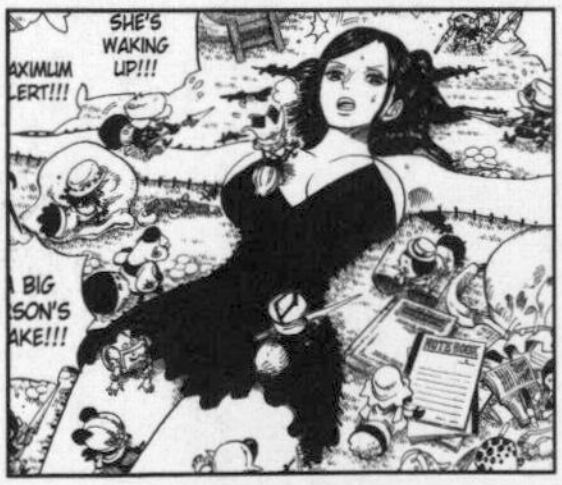
SHE'S WAKING UP!!!

A: At first I just wrote it as "Region Boobs" and laughed my butt off. But then my editor said it wasn't allowed, and we got into a big fight. Since I'm out of shape, I wound up with a skull fracture. What's wrong with the world that I'm the dang author and I can't even write what I want! I get no respect, I tell ya!

Chapter 715:
THE BATTLEGROUND OF BLOCK C

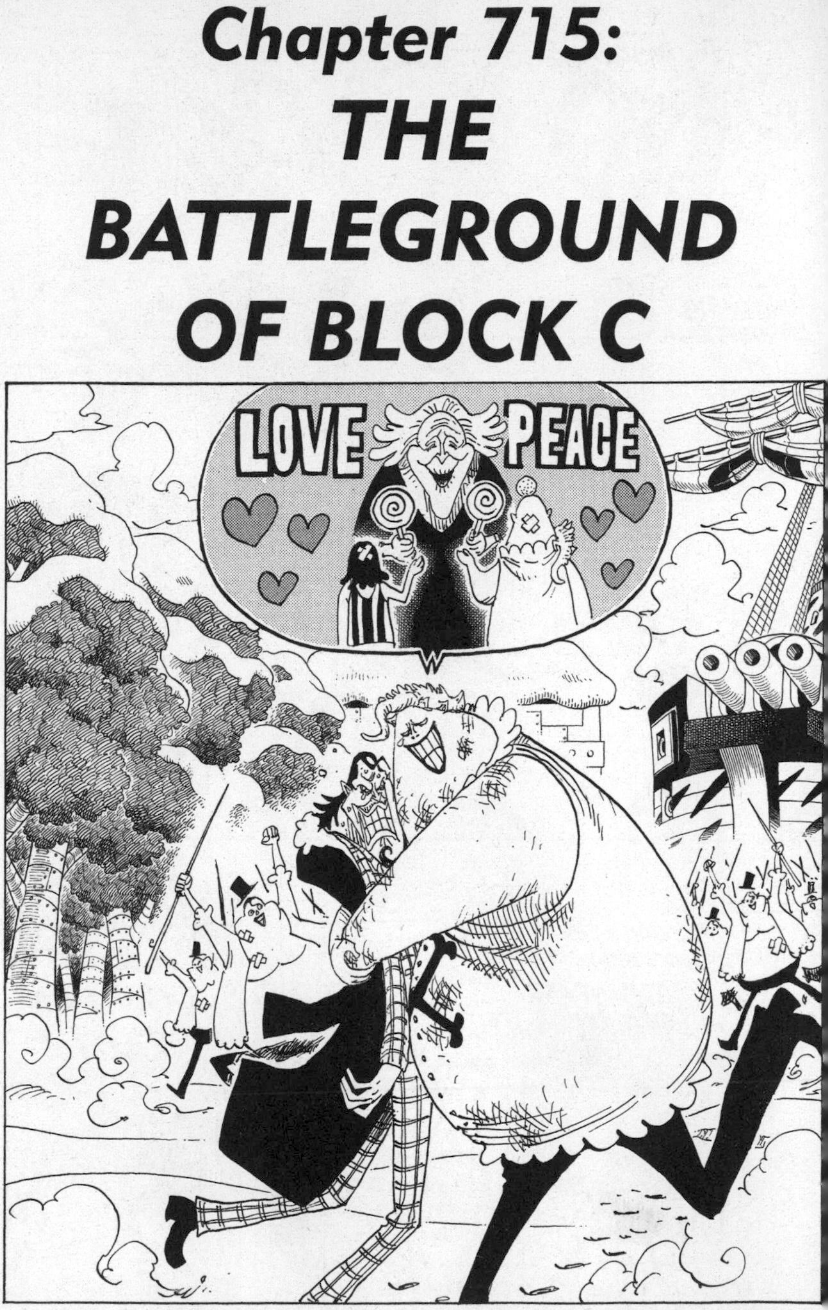
LOVE
PEACE

CARIBOU'S NEW WORLD KEE HEE HEE, VOL. 33: "REMEMBER WHAT OUR DEAD GRANDMA ALWAYS SAID: BROTHERS NEED TO GET ALONG!"

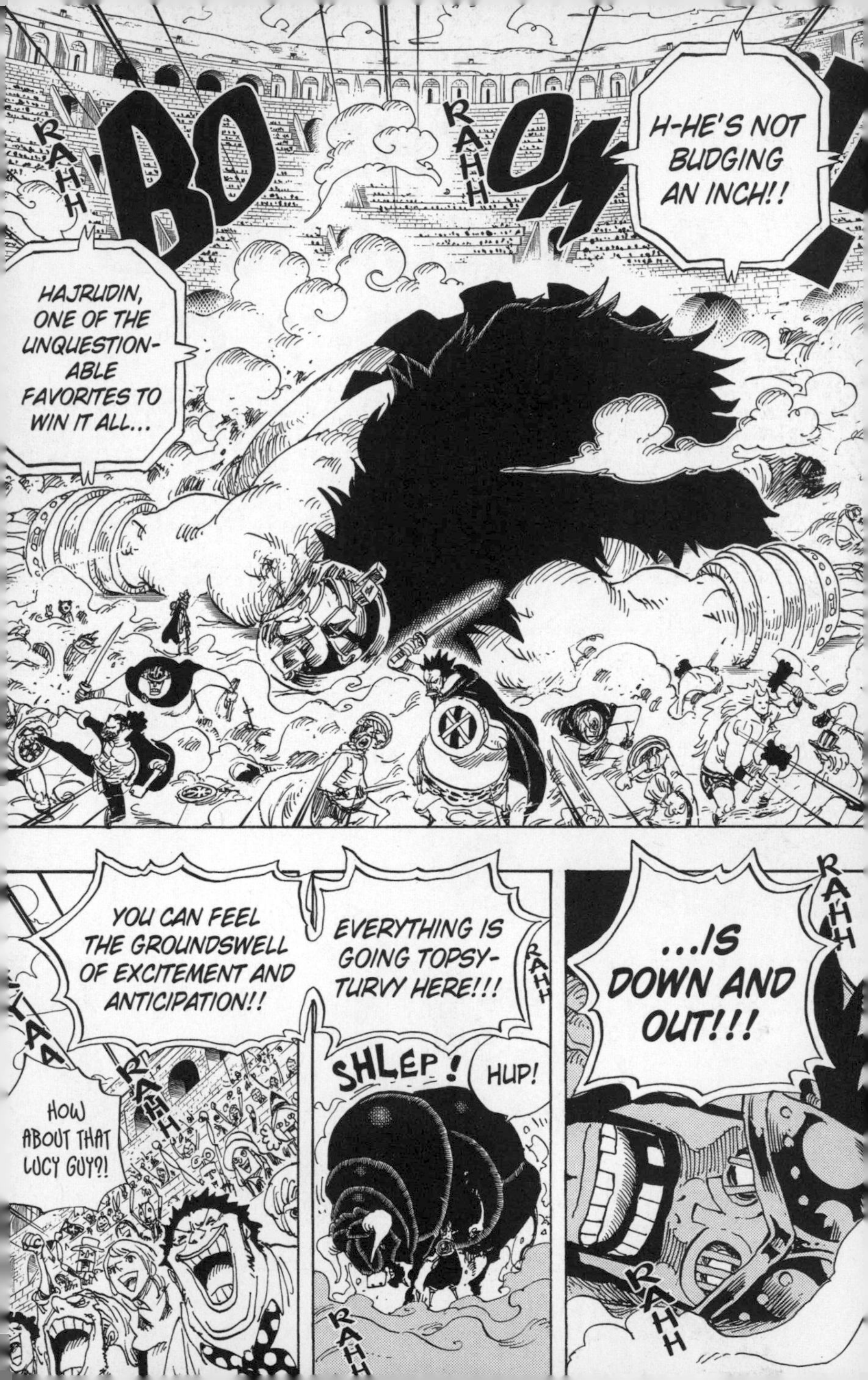
H-HE'S NOT BUDGING AN INCH!!
BOOM
RAHH
RAHH
HAJRUDIN, ONE OF THE UNQUESTION-ABLE FAVORITES TO WIN IT ALL...
RAHH
...IS DOWN AND OUT!!!
RAHH
EVERYTHING IS GOING TOPSY-TURVY HERE!!!
RAHH
HUP!
SHLEP!
RAHH
YOU CAN FEEL THE GROUNDSWELL OF EXCITEMENT AND ANTICIPATION!!
RAHH
HOW ABOUT THAT LUCY GUY?!

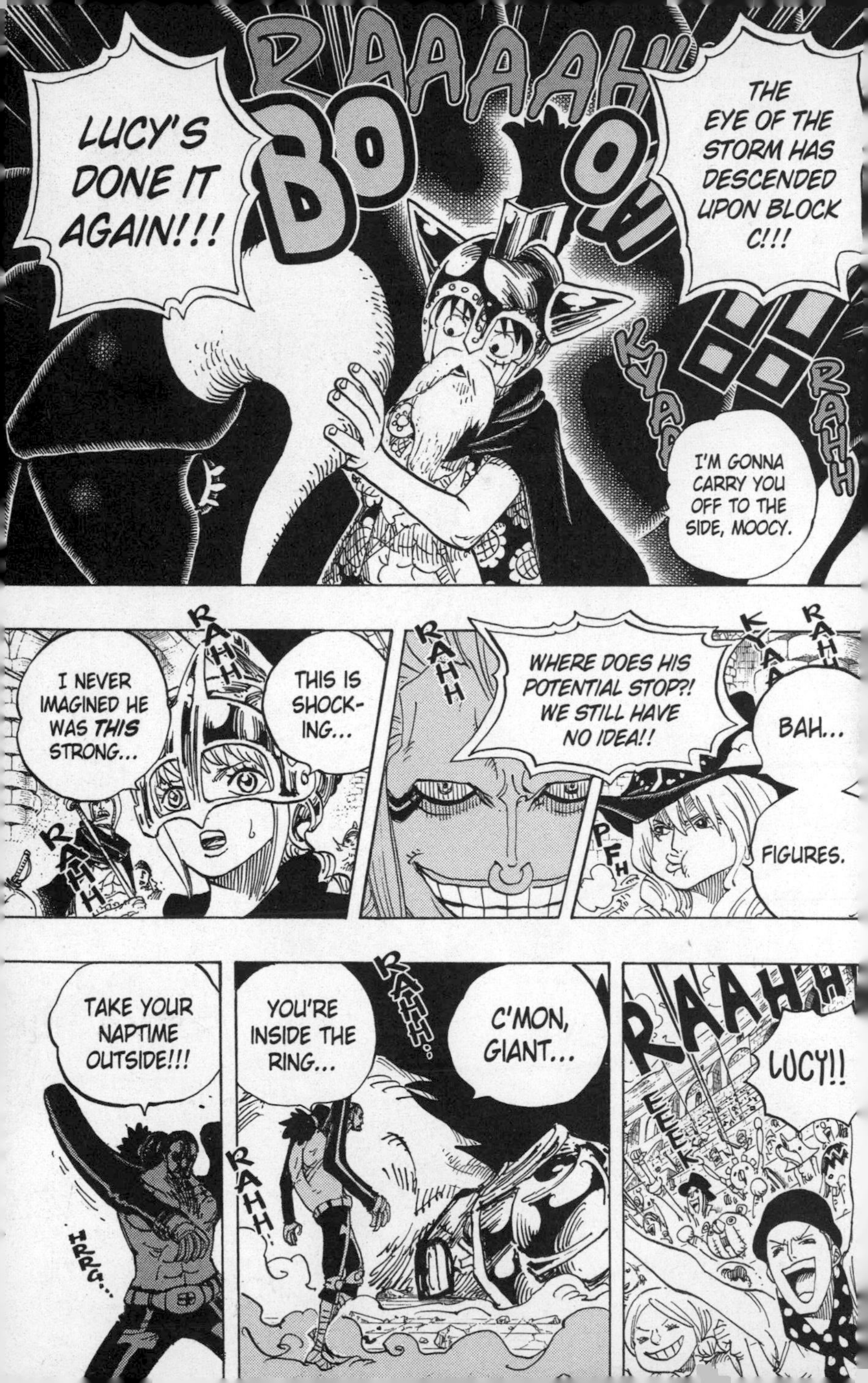
RAAAAH!!
THE EYE OF THE STORM HAS DESCENDED UPON BLOCK C!!!
BOOOM
LUCY'S DONE IT AGAIN!!!
KYAA
RAHH
I'M GONNA CARRY YOU OFF TO THE SIDE, MOOCY.
RAHH
KYAA
BAH...
FIGURES.
PFH
WHERE DOES HIS POTENTIAL STOP?! WE STILL HAVE NO IDEA!!
RAHH
THIS IS SHOCKING...
RAHH
I NEVER IMAGINED HE WAS *THIS* STRONG...
RAHH
RAAHH
LUCY!!
EEEEK
C'MON, GIANT...
RAHH...
YOU'RE INSIDE THE RING...
RAHH
TAKE YOUR NAPTIME OUTSIDE!!!
HRRG...

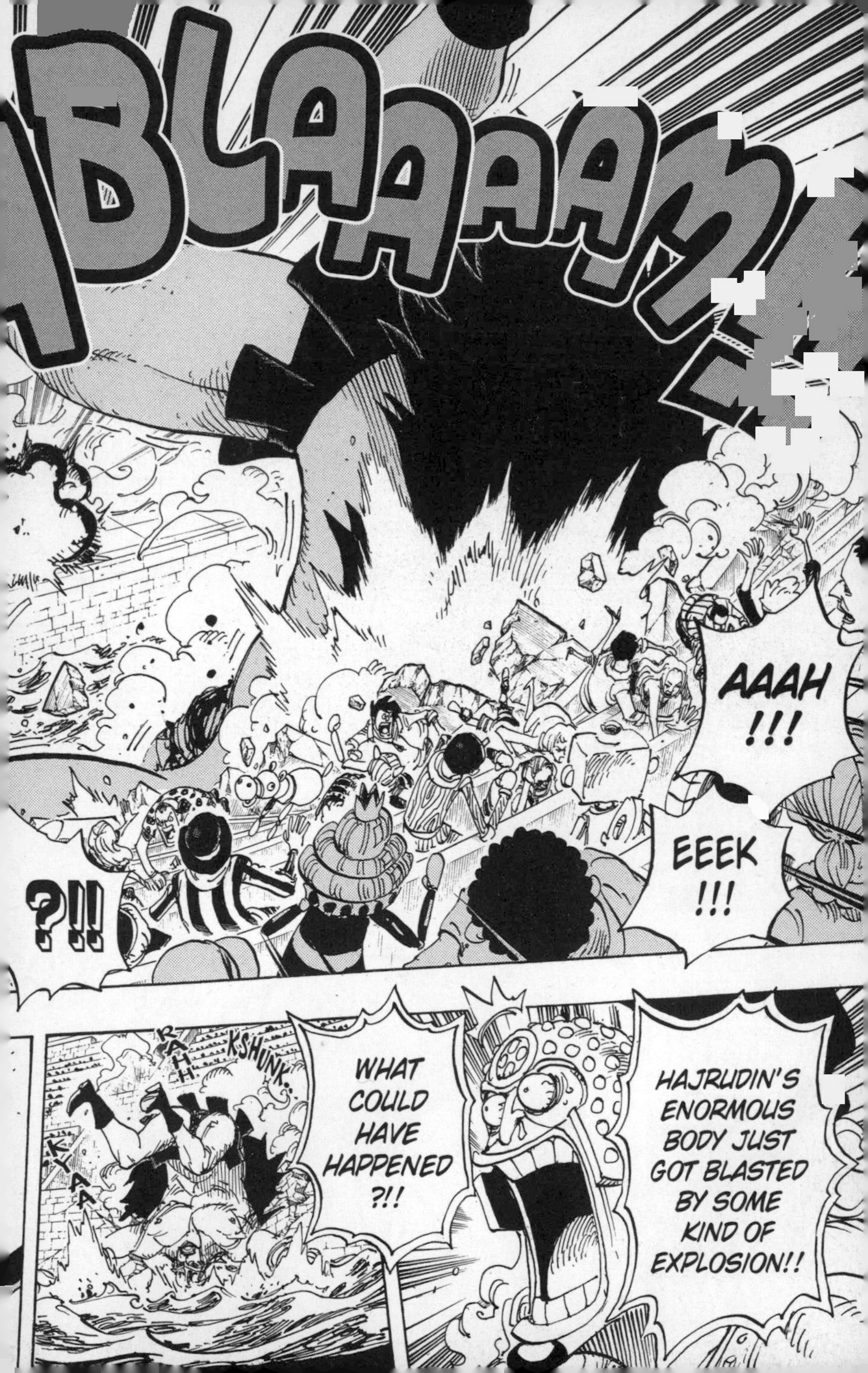
BLAAAAM
AAAH!!!
EEEK!!!
?!!
HAJRUDIN'S ENORMOUS BODY JUST GOT BLASTED BY SOME KIND OF EXPLOSION!!
WHAT COULD HAVE HAPPENED?!!
RAHH
KSHUNK..
KYAA

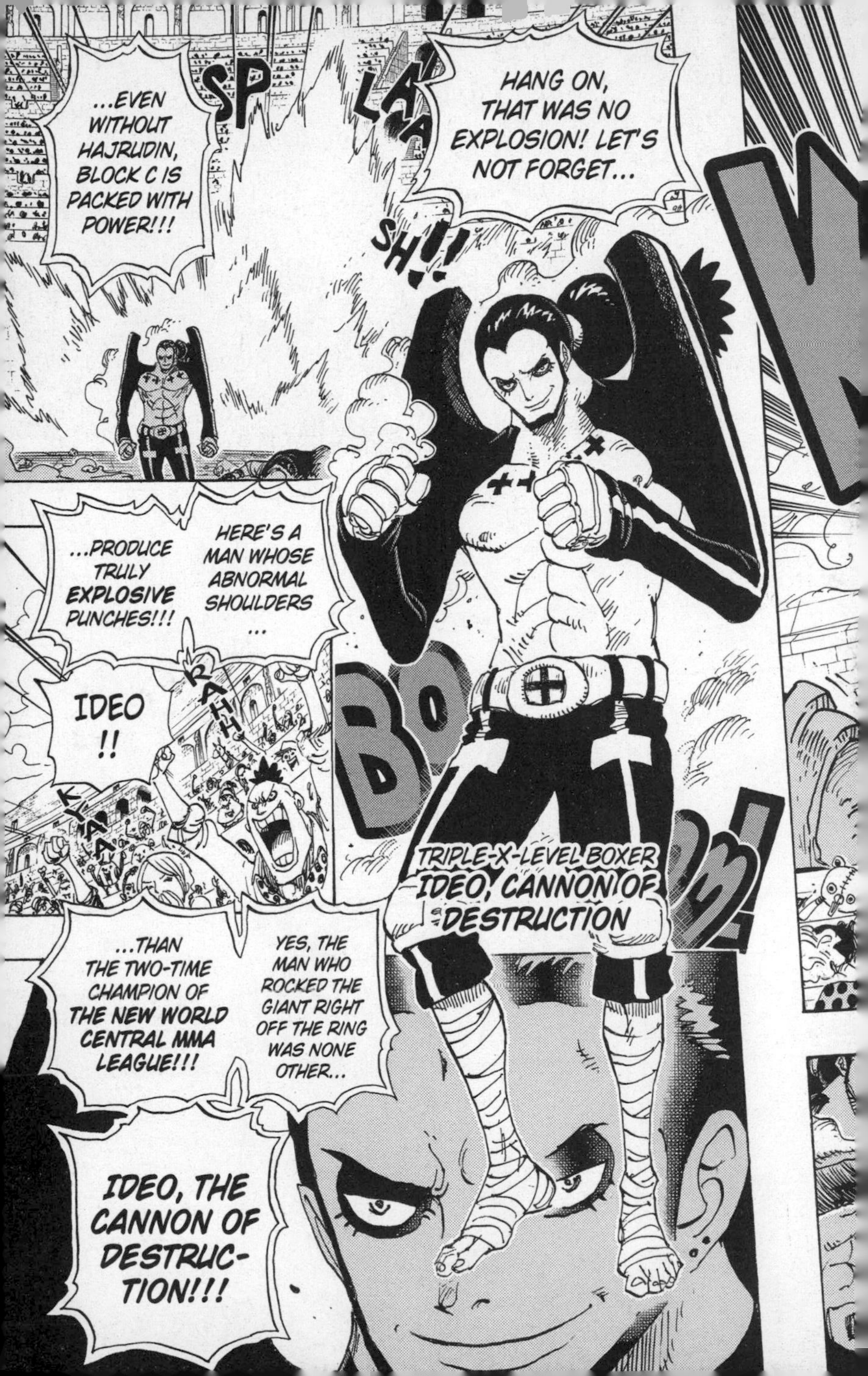

HANG ON, THAT WAS NO EXPLOSION! LET'S NOT FORGET...
...EVEN WITHOUT HAJRUDIN, BLOCK C IS PACKED WITH POWER!!!
SPLAASH!!
HERE'S A MAN WHOSE ABNORMAL SHOULDERS ...
...PRODUCE TRULY EXPLOSIVE PUNCHES!!!
RAHH
IDEO !!
KYAA
BOOM!
TRIPLE-X-LEVEL BOXER IDEO, CANNON OF DESTRUCTION
YES, THE MAN WHO ROCKED THE GIANT RIGHT OFF THE RING WAS NONE OTHER...
...THAN THE TWO-TIME CHAMPION OF THE NEW WORLD CENTRAL MMA LEAGUE!!!
IDEO, THE CANNON OF DESTRUC-TION!!!

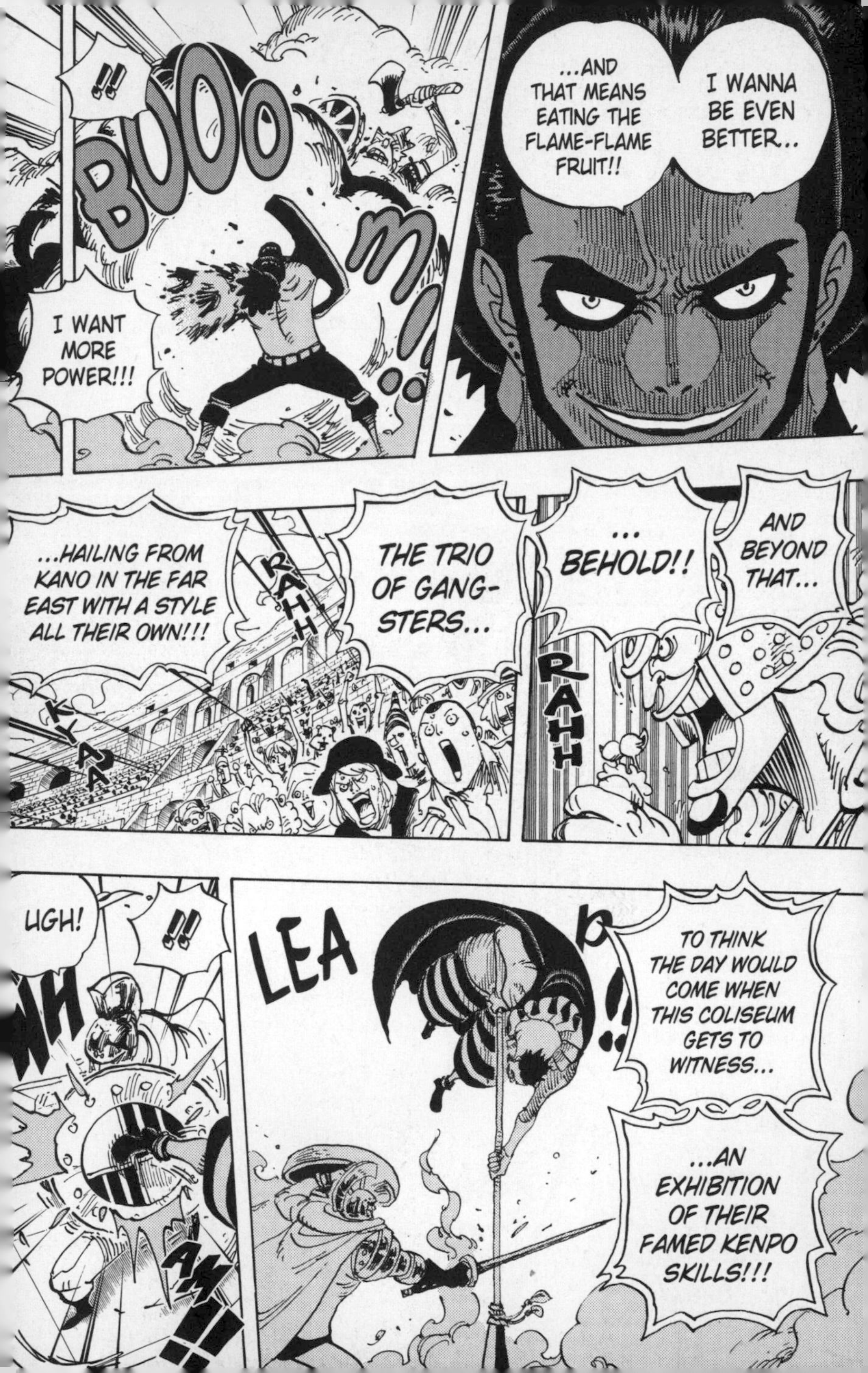
I WANNA BE EVEN BETTER...
...AND THAT MEANS EATING THE FLAME-FLAME FRUIT!!
!!
BUOOOM
I WANT MORE POWER!!!
AND BEYOND THAT...
...BEHOLD!!
RAHH
THE TRIO OF GANG-STERS...
...HAILING FROM KANO IN THE FAR EAST WITH A STYLE ALL THEIR OWN!!!
RAHH
KYAA
TO THINK THE DAY WOULD COME WHEN THIS COLISEUM GETS TO WITNESS...
...AN EXHIBITION OF THEIR FAMED KENPO SKILLS!!!
LEAP
!!
!!
UGH!

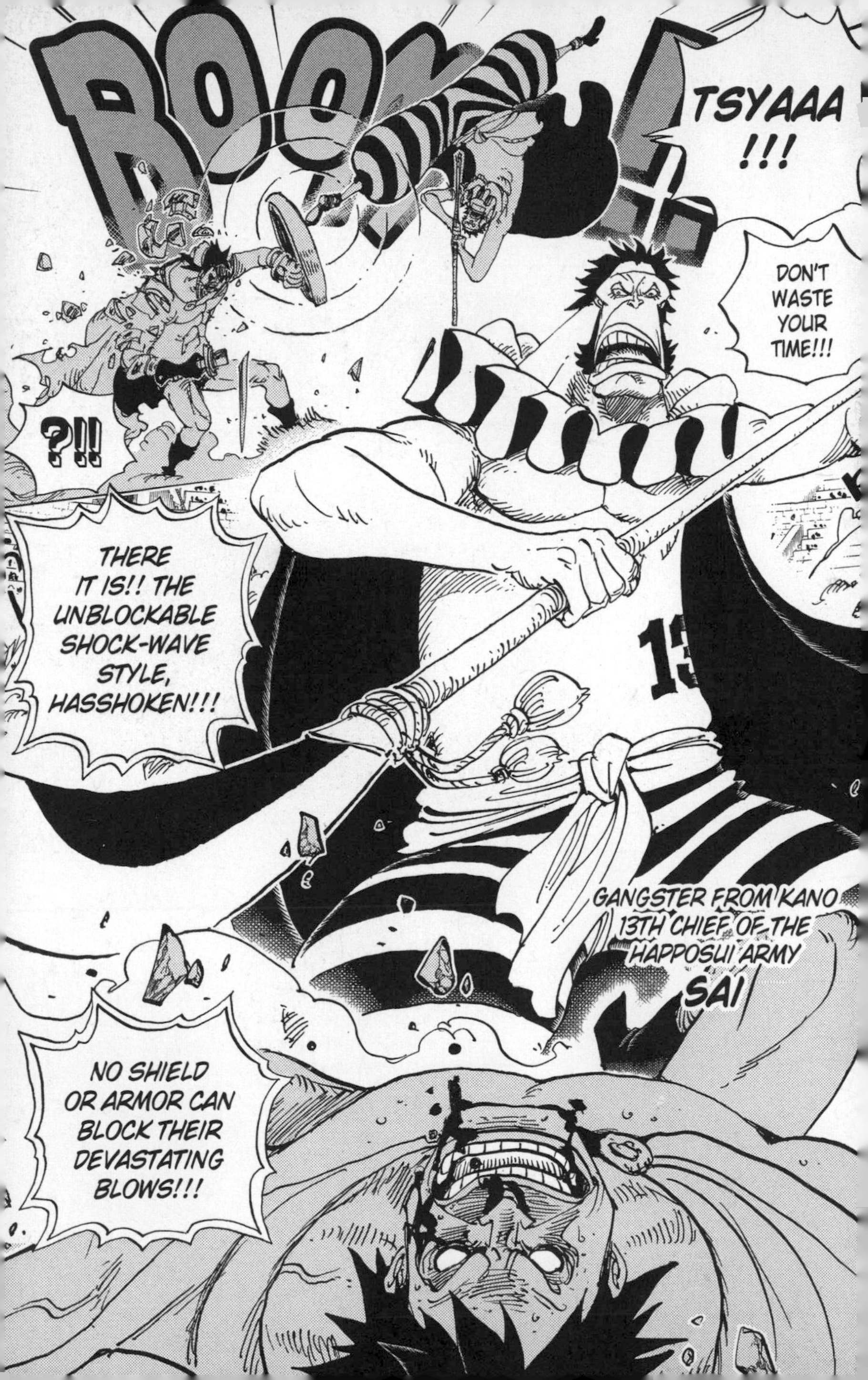
BOOM!
TSYAAA!!!
DON'T WASTE YOUR TIME!!!
?!!
THERE IT IS!! THE UNBLOCKABLE SHOCK-WAVE STYLE, HASSHOKEN!!!
GANGSTER FROM KANO
13TH CHIEF OF THE HAPPOSUI ARMY
SAI
NO SHIELD OR ARMOR CAN BLOCK THEIR DEVASTATING BLOWS!!!
13

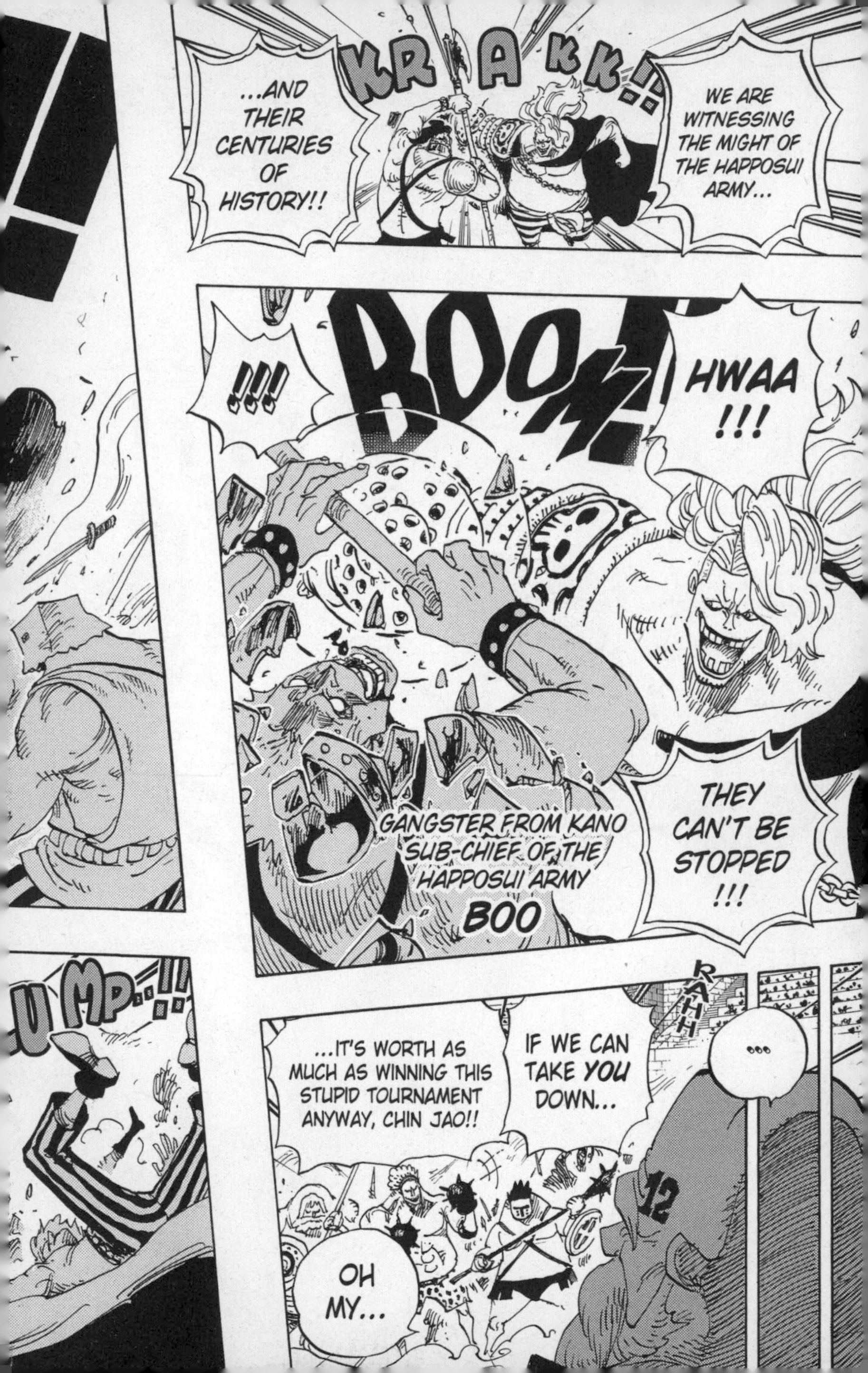

WE ARE WITNESSING THE MIGHT OF THE HAPPOSUI ARMY...
KRAKK!!
...AND THEIR CENTURIES OF HISTORY!!
HWAA !!!
BOOM
!!!
THEY CAN'T BE STOPPED !!!
GANGSTER FROM KANO SUB-CHIEF OF THE HAPPOSUI ARMY BOO
RAHH
...
IF WE CAN TAKE YOU DOWN...
...IT'S WORTH AS MUCH AS WINNING THIS STUPID TOURNAMENT ANYWAY, CHIN JAO!!
OH MY...
12
UMP..!!!

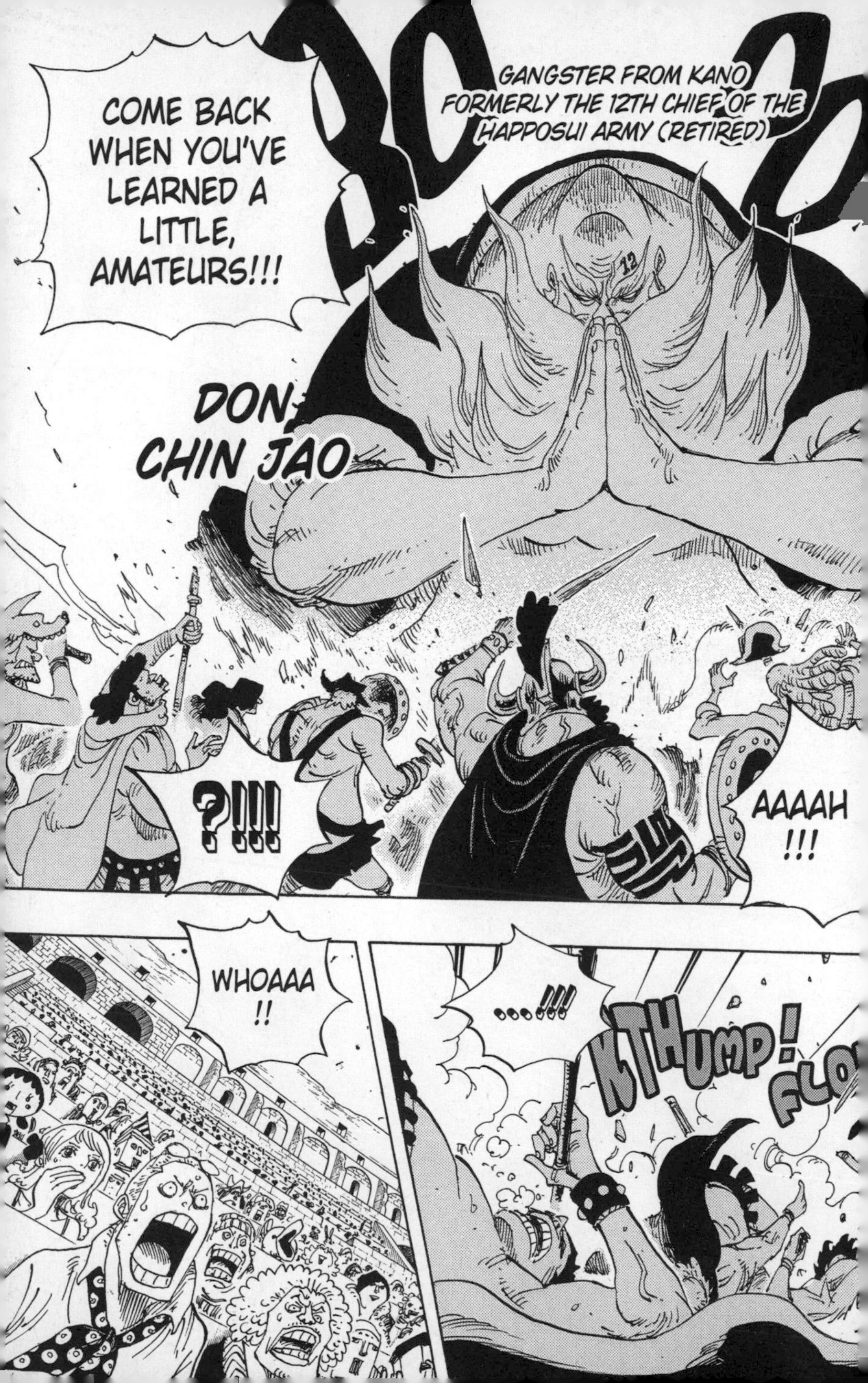

GANGSTER FROM KANO FORMERLY THE 12TH CHIEF OF THE HAPPOSUI ARMY (RETIRED)
COME BACK WHEN YOU'VE LEARNED A LITTLE, AMATEURS!!!
DON CHIN JAO
AAAAH !!!
?!!!
...!!!
KTHUMP!
WHOAAA !!

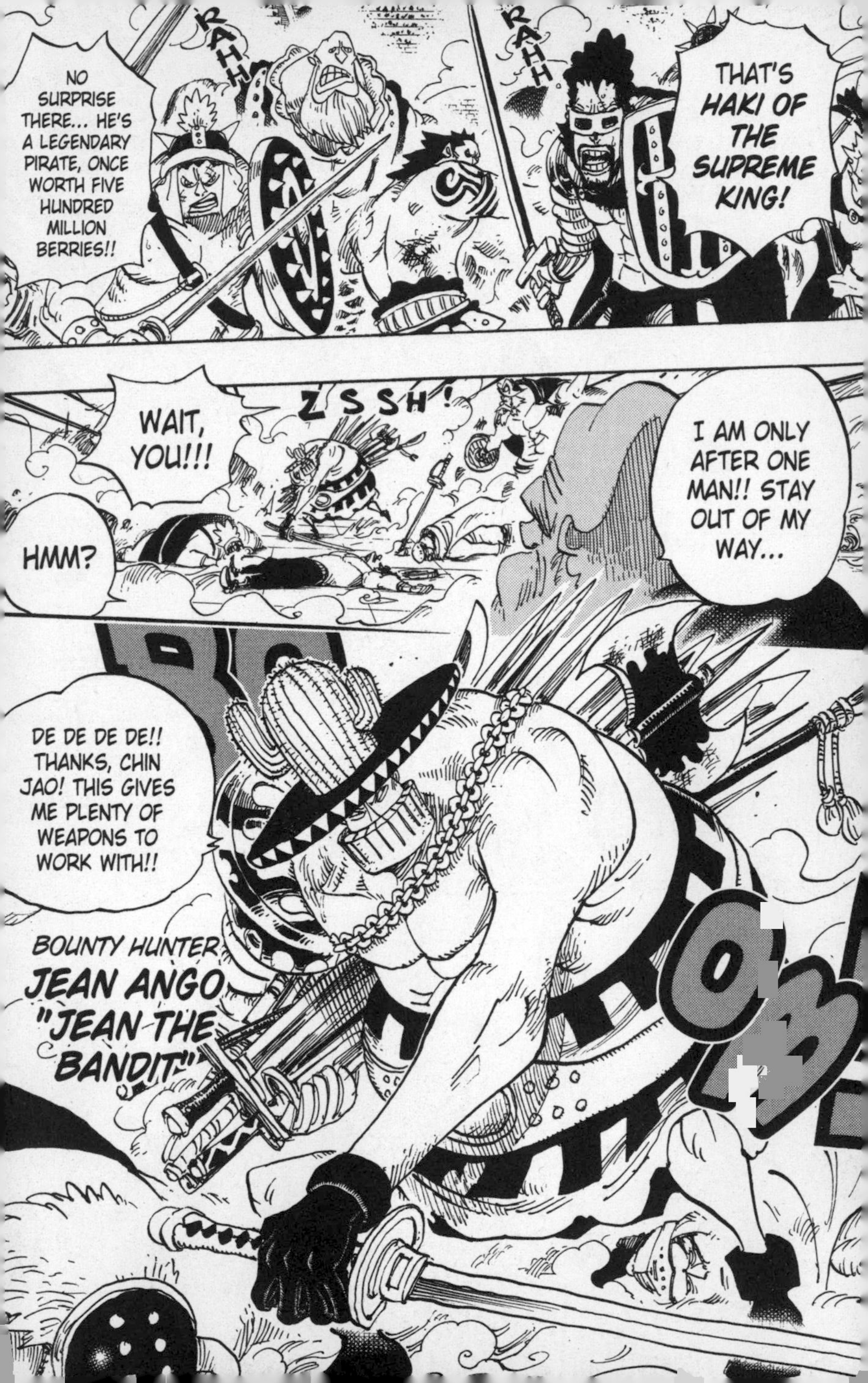
RAHH
THAT'S HAKI OF THE SUPREME KING!
RAHH
NO SURPRISE THERE... HE'S A LEGENDARY PIRATE, ONCE WORTH FIVE HUNDRED MILLION BERRIES!!
I AM ONLY AFTER ONE MAN!! STAY OUT OF MY WAY...
ZSSH!
WAIT, YOU!!!
HMM?
DE DE DE DE!! THANKS, CHIN JAO! THIS GIVES ME PLENTY OF WEAPONS TO WORK WITH!!
BOUNTY HUNTER
JEAN ANGO "JEAN THE BANDIT"

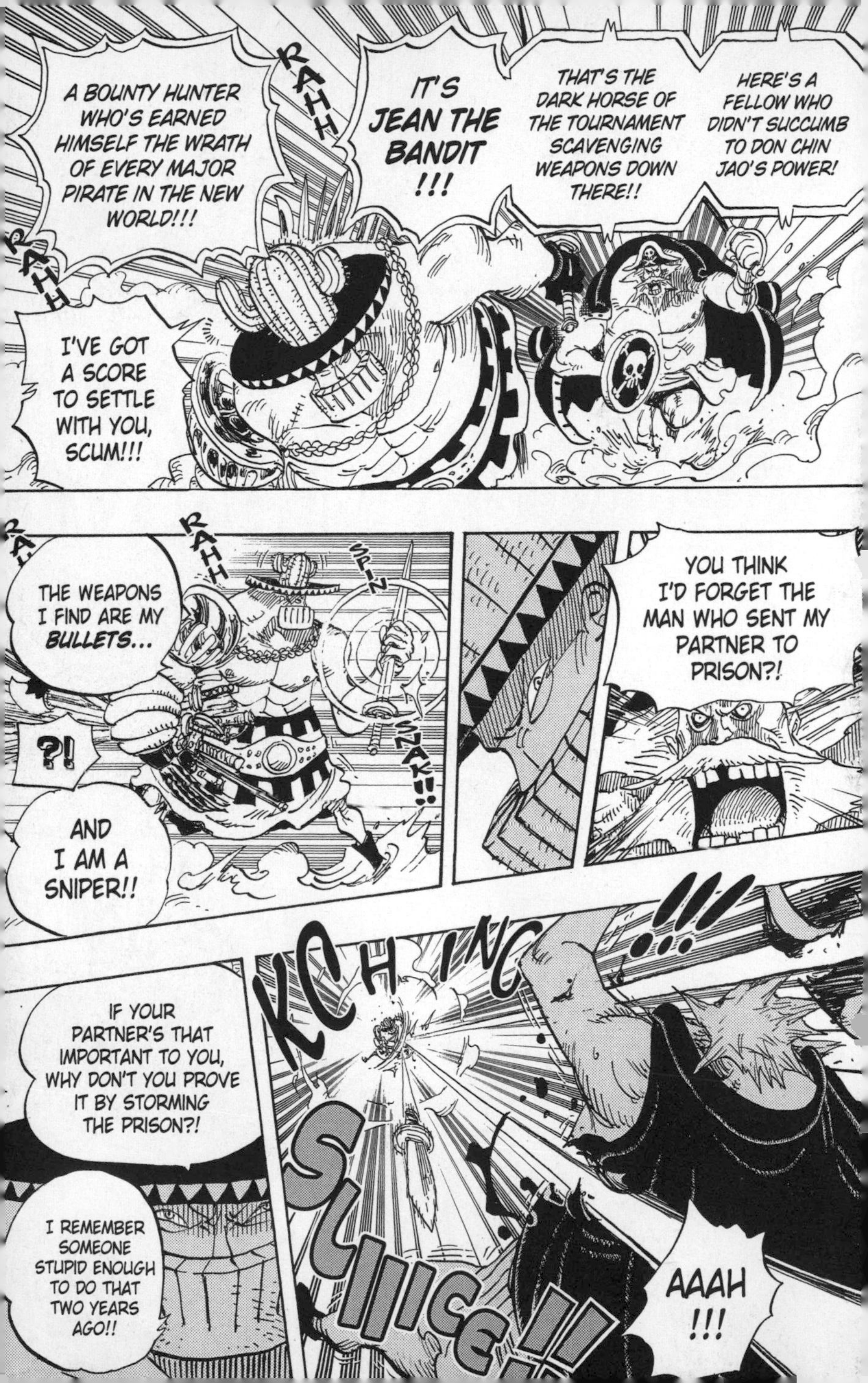
HERE'S A FELLOW WHO DIDN'T SUCCUMB TO DON CHIN JAO'S POWER!
THAT'S THE DARK HORSE OF THE TOURNAMENT SCAVENGING WEAPONS DOWN THERE!!
IT'S JEAN THE BANDIT!!!
RAHH
A BOUNTY HUNTER WHO'S EARNED HIMSELF THE WRATH OF EVERY MAJOR PIRATE IN THE NEW WORLD!!!
RAHH
I'VE GOT A SCORE TO SETTLE WITH YOU, SCUM!!!
YOU THINK I'D FORGET THE MAN WHO SENT MY PARTNER TO PRISON?!
RAHH
SPIN
THE WEAPONS I FIND ARE MY BULLETS...
SNAK!!
?!
AND I AM A SNIPER!!
!!!
KCHING
AAAH!!!
SLIIICE!!
IF YOUR PARTNER'S THAT IMPORTANT TO YOU, WHY DON'T YOU PROVE IT BY STORMING THE PRISON?!
I REMEMBER SOMEONE STUPID ENOUGH TO DO THAT TWO YEARS AGO!!

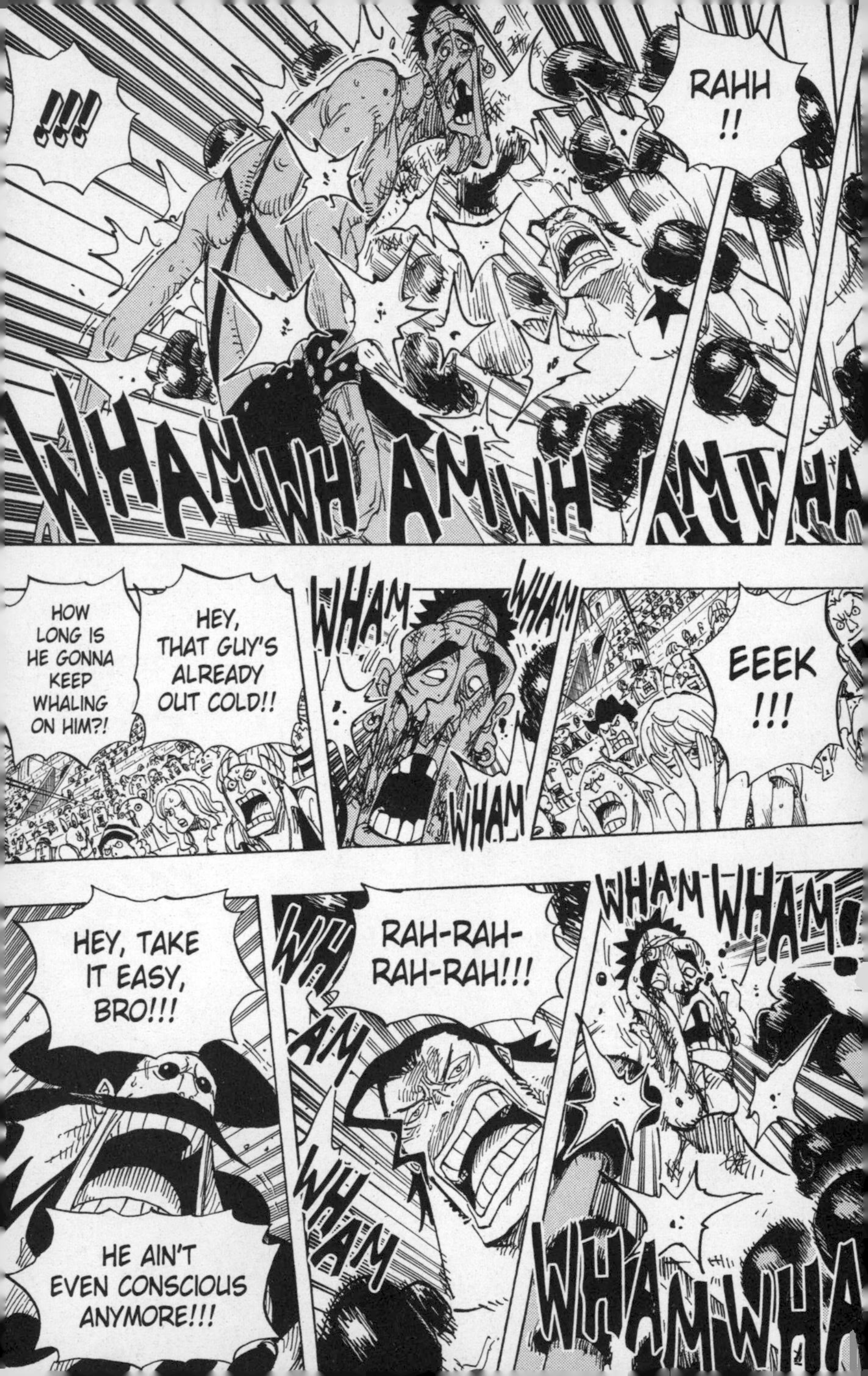

RAHH !!
!!!
WHAM WHAM WHAM
EEEK !!!
WHAM
WHAM
WHAM
HEY, THAT GUY'S ALREADY OUT COLD!!
HOW LONG IS HE GONNA KEEP WHALING ON HIM?!
WHAM WHAM
WHAM
RAH-RAH-RAH-RAH!!!
WHAM
WHAM
HEY, TAKE IT EASY, BRO!!!
HE AIN'T EVEN CONSCIOUS ANYMORE!!!

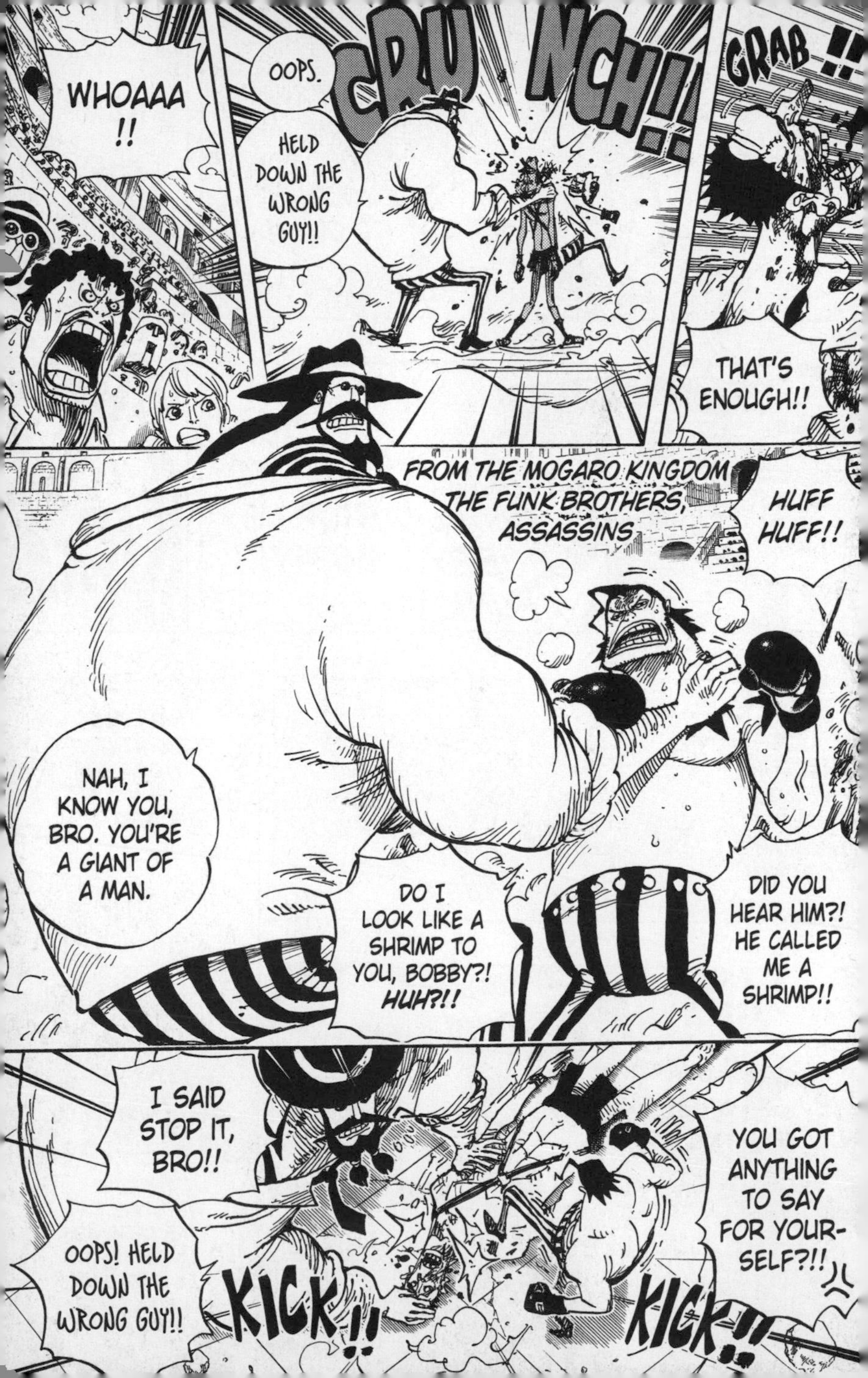
GRAB!!
THAT'S ENOUGH!!
CRUNCH!!
OOPS.
HELD DOWN THE WRONG GUY!!
WHOAAA!!
FROM THE MOGARO KINGDOM THE FUNK BROTHERS, ASSASSINS
HUFF HUFF!!
DID YOU HEAR HIM?! HE CALLED ME A SHRIMP!!
DO I LOOK LIKE A SHRIMP TO YOU, BOBBY?! HUH?!!
NAH, I KNOW YOU, BRO. YOU'RE A GIANT OF A MAN.
YOU GOT ANYTHING TO SAY FOR YOUR-SELF?!!
KICK!!
I SAID STOP IT, BRO!!
OOPS! HELD DOWN THE WRONG GUY!!
KICK!!

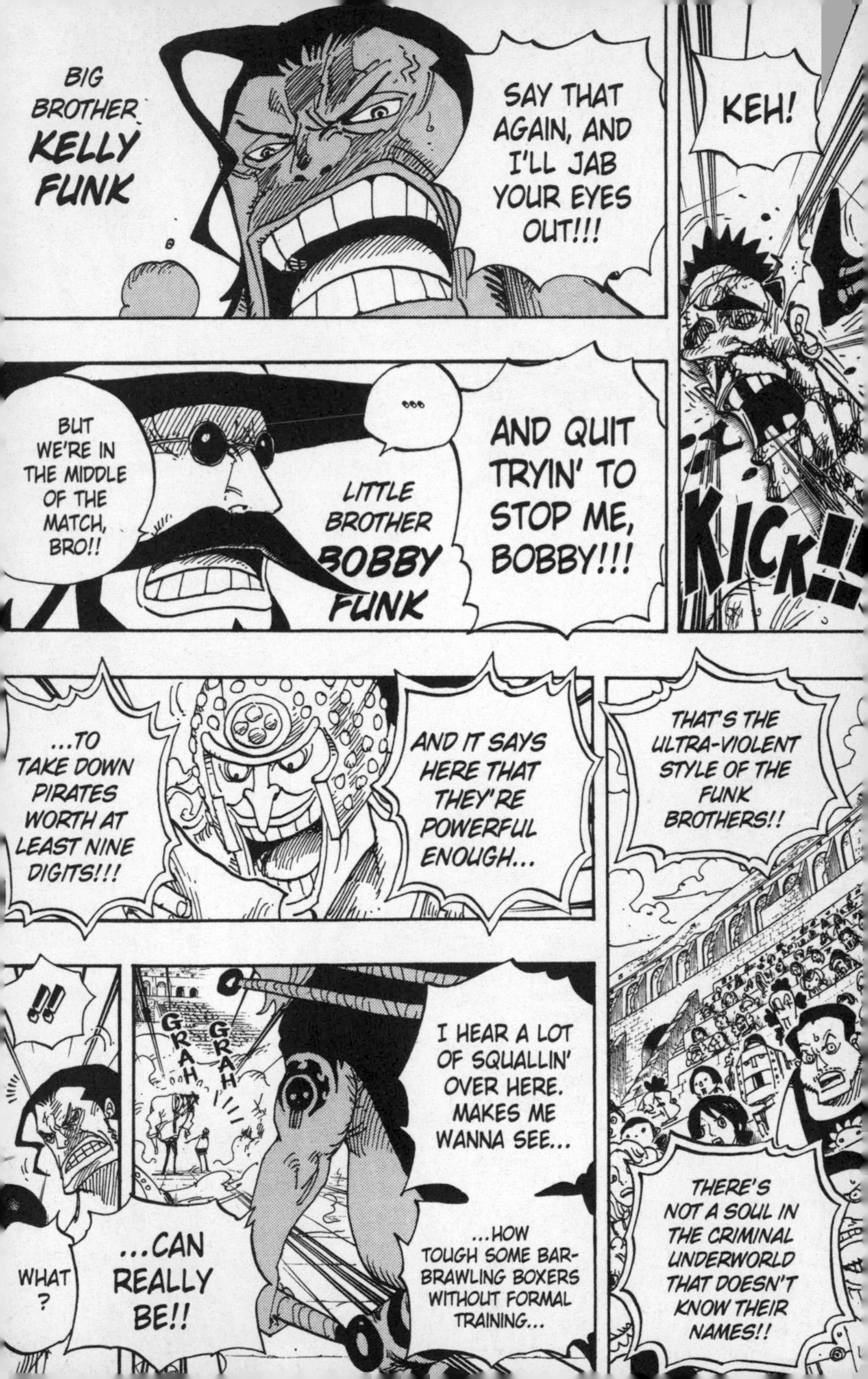
KEH!
KICK!!
SAY THAT AGAIN, AND I'LL JAB YOUR EYES OUT!!!
BIG BROTHER KELLY FUNK
AND QUIT TRYIN' TO STOP ME, BOBBY!!!
...
LITTLE BROTHER BOBBY FUNK
BUT WE'RE IN THE MIDDLE OF THE MATCH, BRO!!
THAT'S THE ULTRA-VIOLENT STYLE OF THE FUNK BROTHERS!!
THERE'S NOT A SOUL IN THE CRIMINAL UNDERWORLD THAT DOESN'T KNOW THEIR NAMES!!
AND IT SAYS HERE THAT THEY'RE POWERFUL ENOUGH...
...TO TAKE DOWN PIRATES WORTH AT LEAST NINE DIGITS!!!
I HEAR A LOT OF SQUALLIN' OVER HERE. MAKES ME WANNA SEE...
...HOW TOUGH SOME BAR-BRAWLING BOXERS WITHOUT FORMAL TRAINING...
GRAH
GRAH
...CAN REALLY BE!!
!!
WHAT?

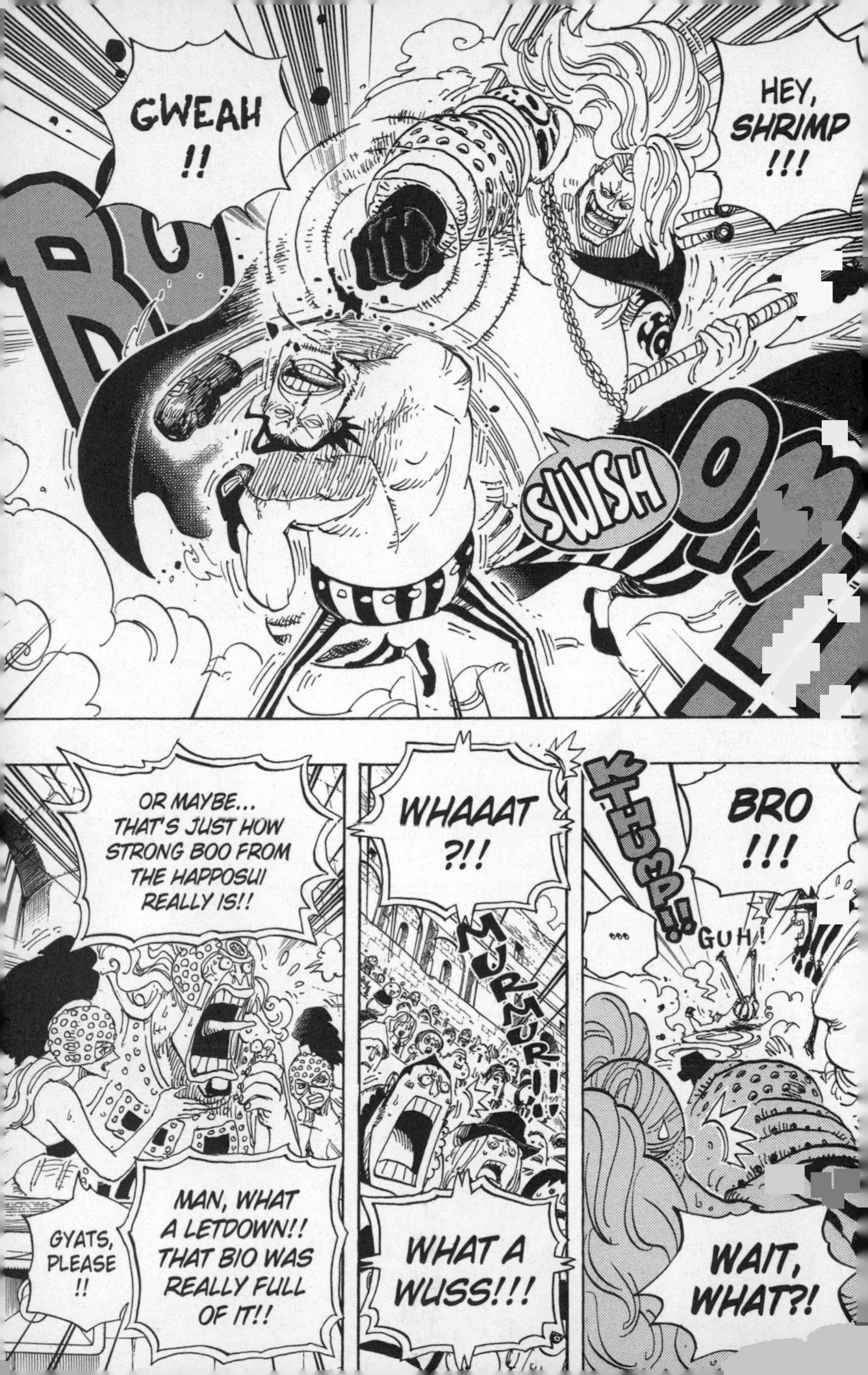
HEY, SHRIMP!!!
SWISH
GWEAH!!
BRO!!!
K-THUMP!!
GUH!
...
WAIT, WHAT?!
WHAAAT?!!
MURMUR!!
WHAT A WUSS!!!
OR MAYBE... THAT'S JUST HOW STRONG BOO FROM THE HAPPOSUI REALLY IS!!
MAN, WHAT A LETDOWN!! THAT BIO WAS REALLY FULL OF IT!!
GYATS, PLEASE!!

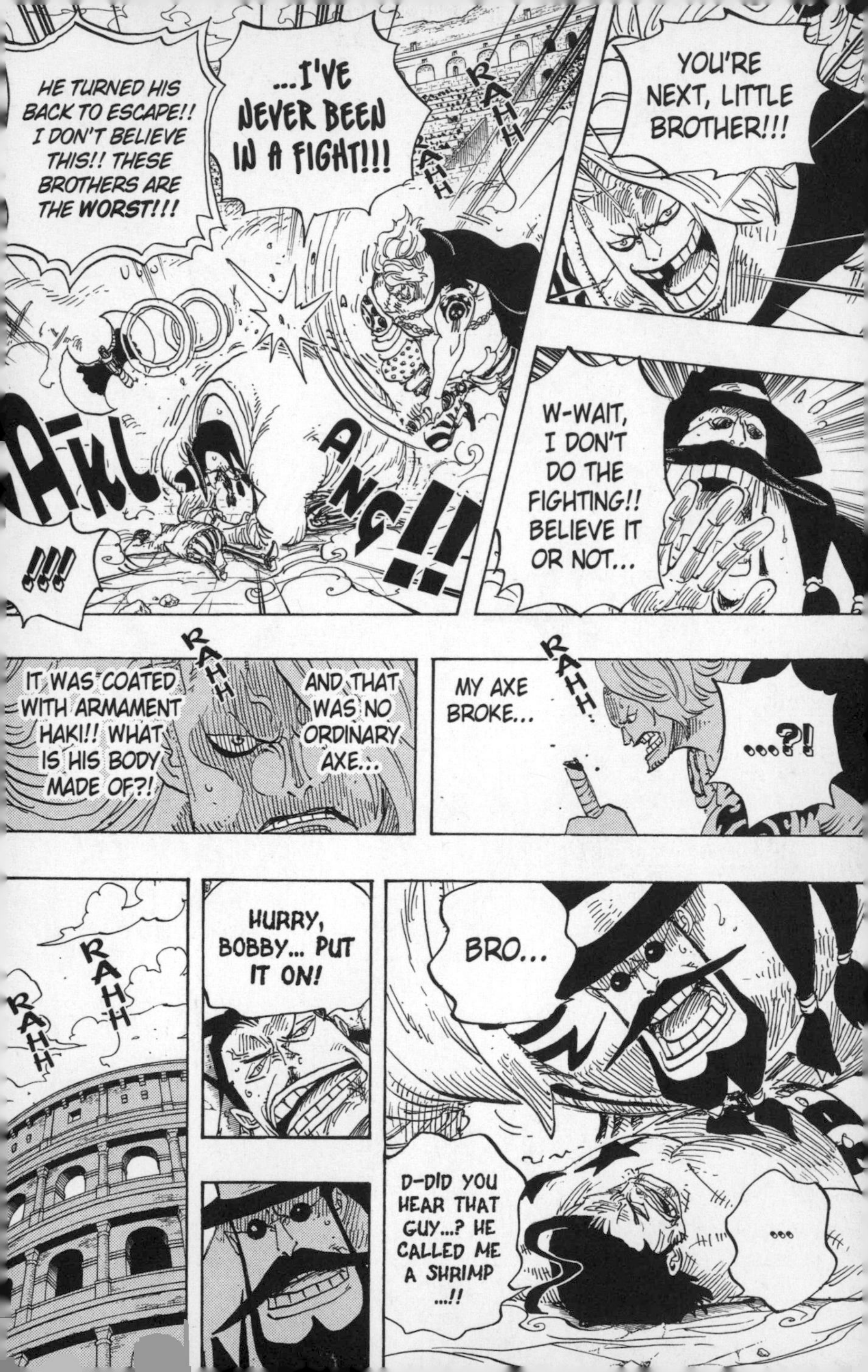
YOU'RE NEXT, LITTLE BROTHER!!!
W-WAIT, I DON'T DO THE FIGHTING!! BELIEVE IT OR NOT...
...I'VE NEVER BEEN IN A FIGHT!!!
RAHH
RAHH
HE TURNED HIS BACK TO ESCAPE!! I DON'T BELIEVE THIS!! THESE BROTHERS ARE THE WORST!!!
RAHH
MY AXE BROKE...
...?!
RAHH
AND THAT WAS NO ORDINARY AXE...
IT WAS COATED WITH ARMAMENT HAKI!! WHAT IS HIS BODY MADE OF?!
BRO...
D-DID YOU HEAR THAT GUY...? HE CALLED ME A SHRIMP ...!!
...
HURRY, BOBBY... PUT IT ON!
RAHH
RAHH

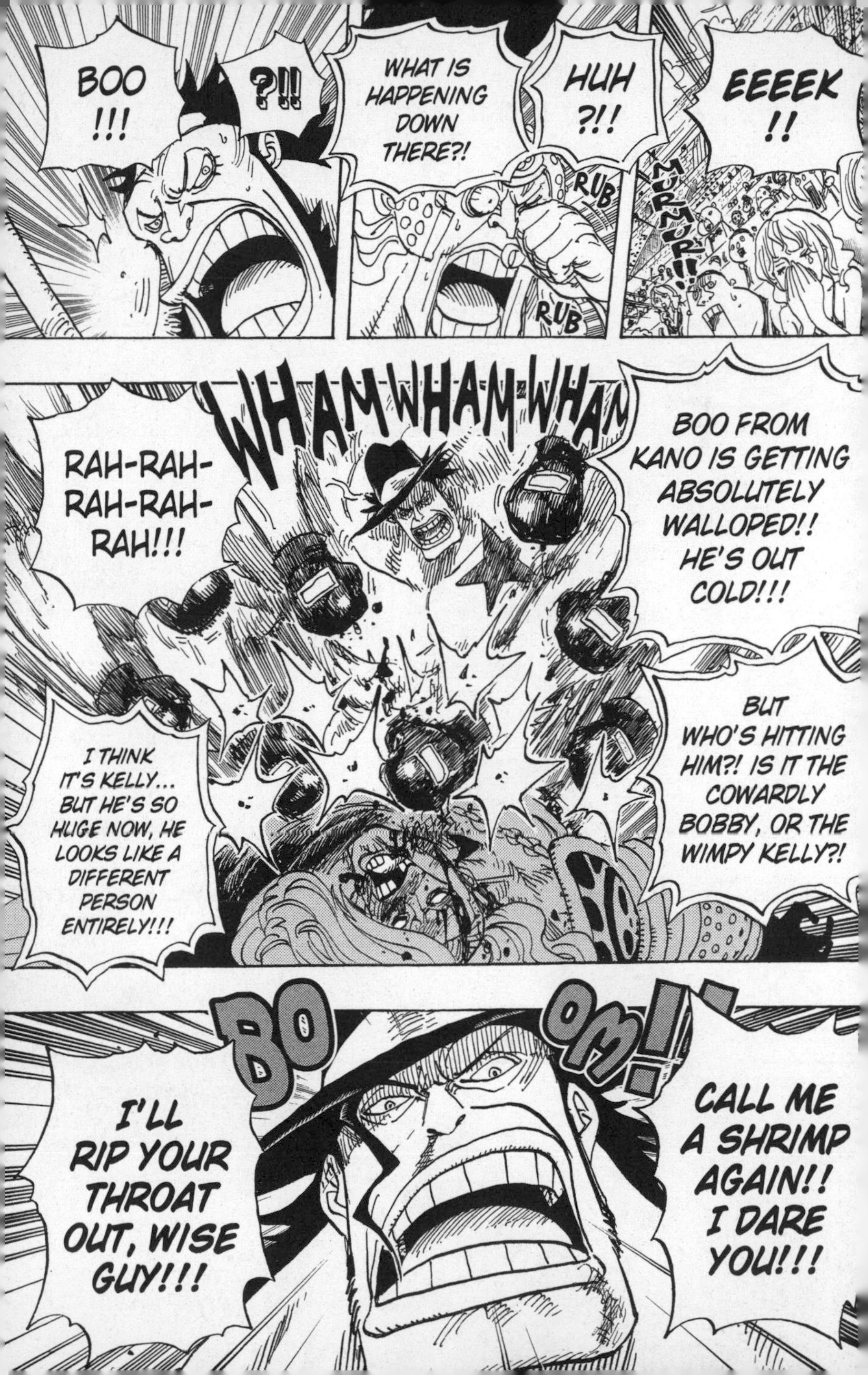
EEEEK !!
MURMUR!!
HUH ?!!
WHAT IS HAPPENING DOWN THERE?!
RUB
RUB
?!!
BOO !!!
WHAM WHAM WHAM
BOO FROM KANO IS GETTING ABSOLUTELY WALLOPED!! HE'S OUT COLD!!!
RAH-RAH-RAH-RAH-RAH!!!
BUT WHO'S HITTING HIM?! IS IT THE COWARDLY BOBBY, OR THE WIMPY KELLY?!
I THINK IT'S KELLY... BUT HE'S SO HUGE NOW, HE LOOKS LIKE A DIFFERENT PERSON ENTIRELY!!!
BOOM!!
CALL ME A SHRIMP AGAIN!! I DARE YOU!!!
I'LL RIP YOUR THROAT OUT, WISE GUY!!!

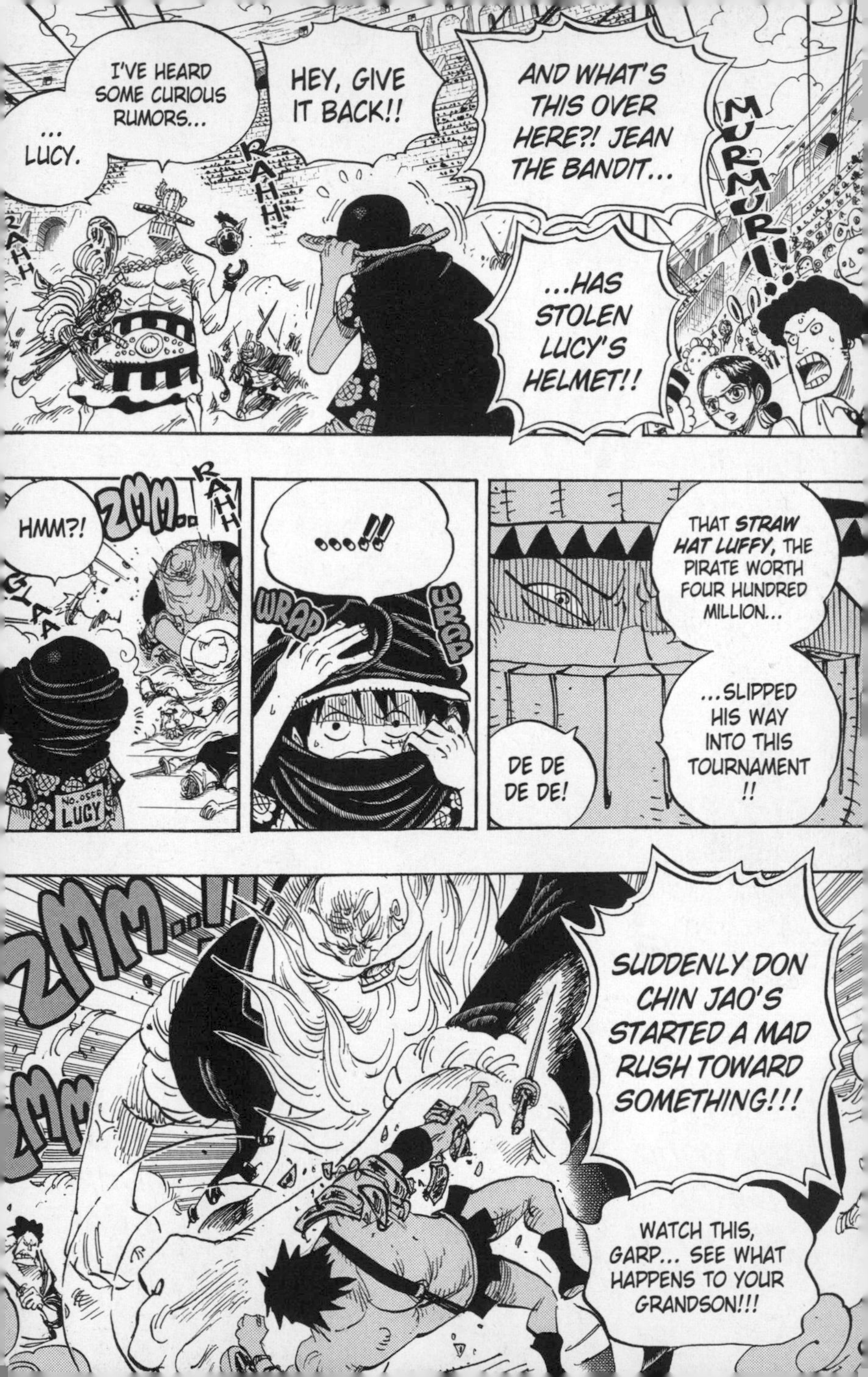
AND WHAT'S THIS OVER HERE?! JEAN THE BANDIT...
MURMUR!!
...HAS STOLEN LUCY'S HELMET!!
HEY, GIVE IT BACK!!
RAHHH
I'VE HEARD SOME CURIOUS RUMORS...
... LUCY.
RAHH
THAT STRAW HAT LUFFY, THE PIRATE WORTH FOUR HUNDRED MILLION...
...SLIPPED HIS WAY INTO THIS TOURNAMENT!!
DE DE DE DE!
....!!
WRAP
WRAP
RAHH
ZMM..
HMM?!
GYAA
No.0556 LUCY
SUDDENLY DON CHIN JAO'S STARTED A MAD RUSH TOWARD SOMETHING!!!
ZMM..!!
WATCH THIS, GARP... SEE WHAT HAPPENS TO YOUR GRANDSON!!!
ZMM

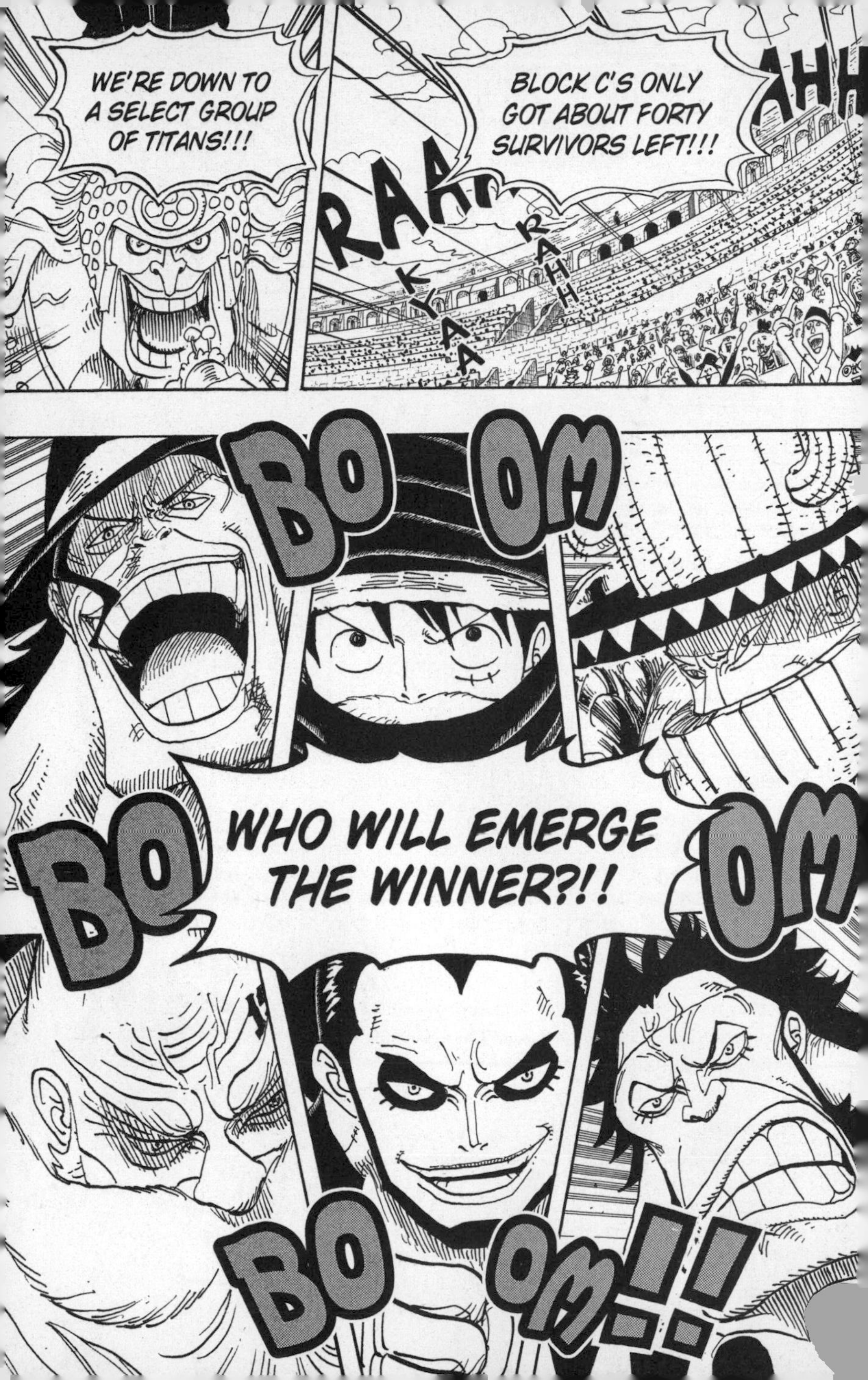
BLOCK C'S ONLY GOT ABOUT FORTY SURVIVORS LEFT!!!
AHH
RAAAH
RAHH
KYAA
WE'RE DOWN TO A SELECT GROUP OF TITANS!!!
BOOM
BOOM
WHO WILL EMERGE THE WINNER?!!
BOOM!!

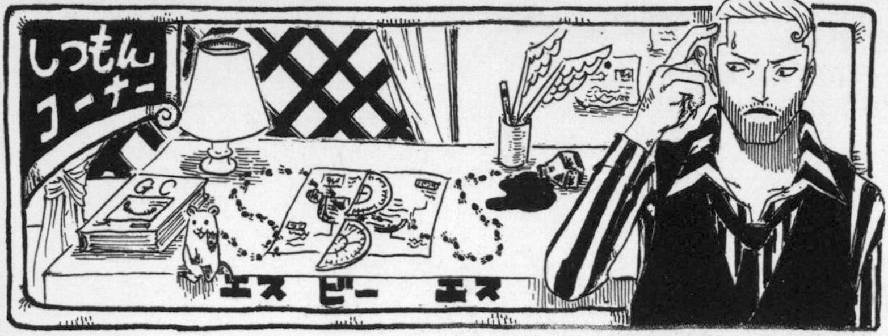
しつもん
コーナー
エス ビー エス
(Coral, Fukuoka)

Q: Which one is a cat

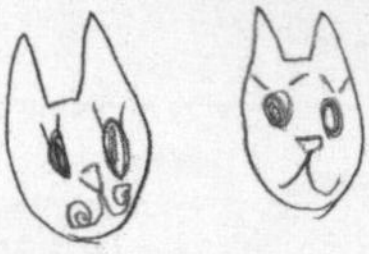

--Milk

A: Okay, um... Hmmm. Which one? Well...they both look like cats to me... Plus, if those aren't cats, what would they be? I'm gonna guess...the left one? Let's check the answer...
They didn't write an answer!!!

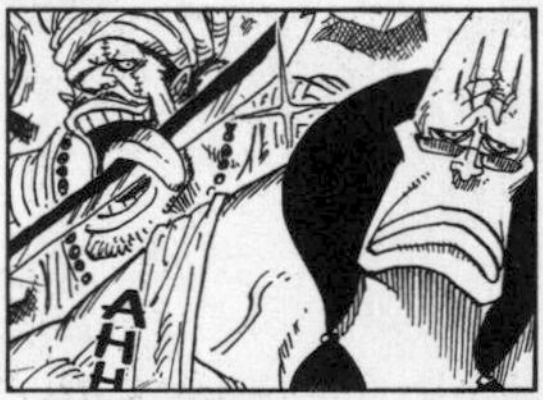

Q: Take this, Odacchi!! Western Lariat!!! And now, my question! In Chapter 704, you introduced the former bounty hunters Abdullah and Jeet. Are they former pro wrestlers, Abdullah the Butcher and Tiger Jeet Singh?! Abdullah's the one who gouged his forehead with forks!! You like pro wrestling, Odacchi? Are you in the pro-wrestling generation?

--Joker

A: That lariat hurt!! Well thanks, you just broke my neck. You're right, that is correct. Japan was in the midst of its pro wrestling craze when I was in elementary school. I loved that stuff, so this is my tribute to the greatest heels who ever menaced the ring, The Butcher and Jeet Singh!!

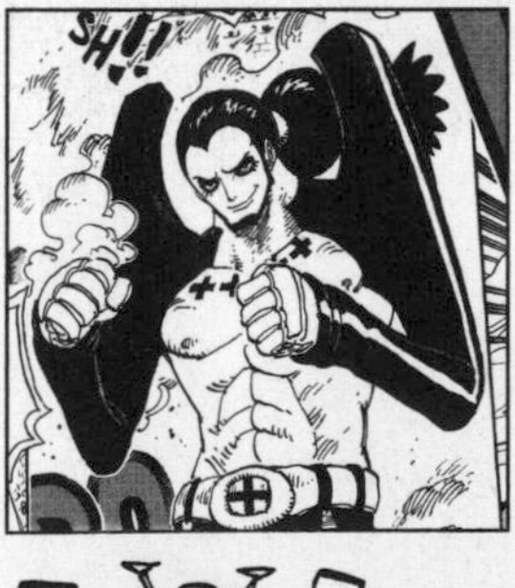

Q: Nice to meet you, Mr. Oda! I've been wondering, is Idea the Boxer based on *Ideon?* That got me really excited, despite my age.

--Astro Robo Sasa (age 38)

A: That's right. I took the idea from the old robot anime show, *Ideon*. Sorry, I had so many characters to introduce, I started having a bit too much fun with them. It was a robot with extended shoulders like this on the right. It was the very first plastic model I got as a kid.

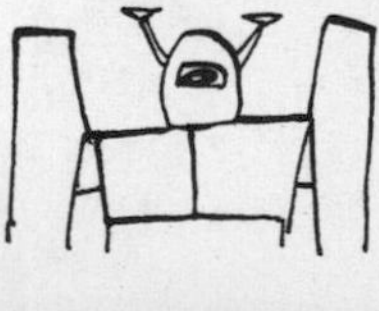
Ideon

Chapter 716:
DON CHIN JAO

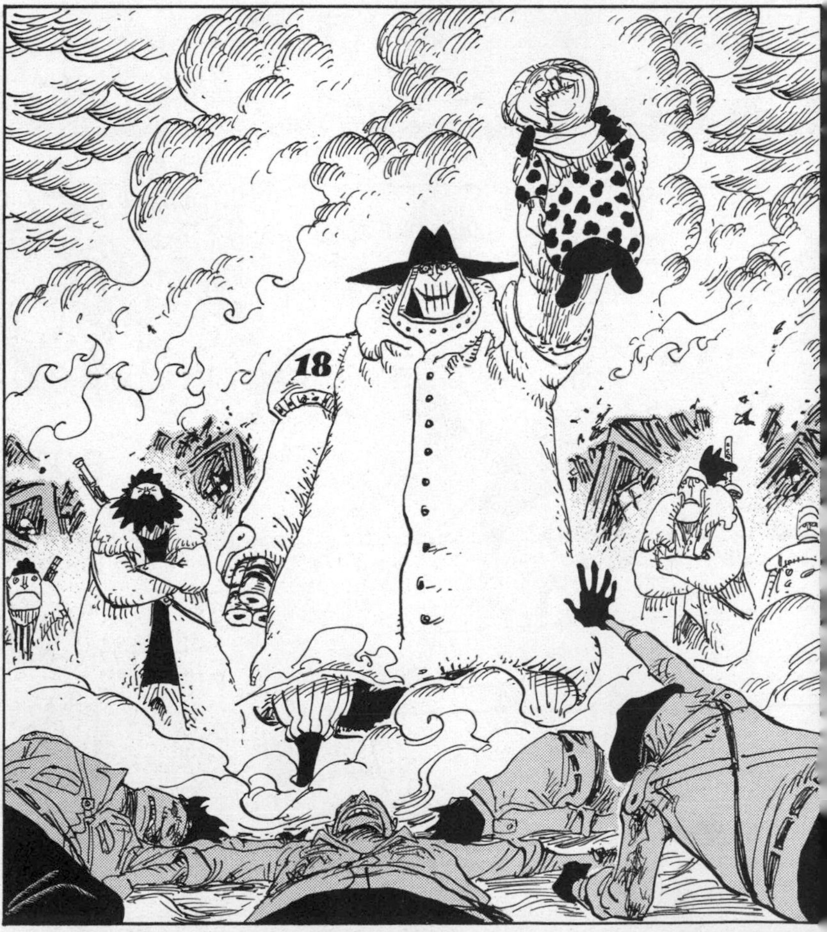
18

CARIBOU'S NEW WORLD KEE HEE HEE, VOL. 34: "BEHOLD THE FATE OF THE GRANDMOTHER OF REVOLUTION ARMY CAPTAIN GABURU"

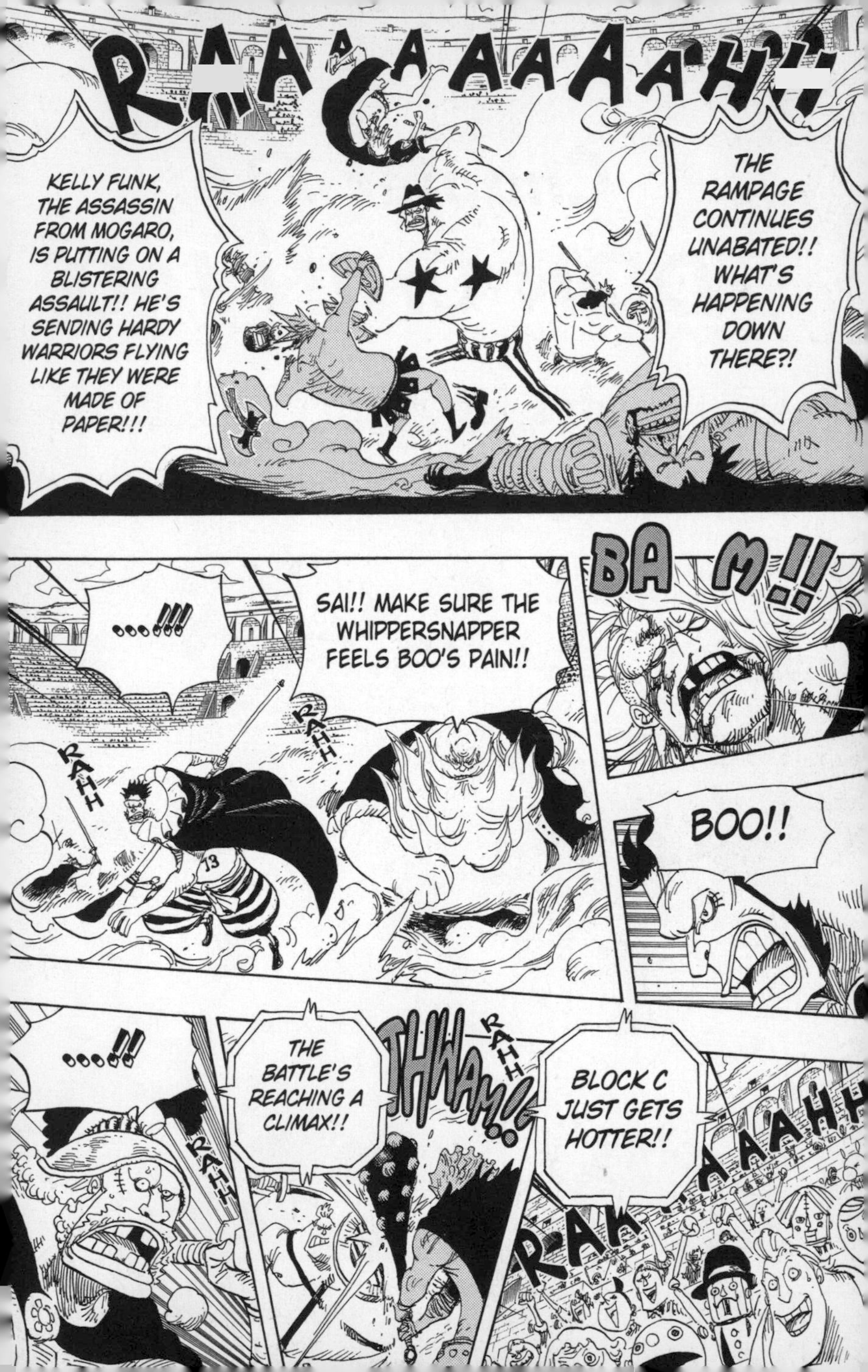
THE RAMPAGE CONTINUES UNABATED!! WHAT'S HAPPENING DOWN THERE?!
KELLY FUNK, THE ASSASSIN FROM MOGARO, IS PUTTING ON A BLISTERING ASSAULT!! HE'S SENDING HARDY WARRIORS FLYING LIKE THEY WERE MADE OF PAPER!!!
BAM!!
BOO!!
SAI!! MAKE SURE THE WHIPPERSNAPPER FEELS BOO'S PAIN!!
RAHH
...!!!
RAHH
BLOCK C JUST GETS HOTTER!!
RAHH
THWAM!!
THE BATTLE'S REACHING A CLIMAX!!
...!!
RAHH

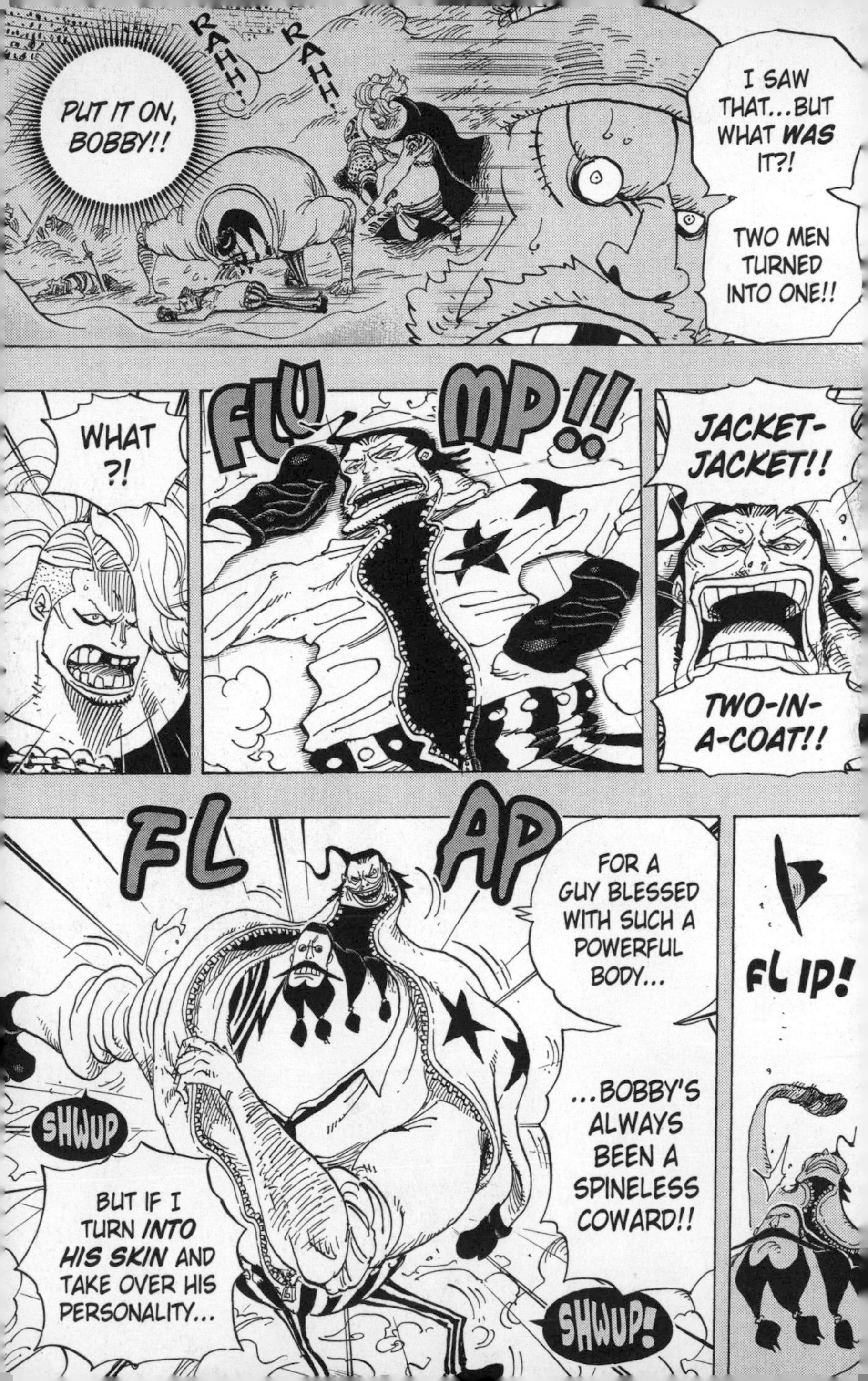
I SAW THAT...BUT WHAT WAS IT?!
TWO MEN TURNED INTO ONE!!
RAHH! RAHH!
PUT IT ON, BOBBY!!
JACKET-JACKET!!
TWO-IN-A-COAT!!
FLUMP!!
WHAT?!
FLIP!
FLAP
FOR A GUY BLESSED WITH SUCH A POWERFUL BODY...
...BOBBY'S ALWAYS BEEN A SPINELESS COWARD!!
SHWUP!
BUT IF I TURN INTO HIS SKIN AND TAKE OVER HIS PERSONALITY...
SHWUP

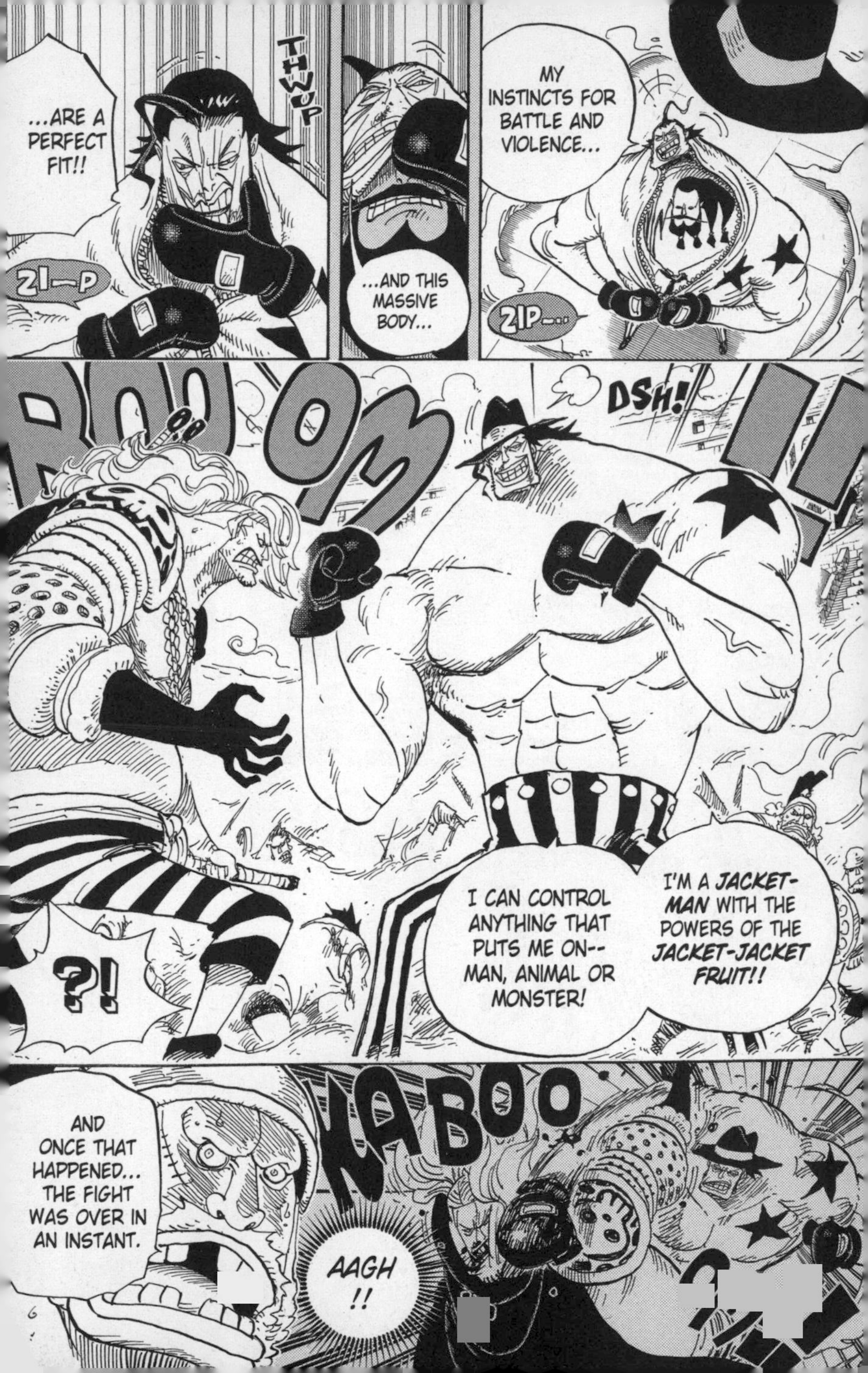
MY INSTINCTS FOR BATTLE AND VIOLENCE...
ZIP...
THWOP
...AND THIS MASSIVE BODY...
...ARE A PERFECT FIT!!
ZI-P
DSH!
BOOOM!!
I'M A JACKET-MAN WITH THE POWERS OF THE JACKET-JACKET FRUIT!!
I CAN CONTROL ANYTHING THAT PUTS ME ON-- MAN, ANIMAL OR MONSTER!
?!
KABOO
AAGH !!
AND ONCE THAT HAPPENED... THE FIGHT WAS OVER IN AN INSTANT.

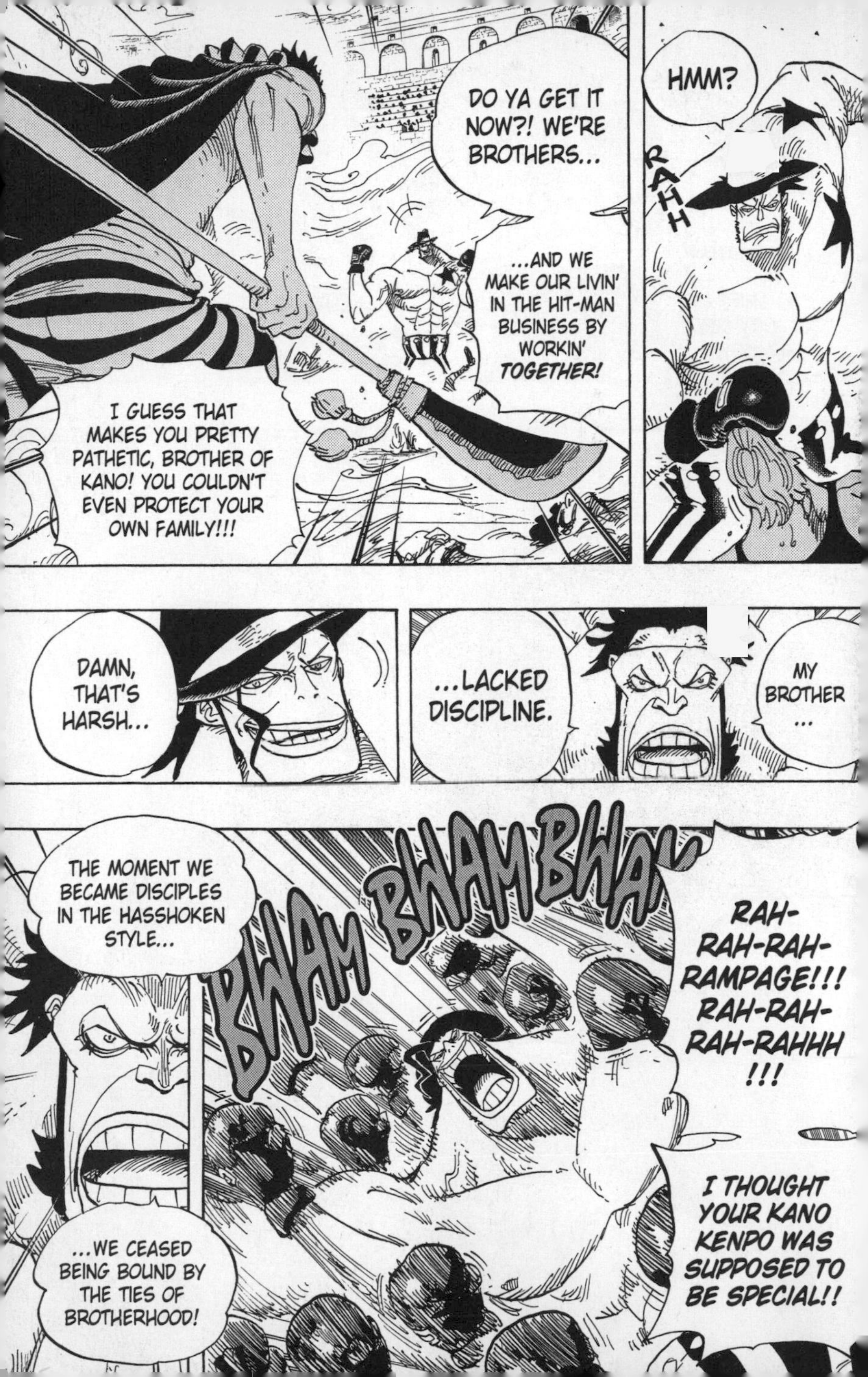
HMM?
RAHH
DO YA GET IT NOW?! WE'RE BROTHERS...
...AND WE MAKE OUR LIVIN' IN THE HIT-MAN BUSINESS BY WORKIN' *TOGETHER!*
I GUESS THAT MAKES YOU PRETTY PATHETIC, BROTHER OF KANO! YOU COULDN'T EVEN PROTECT YOUR OWN FAMILY!!!
MY BROTHER ...
...LACKED DISCIPLINE.
DAMN, THAT'S HARSH...
RAH-RAH-RAH-RAMPAGE!!! RAH-RAH-RAH-RAHHH!!!
BHAM BHAM BHAM BHAM
THE MOMENT WE BECAME DISCIPLES IN THE HASSHOKEN STYLE...
I THOUGHT YOUR KANO KENPO WAS SUPPOSED TO BE SPECIAL!!
...WE CEASED BEING BOUND BY THE TIES OF BROTHERHOOD!

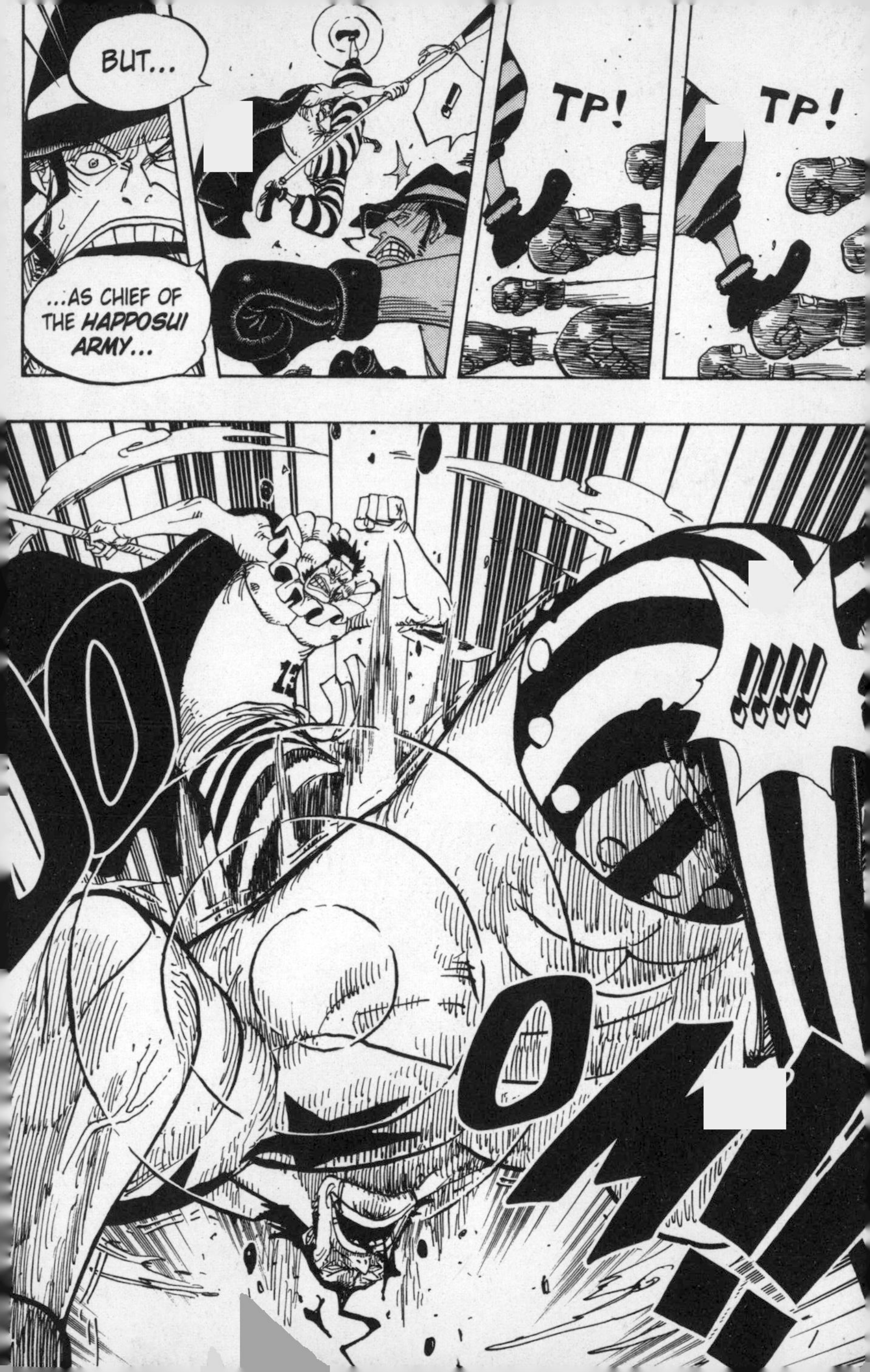
TP!
TP!
!
BUT...
...AS CHIEF OF THE HAPPOSUI ARMY...
!!!!

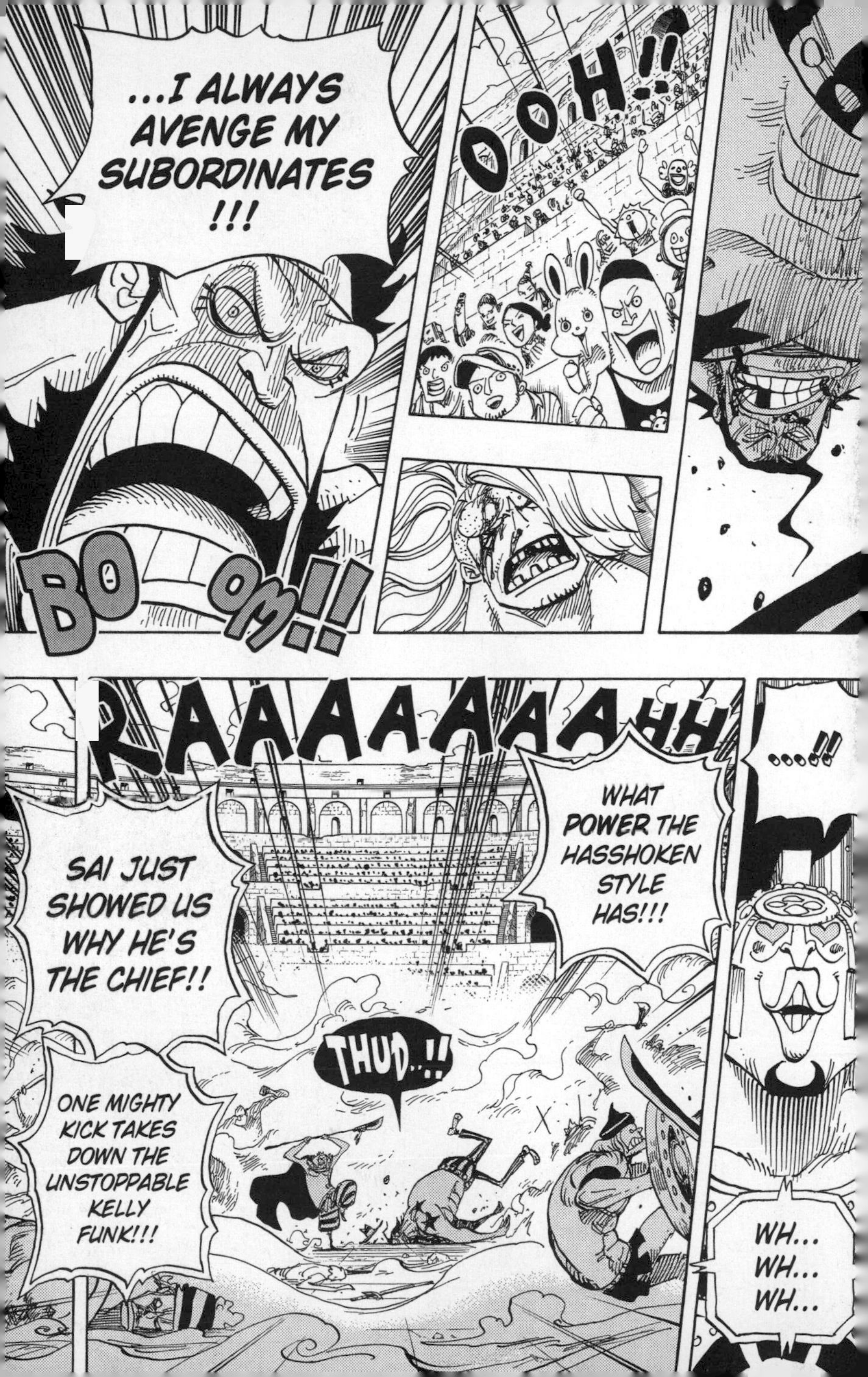
OOOH!!
...I ALWAYS AVENGE MY SUBORDINATES!!!
BOOM!!
...!!
WH... WH... WH...
RAAAAAAAAHH
WHAT POWER THE HASSHOKEN STYLE HAS!!!
SAI JUST SHOWED US WHY HE'S THE CHIEF!!
THUD..!!
ONE MIGHTY KICK TAKES DOWN THE UNSTOPPABLE KELLY FUNK!!!

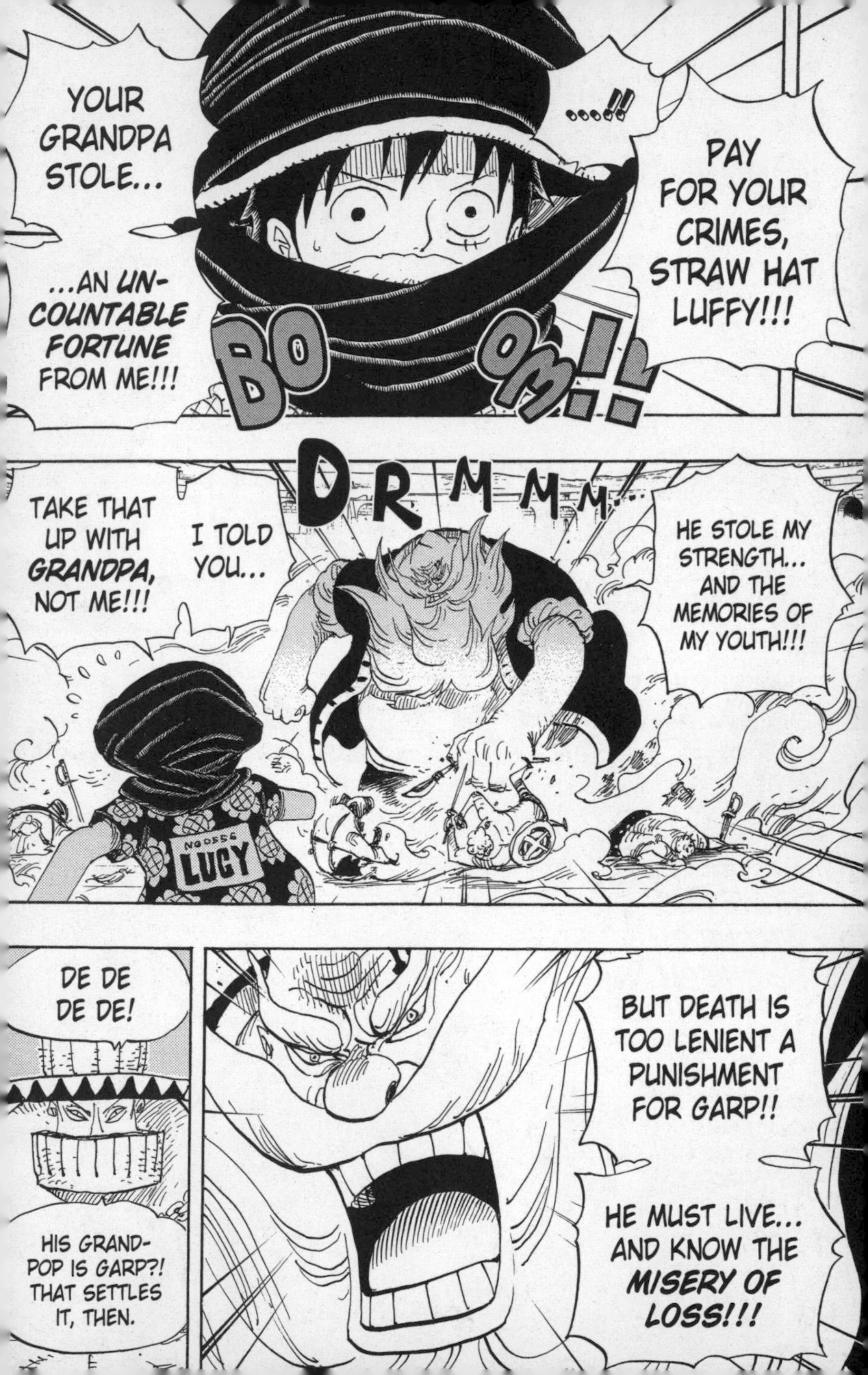

....!!
PAY FOR YOUR CRIMES, STRAW HAT LUFFY!!!
YOUR GRANDPA STOLE...
...AN *UN-COUNTABLE* FORTUNE FROM ME!!!
BOOM!!
DRMMM...
HE STOLE MY STRENGTH... AND THE MEMORIES OF MY YOUTH!!!
I TOLD YOU...
TAKE THAT UP WITH *GRANDPA*, NOT ME!!!
LUCY
BUT DEATH IS TOO LENIENT A PUNISHMENT FOR GARP!!
HE MUST LIVE... AND KNOW THE *MISERY OF LOSS!!!*
DE DE DE DE!
HIS GRAND-POP IS GARP?! THAT SETTLES IT, THEN.

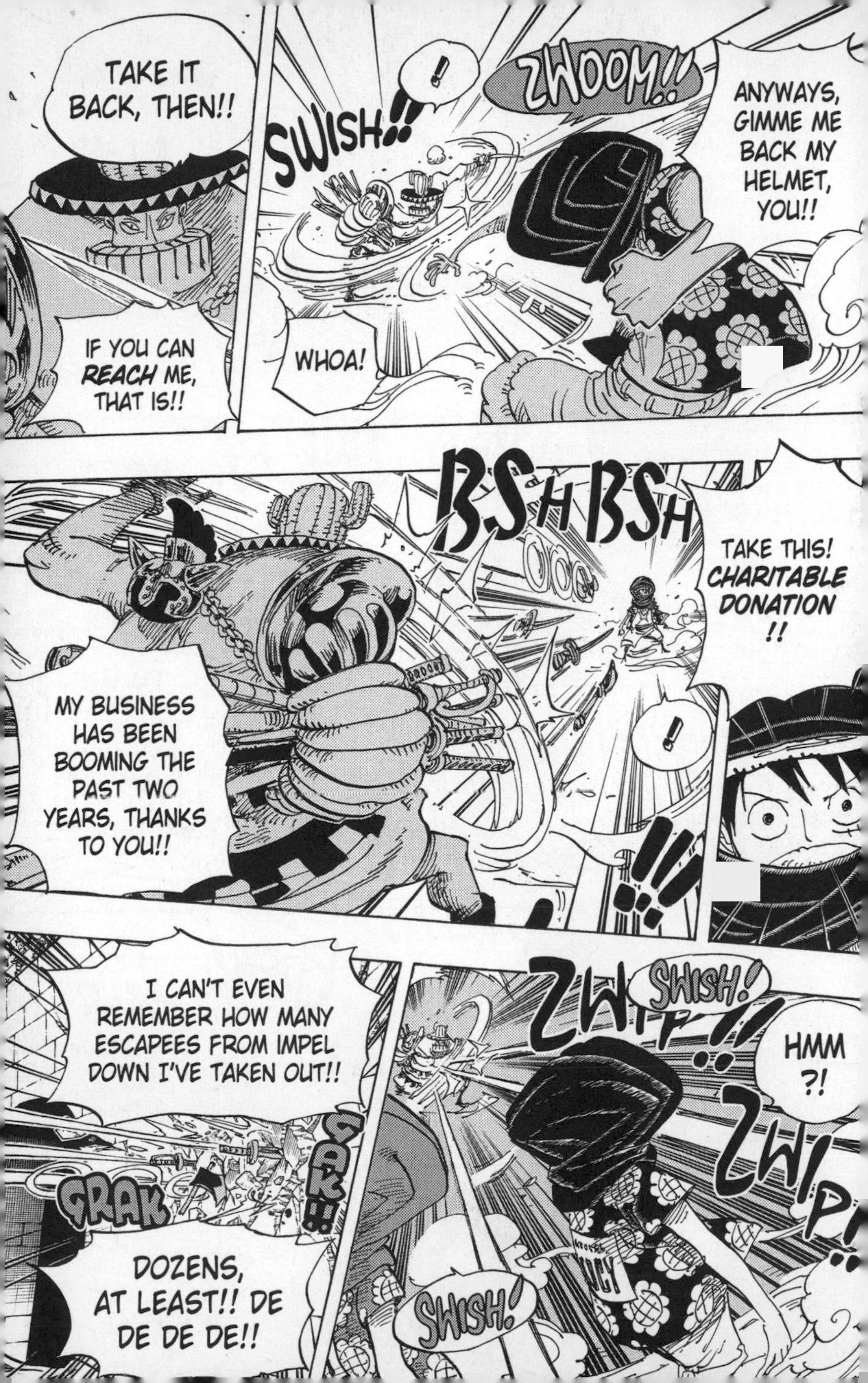
ANYWAYS, GIMME ME BACK MY HELMET, YOU!!
ZWOOM!!
!
SWISH!!
WHOA!
TAKE IT BACK, THEN!!
IF YOU CAN *REACH* ME, THAT IS!!
BSH BSH
TAKE THIS! CHARITABLE DONATION !!
!
MY BUSINESS HAS BEEN BOOMING THE PAST TWO YEARS, THANKS TO YOU!!
HMM ?!
SWISH!
ZWIP!!
ZWIP!
SWISH!
I CAN'T EVEN REMEMBER HOW MANY ESCAPEES FROM IMPEL DOWN I'VE TAKEN OUT!!
GAK!!
GRAK
DOZENS, AT LEAST!! DE DE DE DE!!

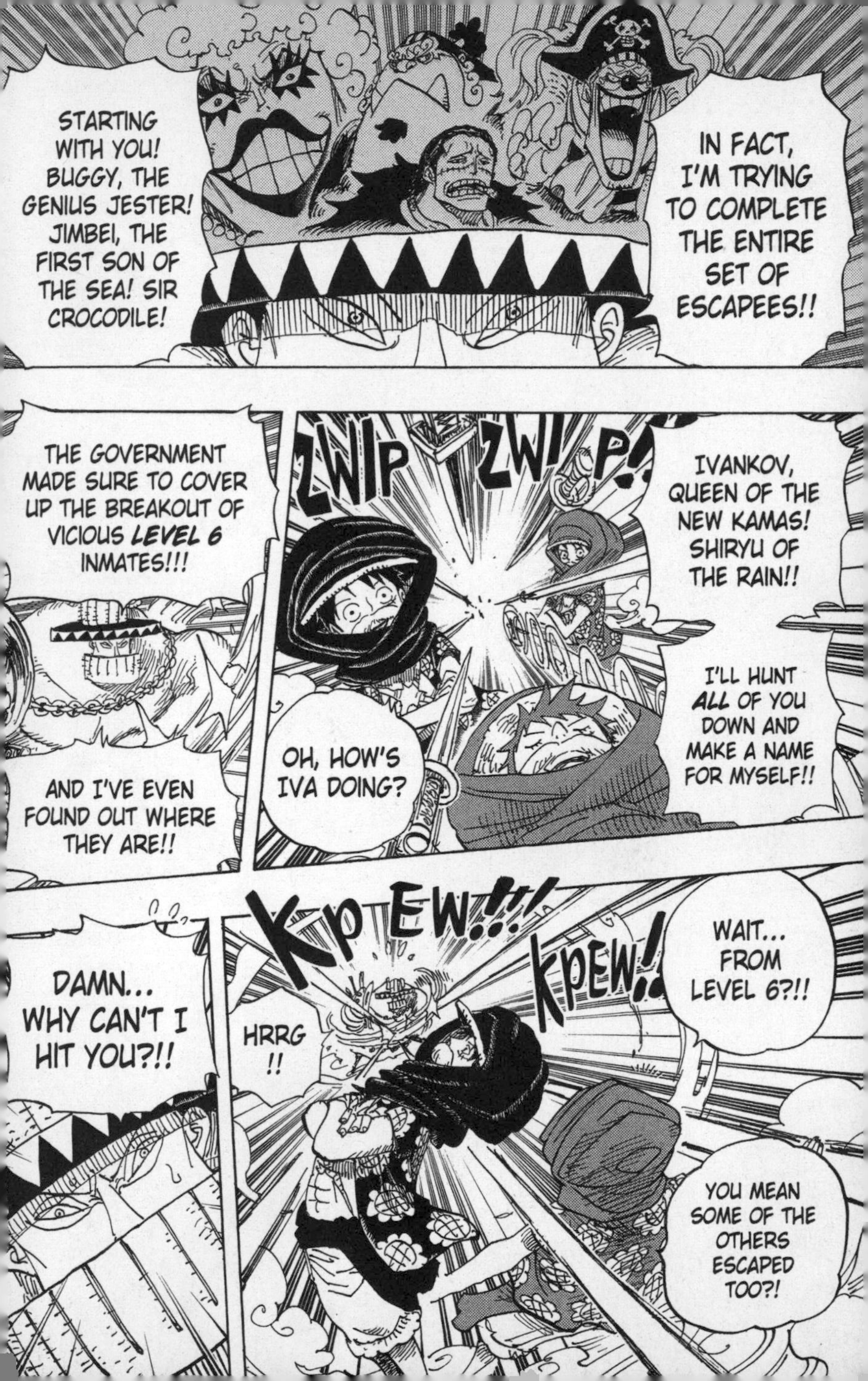
IN FACT, I'M TRYING TO COMPLETE THE ENTIRE SET OF ESCAPEES!!
STARTING WITH YOU! BUGGY, THE GENIUS JESTER! JIMBEI, THE FIRST SON OF THE SEA! SIR CROCODILE!
ZWIP
ZWIP!
IVANKOV, QUEEN OF THE NEW KAMAS! SHIRYU OF THE RAIN!!
I'LL HUNT ALL OF YOU DOWN AND MAKE A NAME FOR MYSELF!!
OH, HOW'S IVA DOING?
THE GOVERNMENT MADE SURE TO COVER UP THE BREAKOUT OF VICIOUS LEVEL 6 INMATES!!!
AND I'VE EVEN FOUND OUT WHERE THEY ARE!!
WAIT... FROM LEVEL 6?!!
KPEW!!!
KPEW!!
HRRG !!
YOU MEAN SOME OF THE OTHERS ESCAPED TOO?!
DAMN... WHY CAN'T I HIT YOU?!!

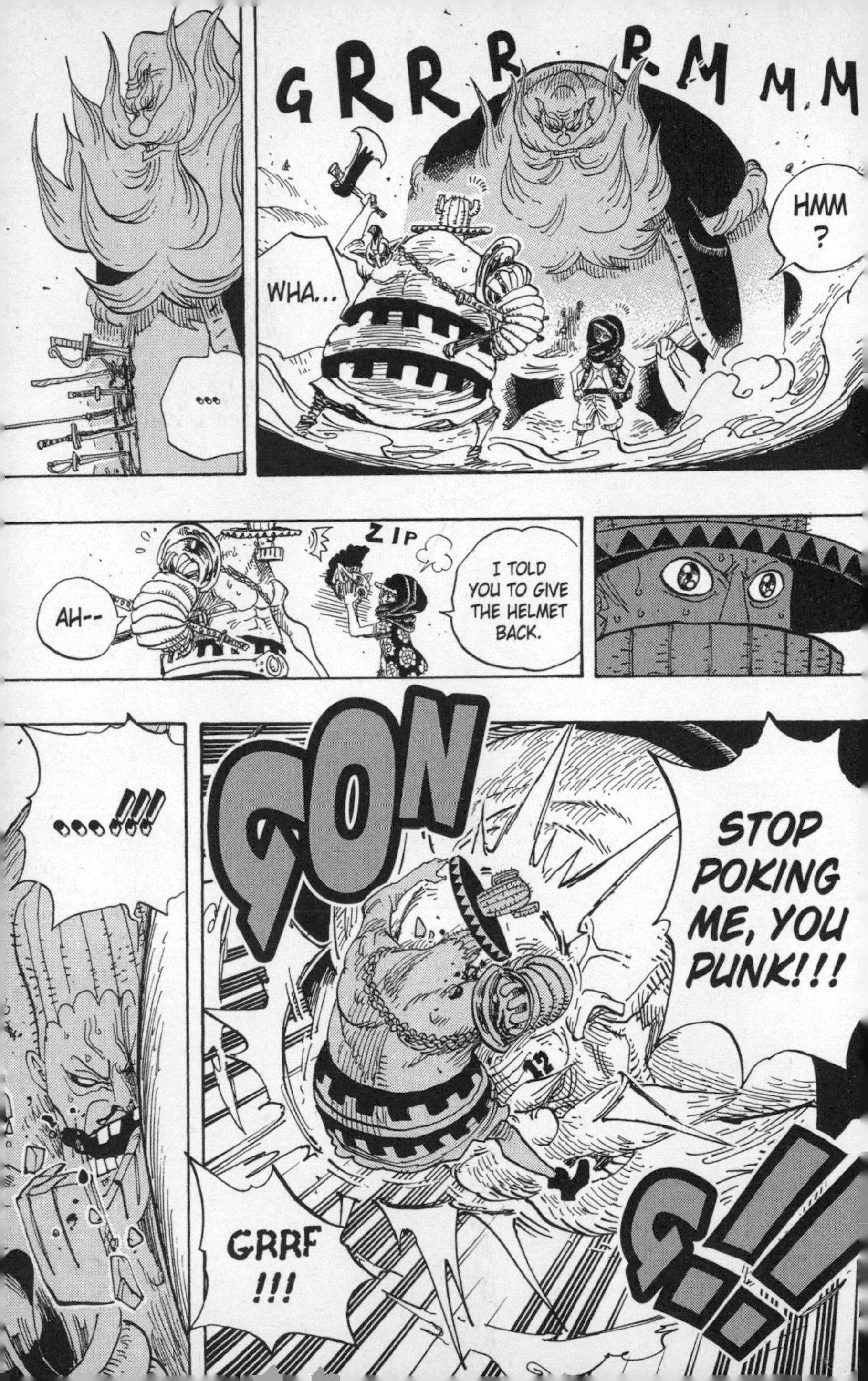
GRRRRMMMM
HMM?
WHA...
...
ZIP
I TOLD YOU TO GIVE THE HELMET BACK.
AH--
GON
STOP POKING ME, YOU PUNK!!!
GRRF!!!
G..!!
...!!!

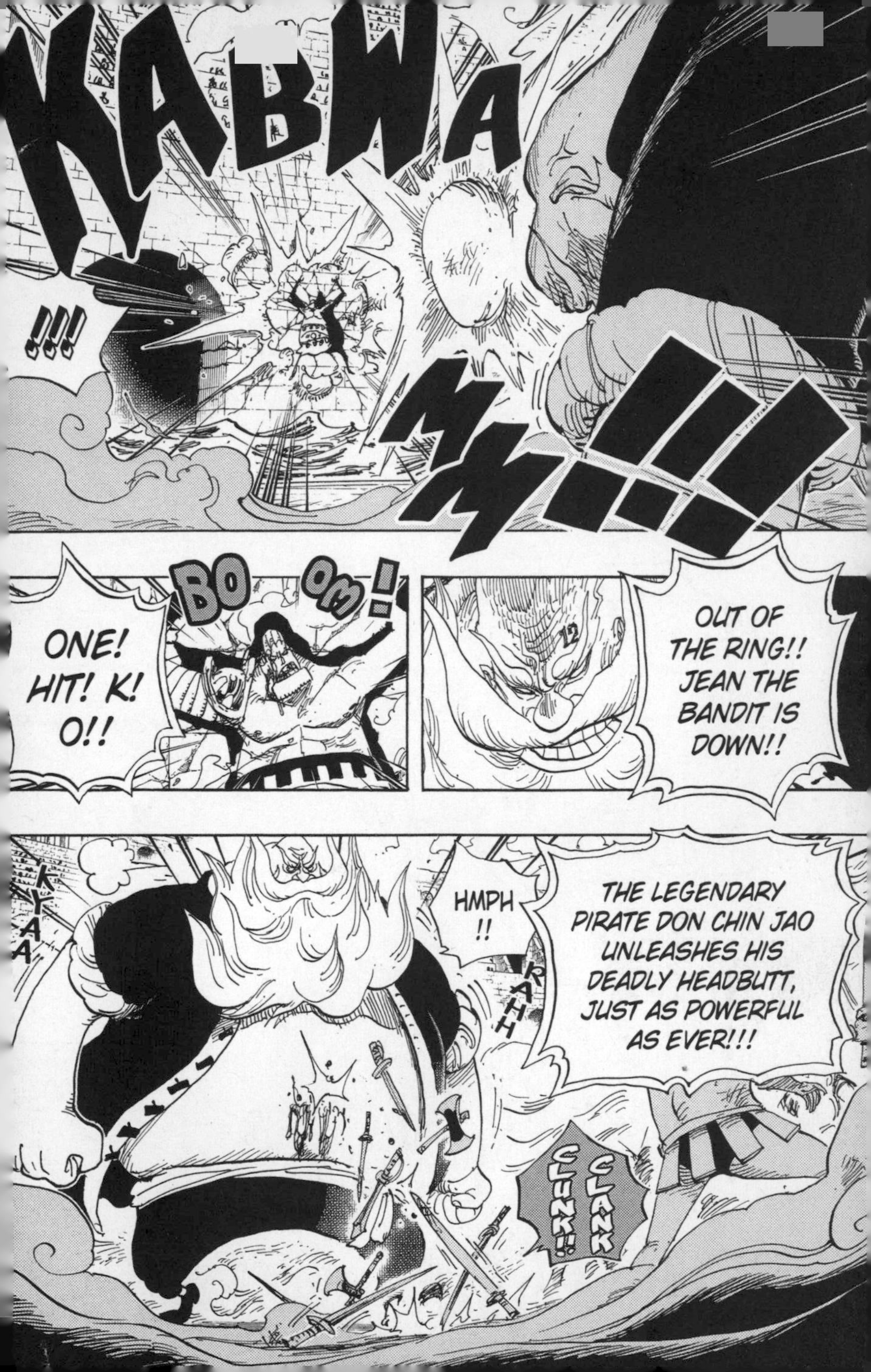
KABWAM!!!
!!!
OUT OF THE RING!! JEAN THE BANDIT IS DOWN!!
BOOM!!
ONE! HIT! K! O!!
THE LEGENDARY PIRATE DON CHIN JAO UNLEASHES HIS DEADLY HEADBUTT, JUST AS POWERFUL AS EVER!!!
HMPH !!
RAHH
CLANK
CLUNK!!
KYAAA

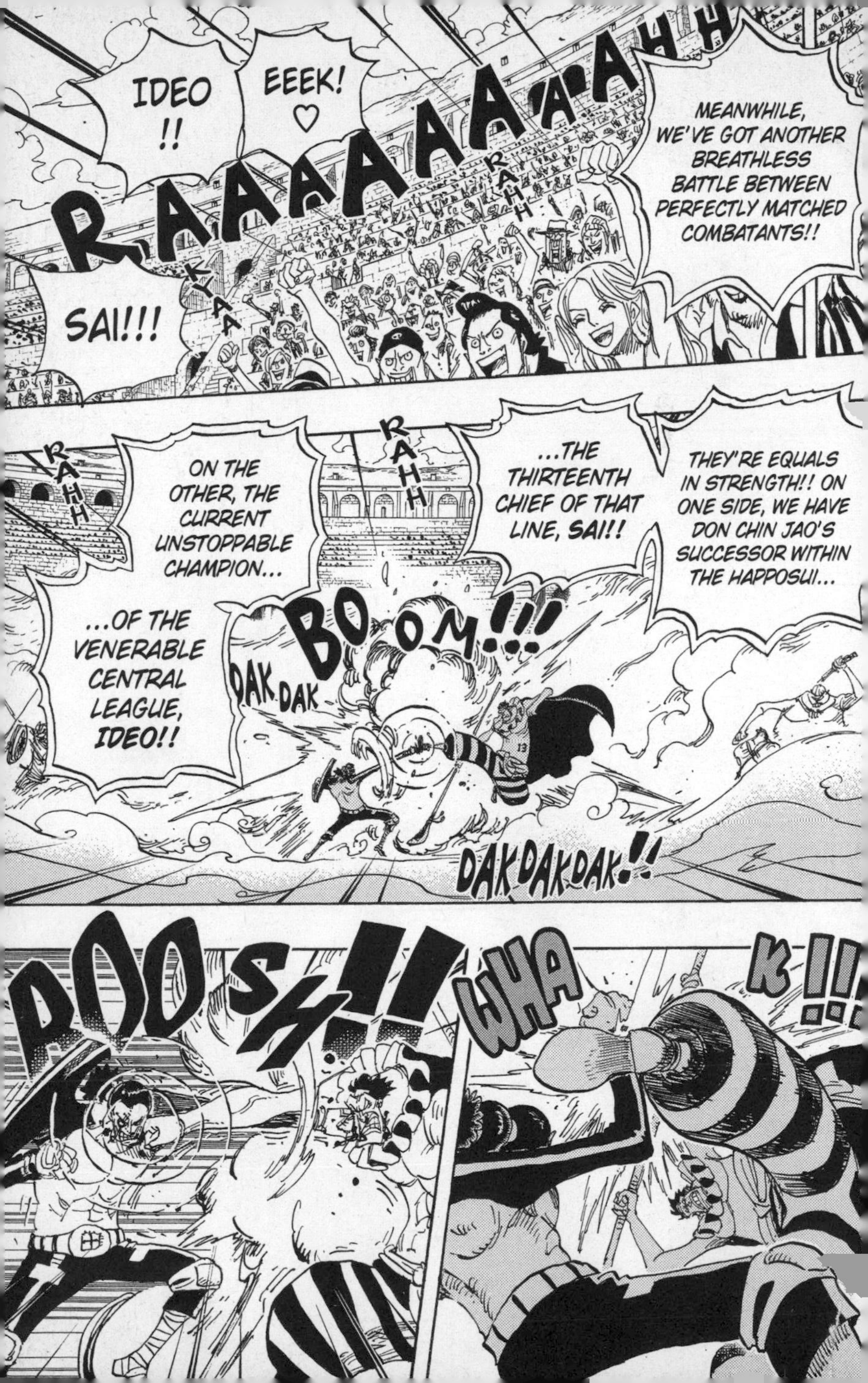
MEANWHILE, WE'VE GOT ANOTHER BREATHLESS BATTLE BETWEEN PERFECTLY MATCHED COMBATANTS!!
RAAAAAAAAHH
RAHH
EEEK! ♡
IDEO !!
KYAA
SAI!!!
THEY'RE EQUALS IN STRENGTH!! ON ONE SIDE, WE HAVE DON CHIN JAO'S SUCCESSOR WITHIN THE HAPPOSUI...
...THE THIRTEENTH CHIEF OF THAT LINE, SAI!!
RAHH
ON THE OTHER, THE CURRENT UNSTOPPABLE CHAMPION...
RAHH
...OF THE VENERABLE CENTRAL LEAGUE, IDEO!!
BOOM!!!
DAK DAK
DAK DAK DAK!!
WHAK!!!
BOOSH!!

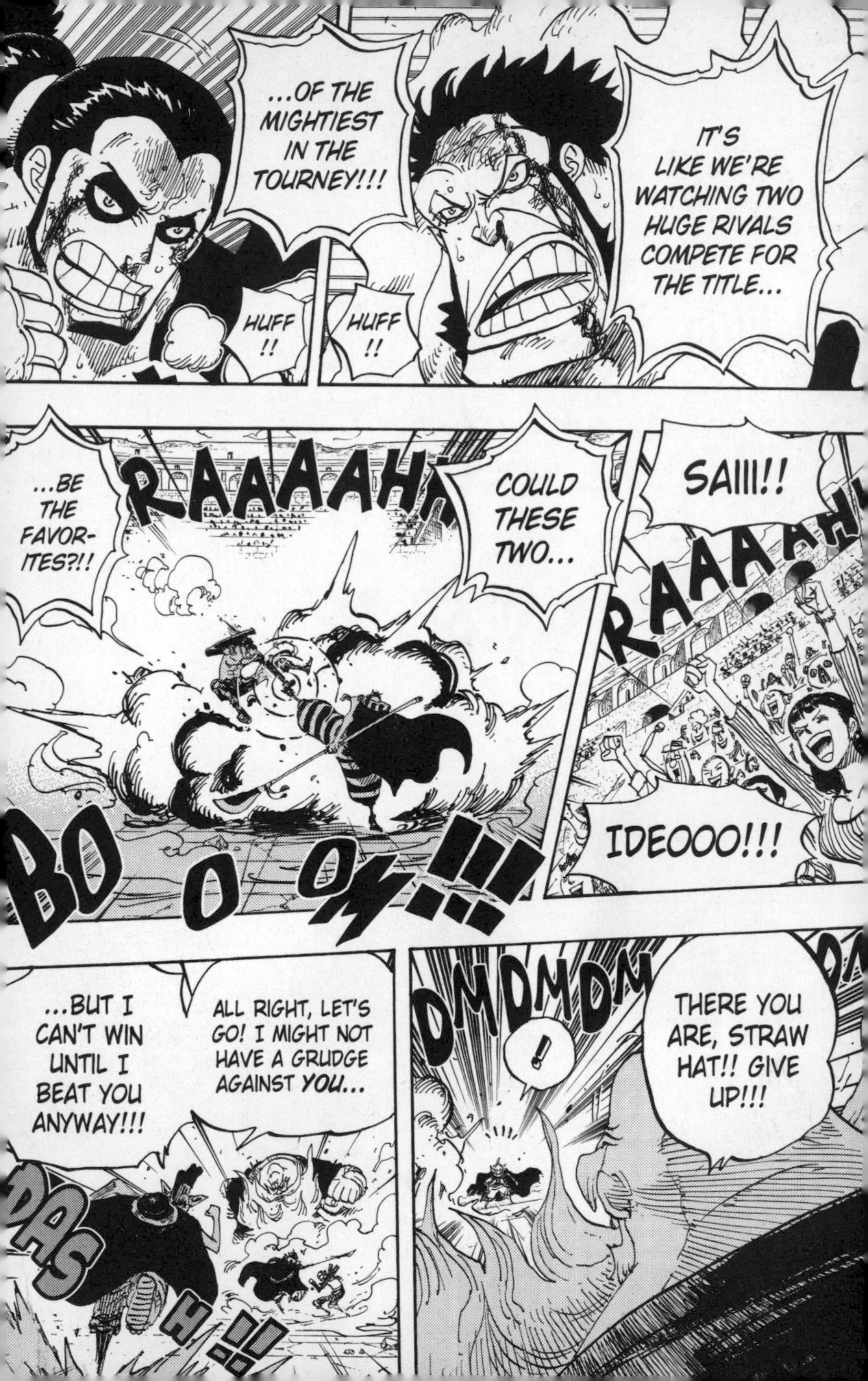
IT'S LIKE WE'RE WATCHING TWO HUGE RIVALS COMPETE FOR THE TITLE...
HUFF!!
...OF THE MIGHTIEST IN THE TOURNEY!!!
HUFF!!
SAIII!!
RAAAAH
IDEOOO!!!
COULD THESE TWO...
...BE THE FAVORITES?!!
RAAAAH
BOOOM!!!
DMDMDM
!
THERE YOU ARE, STRAW HAT!! GIVE UP!!!
ALL RIGHT, LET'S GO! I MIGHT NOT HAVE A GRUDGE AGAINST *YOU*...
...BUT I CAN'T WIN UNTIL I BEAT YOU ANYWAY!!!
DASH!!

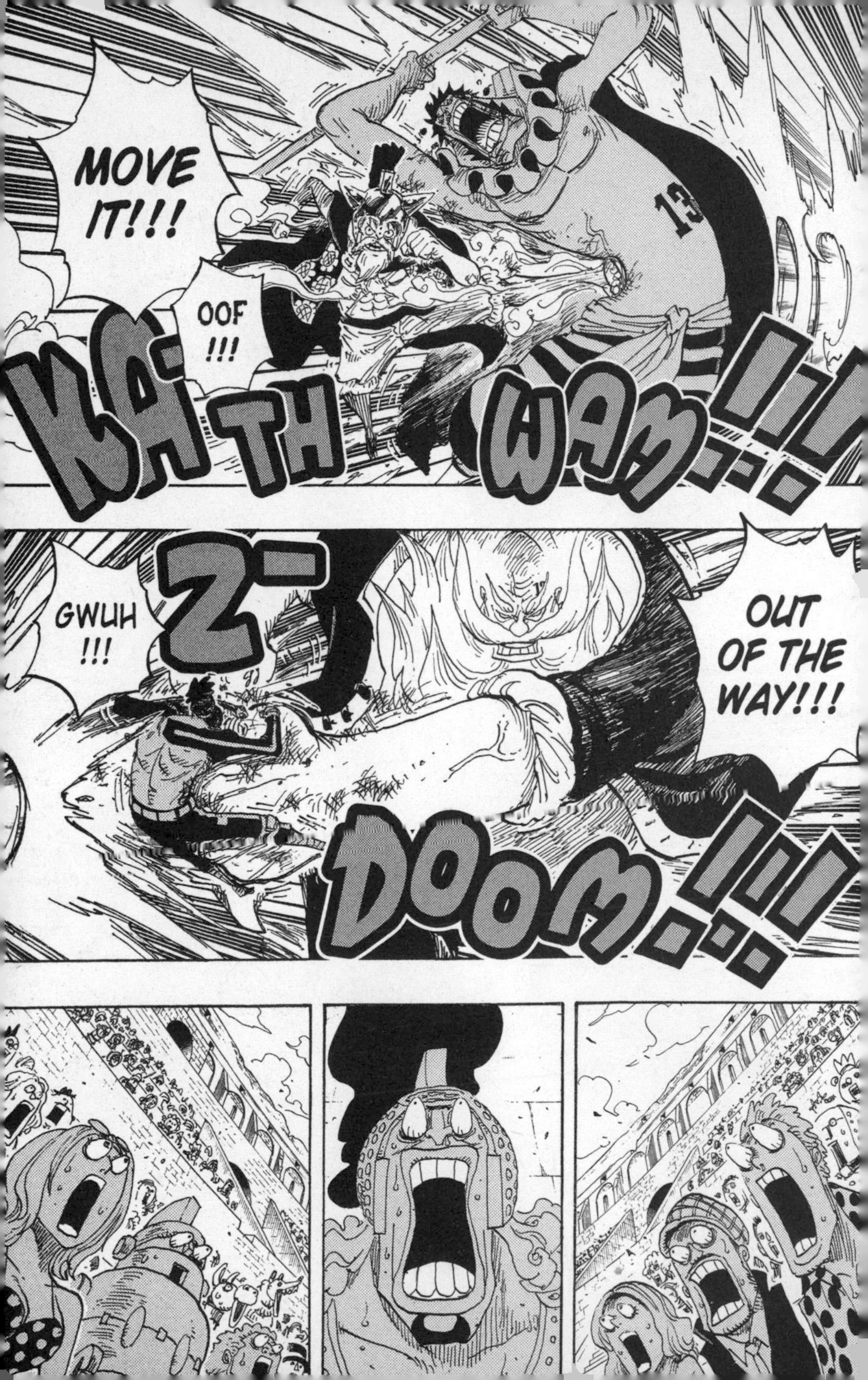
MOVE IT!!!
OOF!!!
KA-TH WAM!!!
OUT OF THE WAY!!!
GWUH!!!
Z-
DOOM!!!

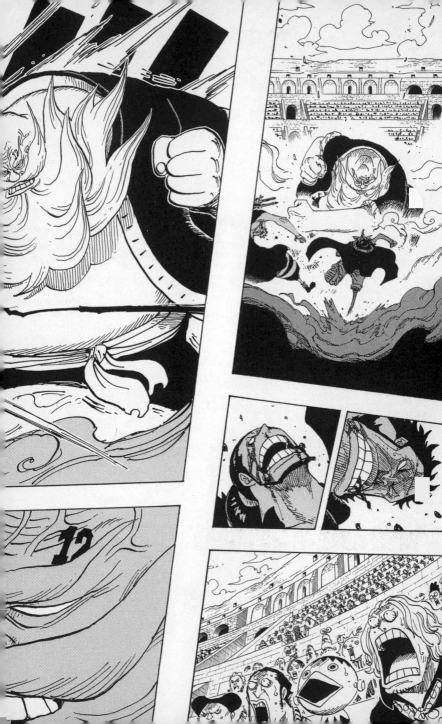

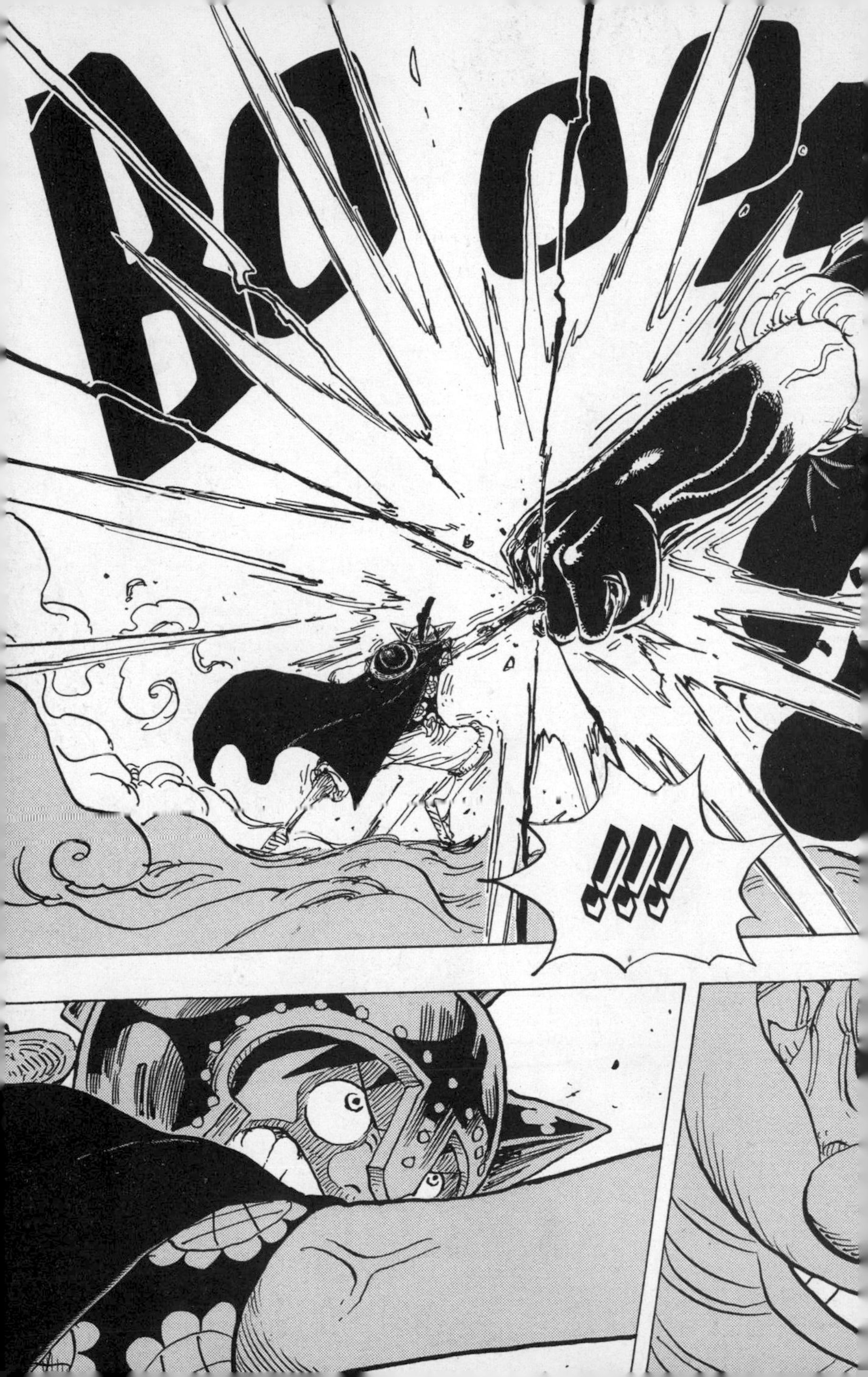
BOO
!!!

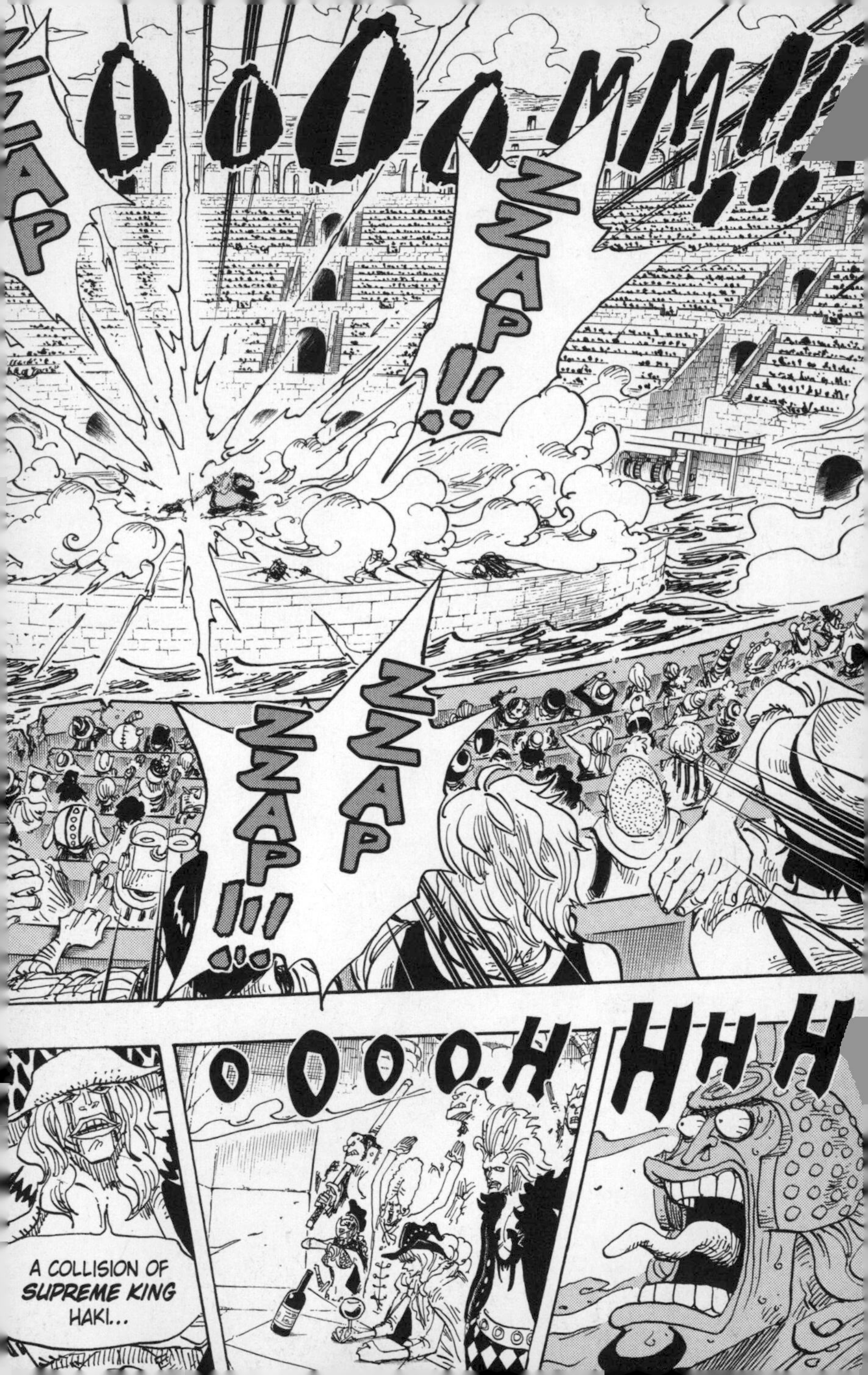

OOOOMM!!!
ZZAP!!!
ZAP
ZZAP
ZZAP!!!
OOOO.HHHHH
A COLLISION OF *SUPREME KING* HAKI...

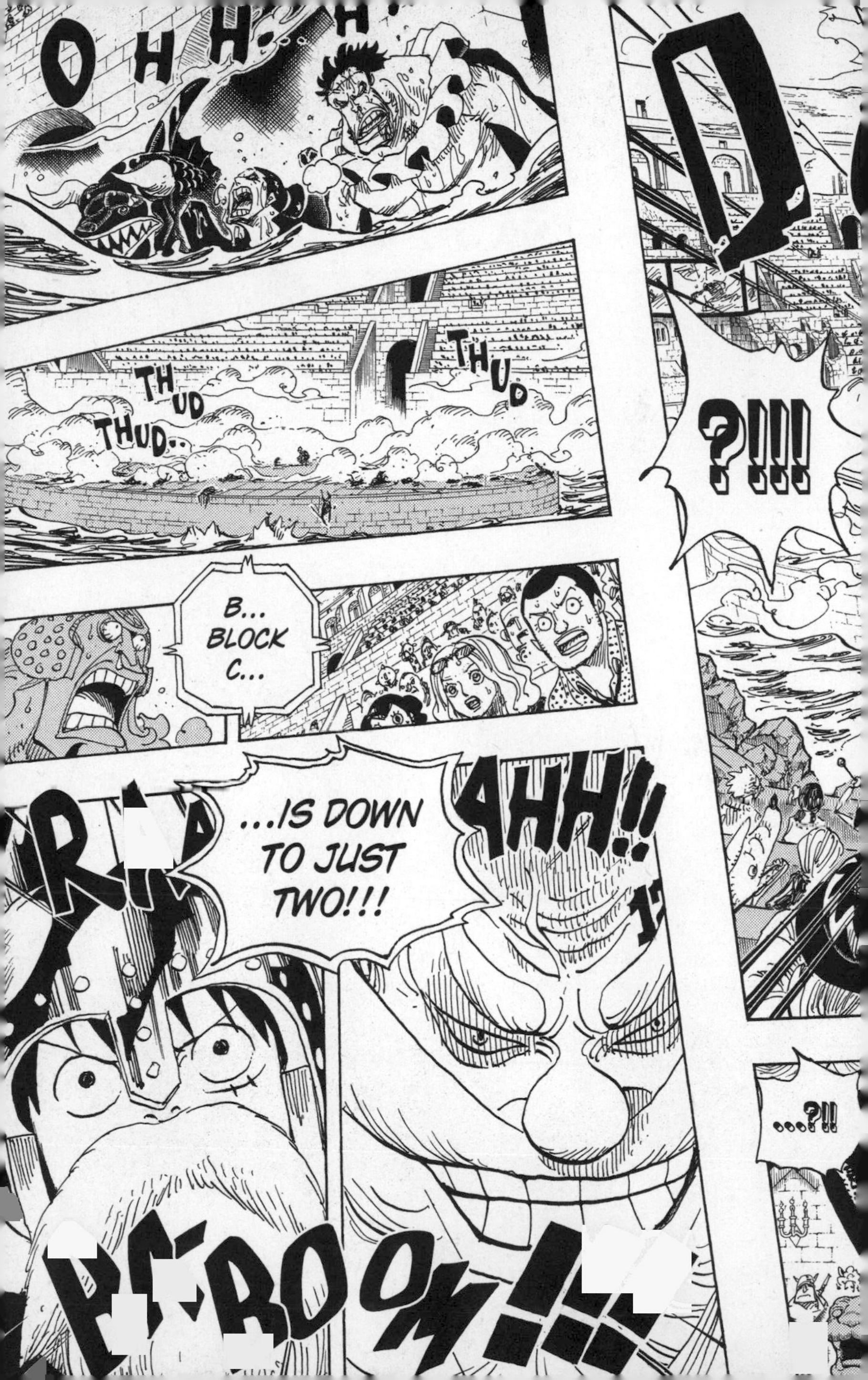

?!!!
...?!!
THUD
THUD
B... BLOCK C...
...IS DOWN TO JUST TWO!!!
AHH!!

DRESSROSA'S FORGOTTEN

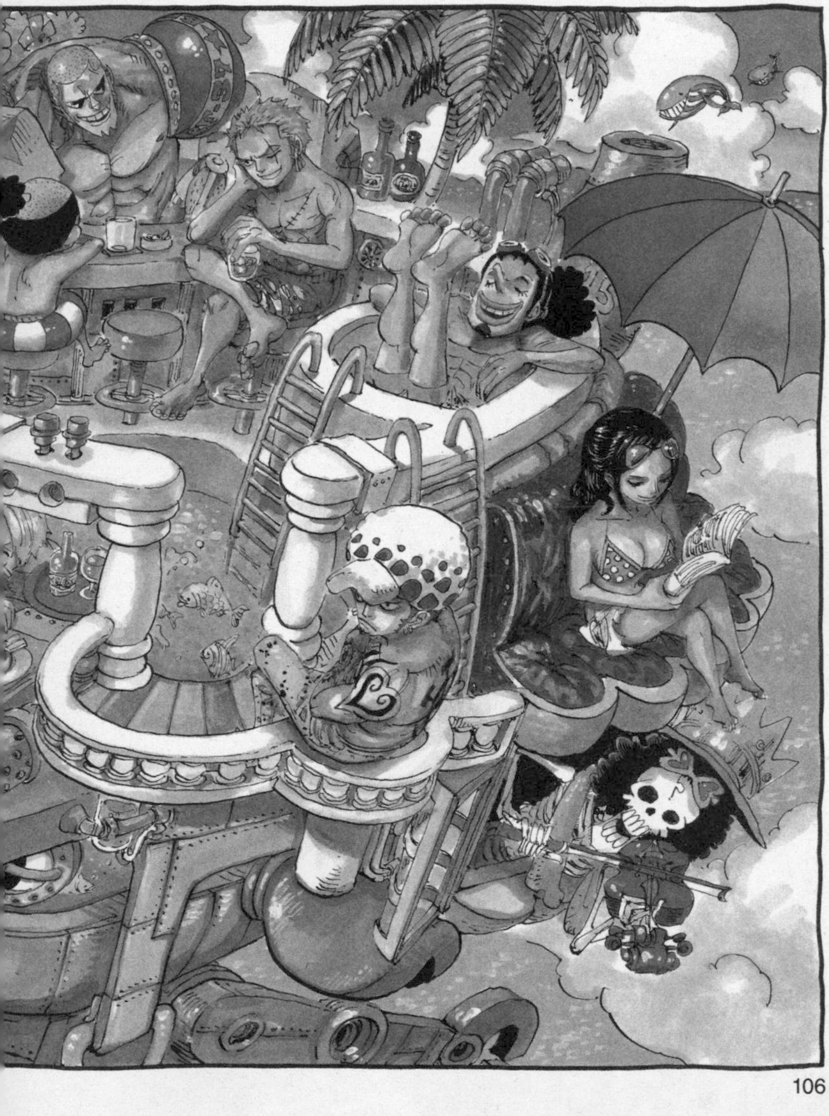

Chapter 717:

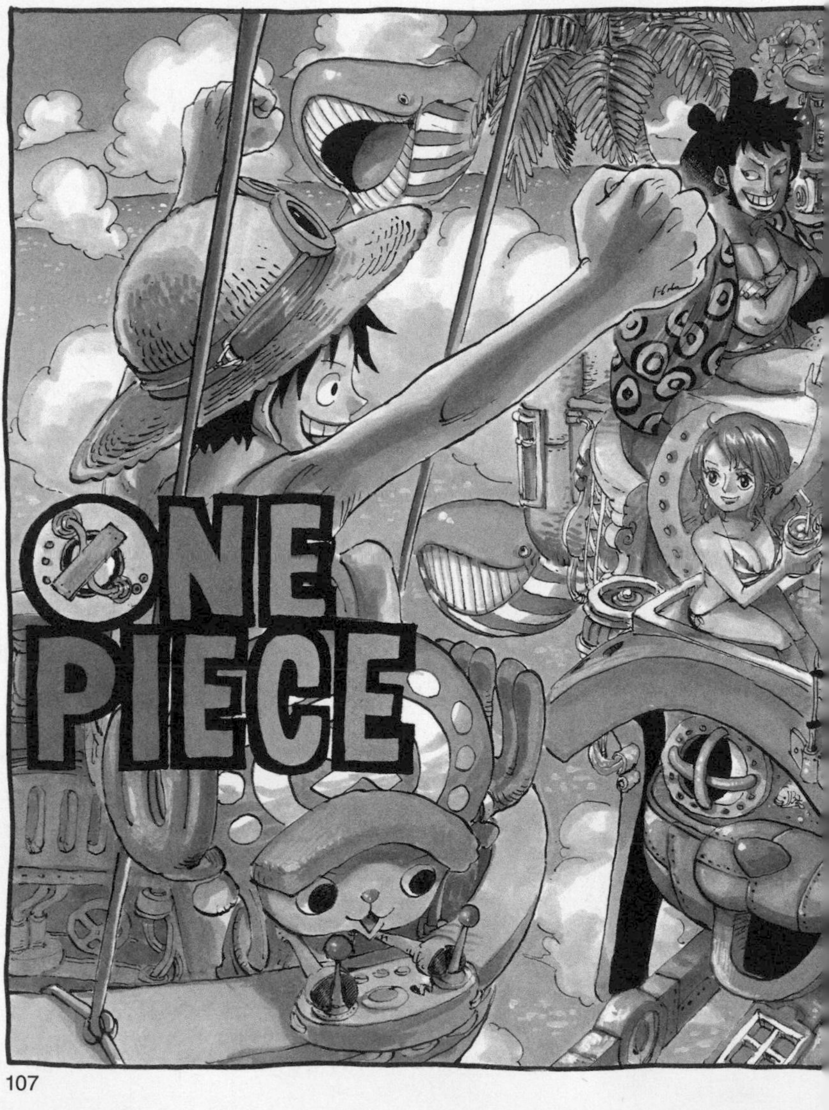
ONE PIECE

vol.72
ONE PIECE

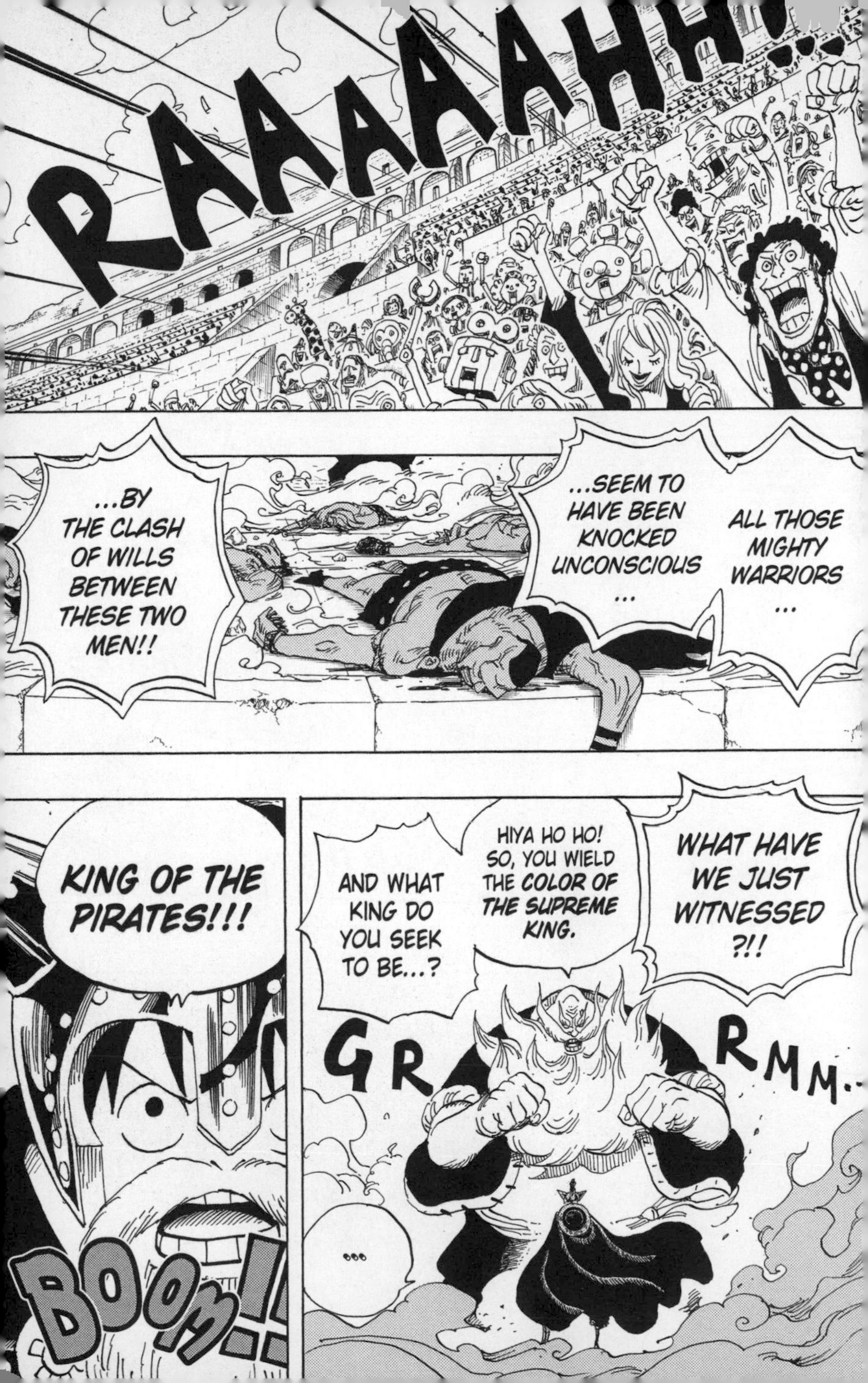
RAAAAHH!...
ALL THOSE MIGHTY WARRIORS ...
...SEEM TO HAVE BEEN KNOCKED UNCONSCIOUS ...
...BY THE CLASH OF WILLS BETWEEN THESE TWO MEN!!
WHAT HAVE WE JUST WITNESSED ?!!
HIYA HO HO! SO, YOU WIELD THE COLOR OF THE SUPREME KING.
AND WHAT KING DO YOU SEEK TO BE...?
GRRMM...
...
KING OF THE PIRATES!!!
BOOM!!

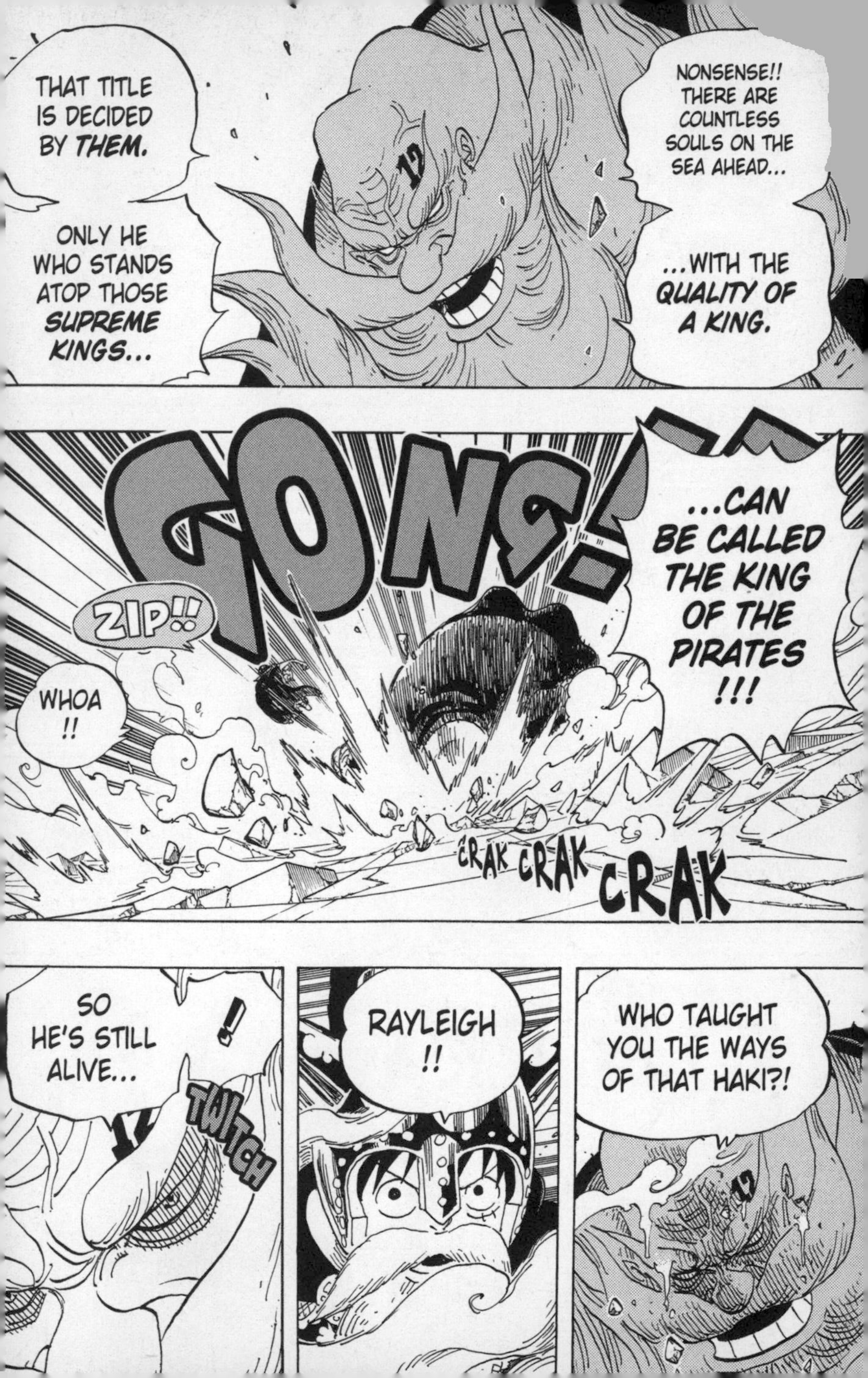
NONSENSE!! THERE ARE COUNTLESS SOULS ON THE SEA AHEAD...
...WITH THE QUALITY OF A KING.
THAT TITLE IS DECIDED BY THEM.
ONLY HE WHO STANDS ATOP THOSE SUPREME KINGS...
...CAN BE CALLED THE KING OF THE PIRATES !!!
GONG!
ZIP!!
WHOA !!
CRAK CRAK CRAK
WHO TAUGHT YOU THE WAYS OF THAT HAKI?!
RAYLEIGH !!
!
SO HE'S STILL ALIVE...
TWITCH

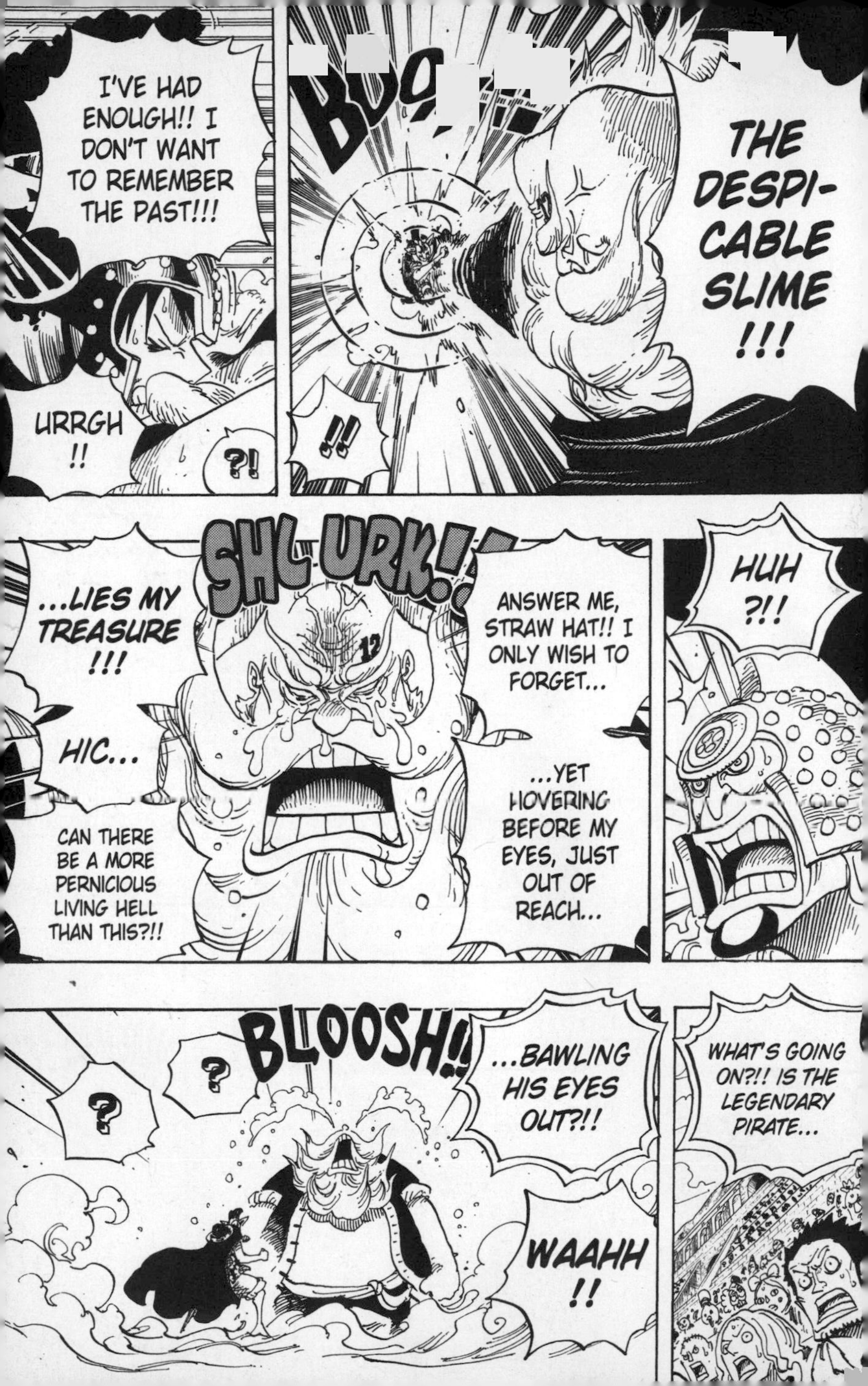
THE DESPI-CABLE SLIME!!!
!!
I'VE HAD ENOUGH!! I DON'T WANT TO REMEMBER THE PAST!!!
URRGH!!
?!
HUH?!!
ANSWER ME, STRAW HAT!! I ONLY WISH TO FORGET...
...YET HOVERING BEFORE MY EYES, JUST OUT OF REACH...
SHLURK!!
...LIES MY TREASURE!!!
HIC...
CAN THERE BE A MORE PERNICIOUS LIVING HELL THAN THIS?!!
WHAT'S GOING ON?!! IS THE LEGENDARY PIRATE...
...BAWLING HIS EYES OUT?!!
BLOOSH!!
WAAHH!!
?
?

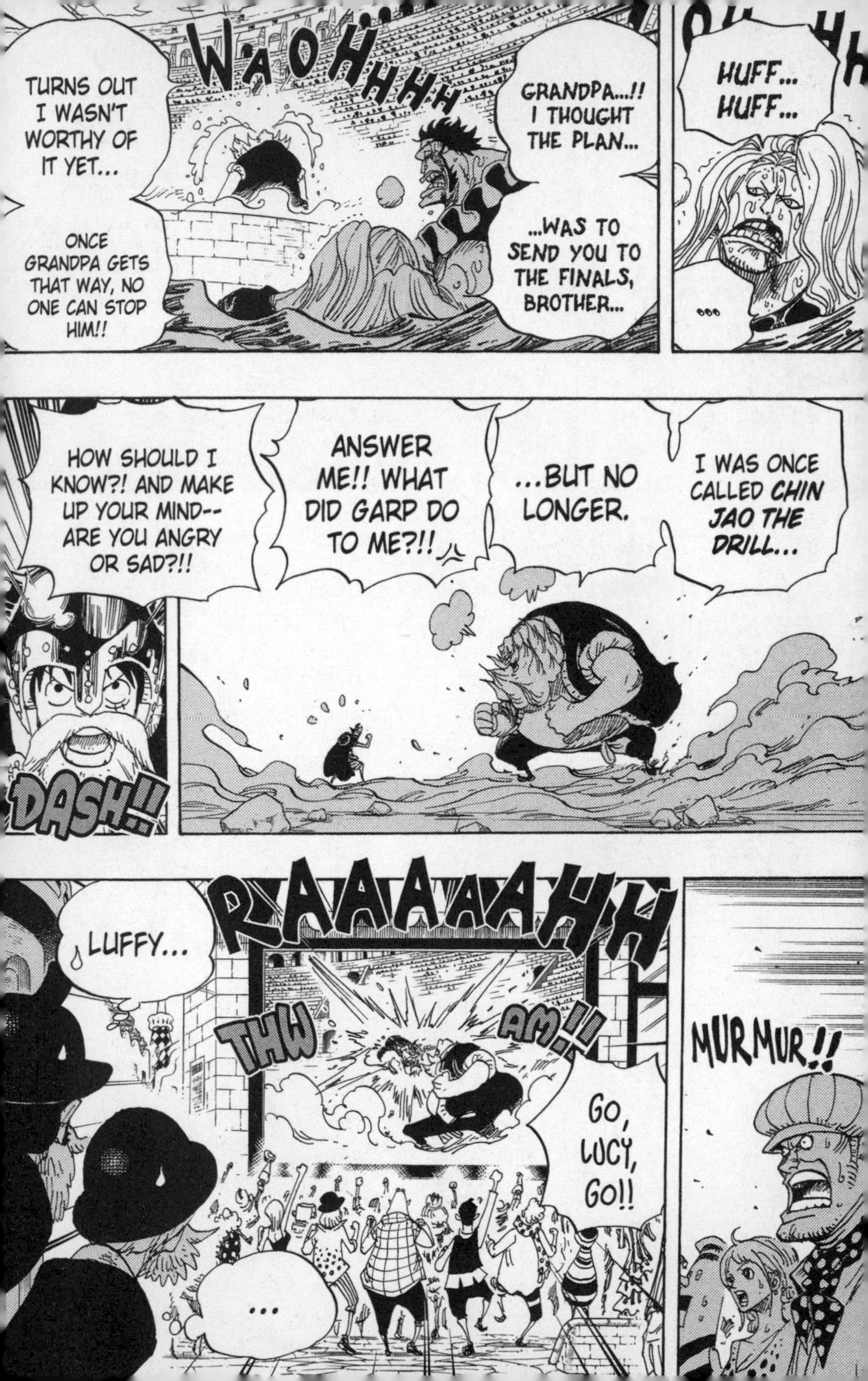
HUFF... HUFF...
WAOHHHH
GRANDPA...!! I THOUGHT THE PLAN...
...WAS TO SEND YOU TO THE FINALS, BROTHER...
TURNS OUT I WASN'T WORTHY OF IT YET...
ONCE GRANDPA GETS THAT WAY, NO ONE CAN STOP HIM!!
I WAS ONCE CALLED CHIN JAO THE DRILL...
...BUT NO LONGER.
ANSWER ME!! WHAT DID GARP DO TO ME?!!
HOW SHOULD I KNOW?! AND MAKE UP YOUR MIND-- ARE YOU ANGRY OR SAD?!!
DASH!!
MURMUR!!
RAAAAAHH
THWAM!!
GO, LUCY, GO!!
LUFFY...
...

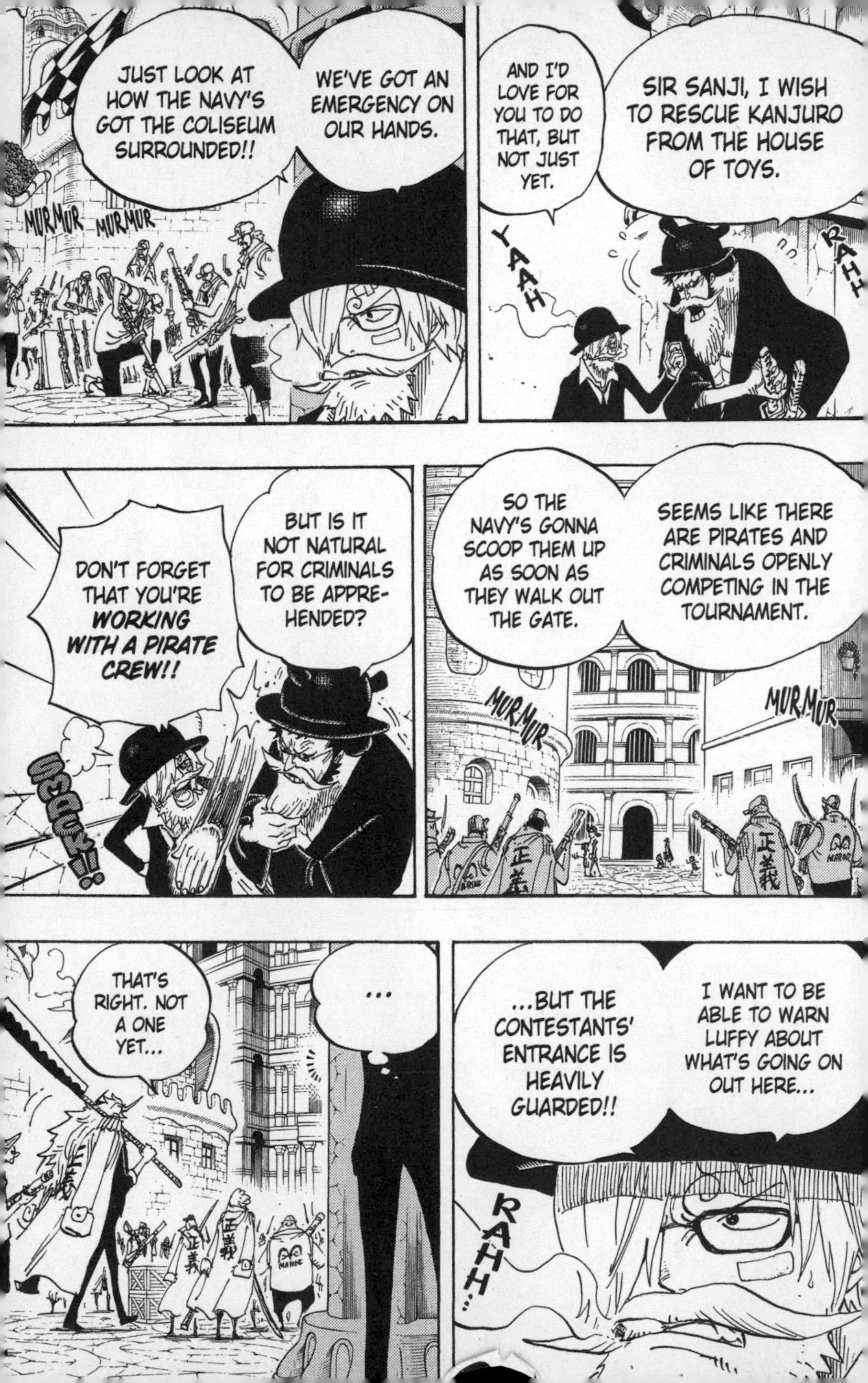
SIR SANJI, I WISH TO RESCUE KANJURO FROM THE HOUSE OF TOYS.
AND I'D LOVE FOR YOU TO DO THAT, BUT NOT JUST YET.
RAHH
YAAH
WE'VE GOT AN EMERGENCY ON OUR HANDS.
JUST LOOK AT HOW THE NAVY'S GOT THE COLISEUM SURROUNDED!!
MURMUR
MURMUR
SEEMS LIKE THERE ARE PIRATES AND CRIMINALS OPENLY COMPETING IN THE TOURNAMENT.
SO THE NAVY'S GONNA SCOOP THEM UP AS SOON AS THEY WALK OUT THE GATE.
MURMUR
MURMUR
BUT IS IT NOT NATURAL FOR CRIMINALS TO BE APPRE-HENDED?
DON'T FORGET THAT YOU'RE *WORKING WITH A PIRATE CREW!!*
SMACK!!
I WANT TO BE ABLE TO WARN LUFFY ABOUT WHAT'S GOING ON OUT HERE...
...BUT THE CONTESTANTS' ENTRANCE IS HEAVILY GUARDED!!
RAHH..
...
THAT'S RIGHT. NOT A ONE YET...

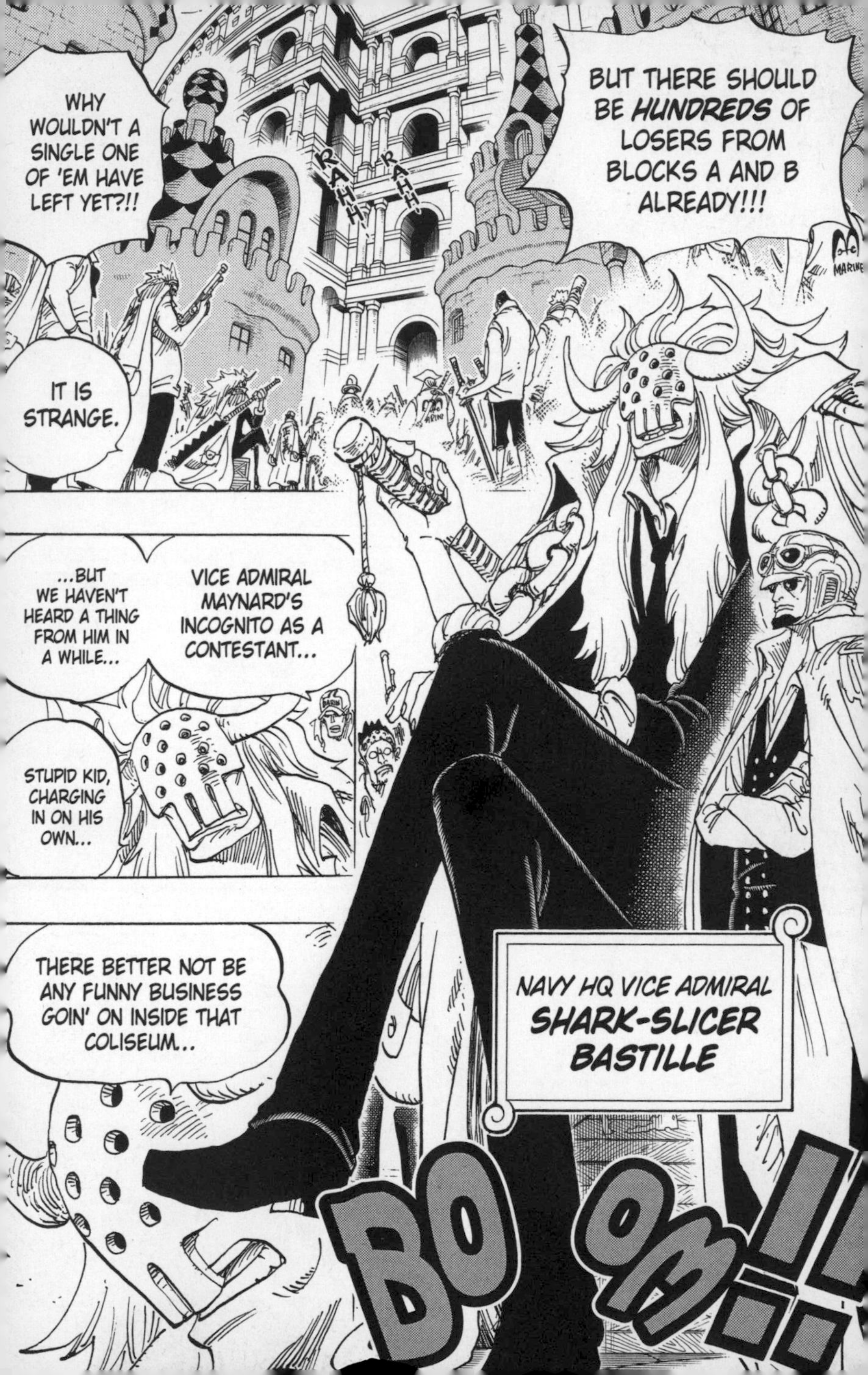
BUT THERE SHOULD BE HUNDREDS OF LOSERS FROM BLOCKS A AND B ALREADY!!!
WHY WOULDN'T A SINGLE ONE OF 'EM HAVE LEFT YET?!!
RAHH RAHH
MARINE
IT IS STRANGE.
VICE ADMIRAL MAYNARD'S INCOGNITO AS A CONTESTANT...
...BUT WE HAVEN'T HEARD A THING FROM HIM IN A WHILE...
STUPID KID, CHARGING IN ON HIS OWN...
THERE BETTER NOT BE ANY FUNNY BUSINESS GOIN' ON INSIDE THAT COLISEUM...
NAVY HQ VICE ADMIRAL SHARK-SLICER BASTILLE
BOOM!!

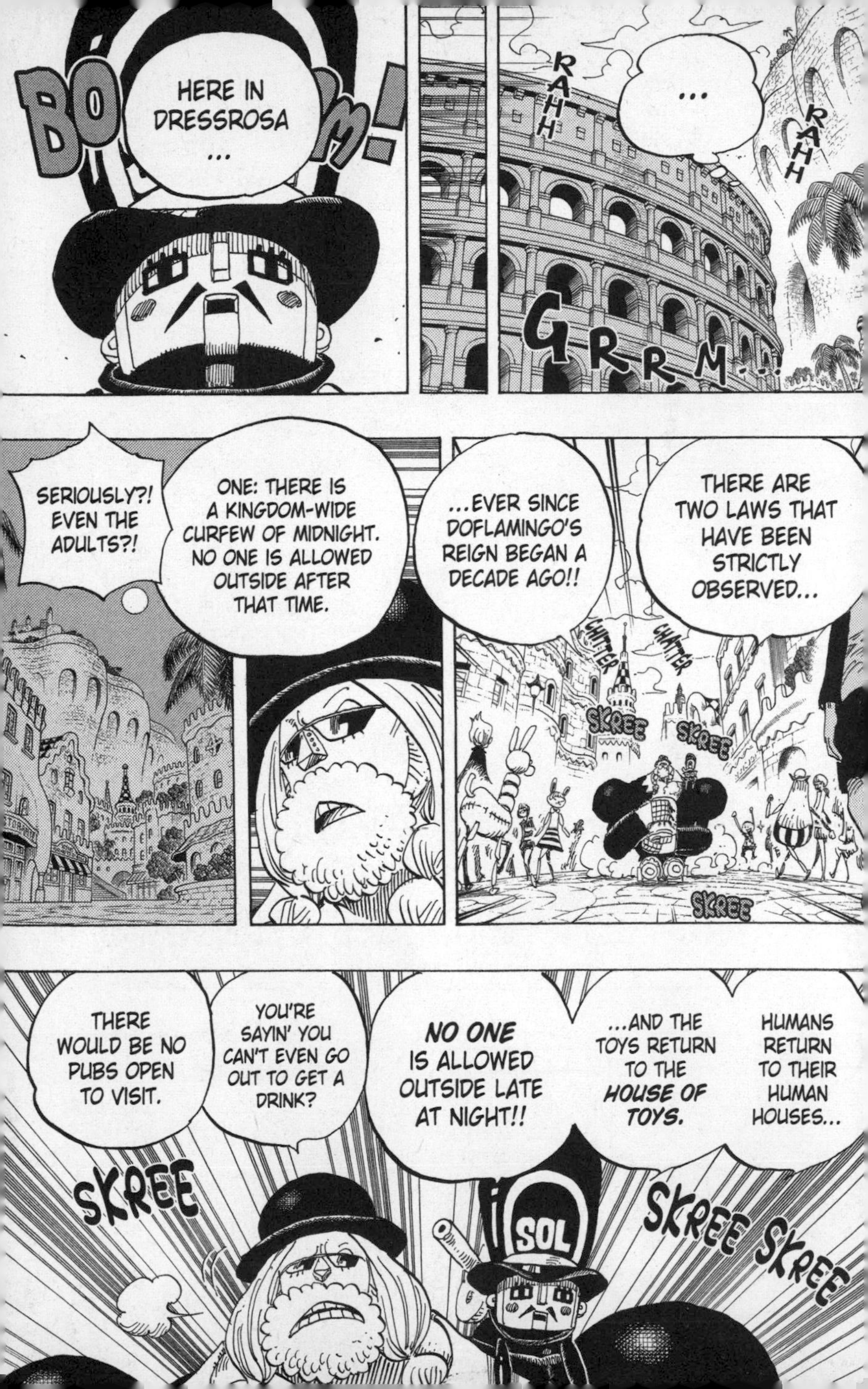
...
RAHH
RAHH
GRRRM..!
BOOM!
HERE IN DRESSROSA ...
THERE ARE TWO LAWS THAT HAVE BEEN STRICTLY OBSERVED...
...EVER SINCE DOFLAMINGO'S REIGN BEGAN A DECADE AGO!!
CHATTER
CHATTER
SKREE
SKREE
SKREE
ONE: THERE IS A KINGDOM-WIDE CURFEW OF MIDNIGHT. NO ONE IS ALLOWED OUTSIDE AFTER THAT TIME.
SERIOUSLY?! EVEN THE ADULTS?!
HUMANS RETURN TO THEIR HUMAN HOUSES...
...AND THE TOYS RETURN TO THE *HOUSE OF TOYS.*
NO ONE IS ALLOWED OUTSIDE LATE AT NIGHT!!
YOU'RE SAYIN' YOU CAN'T EVEN GO OUT TO GET A DRINK?
THERE WOULD BE NO PUBS OPEN TO VISIT.
SKREE SKREE
SOL
SKREE

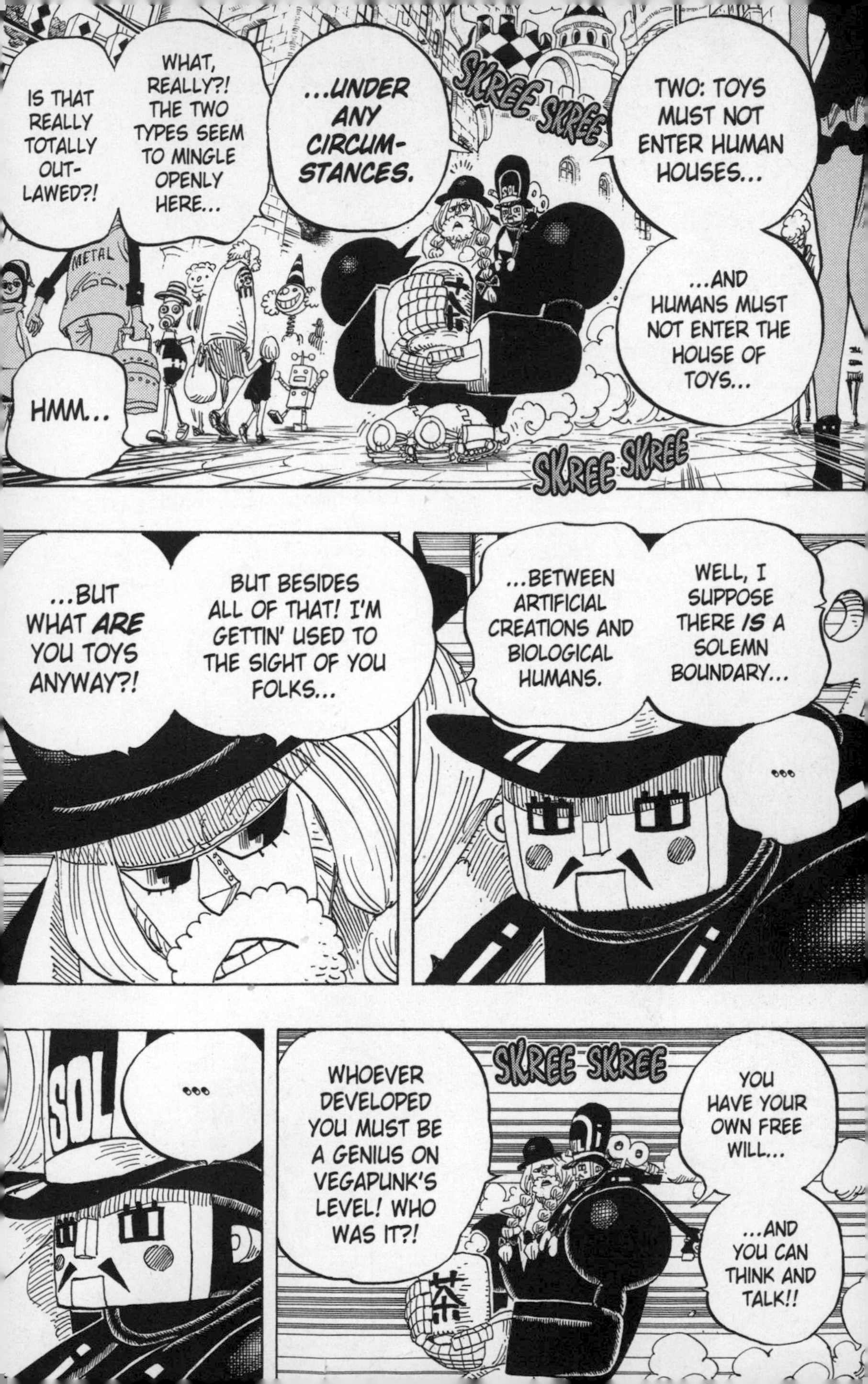
SKREE SKREE
TWO: TOYS MUST NOT ENTER HUMAN HOUSES...
...AND HUMANS MUST NOT ENTER THE HOUSE OF TOYS...
...UNDER ANY CIRCUMSTANCES.
SOL
WHAT, REALLY?! THE TWO TYPES SEEM TO MINGLE OPENLY HERE...
IS THAT REALLY TOTALLY OUT-LAWED?!
METAL
HMM...
SKREE SKREE
WELL, I SUPPOSE THERE IS A SOLEMN BOUNDARY...
...BETWEEN ARTIFICIAL CREATIONS AND BIOLOGICAL HUMANS.
...
BUT BESIDES ALL OF THAT! I'M GETTIN' USED TO THE SIGHT OF YOU FOLKS...
...BUT WHAT ARE YOU TOYS ANYWAY?!
SKREE SKREE
YOU HAVE YOUR OWN FREE WILL...
...AND YOU CAN THINK AND TALK!!
WHOEVER DEVELOPED YOU MUST BE A GENIUS ON VEGAPUNK'S LEVEL! WHO WAS IT?!
...
SOL

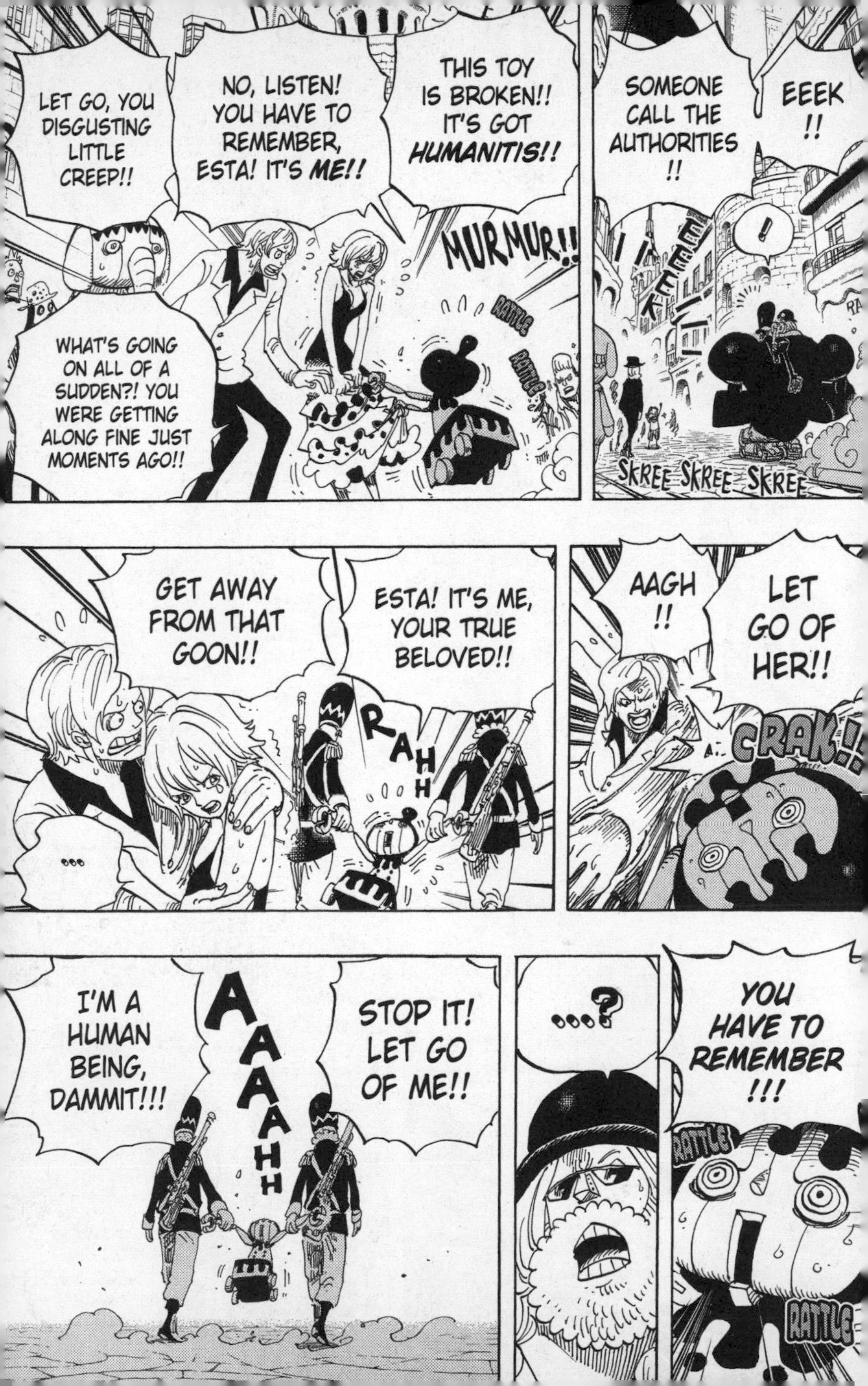
EEEK !!
SOMEONE CALL THE AUTHORITIES !!
!
EEEEK
SKREE SKREE SKREE
THIS TOY IS BROKEN!! IT'S GOT *HUMANITIS!!*
NO, LISTEN! YOU HAVE TO REMEMBER, ESTA! IT'S *ME!!*
LET GO, YOU DISGUSTING LITTLE CREEP!!
MURMUR!!
RATTLE
RATTLE
WHAT'S GOING ON ALL OF A SUDDEN?! YOU WERE GETTING ALONG FINE JUST MOMENTS AGO!!
LET GO OF HER!!
AAGH !!
CRAK!!
ESTA! IT'S ME, YOUR TRUE BELOVED!!
GET AWAY FROM THAT GOON!!
RAHHH
...
YOU HAVE TO REMEMBER !!!
...?
RATTLE
RATTLE
STOP IT! LET GO OF ME!!
AAAAAHH
I'M A HUMAN BEING, DAMMIT!!!

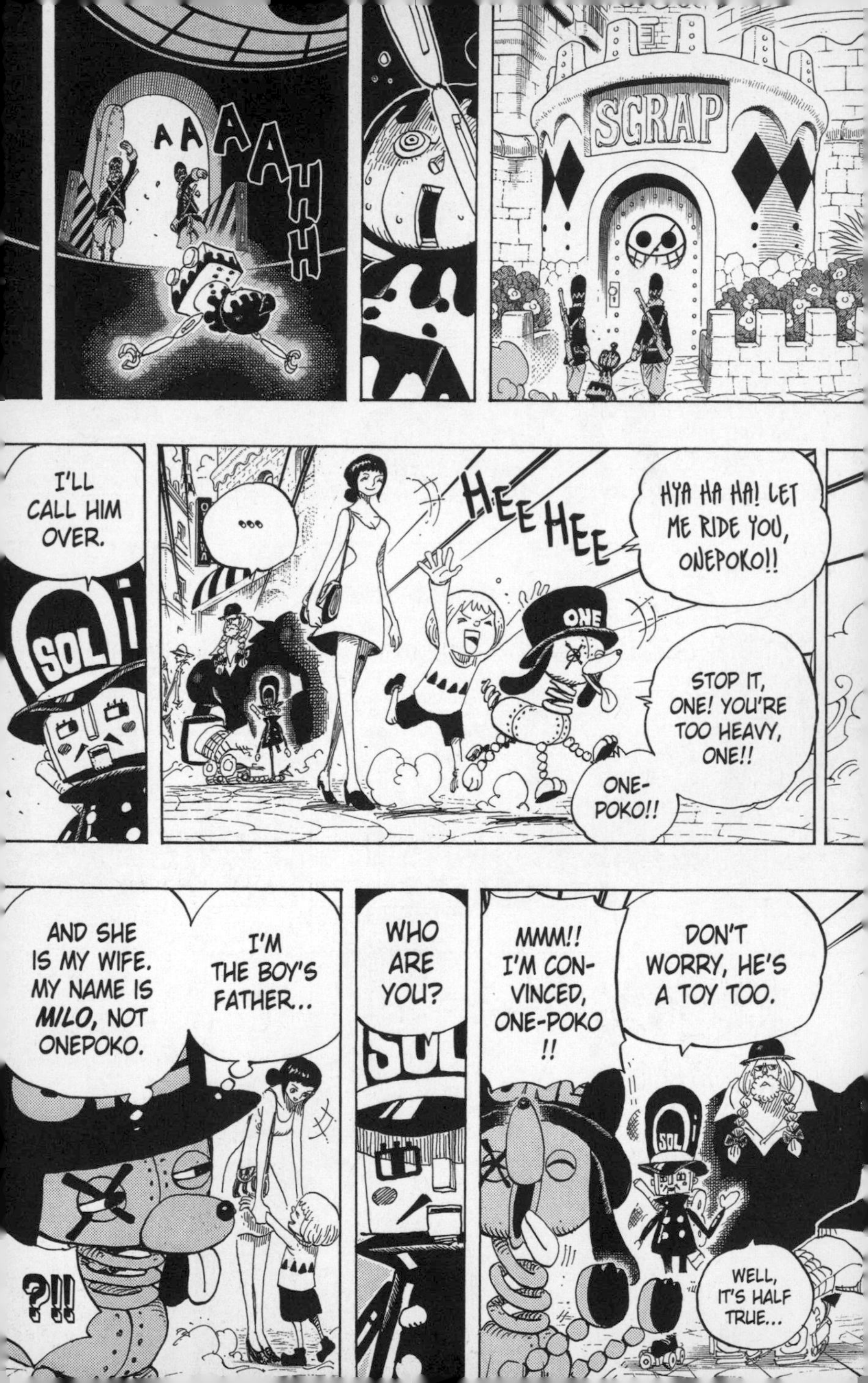
SCRAP
AAAAHHHH
HYA HA HA! LET ME RIDE YOU, ONEPOKO!!
HEE HEE
ONE
STOP IT, ONE! YOU'RE TOO HEAVY, ONE!!
ONE-POKO!!
...
I'LL CALL HIM OVER.
SOL
DON'T WORRY, HE'S A TOY TOO.
MMM!! I'M CON-VINCED, ONE-POKO!!
SOL
WELL, IT'S HALF TRUE...
WHO ARE YOU?
I'M THE BOY'S FATHER...
AND SHE IS MY WIFE. MY NAME IS *MILO*, NOT ONEPOKO.
?!!

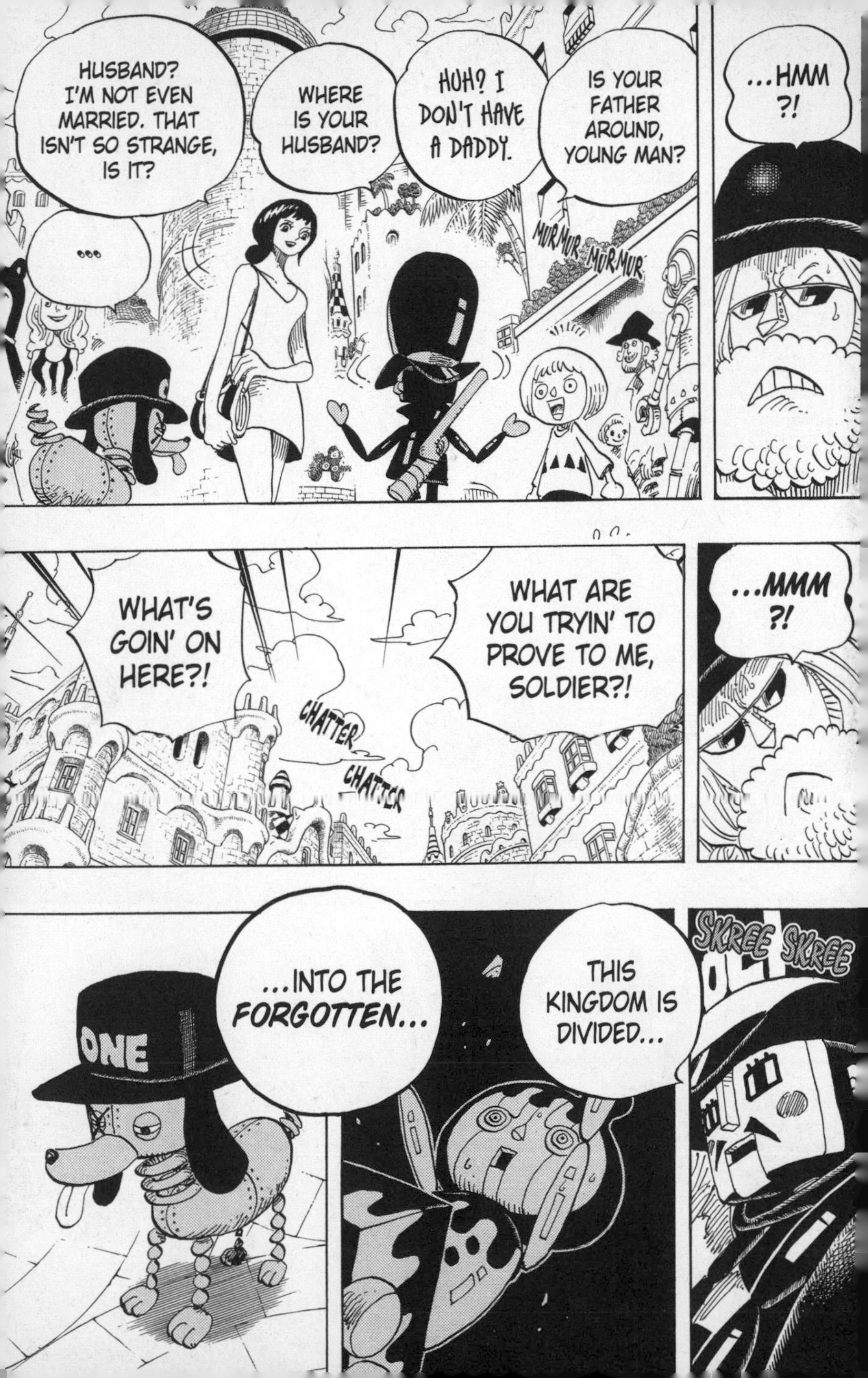
...HMM ?!
IS YOUR FATHER AROUND, YOUNG MAN?
HUH? I DON'T HAVE A DADDY.
MURMUR MURMUR
WHERE IS YOUR HUSBAND?
HUSBAND? I'M NOT EVEN MARRIED. THAT ISN'T SO STRANGE, IS IT?
...
...MMM ?!
WHAT ARE YOU TRYIN' TO PROVE TO ME, SOLDIER?!
CHATTER CHATTER
WHAT'S GOIN' ON HERE?!
SKREE SKREE
THIS KINGDOM IS DIVIDED...
...INTO THE FORGOTTEN...
ONE

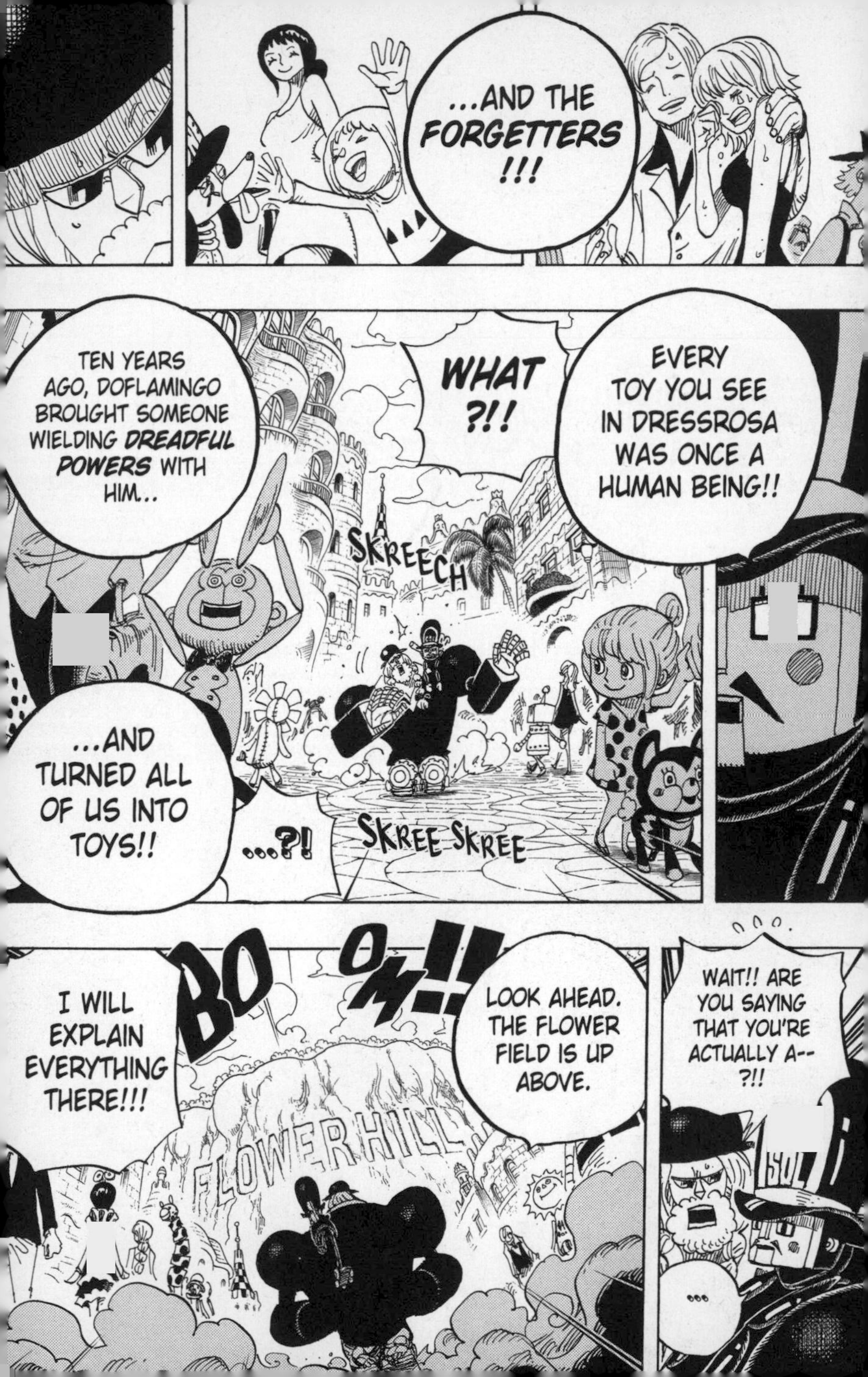
...AND THE FORGETTERS!!!
EVERY TOY YOU SEE IN DRESSROSA WAS ONCE A HUMAN BEING!!
WHAT?!!
TEN YEARS AGO, DOFLAMINGO BROUGHT SOMEONE WIELDING DREADFUL POWERS WITH HIM...
SKREEECH
SKREE SKREE
...?!
...AND TURNED ALL OF US INTO TOYS!!
WAIT!! ARE YOU SAYING THAT YOU'RE ACTUALLY A--?!!
...
LOOK AHEAD. THE FLOWER FIELD IS UP ABOVE.
BOOM!!
I WILL EXPLAIN EVERYTHING THERE!!!
FLOWER HILL

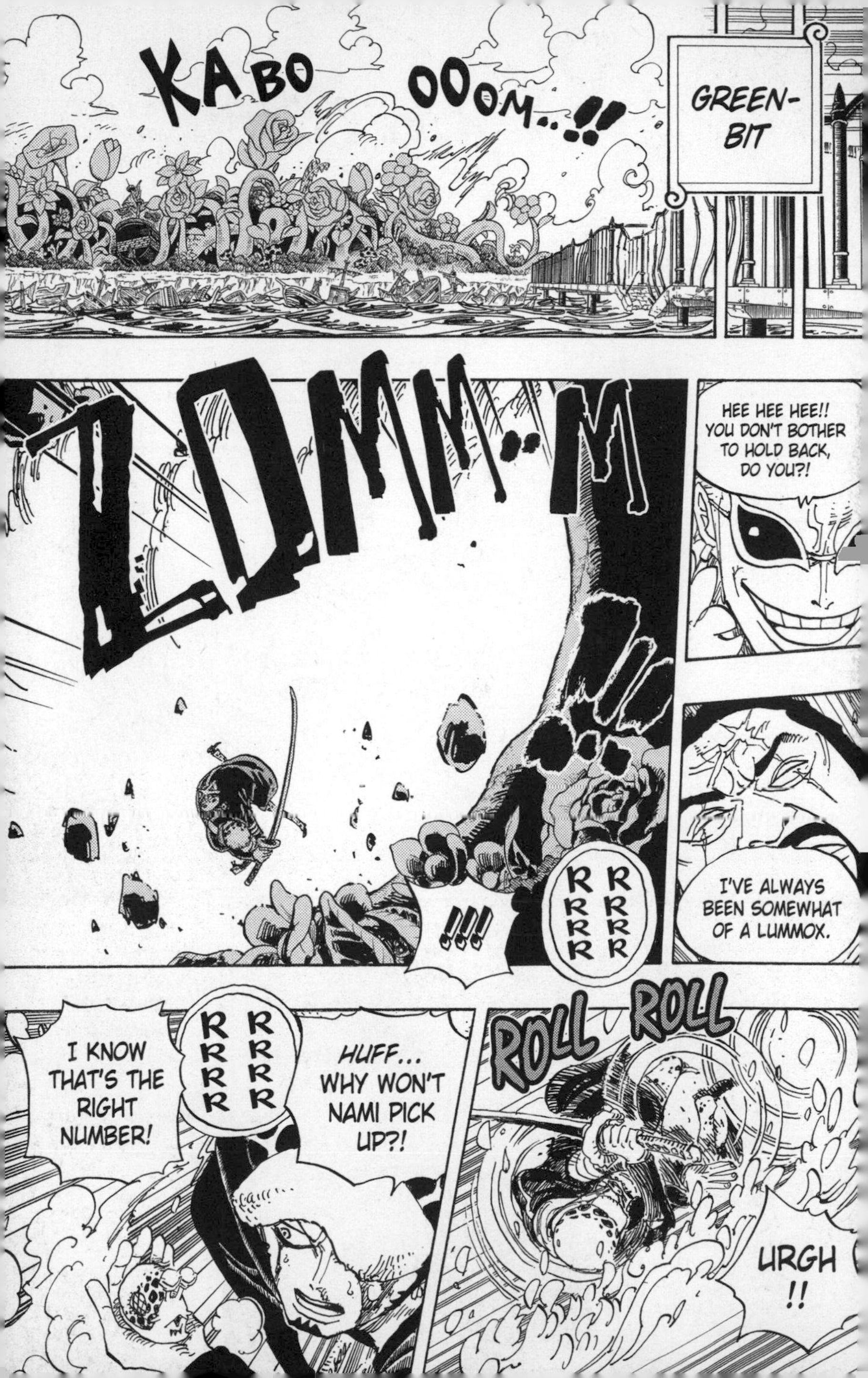
GREEN-BIT
KABOOOOM..!!
HEE HEE HEE!! YOU DON'T BOTHER TO HOLD BACK, DO YOU?!
I'VE ALWAYS BEEN SOMEWHAT OF A LUMMOX.
ZOMM..M
RRRR RRRR
!!!
ROLL ROLL
URGH!!
HUFF... WHY WON'T NAMI PICK UP?!
RRRR RRRR
I KNOW THAT'S THE RIGHT NUMBER!

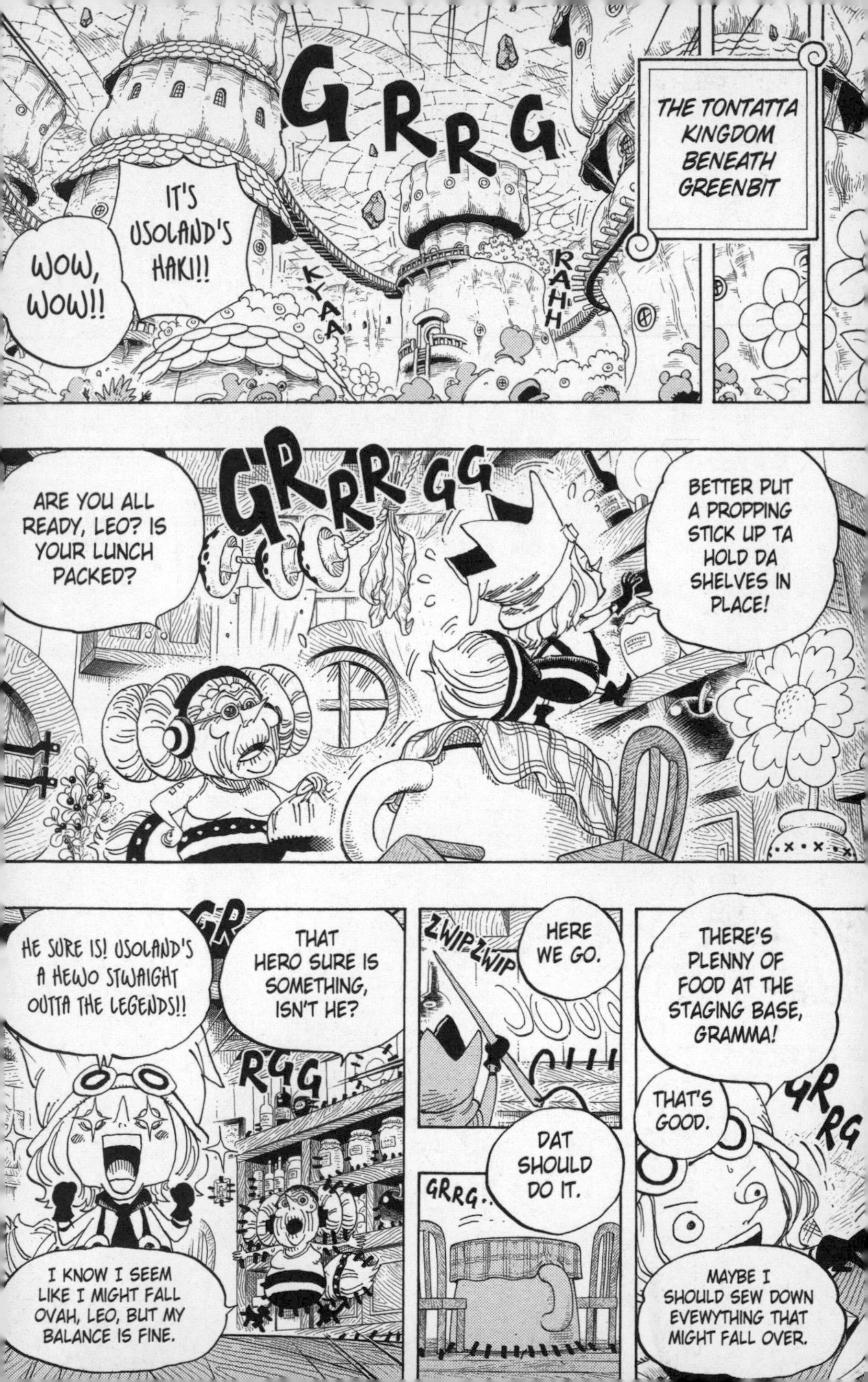
THE TONTATTA KINGDOM BENEATH GREENBIT
GRRG
RAHH
IT'S USOLAND'S HAKI!!
KYAA
WOW, WOW!!
BETTER PUT A PROPPING STICK UP TA HOLD DA SHELVES IN PLACE!
GRRRGG
ARE YOU ALL READY, LEO? IS YOUR LUNCH PACKED?
THERE'S PLENNY OF FOOD AT THE STAGING BASE, GRAMMA!
GRRG
THAT'S GOOD.
MAYBE I SHOULD SEW DOWN EVEWYTHING THAT MIGHT FALL OVER.
HERE WE GO.
ZWIP ZWIP
DAT SHOULD DO IT.
GRRG..
THAT HERO SURE IS SOMETHING, ISN'T HE?
GR
HE SURE IS! USOLAND'S A HEWO STWAIGHT OUTTA THE LEGENDS!!
RGG
I KNOW I SEEM LIKE I MIGHT FALL OVAH, LEO, BUT MY BALANCE IS FINE.

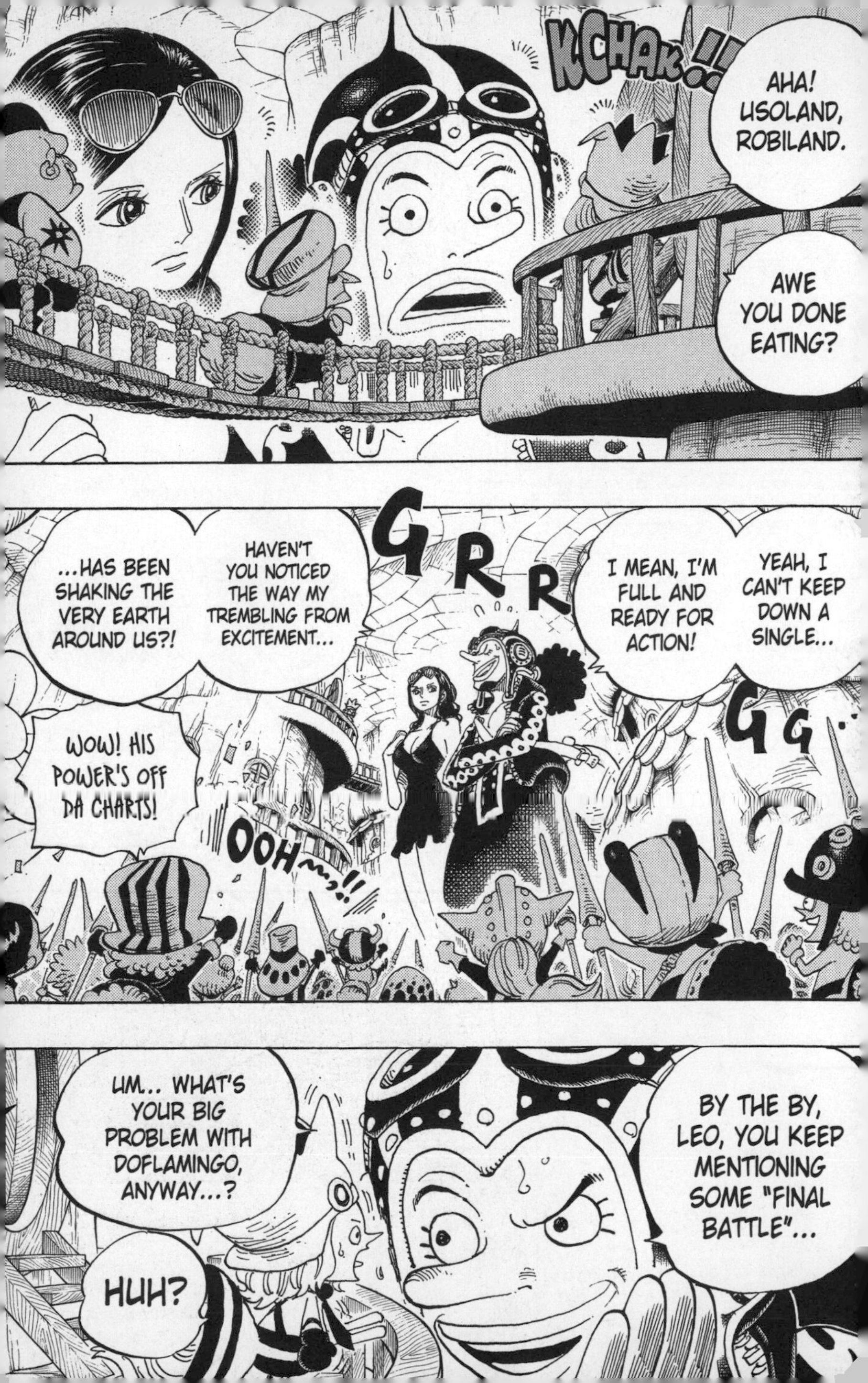

AHA! USOLAND, ROBILAND.
AWE YOU DONE EATING?
K-CHAK!!
YEAH, I CAN'T KEEP DOWN A SINGLE...
I MEAN, I'M FULL AND READY FOR ACTION!
GRR
HAVEN'T YOU NOTICED THE WAY MY TREMBLING FROM EXCITEMENT...
...HAS BEEN SHAKING THE VERY EARTH AROUND US?!
GG
WOW! HIS POWER'S OFF DA CHARTS!
OOH~~!!
BY THE BY, LEO, YOU KEEP MENTIONING SOME "FINAL BATTLE"...
UM... WHAT'S YOUR BIG PROBLEM WITH DOFLAMINGO, ANYWAY...?
HUH?

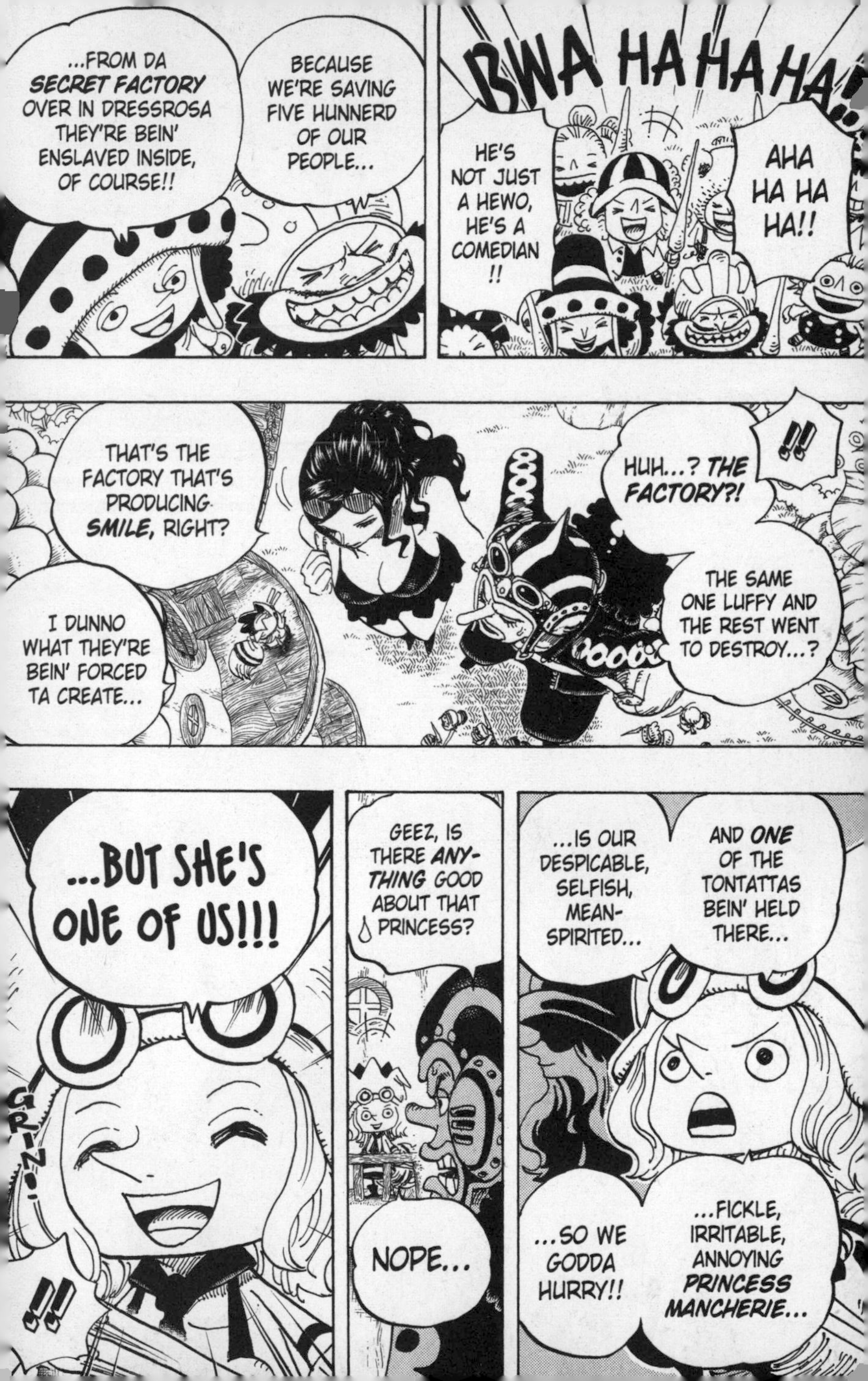
BWA HA HA HA HA!!
AHA HA HA HA!!
HE'S NOT JUST A HEWO, HE'S A COMEDIAN !!
BECAUSE WE'RE SAVING FIVE HUNNERD OF OUR PEOPLE...
...FROM DA SECRET FACTORY OVER IN DRESSROSA THEY'RE BEIN' ENSLAVED INSIDE, OF COURSE!!
!!
HUH...? THE FACTORY?!
THE SAME ONE LUFFY AND THE REST WENT TO DESTROY...?
THAT'S THE FACTORY THAT'S PRODUCING SMILE, RIGHT?
I DUNNO WHAT THEY'RE BEIN' FORCED TA CREATE...
AND ONE OF THE TONTATTAS BEIN' HELD THERE...
...IS OUR DESPICABLE, SELFISH, MEAN-SPIRITED...
...FICKLE, IRRITABLE, ANNOYING PRINCESS MANCHERIE...
...SO WE GODDA HURRY!!
GEEZ, IS THERE ANYTHING GOOD ABOUT THAT PRINCESS?
NOPE...
...BUT SHE'S ONE OF US!!!
GRIN...
!!

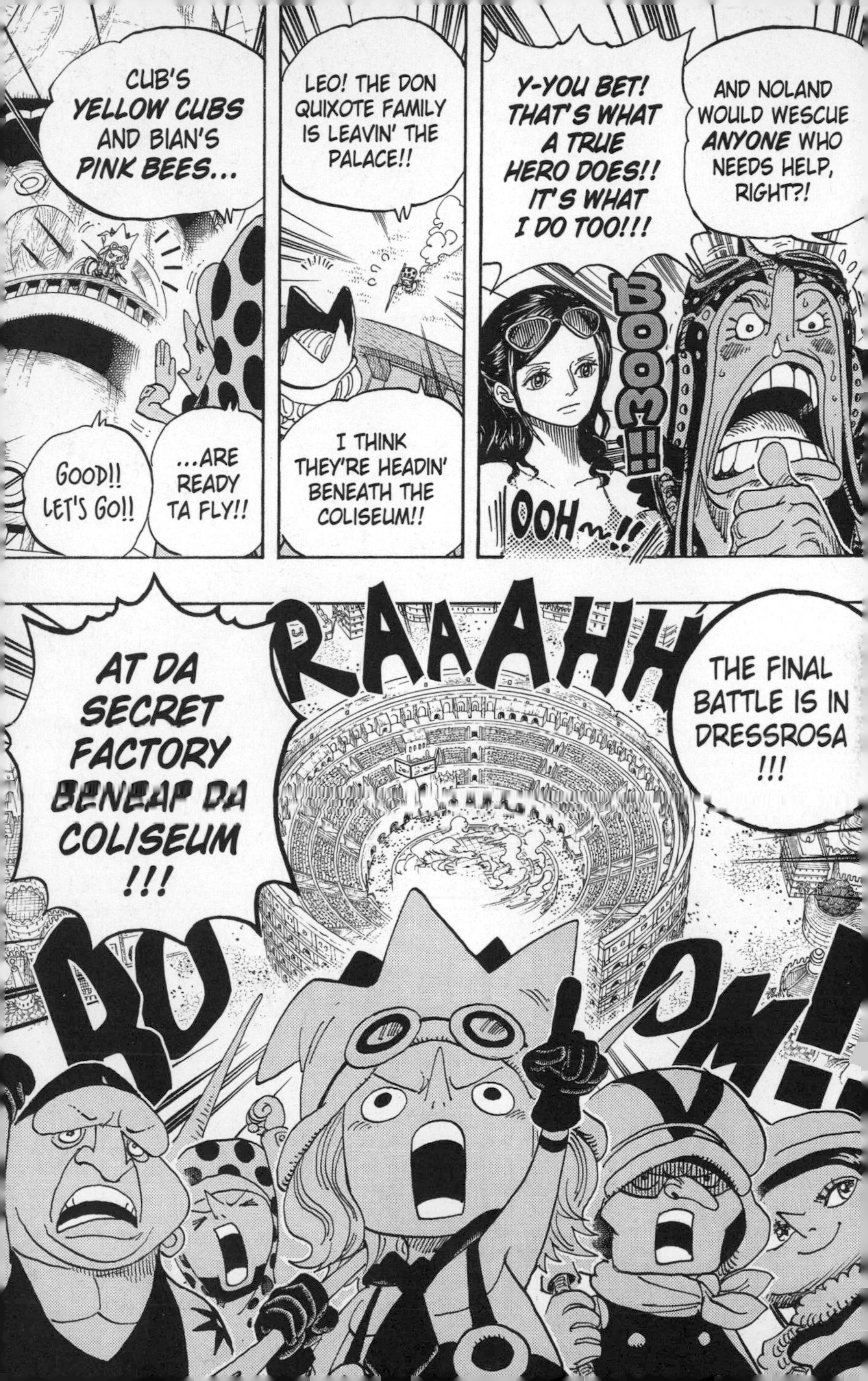
AND NOLAND WOULD WESCUE ANYONE WHO NEEDS HELP, RIGHT?!
Y-YOU BET! THAT'S WHAT A TRUE HERO DOES!! IT'S WHAT I DO TOO!!!
BOOM!!
OOH~!!
LEO! THE DON QUIXOTE FAMILY IS LEAVIN' THE PALACE!!
I THINK THEY'RE HEADIN' BENEATH THE COLISEUM!!
CUB'S YELLOW CUBS AND BIAN'S PINK BEES...
...ARE READY TA FLY!!
GOOD!! LET'S GO!!
THE FINAL BATTLE IS IN DRESSROSA!!!
RAAAHH
AT DA SECRET FACTORY BENEAP DA COLISEUM!!!
BOOM!!

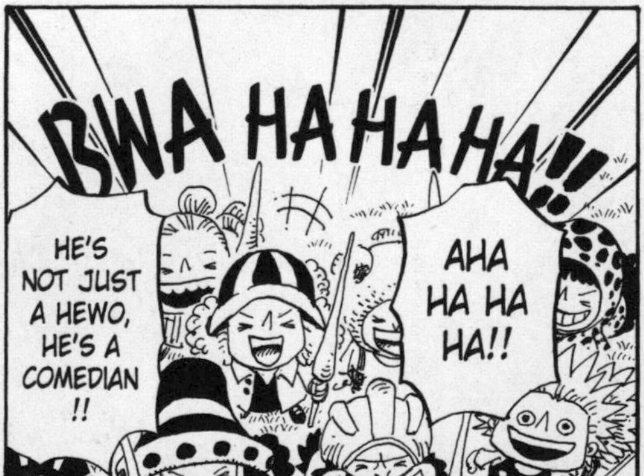
BWA HA HA HA HA!!
AHA HA HA HA!!
HE'S NOT JUST A HEWO, HE'S A COMEDIAN!!

Chapter 718:

RIKU ARMY AT THE FLOWER FIELD

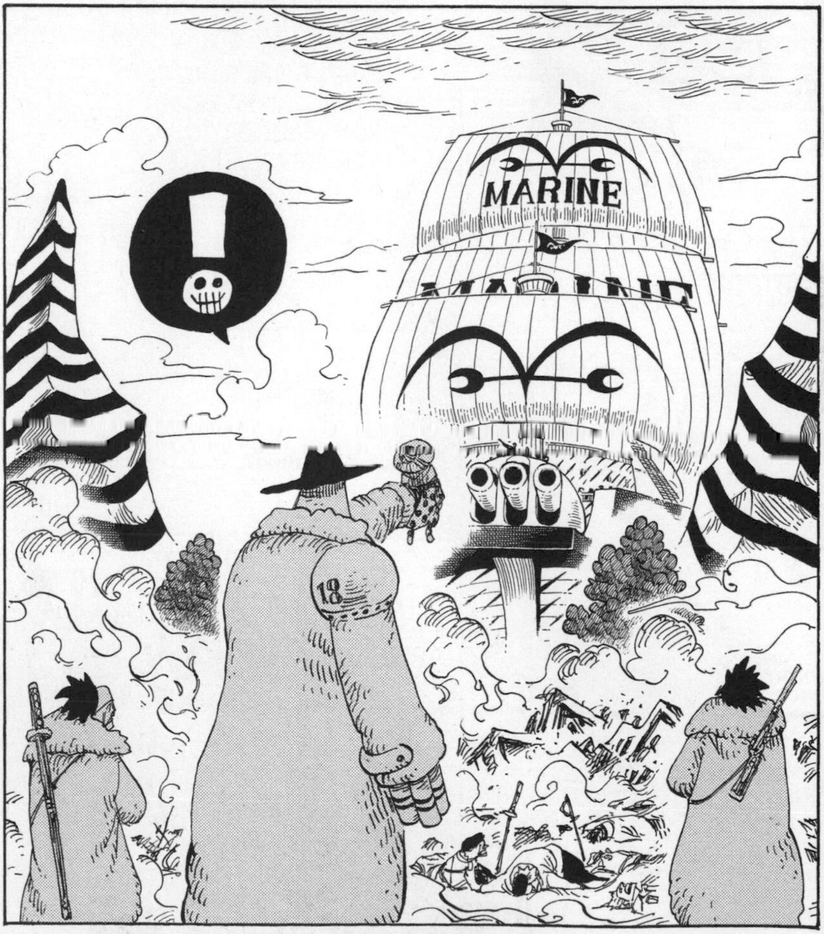
MARINE
!
18

CARIBOU'S NEW WORLD KEE HEE HEE, VOL. 35:
"A BATTLESHIP AT THE SHORE!!"

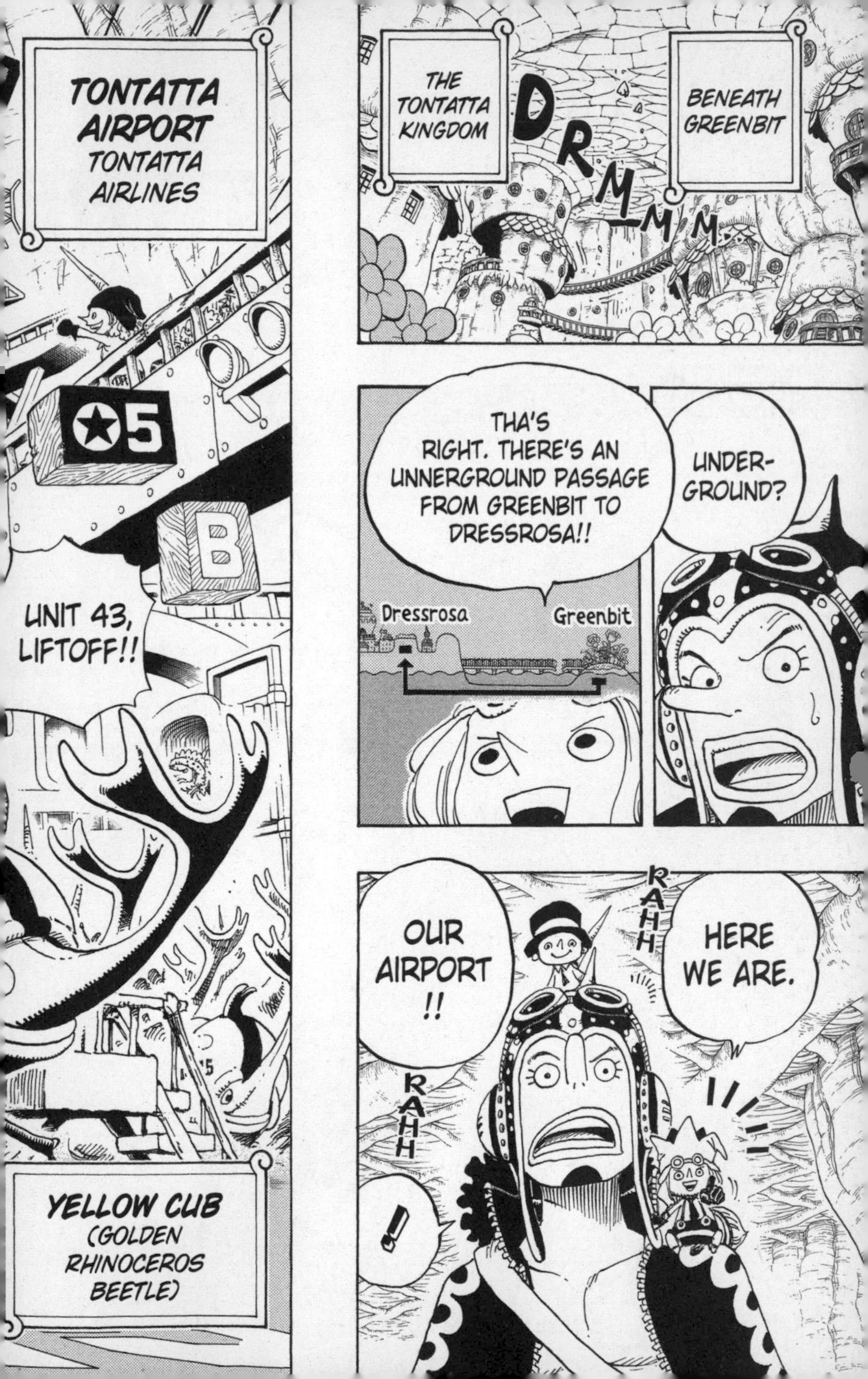
BENEATH GREENBIT
THE TONTATTA KINGDOM
DRMMMM
UNDER-GROUND?
THA'S RIGHT. THERE'S AN UNNERGROUND PASSAGE FROM GREENBIT TO DRESSROSA!!
Greenbit
Dressrosa
HERE WE ARE.
RAHH
OUR AIRPORT!!
RAHH
!!!
!
TONTATTA AIRPORT TONTATTA AIRLINES
5
B
UNIT 43, LIFTOFF!!
YELLOW CUB (GOLDEN RHINOCEROS BEETLE)

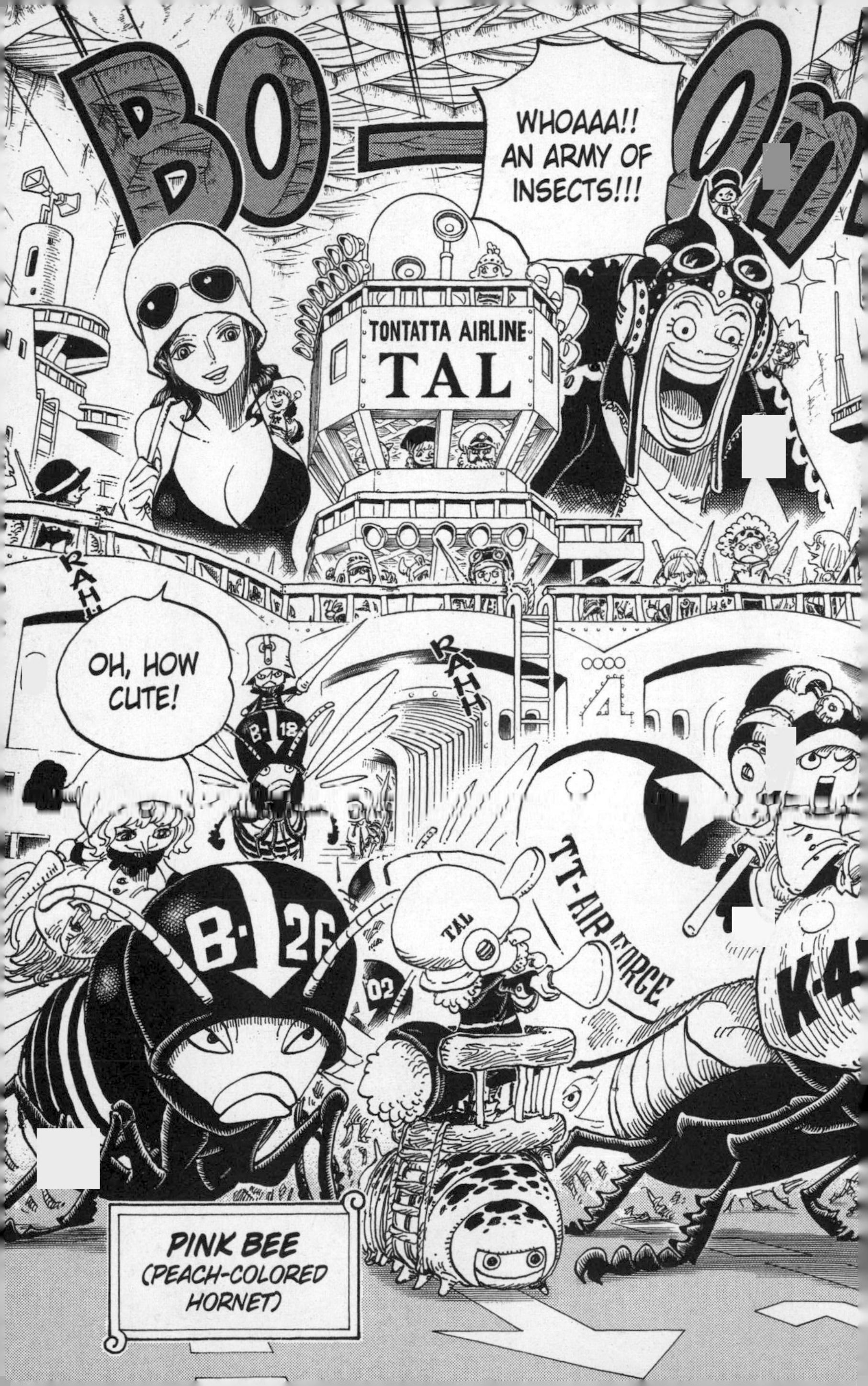
BO-OM
WHOAAA!! AN ARMY OF INSECTS!!!
TONTATTA AIRLINE
TAL
RAHH
OH, HOW CUTE!
RAHH
B-18
TT-AIR FORCE
TAL
B-26
02
K-4
PINK BEE (PEACH-COLORED HORNET)

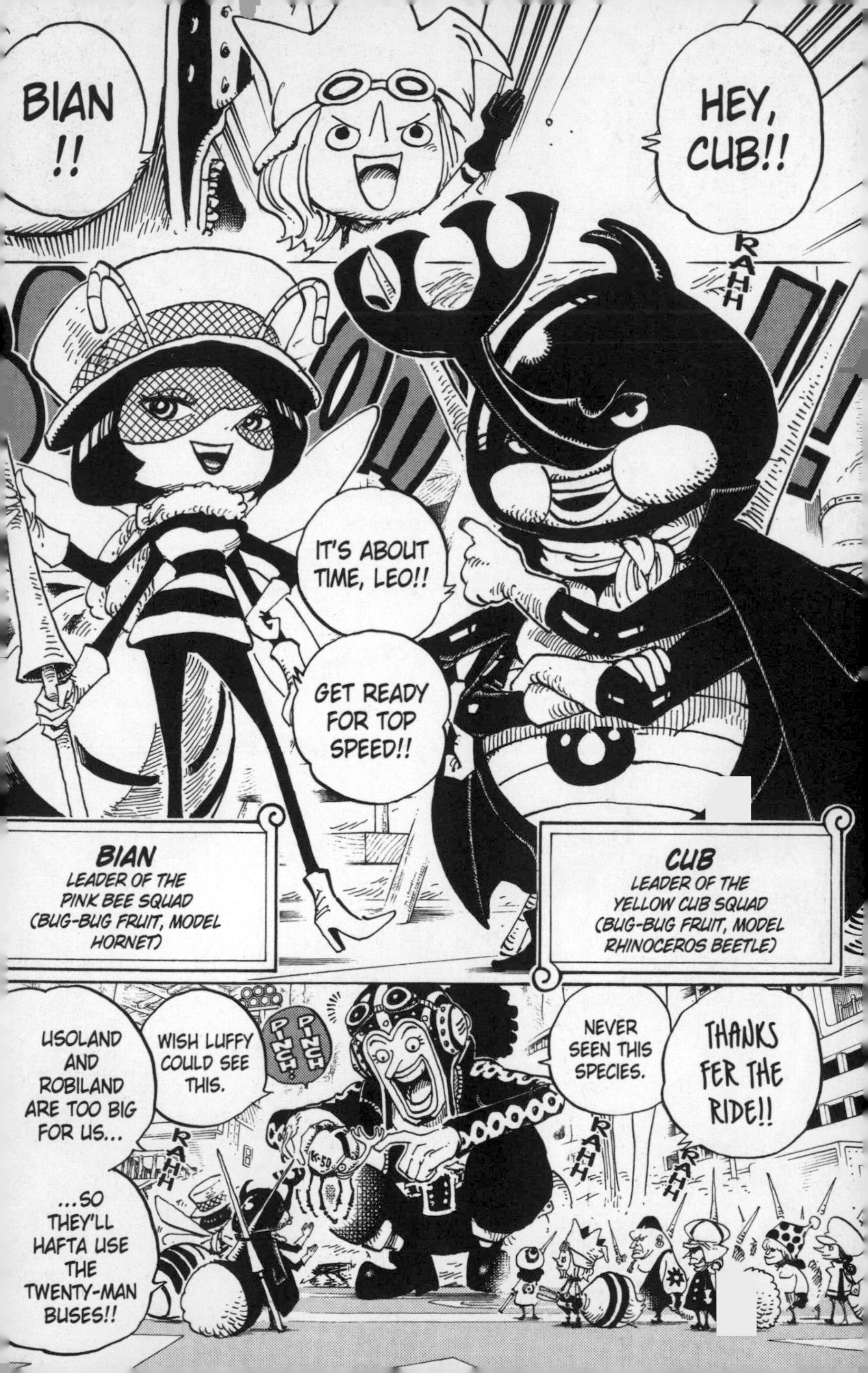
HEY, CUB!!
RAHH
BIAN !!
IT'S ABOUT TIME, LEO!!
GET READY FOR TOP SPEED!!
CUB
LEADER OF THE YELLOW CUB SQUAD (BUG-BUG FRUIT, MODEL RHINOCEROS BEETLE)
BIAN
LEADER OF THE PINK BEE SQUAD (BUG-BUG FRUIT, MODEL HORNET)
THANKS FER THE RIDE!!
RAHH
NEVER SEEN THIS SPECIES.
RAHH
PINCH PINCH
WISH LUFFY COULD SEE THIS.
USOLAND AND ROBILAND ARE TOO BIG FOR US...
RAHH
...SO THEY'LL HAFTA USE THE TWENTY-MAN BUSES!!

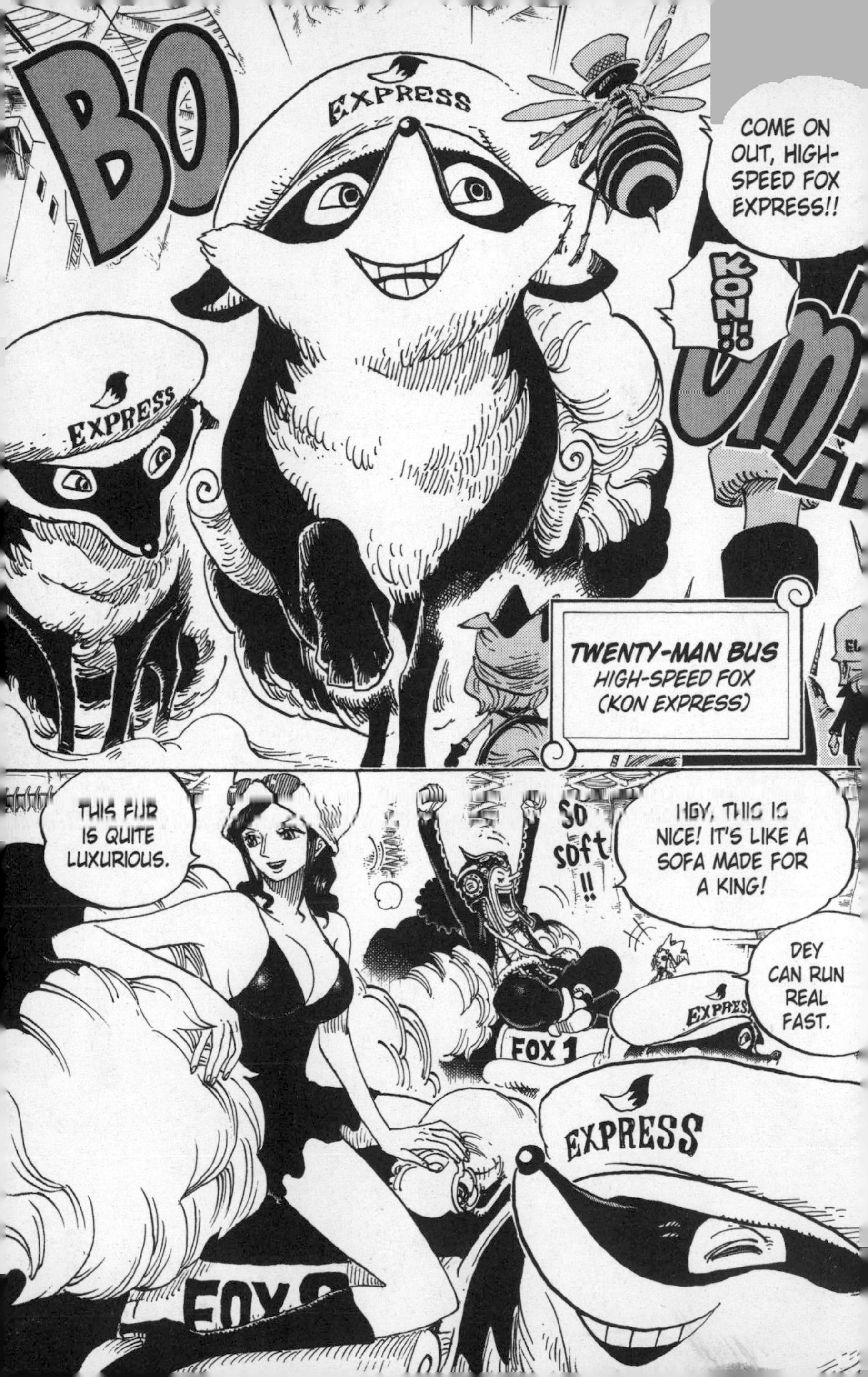

COME ON OUT, HIGH-SPEED FOX EXPRESS!!
KON!!
BO
EXPRESS
EXPRESS
TWENTY-MAN BUS
HIGH-SPEED FOX
(KON EXPRESS)
HEY, THIS IS NICE! IT'S LIKE A SOFA MADE FOR A KING!
SO soft!!
THIS FUR IS QUITE LUXURIOUS.
DEY CAN RUN REAL FAST.
EXPRES
FOX 1
EXPRESS

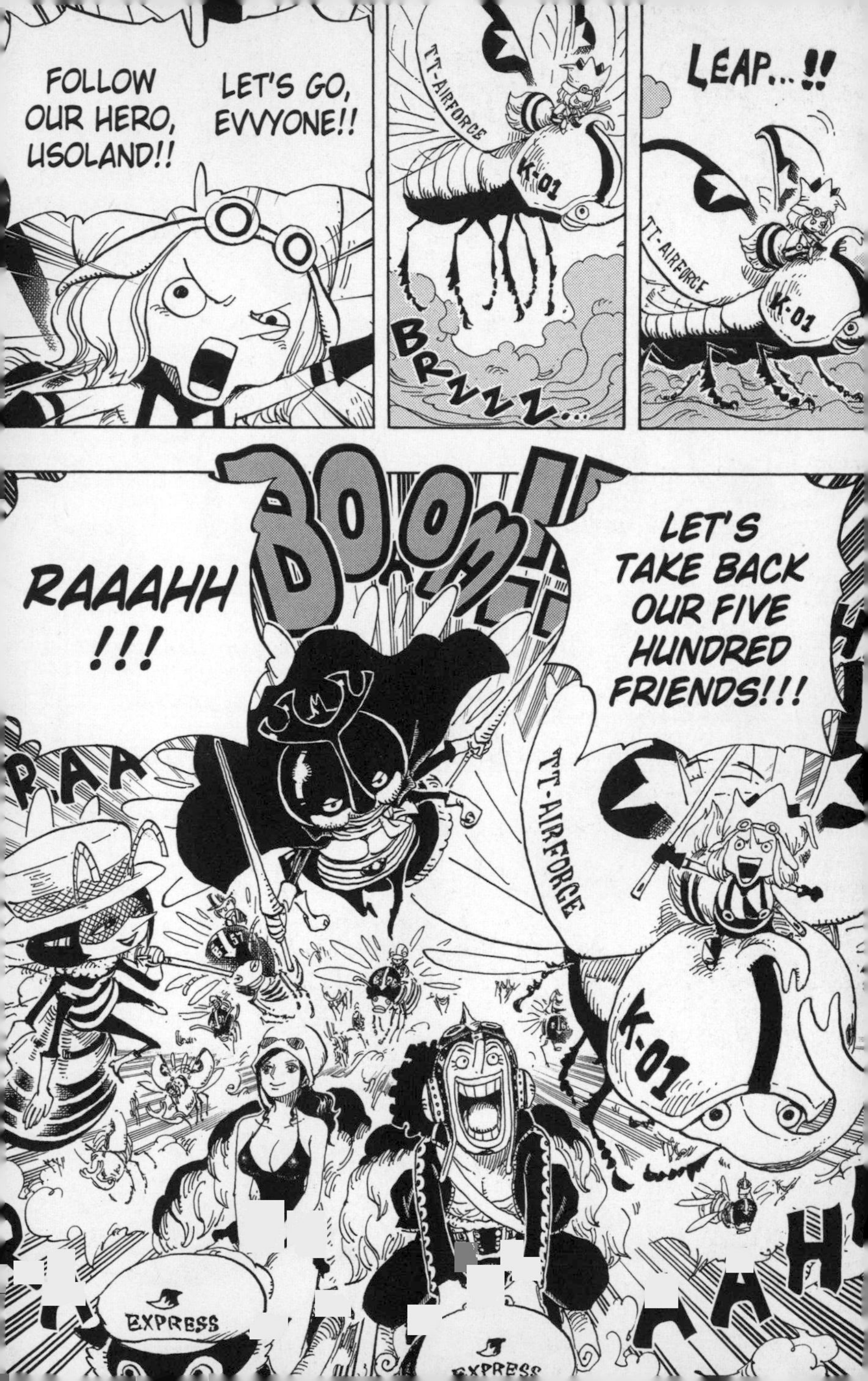
LEAP...!!
TT-AIRFORCE
K-01
BRZZZZ...
TT-AIRFORCE
K-01
LET'S GO, EVVYONE!!
FOLLOW OUR HERO, USOLAND!!
LET'S TAKE BACK OUR FIVE HUNDRED FRIENDS!!!
TT-AIRFORCE
K-01
BOOM
RAAAHH!!!
EXPRESS
EXPRESS

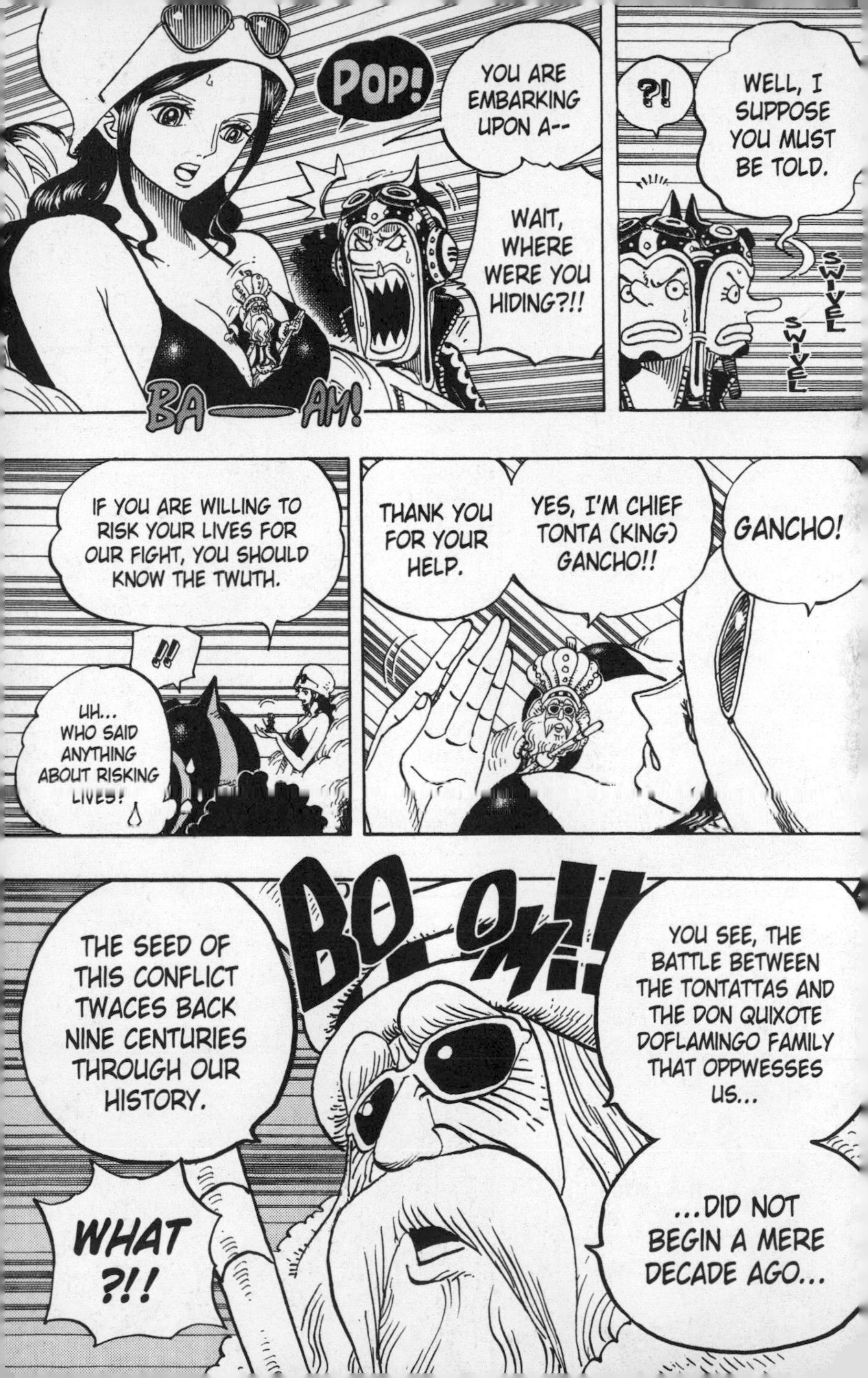
?!
WELL, I SUPPOSE YOU MUST BE TOLD.
SWIVEL
SWIVEL
YOU ARE EMBARKING UPON A--
POP!
WAIT, WHERE WERE YOU HIDING?!!
BA—AM!
GANCHO!
YES, I'M CHIEF TONTA (KING) GANCHO!!
THANK YOU FOR YOUR HELP.
IF YOU ARE WILLING TO RISK YOUR LIVES FOR OUR FIGHT, YOU SHOULD KNOW THE TWUTH.
!!
UH... WHO SAID ANYTHING ABOUT RISKING LIVES!
YOU SEE, THE BATTLE BETWEEN THE TONTATTAS AND THE DON QUIXOTE DOFLAMINGO FAMILY THAT OPPWESSES US...
...DID NOT BEGIN A MERE DECADE AGO...
BO—OM!!
THE SEED OF THIS CONFLICT TWACES BACK NINE CENTURIES THROUGH OUR HISTORY.
WHAT ?!!

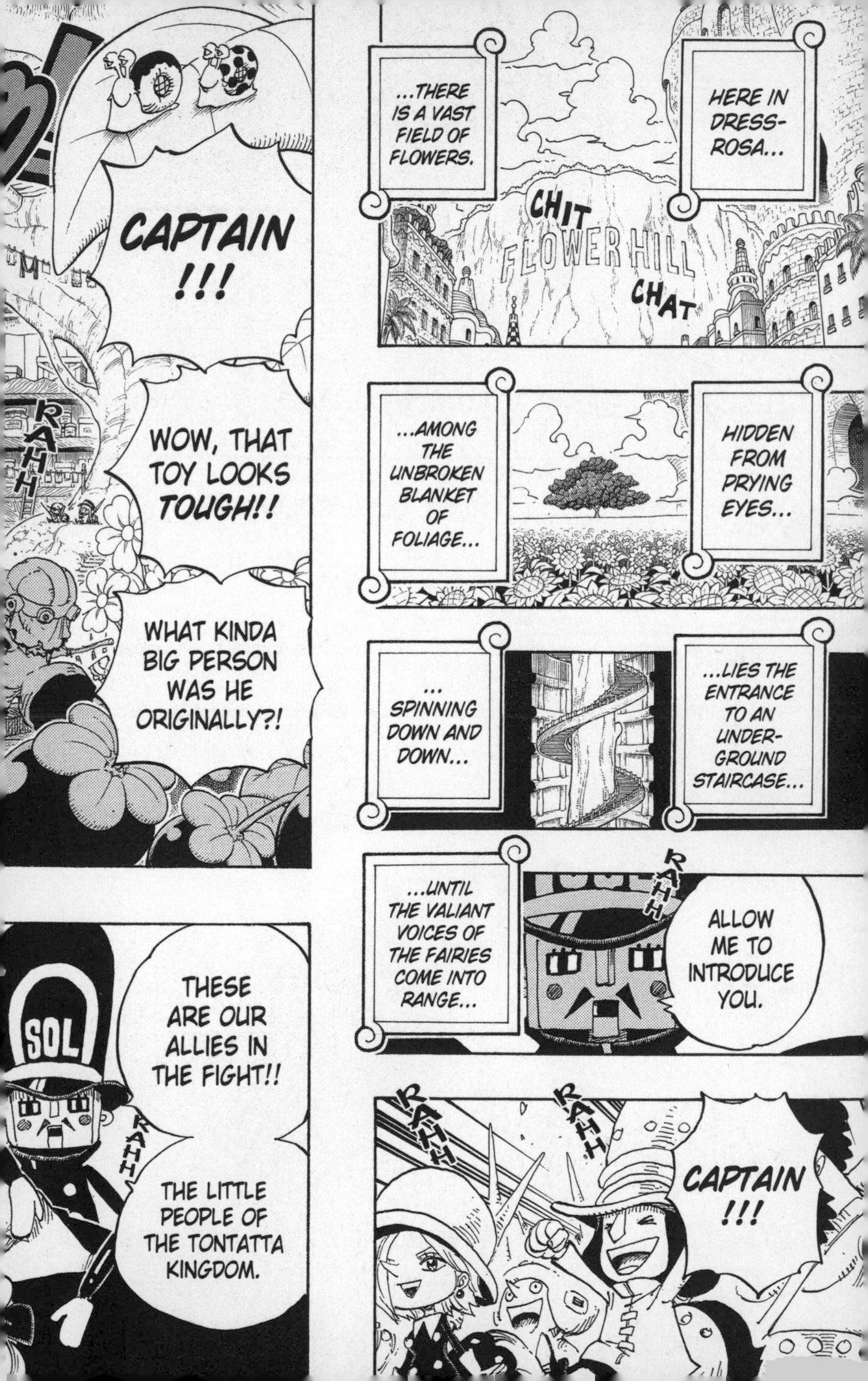
HERE IN DRESS-ROSA...
...THERE IS A VAST FIELD OF FLOWERS.
CHIT
FLOWER HILL
CHAT
HIDDEN FROM PRYING EYES...
...AMONG THE UNBROKEN BLANKET OF FOLIAGE...
...LIES THE ENTRANCE TO AN UNDER-GROUND STAIRCASE...
... SPINNING DOWN AND DOWN...
RAHH
ALLOW ME TO INTRODUCE YOU.
...UNTIL THE VALIANT VOICES OF THE FAIRIES COME INTO RANGE...
CAPTAIN!!!
RAHH
WOW, THAT TOY LOOKS TOUGH!!
WHAT KINDA BIG PERSON WAS HE ORIGINALLY?!
CAPTAIN!!!
RAHH
RAHH
THESE ARE OUR ALLIES IN THE FIGHT!!
SOL
RAHH
THE LITTLE PEOPLE OF THE TONTATTA KINGDOM.

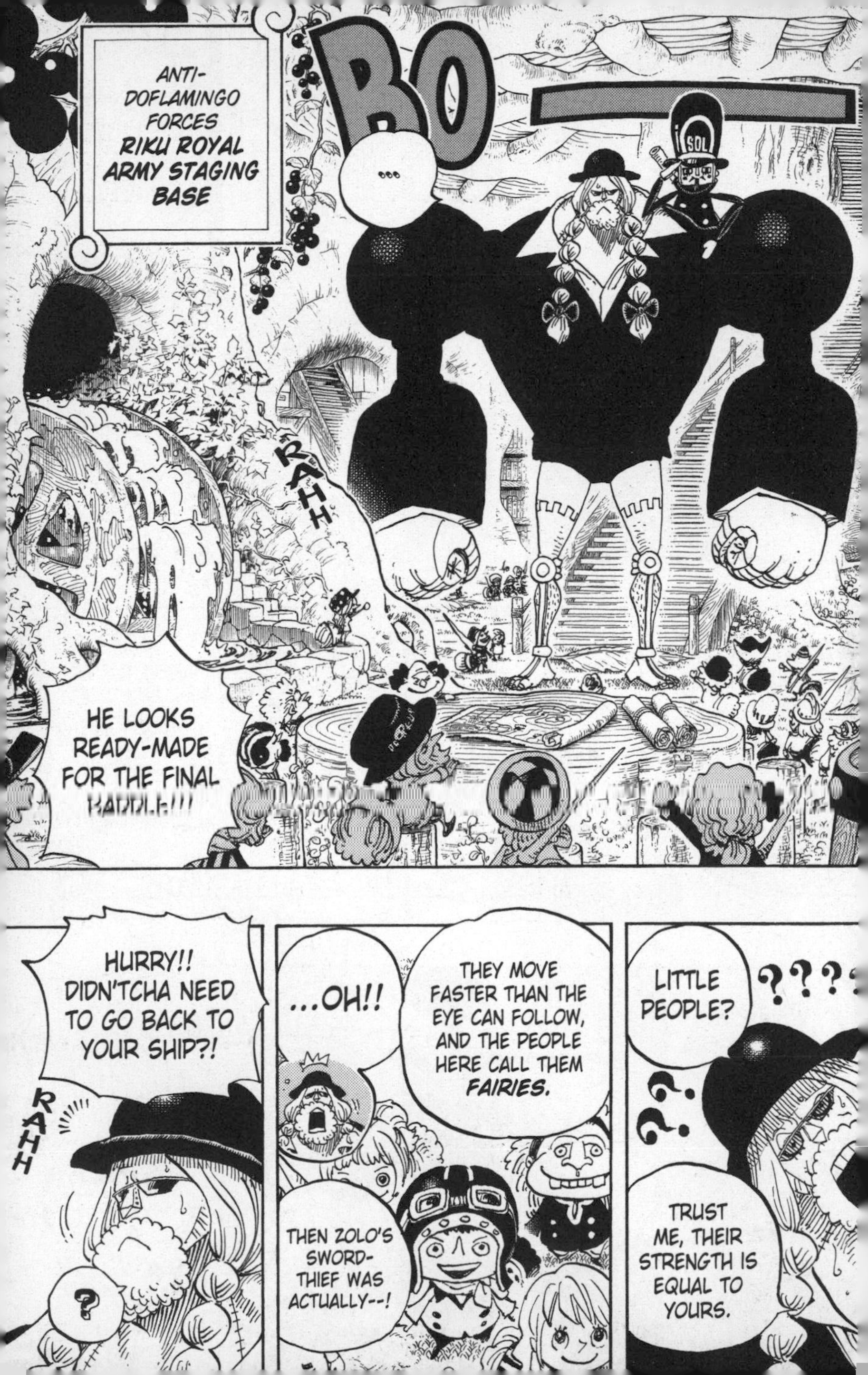
BO—T
...
ANTI-DOFLAMINGO FORCES RIKU ROYAL ARMY STAGING BASE
RAHH
HE LOOKS READY-MADE FOR THE FINAL BATTLE!!!
LITTLE PEOPLE?
????
??
TRUST ME, THEIR STRENGTH IS EQUAL TO YOURS.
THEY MOVE FASTER THAN THE EYE CAN FOLLOW, AND THE PEOPLE HERE CALL THEM FAIRIES.
...OH!!
THEN ZOLO'S SWORD-THIEF WAS ACTUALLY--!
HURRY!! DIDN'TCHA NEED TO GO BACK TO YOUR SHIP?!
RAHH
?

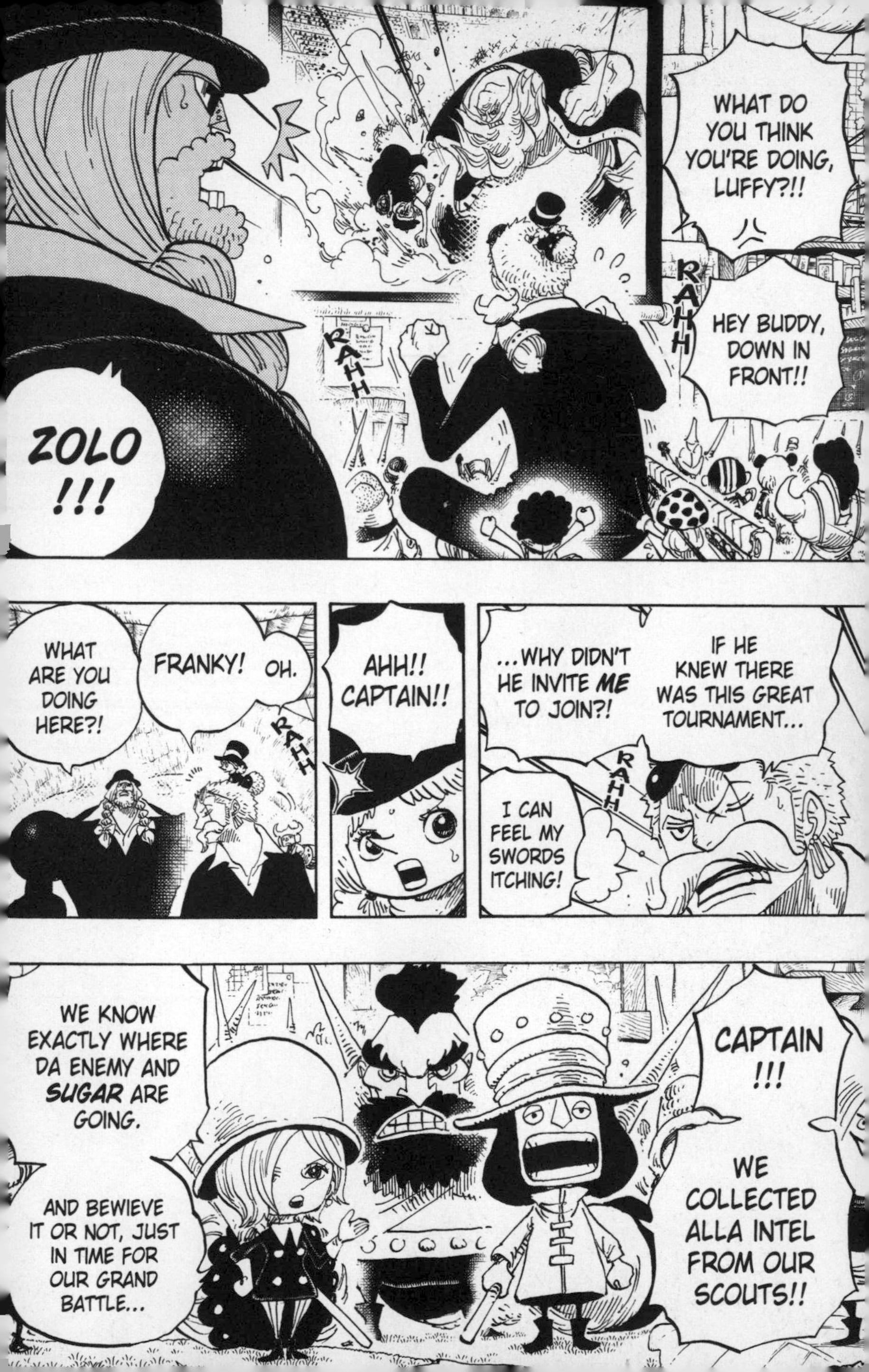
WHAT DO YOU THINK YOU'RE DOING, LUFFY?!!
RAHH
HEY BUDDY, DOWN IN FRONT!!
RAHH
ZOLO !!!
IF HE KNEW THERE WAS THIS GREAT TOURNAMENT...
...WHY DIDN'T HE INVITE ME TO JOIN?!
RAHH
I CAN FEEL MY SWORDS ITCHING!
AHH!! CAPTAIN!!
OH.
FRANKY!
WHAT ARE YOU DOING HERE?!
RAHH
CAPTAIN !!!
WE COLLECTED ALLA INTEL FROM OUR SCOUTS!!
WE KNOW EXACTLY WHERE DA ENEMY AND SUGAR ARE GOING.
AND BEWIEVE IT OR NOT, JUST IN TIME FOR OUR GRAND BATTLE...

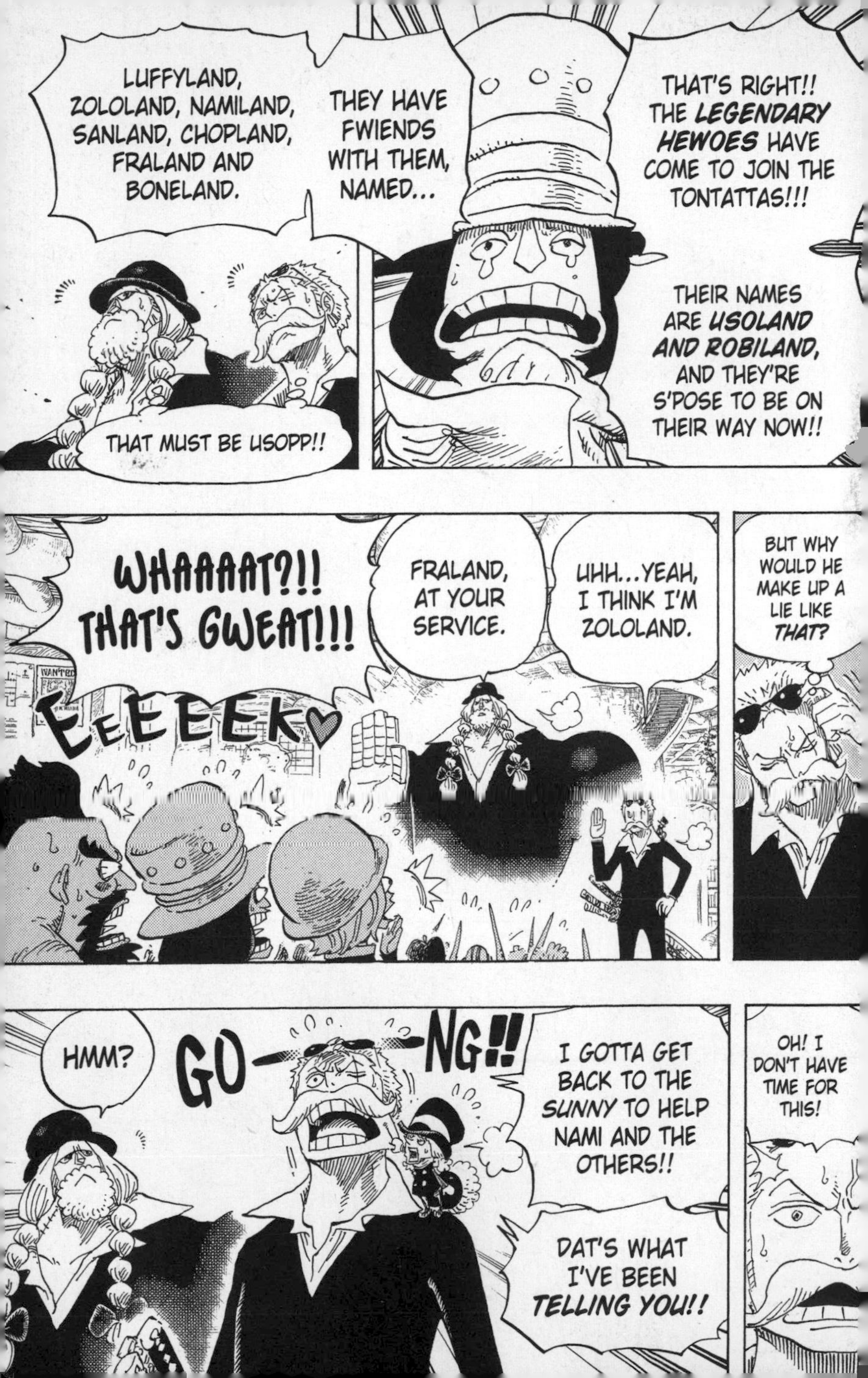
LUFFYLAND, ZOLOLAND, NAMILAND, SANLAND, CHOPLAND, FRALAND AND BONELAND.
THEY HAVE FWIENDS WITH THEM, NAMED...
THAT'S RIGHT!! THE LEGENDARY HEWOES HAVE COME TO JOIN THE TONTATTAS!!!
THEIR NAMES ARE USOLAND AND ROBILAND, AND THEY'RE S'POSE TO BE ON THEIR WAY NOW!!
THAT MUST BE USOPP!!
BUT WHY WOULD HE MAKE UP A LIE LIKE THAT?
UHH...YEAH, I THINK I'M ZOLOLAND.
FRALAND, AT YOUR SERVICE.
WHAAAAT?!! THAT'S GWEAT!!!
EEEEEK♥
OH! I DON'T HAVE TIME FOR THIS!
I GOTTA GET BACK TO THE SUNNY TO HELP NAMI AND THE OTHERS!!
DAT'S WHAT I'VE BEEN TELLING YOU!!
GO-NG!!
HMM?

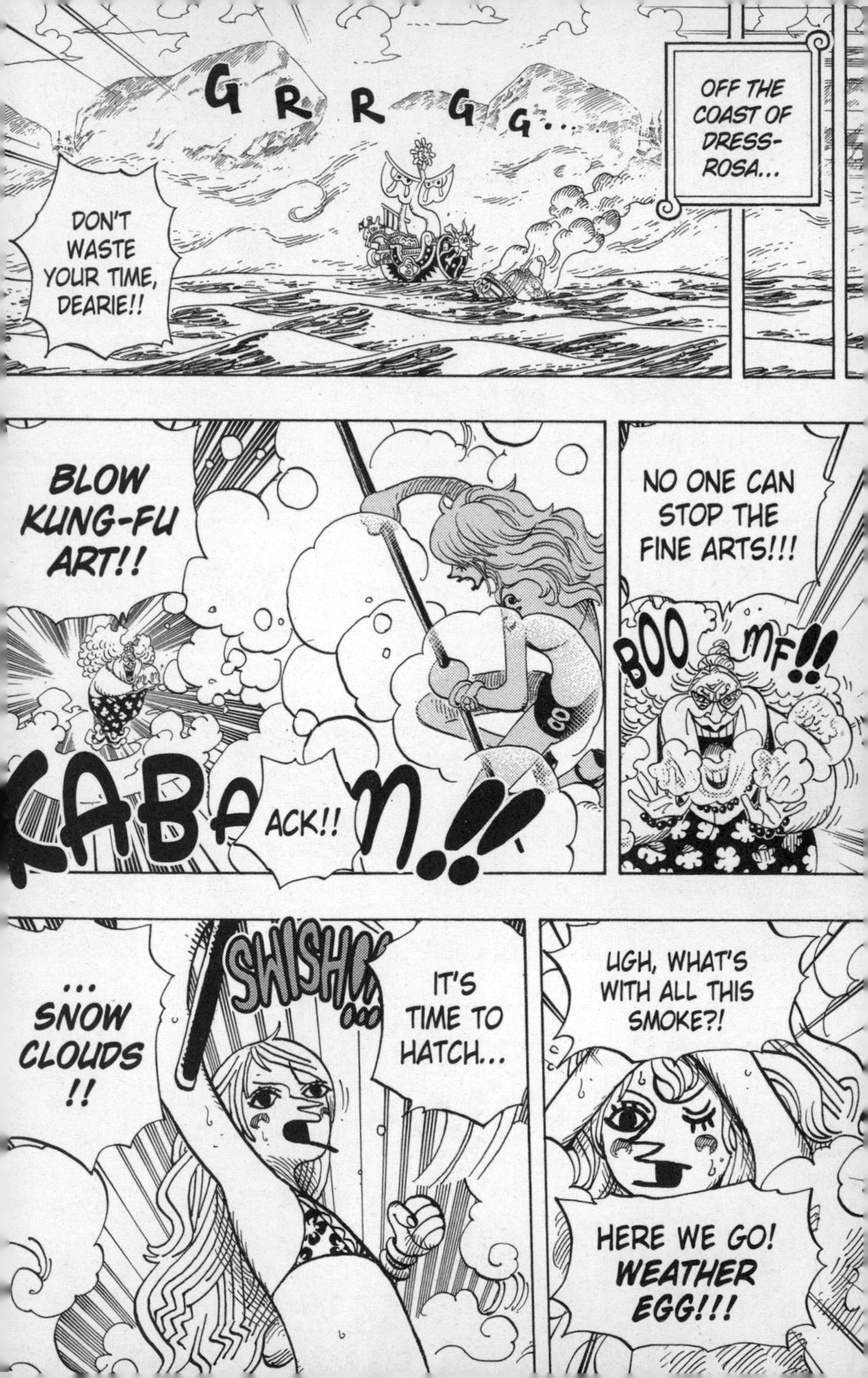
OFF THE COAST OF DRESS-ROSA...
GRRRGG...
DON'T WASTE YOUR TIME, DEARIE!!
NO ONE CAN STOP THE FINE ARTS!!!
BOOMF!!
BLOW KUNG-FU ART!!
ACK!!
KABA N!!
UGH, WHAT'S WITH ALL THIS SMOKE?!
HERE WE GO! WEATHER EGG!!!
IT'S TIME TO HATCH...
SWISH
... SNOW CLOUDS !!

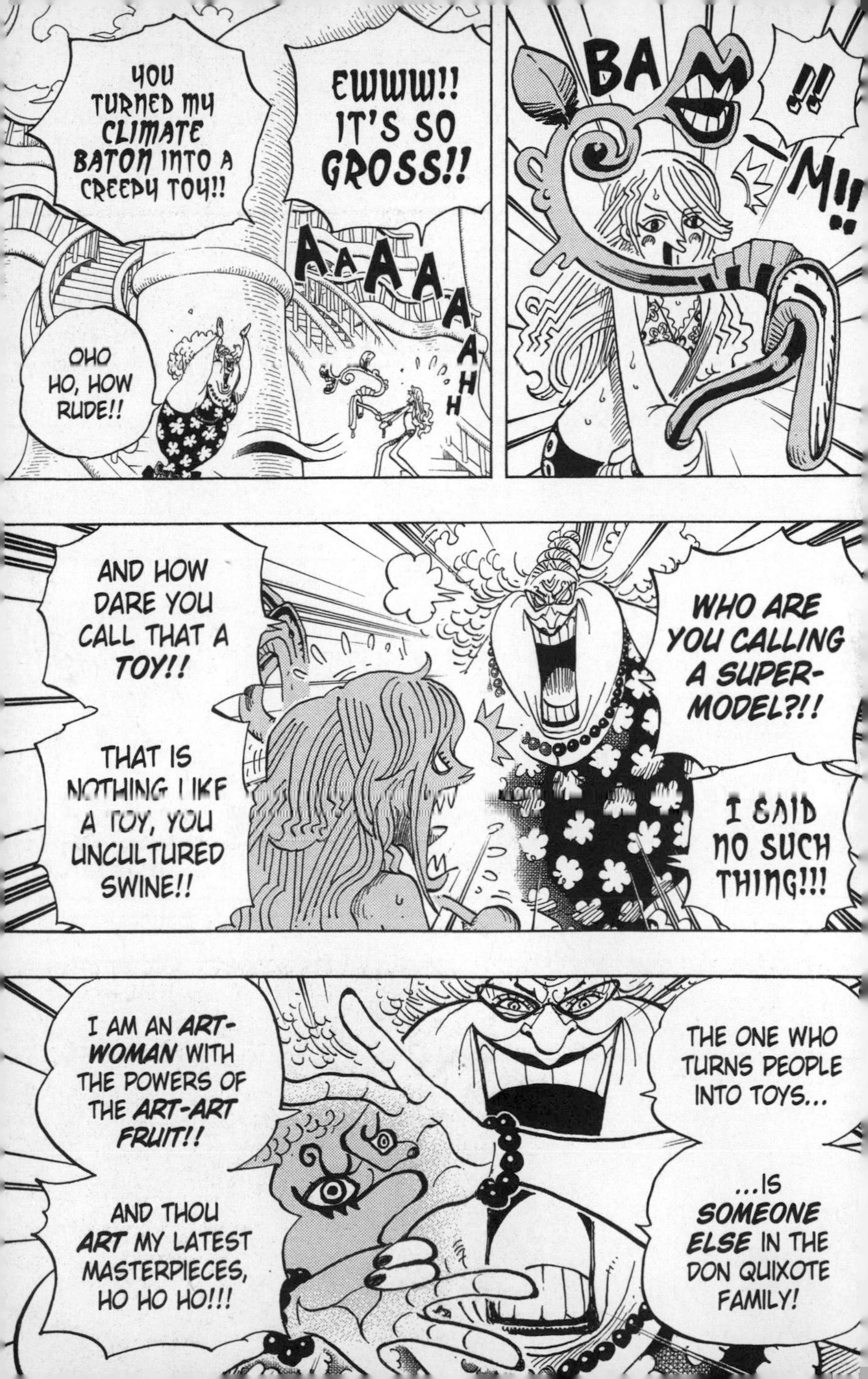
BAM M!!
EWWW!! IT'S SO GROSS!!
AAAAAAAAH
YOU TURNED MY CLIMATE BATON INTO A CREEPY TOY!!
OHO HO, HOW RUDE!!
WHO ARE YOU CALLING A SUPER-MODEL?!!
I SAID NO SUCH THING!!!
AND HOW DARE YOU CALL THAT A TOY!!
THAT IS NOTHING LIKE A TOY, YOU UNCULTURED SWINE!!
THE ONE WHO TURNS PEOPLE INTO TOYS...
...IS SOMEONE ELSE IN THE DON QUIXOTE FAMILY!
I AM AN ART-WOMAN WITH THE POWERS OF THE ART-ART FRUIT!!
AND THOU ART MY LATEST MASTERPIECES, HO HO HO!!!

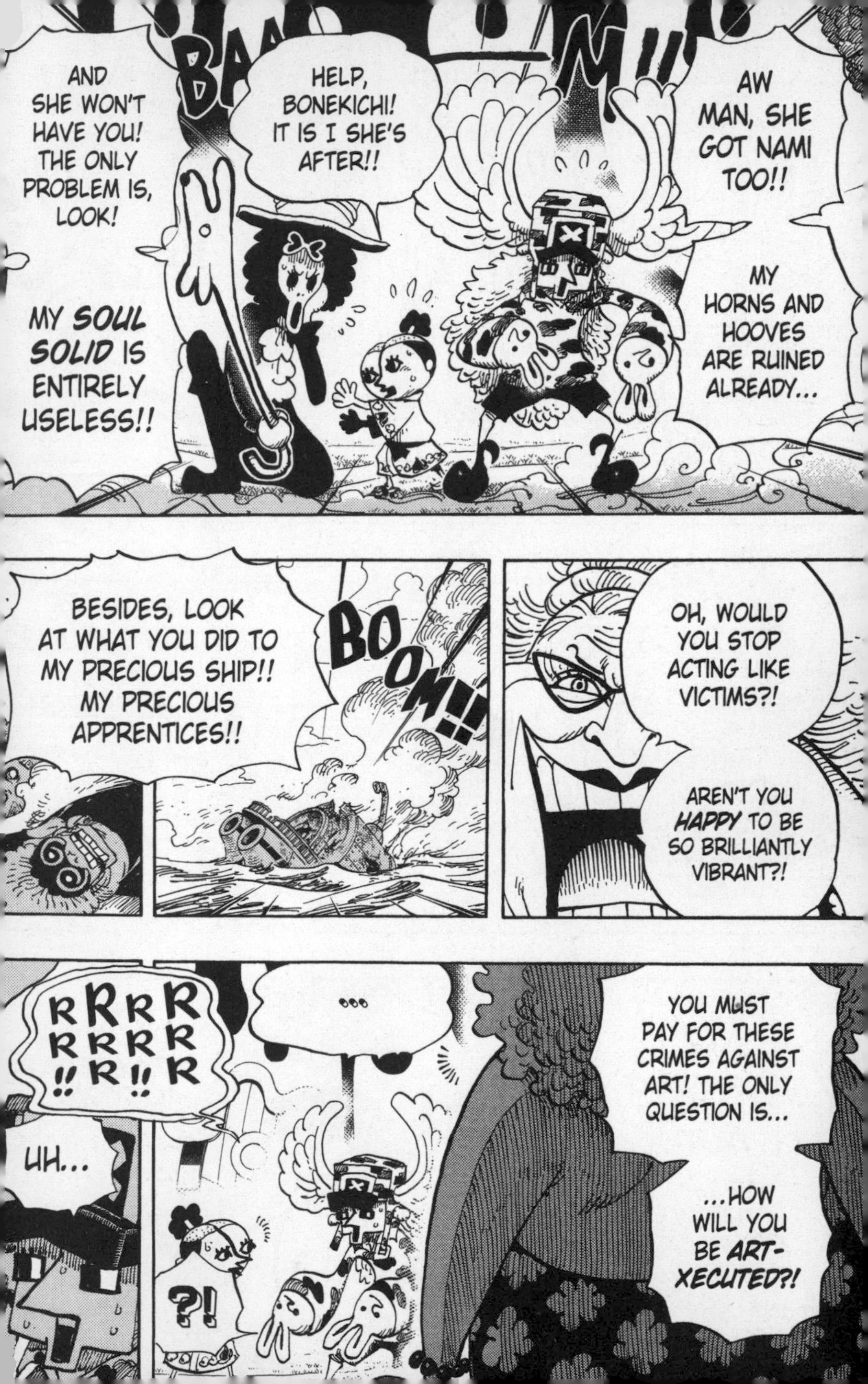
AW MAN, SHE GOT NAMI TOO!!
MY HORNS AND HOOVES ARE RUINED ALREADY...
HELP, BONEKICHI! IT IS I SHE'S AFTER!!
AND SHE WON'T HAVE YOU! THE ONLY PROBLEM IS, LOOK!
MY **SOUL SOLID** IS ENTIRELY USELESS!!
OH, WOULD YOU STOP ACTING LIKE VICTIMS?!
AREN'T YOU *HAPPY* TO BE SO BRILLIANTLY VIBRANT?!
BOOM!!
BESIDES, LOOK AT WHAT YOU DID TO MY PRECIOUS SHIP!! MY PRECIOUS APPRENTICES!!
YOU MUST PAY FOR THESE CRIMES AGAINST ART! THE ONLY QUESTION IS...
...HOW WILL YOU BE ***ART-XECUTED?!***
...
?!
RRRRRRRRRRR!! !!
UH...

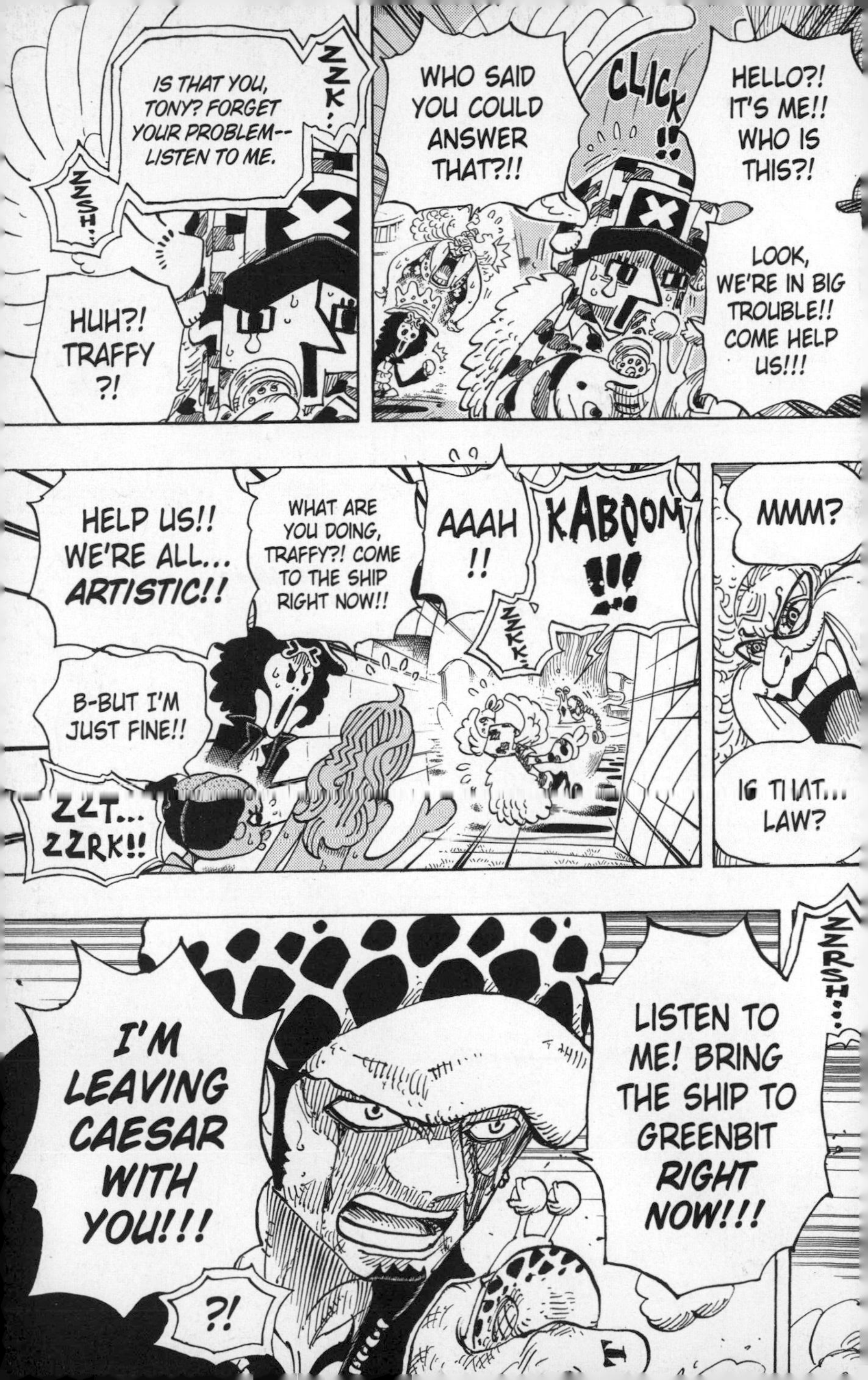
CLICK!!
HELLO?! IT'S ME!! WHO IS THIS?!
WHO SAID YOU COULD ANSWER THAT?!!
LOOK, WE'RE IN BIG TROUBLE!! COME HELP US!!!
ZZK...
IS THAT YOU, TONY? FORGET YOUR PROBLEM-- LISTEN TO ME.
ZZSH...
HUH?! TRAFFY?!
MMM?
IS THAT... LAW?
KABOOM!!!
AAAH!!
ZZKK...
WHAT ARE YOU DOING, TRAFFY?! COME TO THE SHIP RIGHT NOW!!
HELP US!! WE'RE ALL... ARTISTIC!!
B-BUT I'M JUST FINE!!
ZZT... ZZRK!!
ZZRSH...
LISTEN TO ME! BRING THE SHIP TO GREENBIT RIGHT NOW!!!
I'M LEAVING CAESAR WITH YOU!!!
?!

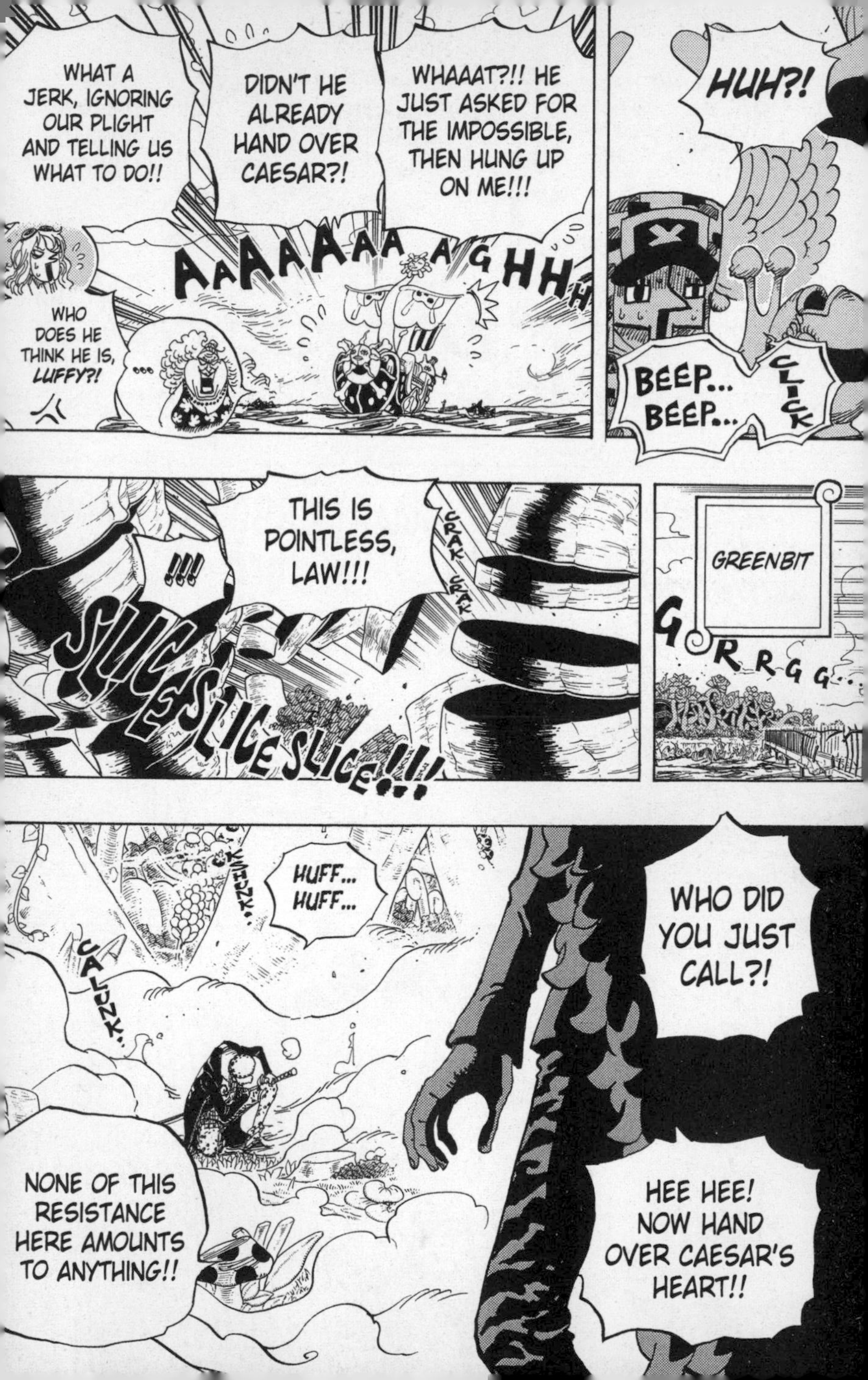
HUH?!
BEEP... BEEP...
CLICK
WHAAAT?!! HE JUST ASKED FOR THE IMPOSSIBLE, THEN HUNG UP ON ME!!!
DIDN'T HE ALREADY HAND OVER CAESAR?!
WHAT A JERK, IGNORING OUR PLIGHT AND TELLING US WHAT TO DO!!
AAAAAAA AGHHH
WHO DOES HE THINK HE IS, *LUFFY?!*
...
GREENBIT
GRRRGG...
CRAK CRAK
THIS IS POINTLESS, LAW!!!
!!!
SLICE SLICE SLICE SLICE!!!
WHO DID YOU JUST CALL?!
HEE HEE! NOW HAND OVER CAESAR'S HEART!!
HUFF... HUFF...
SHUNK
CALUNK
NONE OF THIS RESISTANCE HERE AMOUNTS TO ANYTHING!!

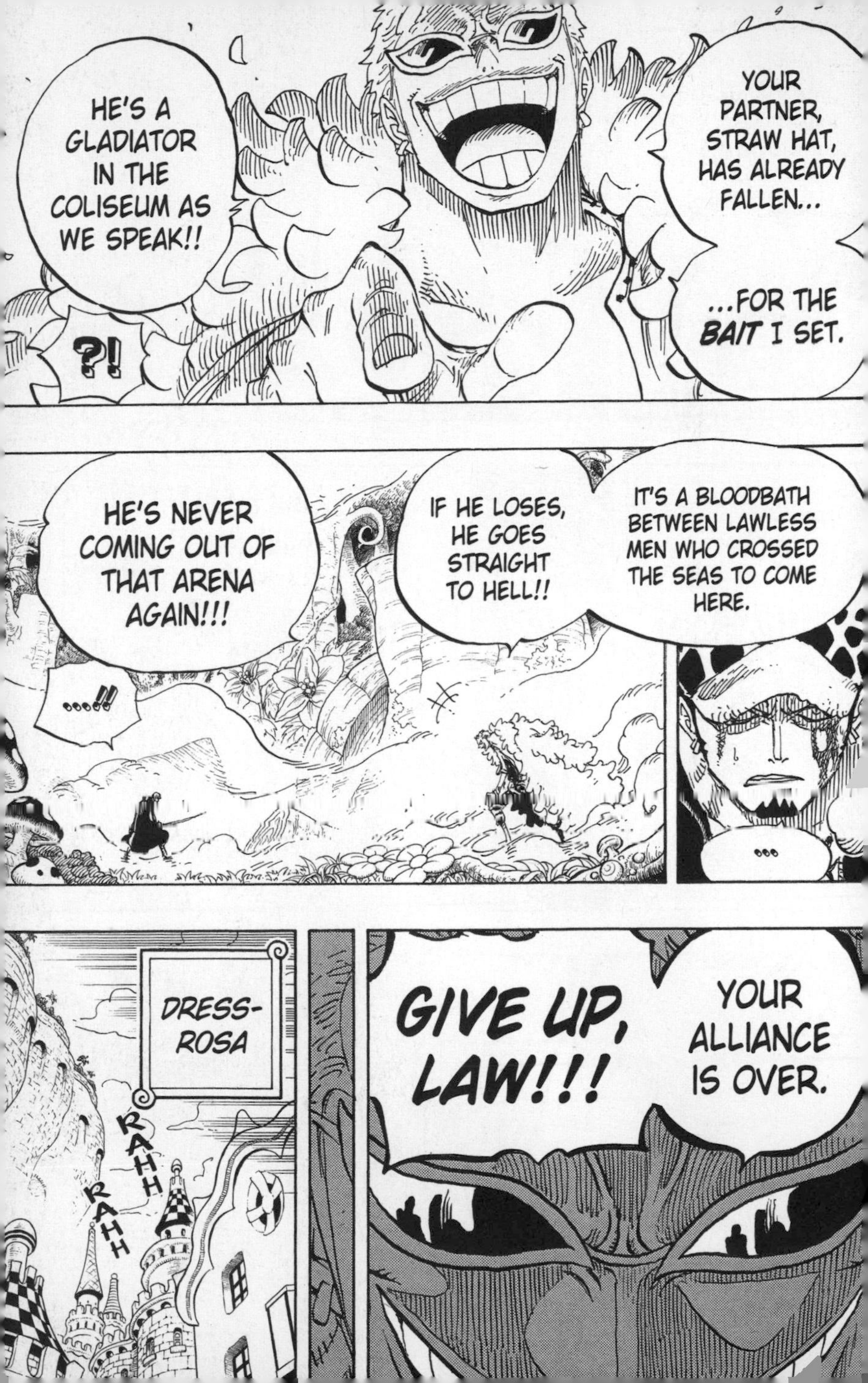
YOUR PARTNER, STRAW HAT, HAS ALREADY FALLEN...
...FOR THE *BAIT* I SET.
HE'S A GLADIATOR IN THE COLISEUM AS WE SPEAK!!
?!
IT'S A BLOODBATH BETWEEN LAWLESS MEN WHO CROSSED THE SEAS TO COME HERE.
IF HE LOSES, HE GOES STRAIGHT TO HELL!!
HE'S NEVER COMING OUT OF THAT ARENA AGAIN!!!
...!!
...
YOUR ALLIANCE IS OVER.
GIVE UP, LAW!!!
DRESS-ROSA
RAHH
RAHH

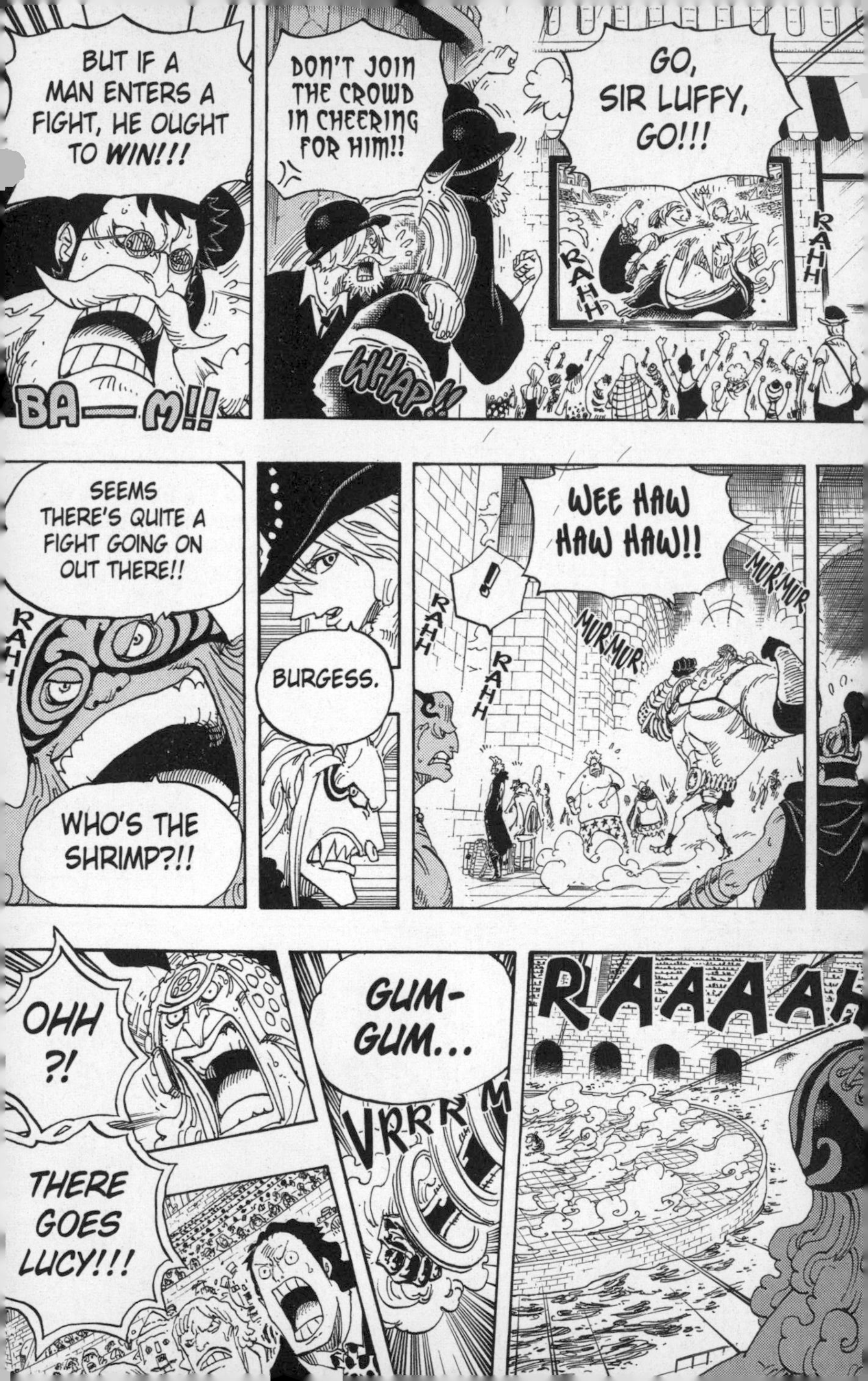
GO, SIR LUFFY, GO!!!
RAHH
RAHH
DON'T JOIN THE CROWD IN CHEERING FOR HIM!!
WHAP!!
BUT IF A MAN ENTERS A FIGHT, HE OUGHT TO WIN!!!
BA—M!!
WEE HAW HAW HAW!!
!
MUR MUR
MUR MUR
RAHH
RAHH
BURGESS.
SEEMS THERE'S QUITE A FIGHT GOING ON OUT THERE!!
RAHH
WHO'S THE SHRIMP?!!
RAAAAH
GUM-GUM...
VRRRRM
OHH ?!
THERE GOES LUCY!!!

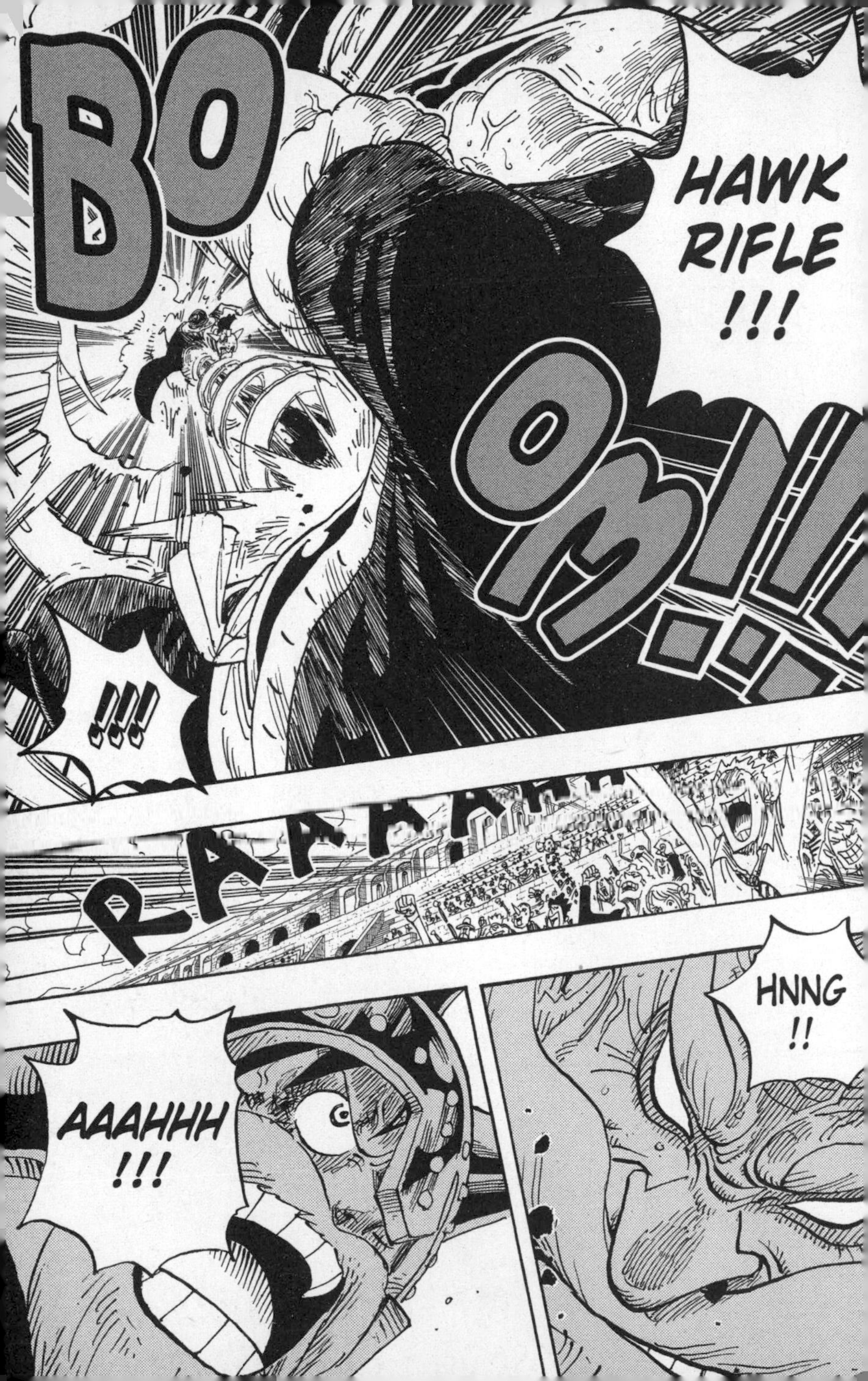
HAWK RIFLE!!!
BOOM!!
!!!
RAAAAH
HNNG!!
AAAHHH!!!

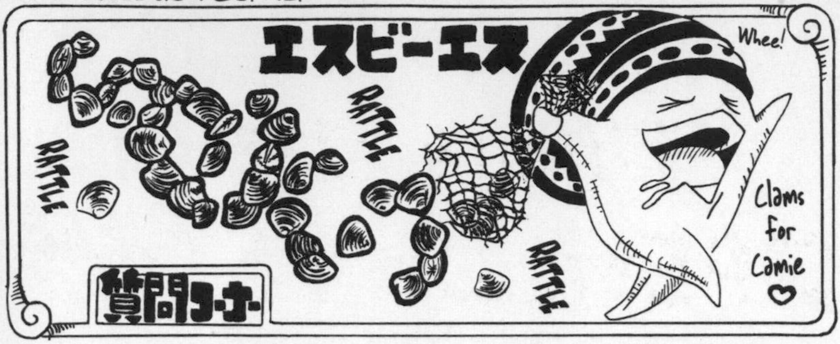
エスビーエス
RATTLE
RATTLE
RATTLE
Whee!
Clams for Camie ♡
質問コーナー

(Michi Nakahara, Tottori)

Q: Hello, Mr. Oda! I noticed that Dressrosa was based on our home of Spain, so I decided to send you this letter as the speaker for our group. Why did you choose Spain? If you ever have reason to visit Spain, I hope you will attend Barcelona's Salon Del Manga (a Spanish manga/anime convention). Nothing to be afraid of! Our women won't stab you!

--Voice of the Pirate King

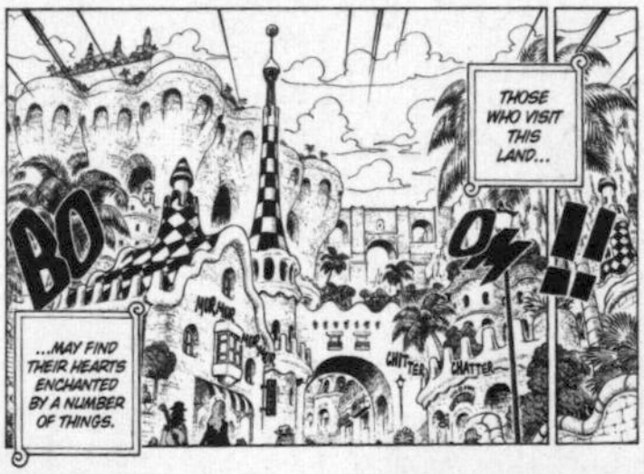
THOSE WHO VISIT THIS LAND...
BO
OM!!
...MAY FIND THEIR HEARTS ENCHANTED BY A NUMBER OF THINGS.
MURMUR
CHITTER
CHATTER

A: This is a condensed version of a letter I received from Spain. The Japanese was strange in a few places, so I think that must have come from one of those auto-translation sites. Thanks for the letter. You're right about Dressrosa. It's based on Spain, and ancient Greece for the coliseum parts. When I took a close look at Doflamingo and tried to think of what kind of country suited him, I arrived at the conclusion of Spain. I've mentioned lands of One Piece being inspired by real countries in the SBS before, but this is the first time I've gotten feedback from residents of that country. I can't be irresponsible in the way I draw, but if you do see anything that seems like a half-baked version of your culture or buildings, please forgive me. Remember, it's just a manga.

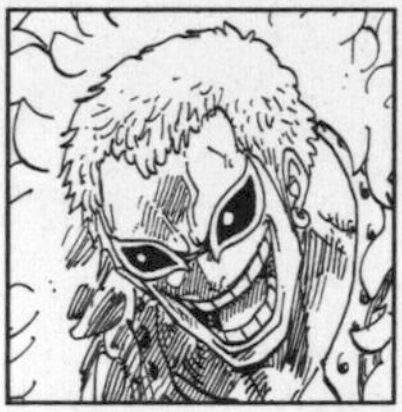

Q: I've been wondering for ages--would you draw gender-swapped versions of the Worst Generation for us? In fact, please do!!!

--Momokichi

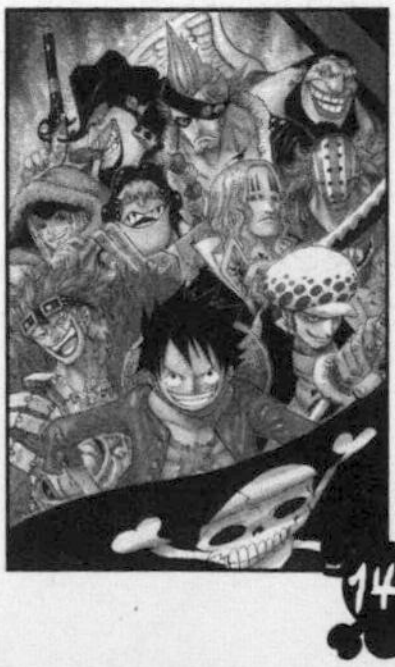

A: I got so many requests for this. I mean, I'll do it, but it's creepy, okay? Check it out on page 166. I haven't shown Blackbeard since the time skip yet, so he's not included. That's all for this SBS. See you next volume!!

Chapter 719:

OPEN, CHIN JAO

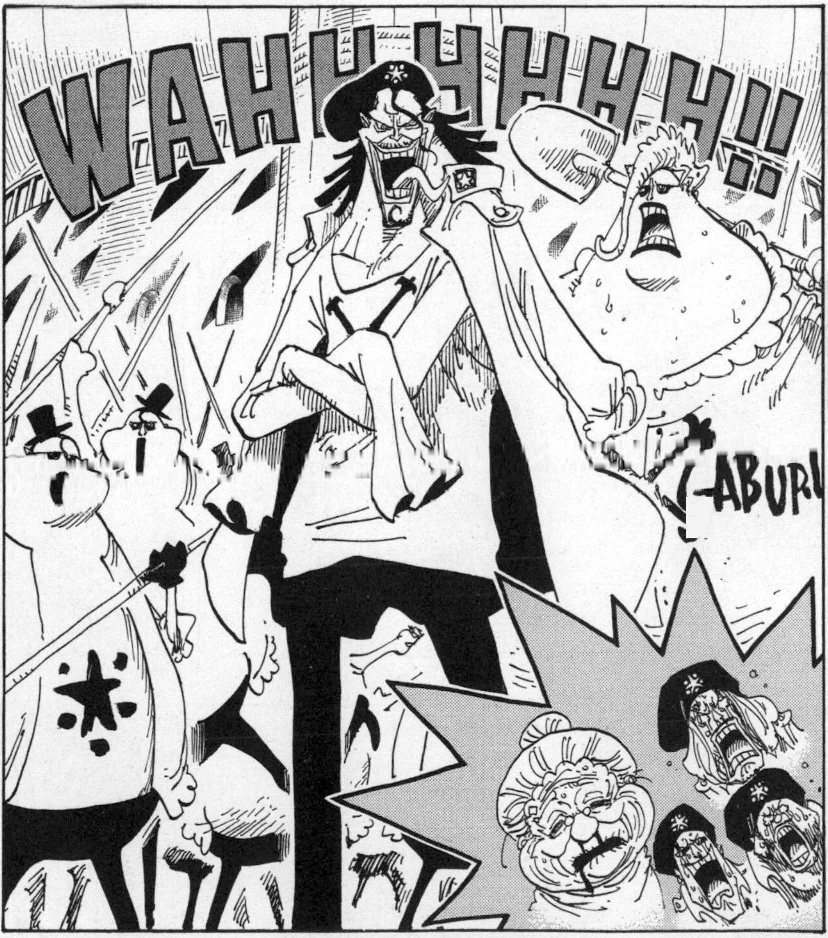
WAHHHHHHH!!
GABURU

CARIBOU'S NEW WORLD KEE HEE HEE, VOL. 36:
"CAPTAIN GABURU IS ALIVE AND ON THE SCENE!!!"

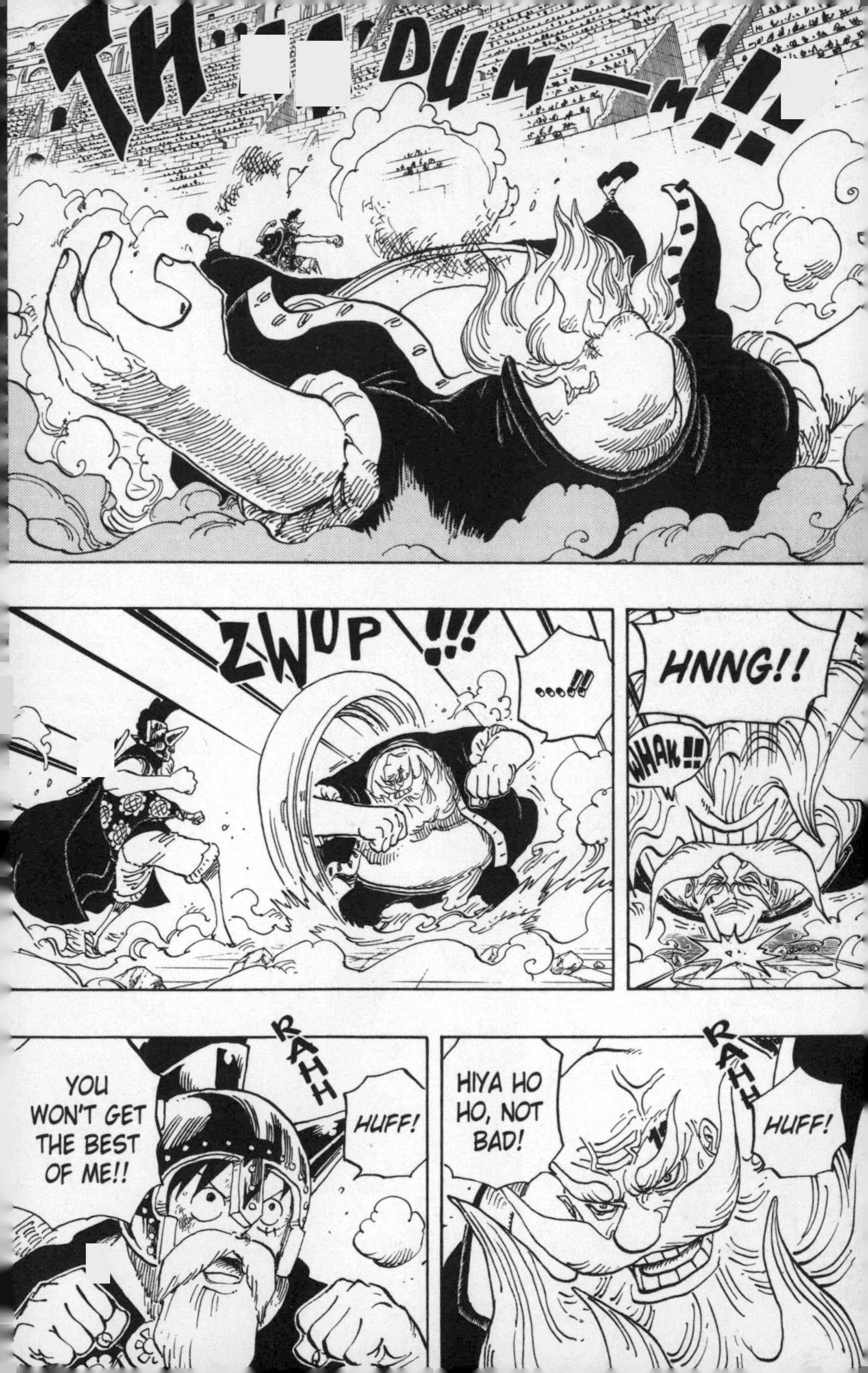
TH
DUM—!!
HNNG!!
WHAK!!
ZWOP!!!
...!!
HIYA HO HO, NOT BAD!
RAHH
HUFF!
RAHH
HUFF!
YOU WON'T GET THE BEST OF ME!!

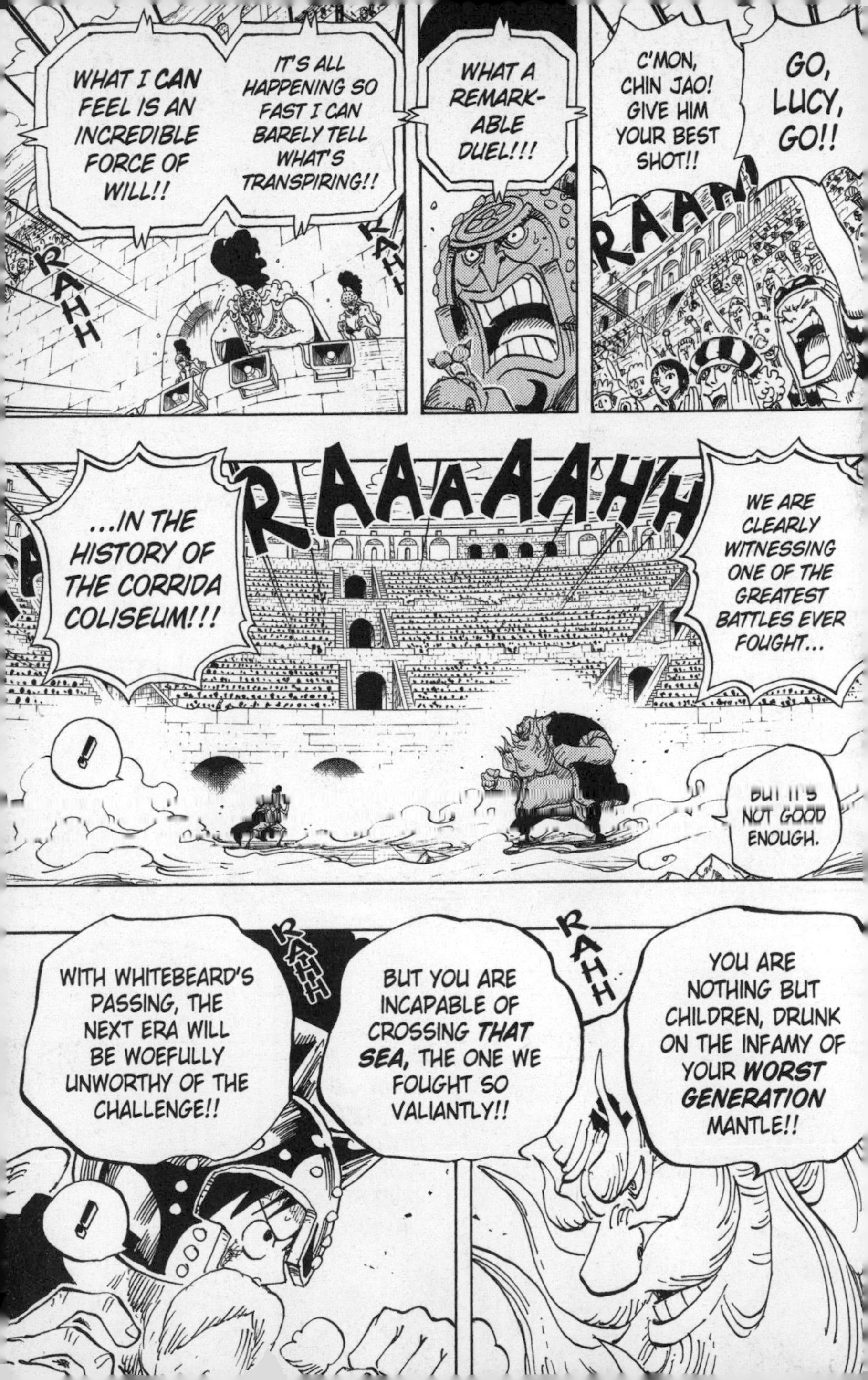
GO, LUCY, GO!!
C'MON, CHIN JAO! GIVE HIM YOUR BEST SHOT!!
RAAAH
WHAT A REMARKABLE DUEL!!!
RAHH
IT'S ALL HAPPENING SO FAST I CAN BARELY TELL WHAT'S TRANSPIRING!!
WHAT I CAN FEEL IS AN INCREDIBLE FORCE OF WILL!!
RAHH
WE ARE CLEARLY WITNESSING ONE OF THE GREATEST BATTLES EVER FOUGHT...
RAAAAAAHH
...IN THE HISTORY OF THE CORRIDA COLISEUM!!!
BUT IT'S NOT GOOD ENOUGH.
!
YOU ARE NOTHING BUT CHILDREN, DRUNK ON THE INFAMY OF YOUR WORST GENERATION MANTLE!!
RAHH
BUT YOU ARE INCAPABLE OF CROSSING THAT SEA, THE ONE WE FOUGHT SO VALIANTLY!!
RAHH
WITH WHITEBEARD'S PASSING, THE NEXT ERA WILL BE WOEFULLY UNWORTHY OF THE CHALLENGE!!
!

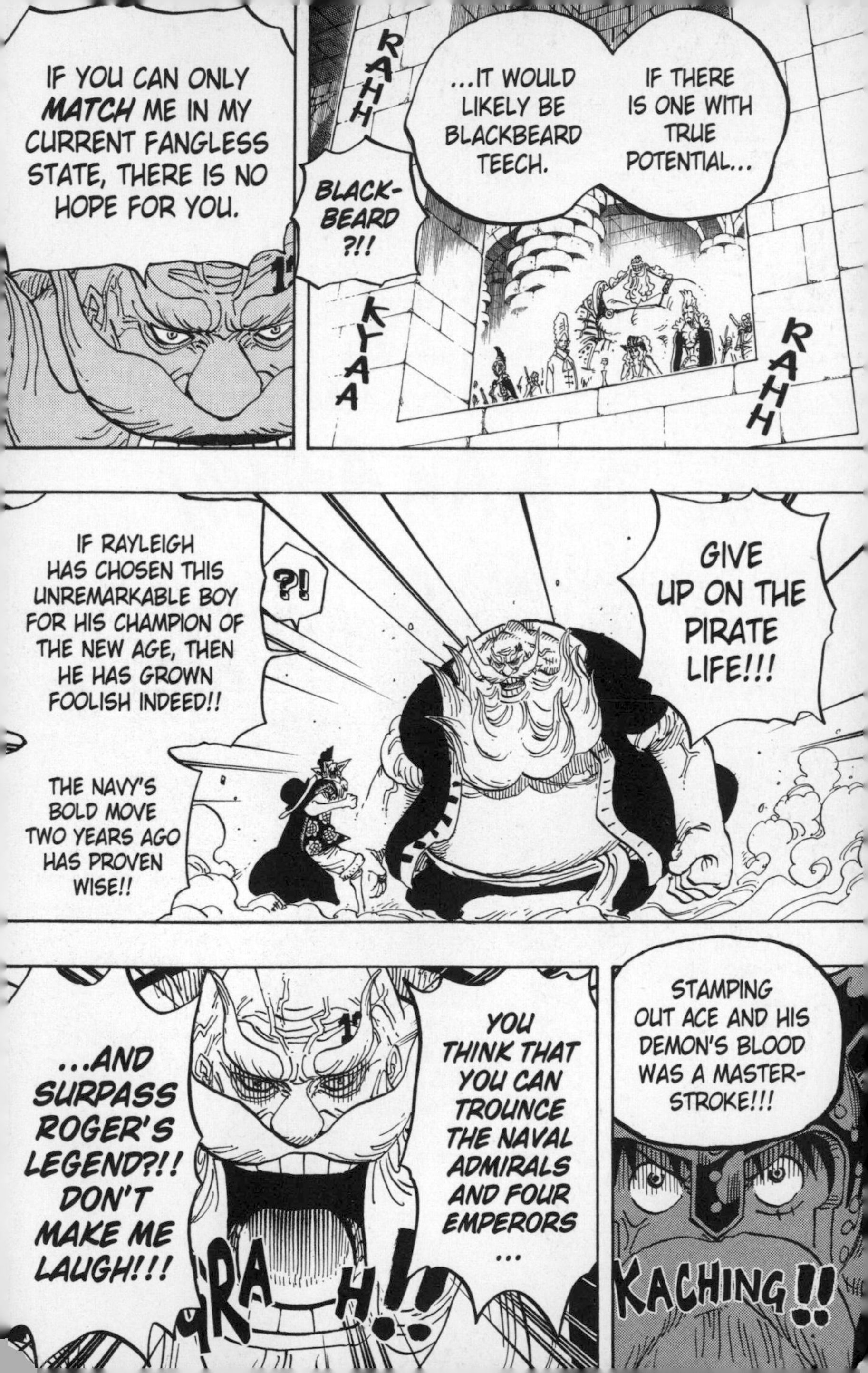

IF THERE IS ONE WITH TRUE POTENTIAL...
...IT WOULD LIKELY BE BLACKBEARD TEECH.
RAHH
BLACK-BEARD ?!!
KYAA
RAHH
IF YOU CAN ONLY MATCH ME IN MY CURRENT FANGLESS STATE, THERE IS NO HOPE FOR YOU.
GIVE UP ON THE PIRATE LIFE!!!
?!
IF RAYLEIGH HAS CHOSEN THIS UNREMARKABLE BOY FOR HIS CHAMPION OF THE NEW AGE, THEN HE HAS GROWN FOOLISH INDEED!!
THE NAVY'S BOLD MOVE TWO YEARS AGO HAS PROVEN WISE!!
STAMPING OUT ACE AND HIS DEMON'S BLOOD WAS A MASTER-STROKE!!!
KACHING!!
YOU THINK THAT YOU CAN TROUNCE THE NAVAL ADMIRALS AND FOUR EMPERORS ...
...AND SURPASS ROGER'S LEGEND?!! DON'T MAKE ME LAUGH!!!
RAH!!

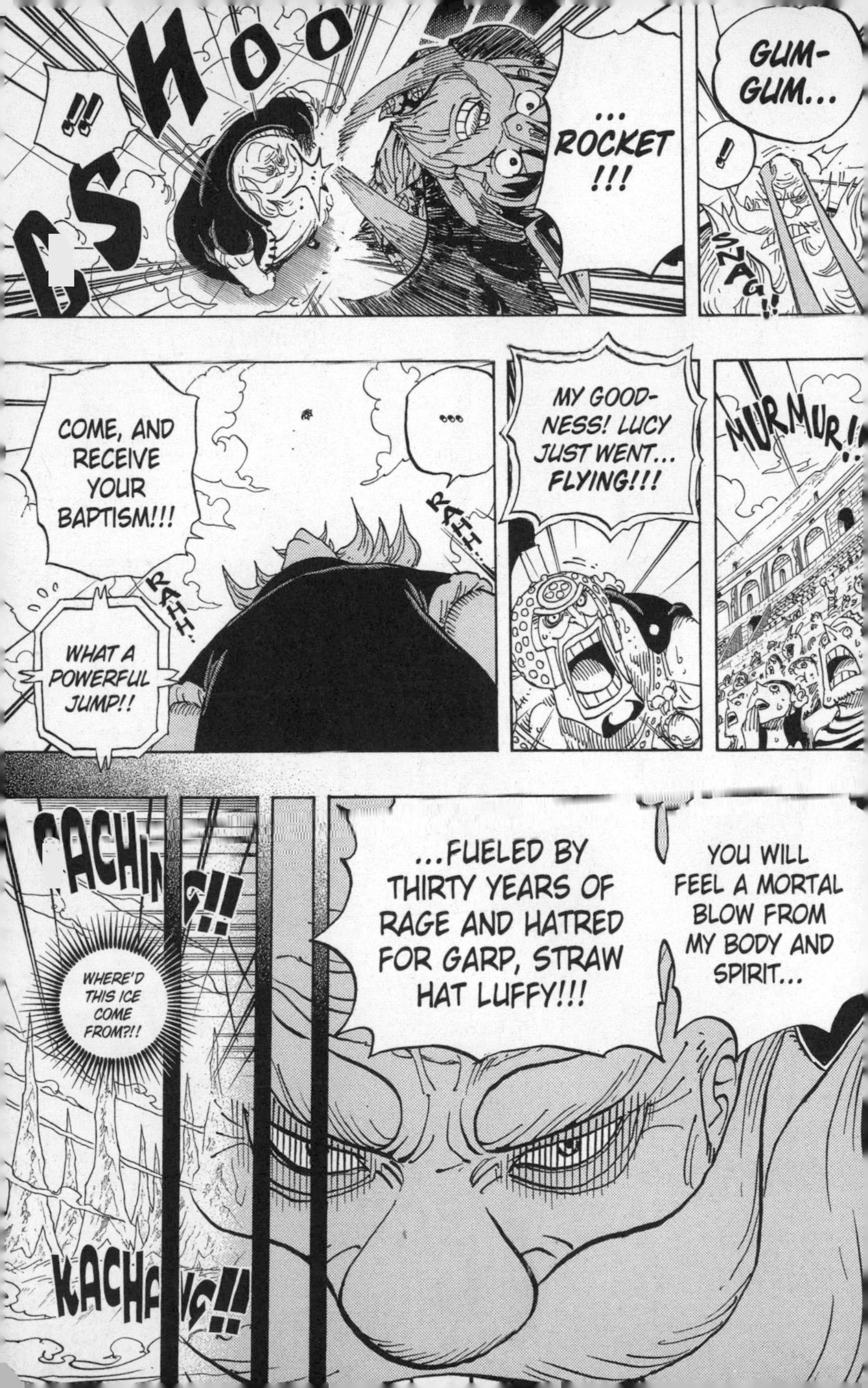
GUM-GUM...
!
SNAG!!
...ROCKET!!!
!!
SHOO
MURMUR!!
MY GOODNESS! LUCY JUST WENT... FLYING!!!
...
RAHH...
COME, AND RECEIVE YOUR BAPTISM!!!
RAHH...
WHAT A POWERFUL JUMP!!
YOU WILL FEEL A MORTAL BLOW FROM MY BODY AND SPIRIT...
...FUELED BY THIRTY YEARS OF RAGE AND HATRED FOR GARP, STRAW HAT LUFFY!!!
ACHING!!
WHERE'D THIS ICE COME FROM?!!
KACHANG!!

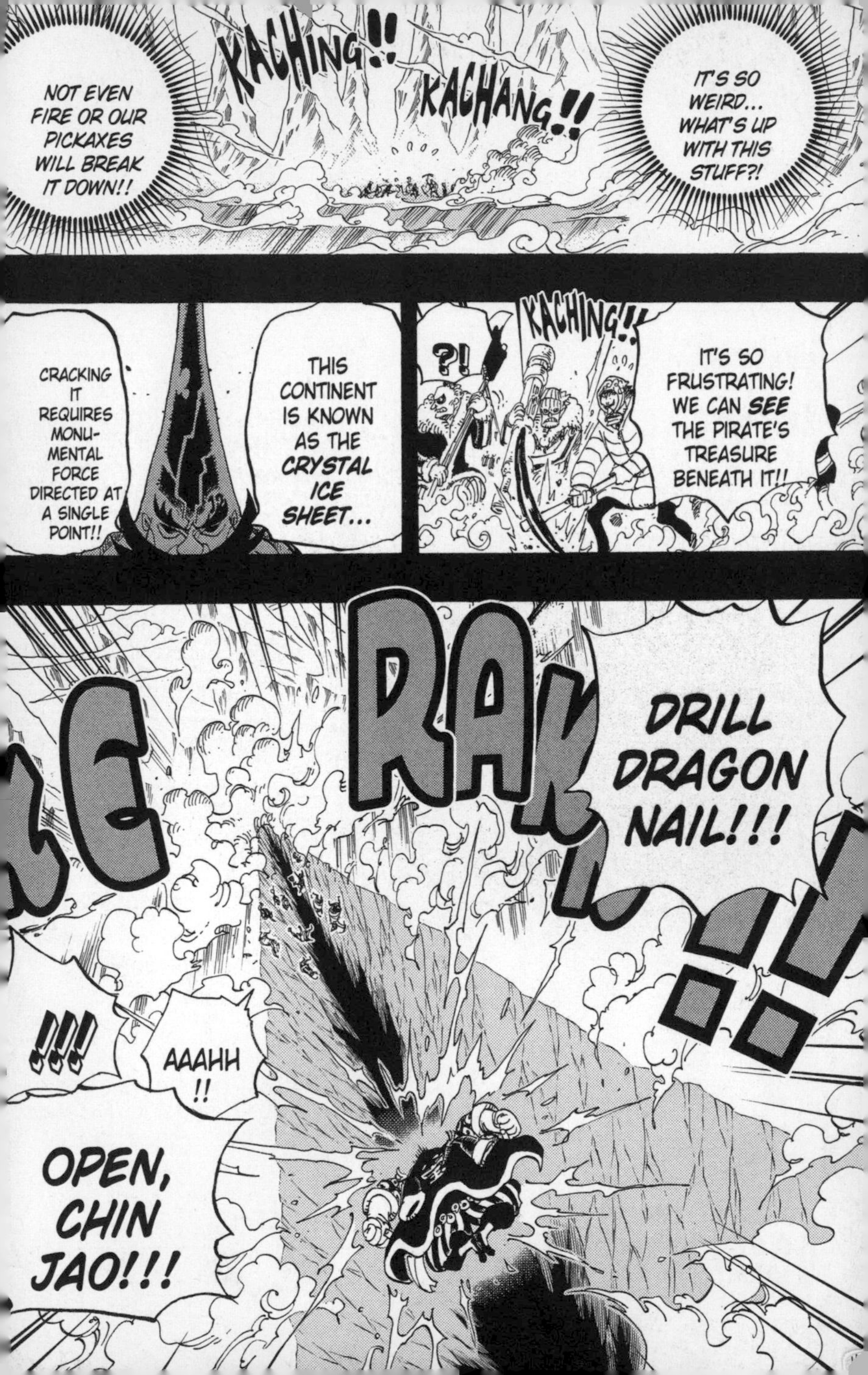
IT'S SO WEIRD... WHAT'S UP WITH THIS STUFF?!
KACHANG!!
KACHING!!
NOT EVEN FIRE OR OUR PICKAXES WILL BREAK IT DOWN!!
KACHING!!
IT'S SO FRUSTRATING! WE CAN **SEE** THE PIRATE'S TREASURE BENEATH IT!!
?!
THIS CONTINENT IS KNOWN AS THE **CRYSTAL ICE SHEET...**
CRACKING IT REQUIRES MONU-MENTAL FORCE DIRECTED AT A SINGLE POINT!!
DRILL DRAGON NAIL!!!
!!
AAAHH!!
!!!
OPEN, CHIN JAO!!!

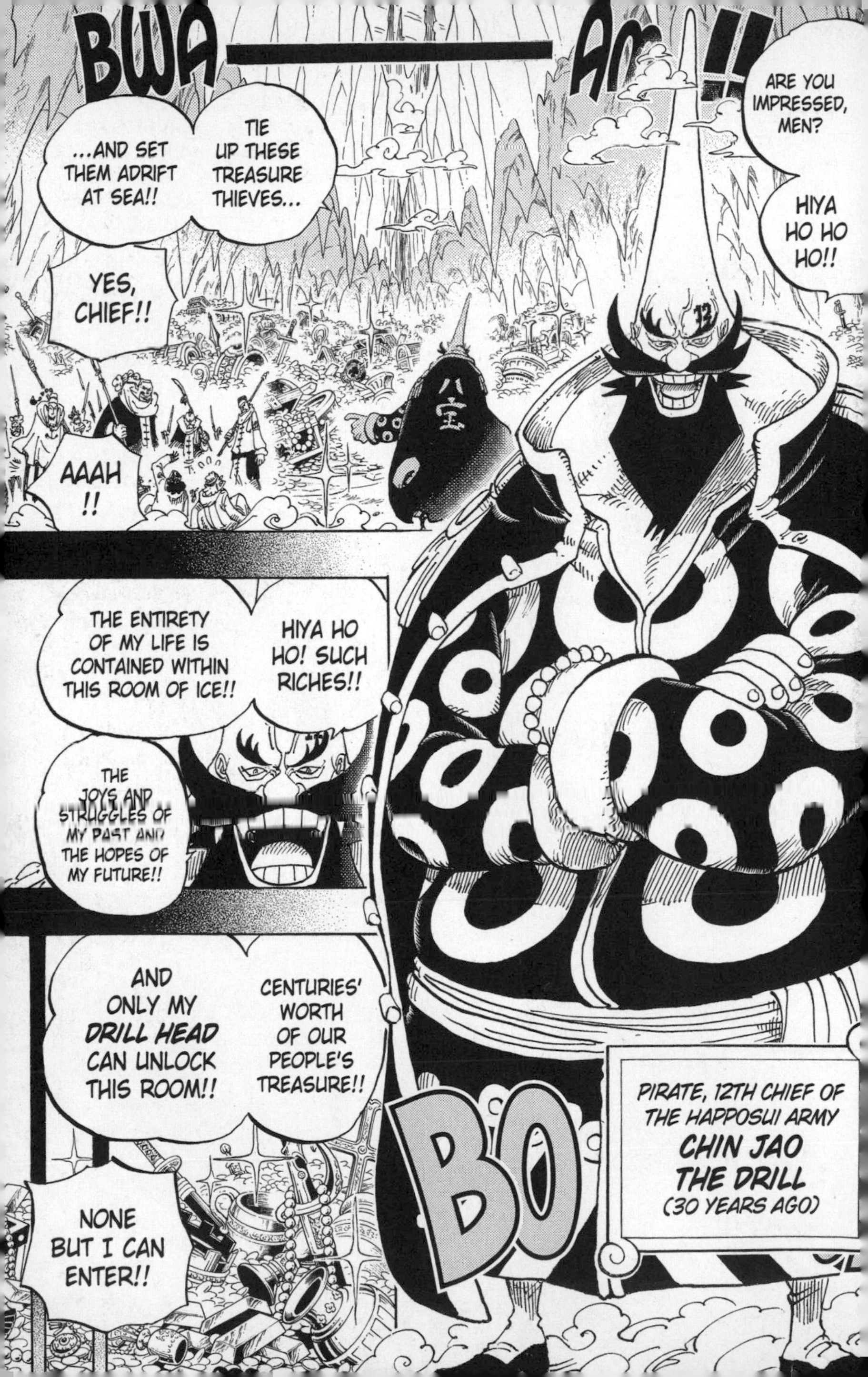
BWA—AM!!
ARE YOU IMPRESSED, MEN?
HIYA HO HO HO!!
TIE UP THESE TREASURE THIEVES...
...AND SET THEM ADRIFT AT SEA!!
YES, CHIEF!!
AAAH!!
PIRATE, 12TH CHIEF OF THE HAPPOSUI ARMY CHIN JAO THE DRILL (30 YEARS AGO)
BO
HIYA HO HO! SUCH RICHES!!
THE ENTIRETY OF MY LIFE IS CONTAINED WITHIN THIS ROOM OF ICE!!
THE JOYS AND STRUGGLES OF MY PAST AND THE HOPES OF MY FUTURE!!
CENTURIES' WORTH OF OUR PEOPLE'S TREASURE!!
AND ONLY MY DRILL HEAD CAN UNLOCK THIS ROOM!!
NONE BUT I CAN ENTER!!

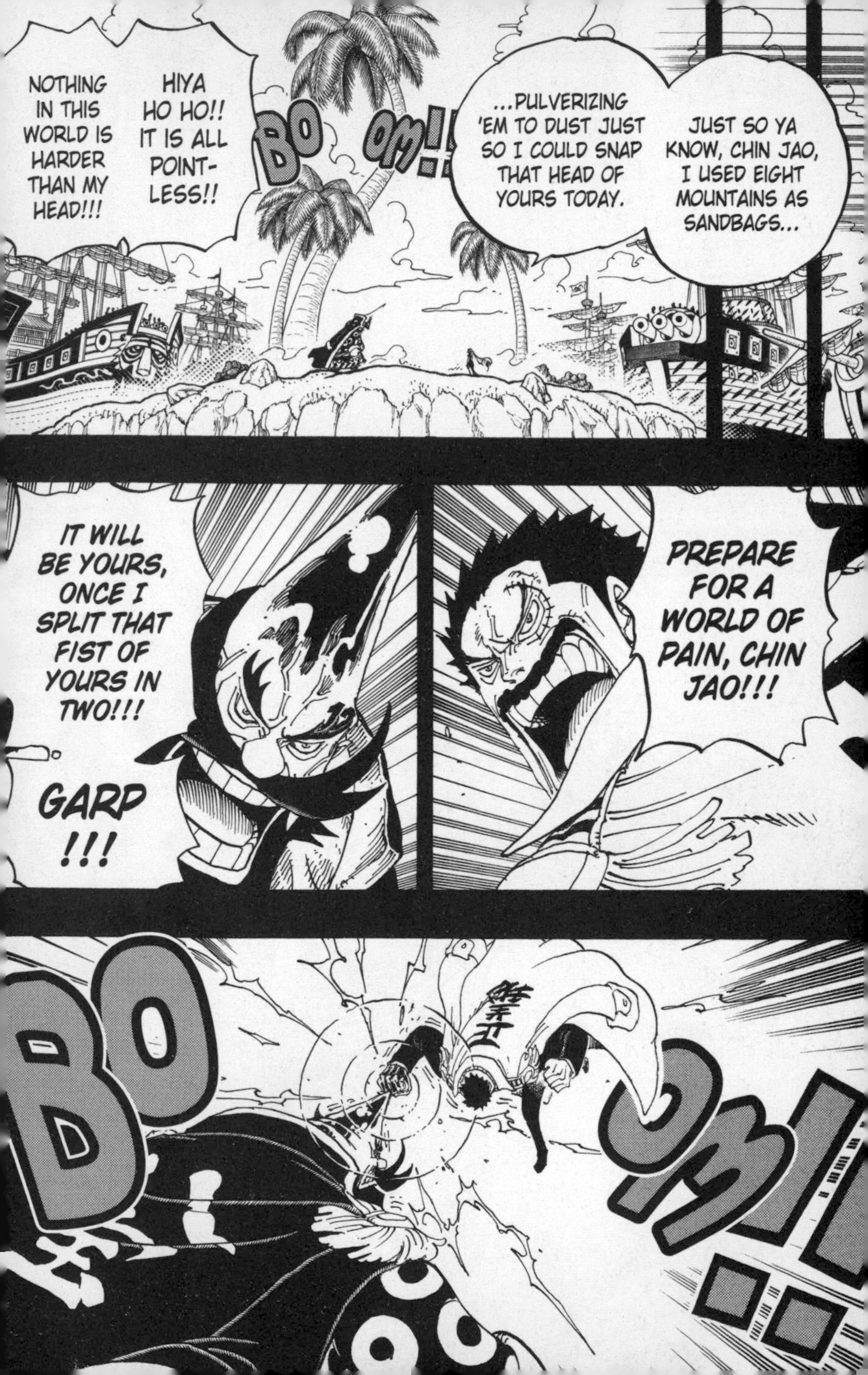
JUST SO YA KNOW, CHIN JAO, I USED EIGHT MOUNTAINS AS SANDBAGS...
...PULVERIZING 'EM TO DUST JUST SO I COULD SNAP THAT HEAD OF YOURS TODAY.
BOOM!!
HIYA HO HO!! IT IS ALL POINTLESS!!
NOTHING IN THIS WORLD IS HARDER THAN MY HEAD!!!
PREPARE FOR A WORLD OF PAIN, CHIN JAO!!!
IT WILL BE YOURS, ONCE I SPLIT THAT FIST OF YOURS IN TWO!!!
GARP!!!
BOOM!!

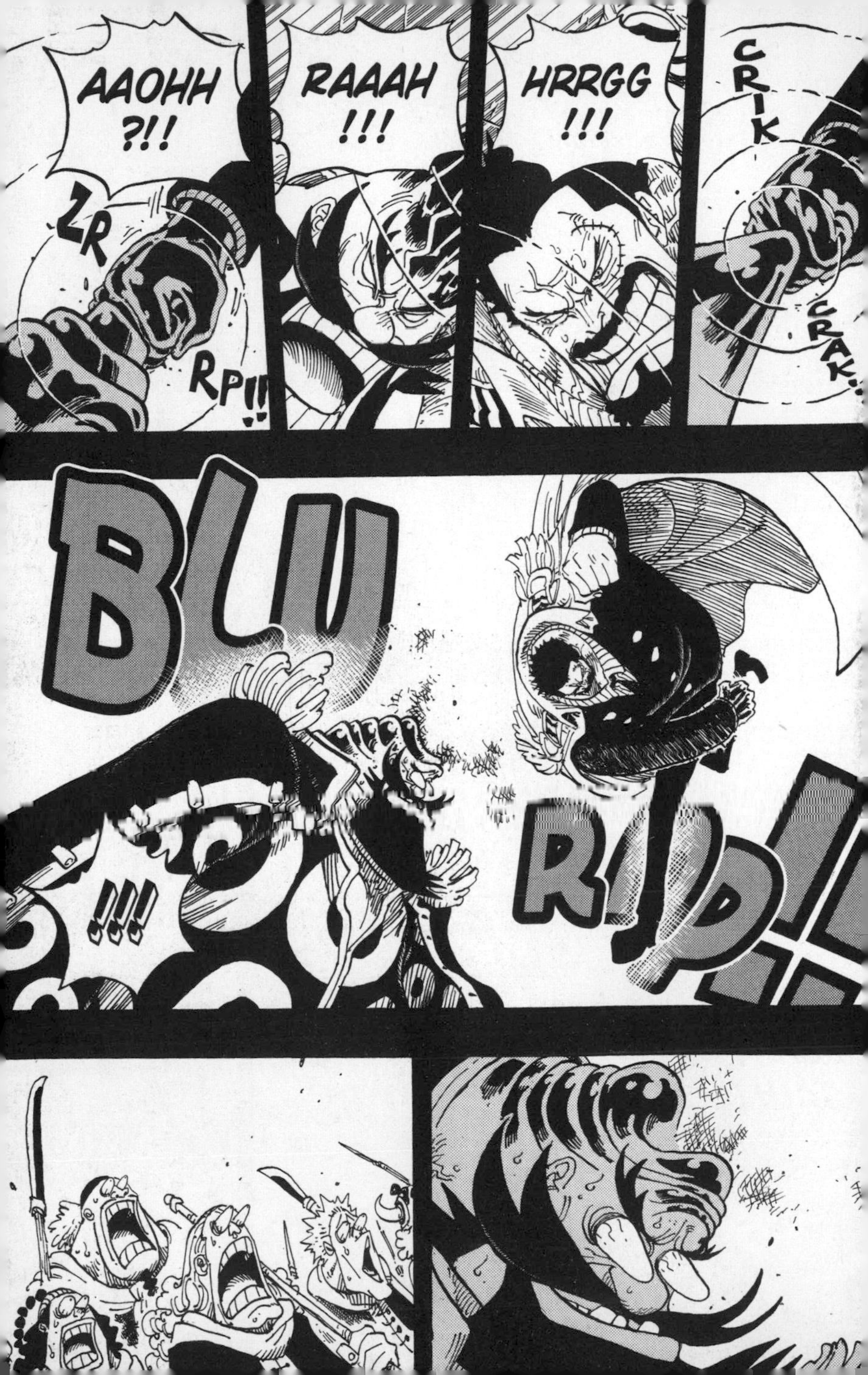
CRIK
CRAK..
HRRGG !!!
RAAAH !!!
AAOHH ?!!
ZR
RP!!
BLU
RIP!
!!!

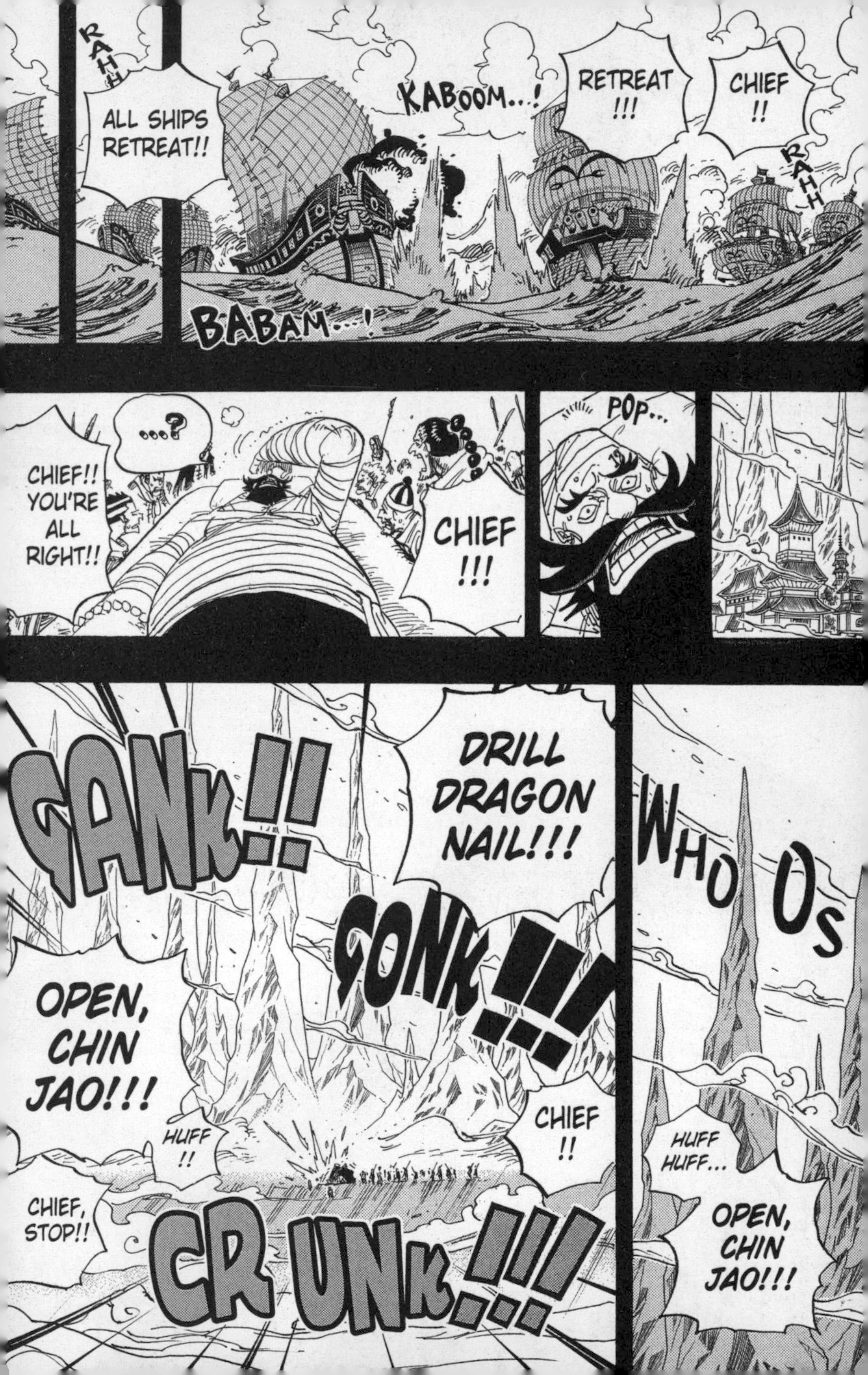
CHIEF!!
RAHH
RETREAT!!!
KABOOM...!
RAHH
ALL SHIPS RETREAT!!
BABAM...!
POP...
CHIEF!!!
...?
CHIEF!! YOU'RE ALL RIGHT!!
WHO OS
HUFF HUFF...
OPEN, CHIN JAO!!!
DRILL DRAGON NAIL!!!
GANK!!
GONK!!!
OPEN, CHIN JAO!!!
CHIEF!!
HUFF!!
CHIEF, STOP!!
CRUNK...!!!

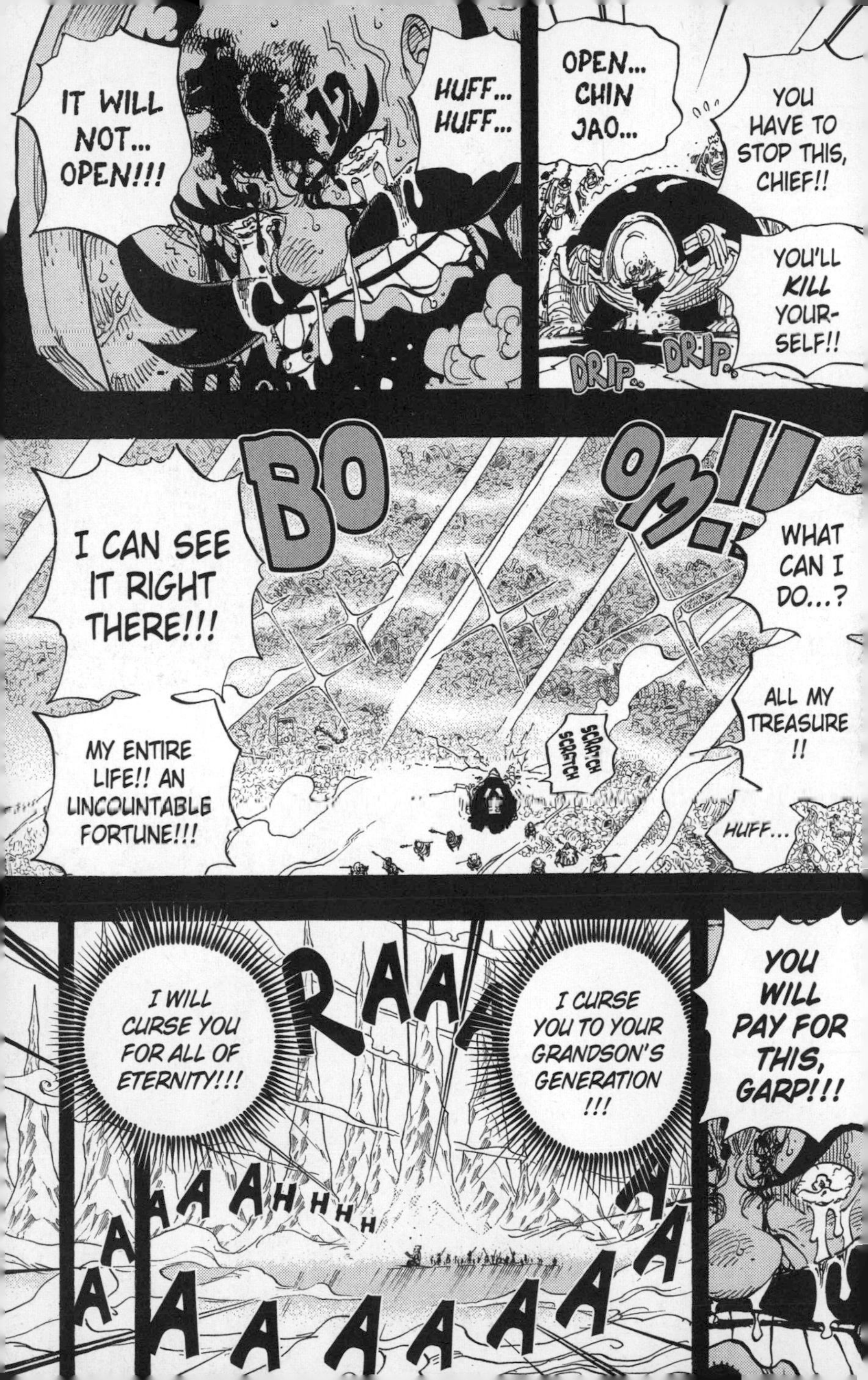
YOU HAVE TO STOP THIS, CHIEF!!
OPEN... CHIN JAO...
YOU'LL KILL YOURSELF!!
DRIP.. DRIP..
HUFF... HUFF...
IT WILL NOT... OPEN!!!
WHAT CAN I DO...?
BOOM!!
I CAN SEE IT RIGHT THERE!!!
ALL MY TREASURE !!
HUFF...
SCRATCH SCRATCH
MY ENTIRE LIFE!! AN UNCOUNTABLE FORTUNE!!!
YOU WILL PAY FOR THIS, GARP!!!
I CURSE YOU TO YOUR GRANDSON'S GENERATION !!!
RAAAAAAAAAAAAAAAAAAHHHHH
I WILL CURSE YOU FOR ALL OF ETERNITY!!!

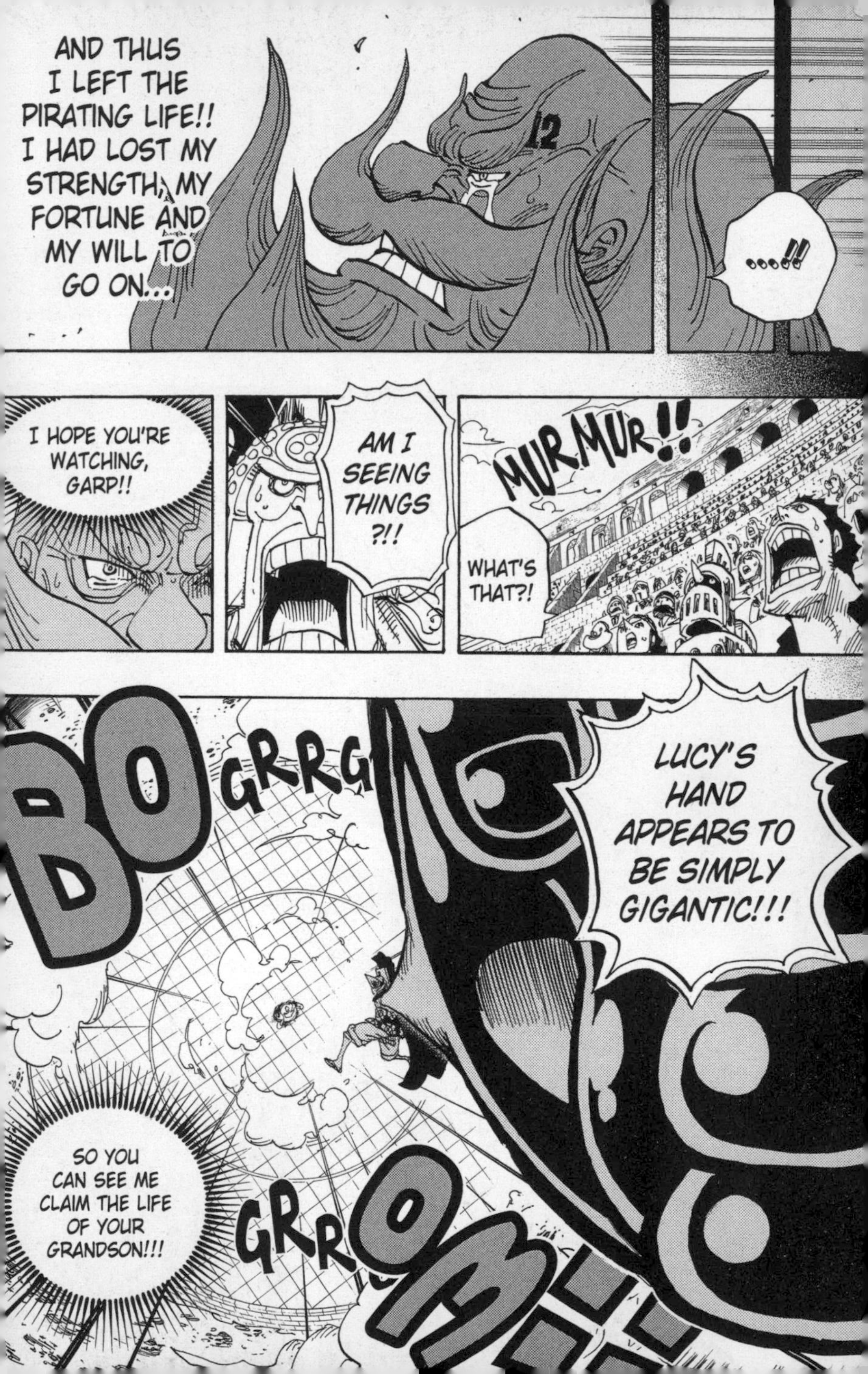
....!!
AND THUS I LEFT THE PIRATING LIFE!! I HAD LOST MY STRENGTH, MY FORTUNE AND MY WILL TO GO ON...
MURMUR!!
WHAT'S THAT?!
AM I SEEING THINGS?!!
I HOPE YOU'RE WATCHING, GARP!!
LUCY'S HAND APPEARS TO BE SIMPLY GIGANTIC!!!
BO GRRG
GRROOM
SO YOU CAN SEE ME CLAIM THE LIFE OF YOUR GRANDSON!!!

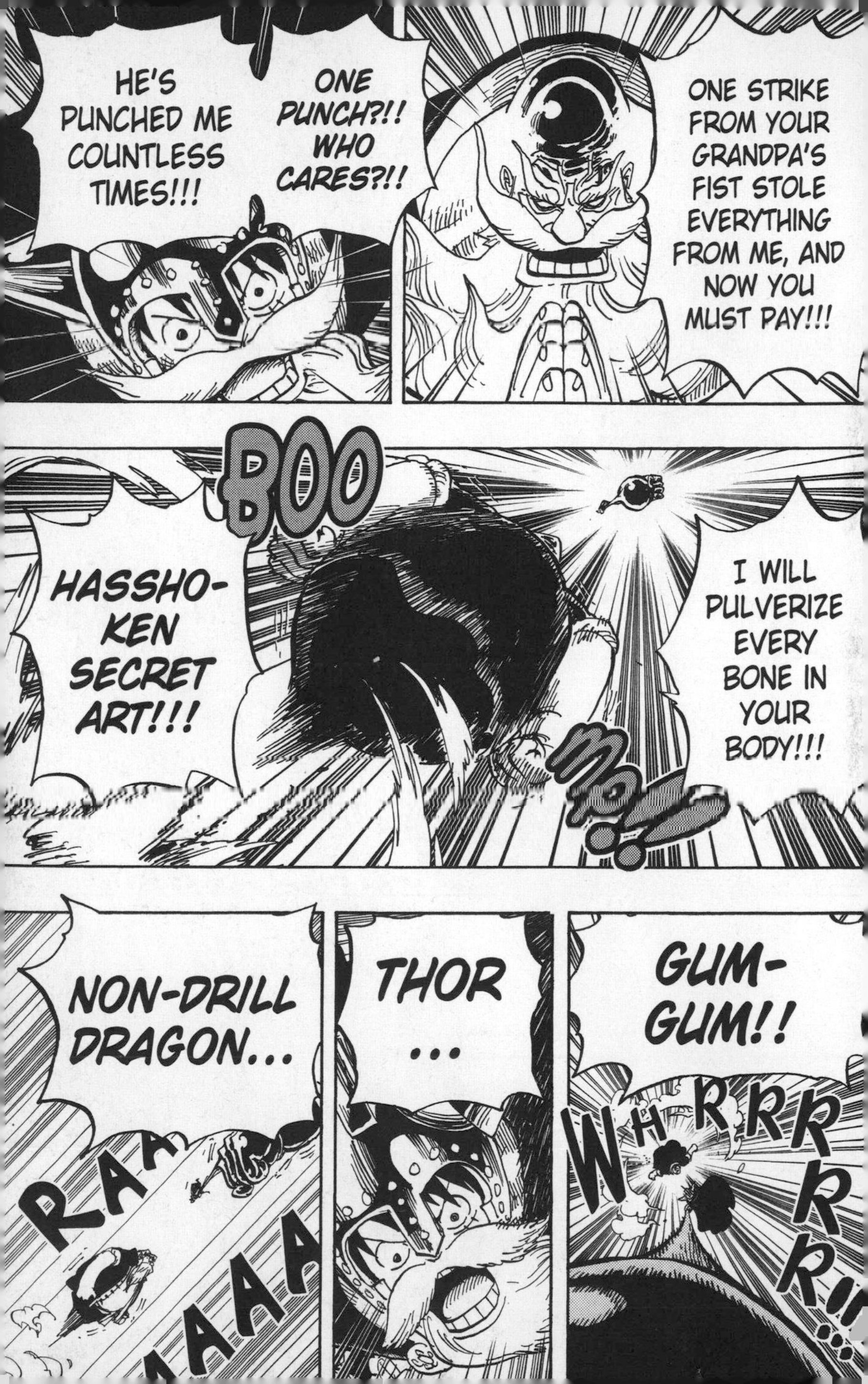
ONE STRIKE FROM YOUR GRANDPA'S FIST STOLE EVERYTHING FROM ME, AND NOW YOU MUST PAY!!!
ONE PUNCH?!! WHO CARES?!!
HE'S PUNCHED ME COUNTLESS TIMES!!!
BOO
I WILL PULVERIZE EVERY BONE IN YOUR BODY!!!
HASSHO-KEN SECRET ART!!!
MP!!
GUM-GUM!!
WHRRRRRRR!!...
THOR ...
NON-DRILL DRAGON...
RAAAAAAAA

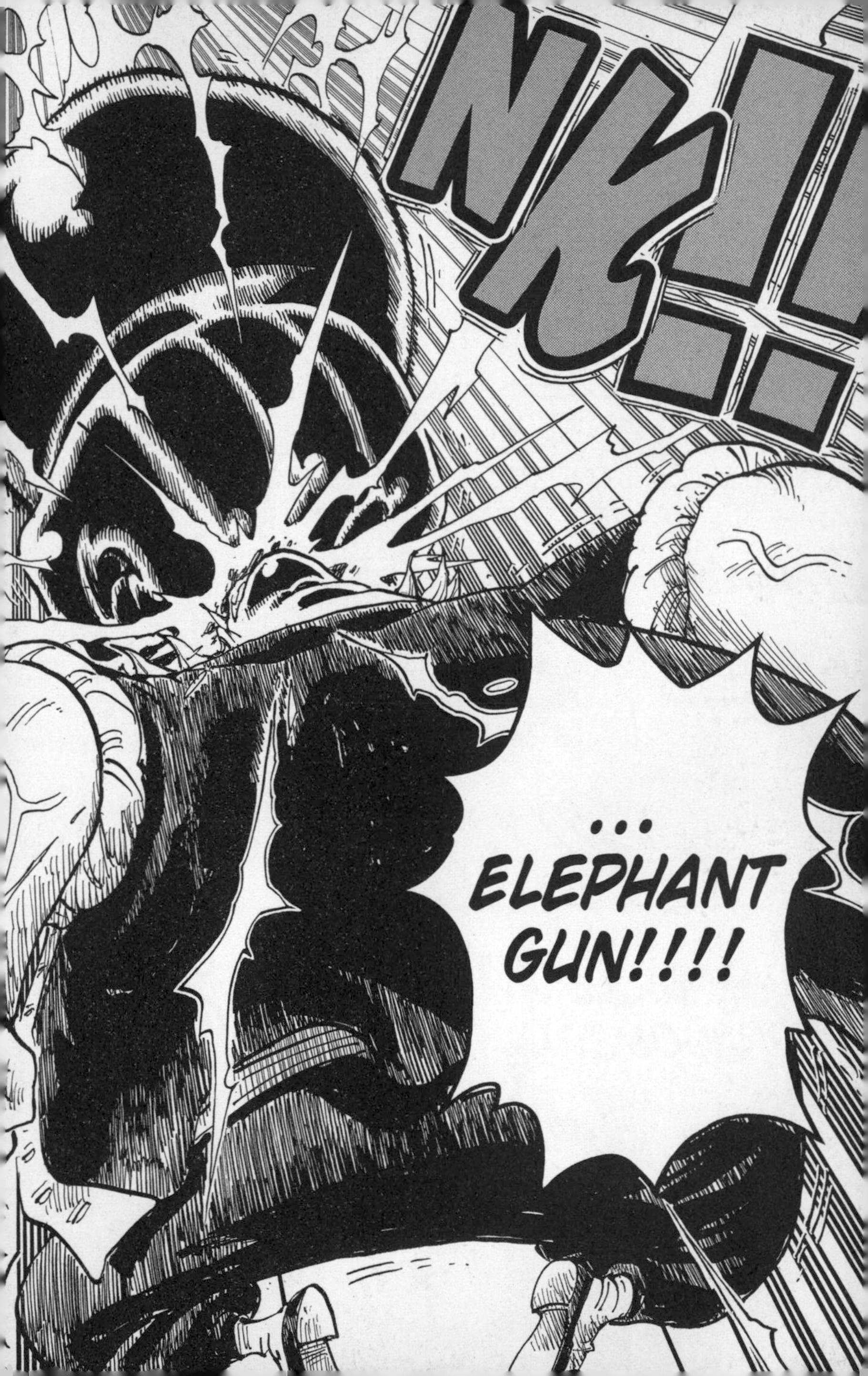
NN!!
...ELEPHANT GUN!!!!

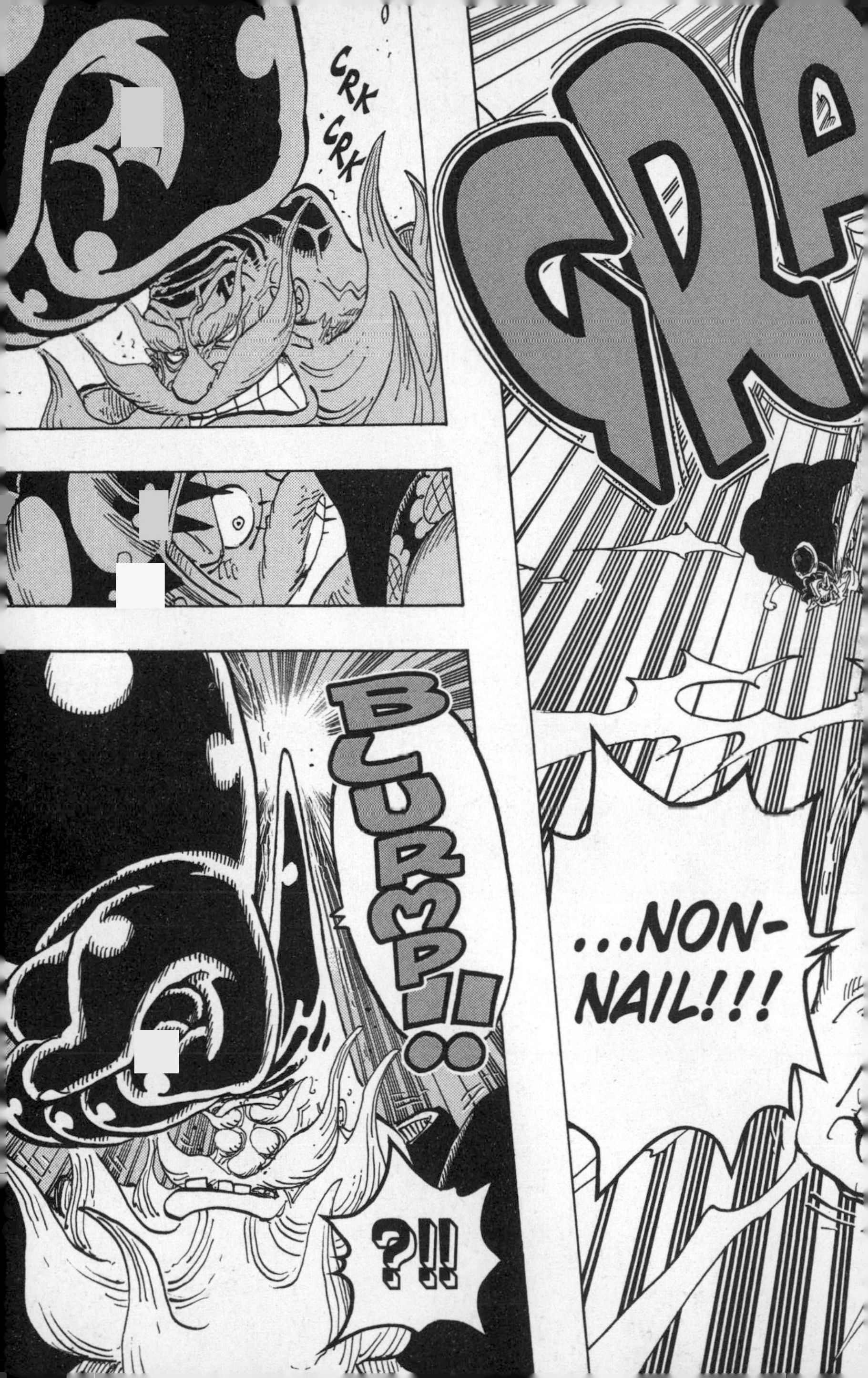
...NON-
NAIL!!!
CRK
CRK
BLURMP!!
?!!

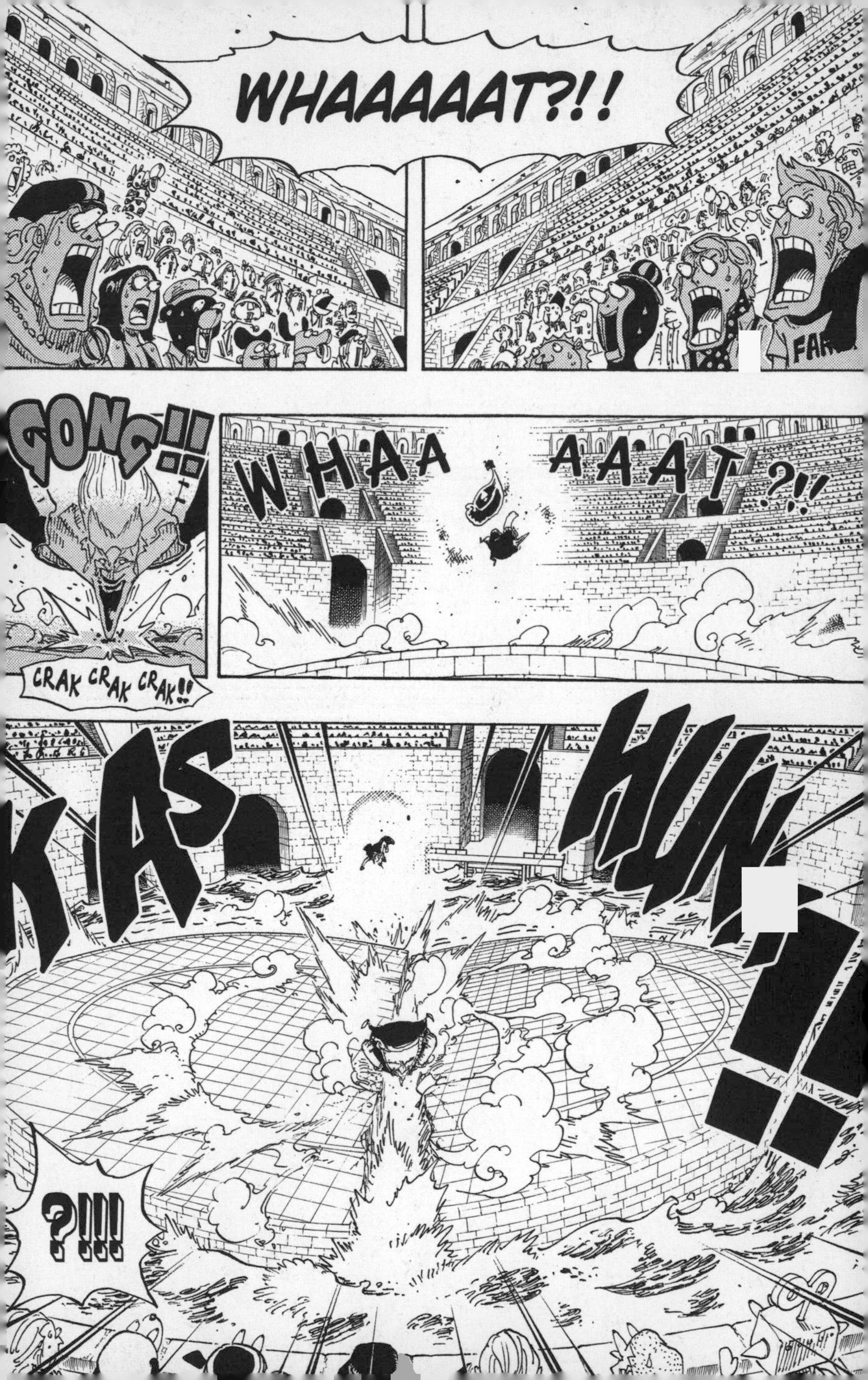
WHAAAAAT?!!
WHAA AAAT?!!
GONG!!
CRAK CRAK CRAK!!
KASHUN!!
?!!!

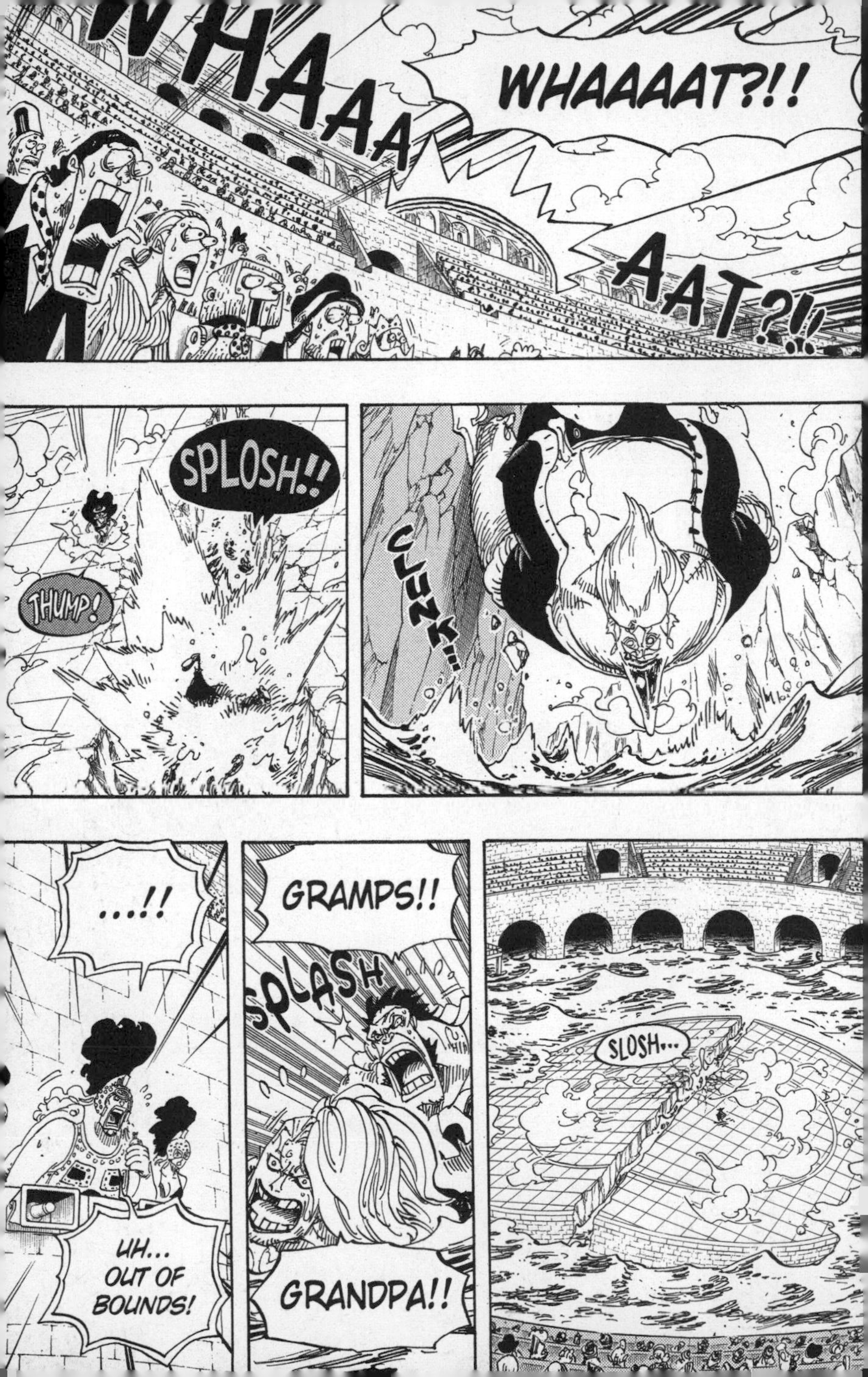
WHAAAAT?!!
WHAAAA
AAT?!!
CLUNK!!
SPLOSH!!
THUMP!
SLOSH...
GRAMPS!!
SPLASH
GRANDPA!!
...!!
UH... OUT OF BOUNDS!

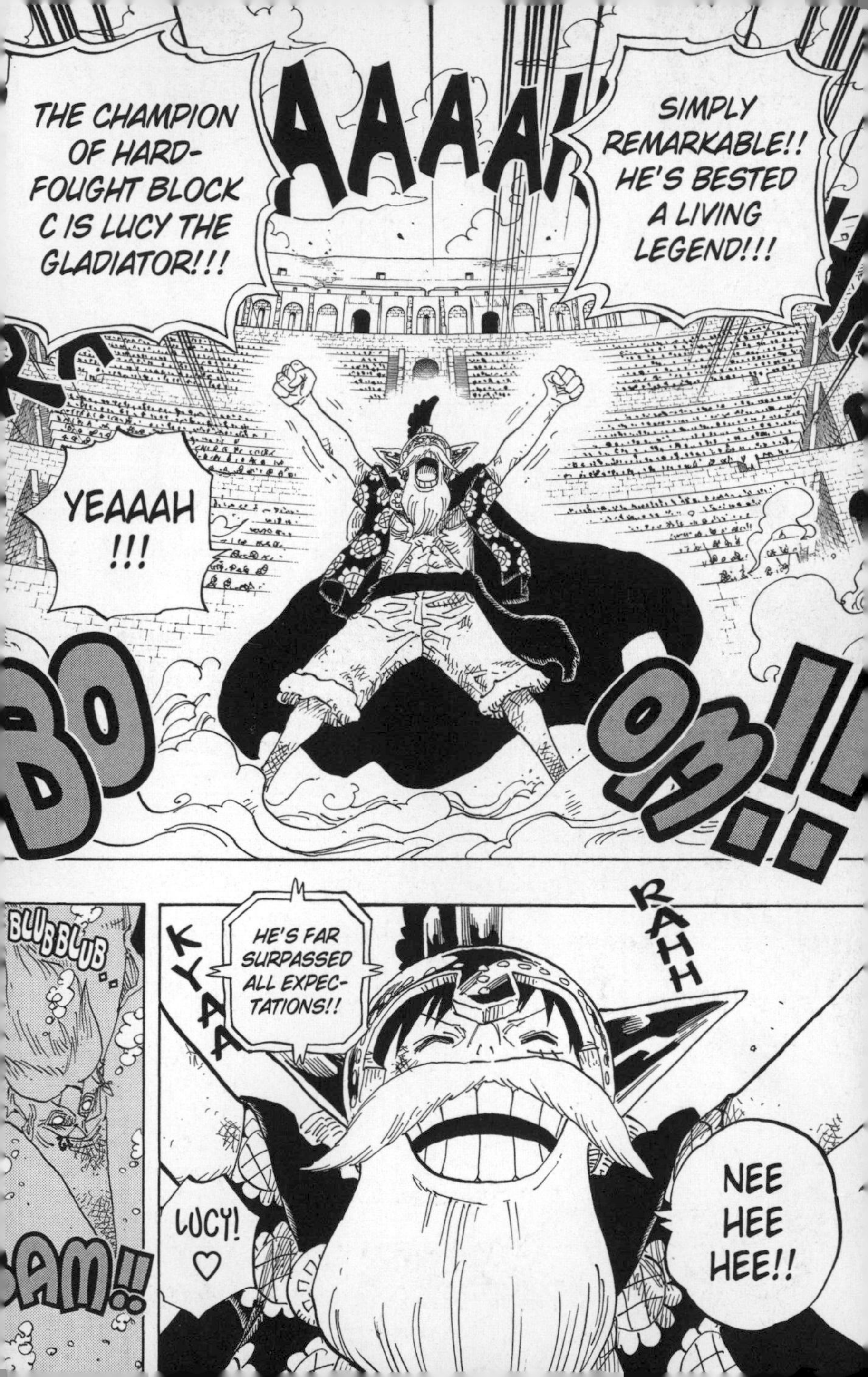
SIMPLY REMARKABLE!! HE'S BESTED A LIVING LEGEND!!!
AAAA
THE CHAMPION OF HARD-FOUGHT BLOCK C IS LUCY THE GLADIATOR!!!
YEAAAH !!!
BOOM!!
RAHH
HE'S FAR SURPASSED ALL EXPECTATIONS!!
KYAA
NEE HEE HEE!!
LUCY! ♡
BLUB BLUB

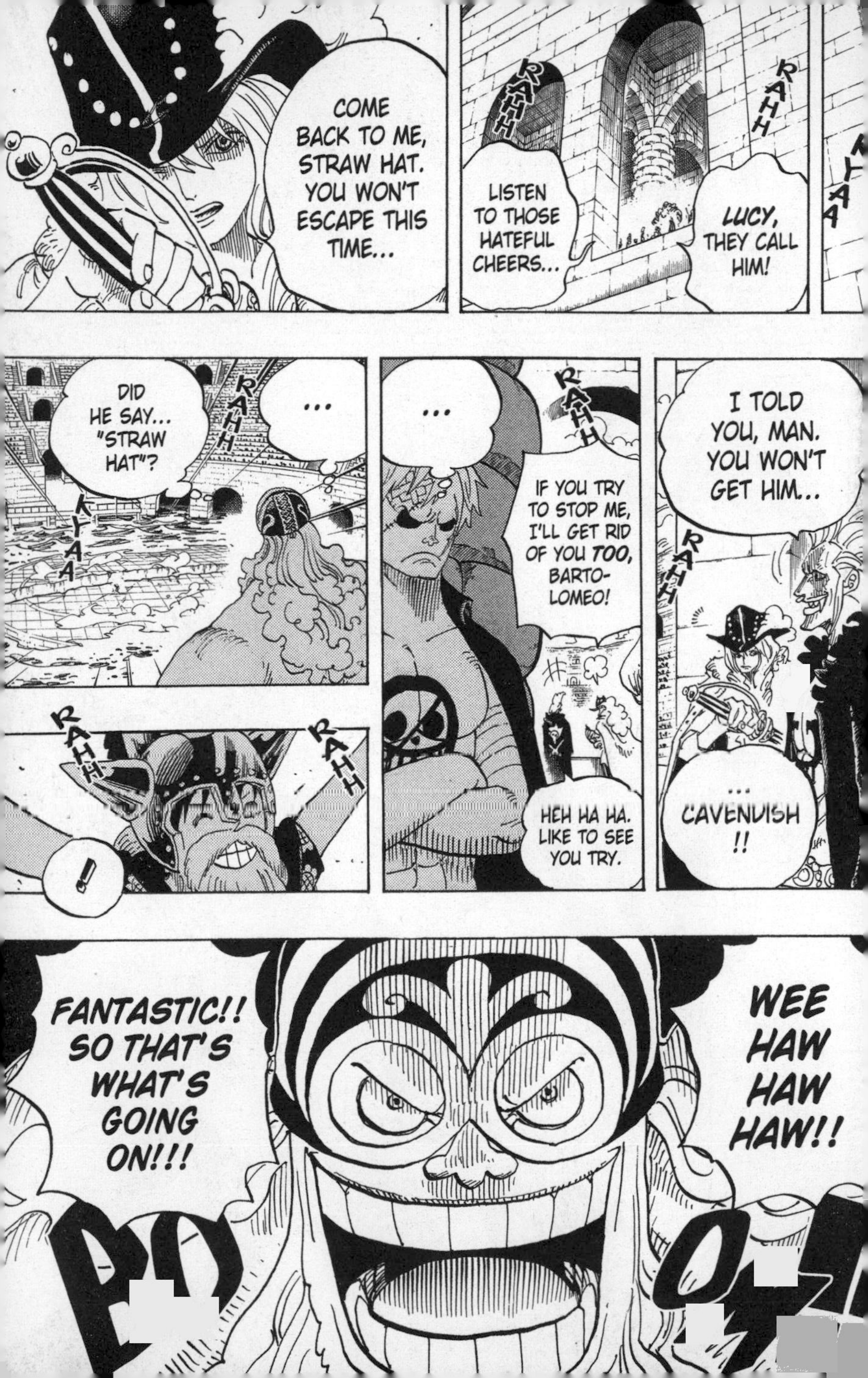
RAHH
RAHH
KYAA
LISTEN TO THOSE HATEFUL CHEERS...
LUCY, THEY CALL HIM!
COME BACK TO ME, STRAW HAT. YOU WON'T ESCAPE THIS TIME...
I TOLD YOU, MAN. YOU WON'T GET HIM...
RAHH
... CAVENDISH !!
RAHH
...
IF YOU TRY TO STOP ME, I'LL GET RID OF YOU *TOO*, BARTO-LOMEO!
HEH HA HA. LIKE TO SEE YOU TRY.
...
RAHH
DID HE SAY... "STRAW HAT"?
KYAA
RAHH
RAHH
!
WEE HAW HAW HAW!!
FANTASTIC!! SO THAT'S WHAT'S GOING ON!!!

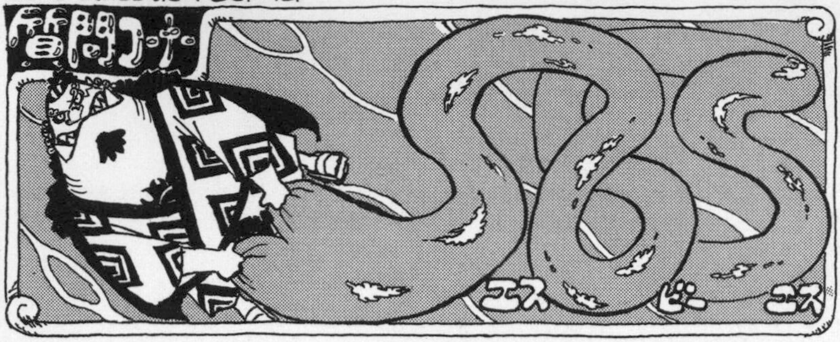
SBS
エス ビー エス

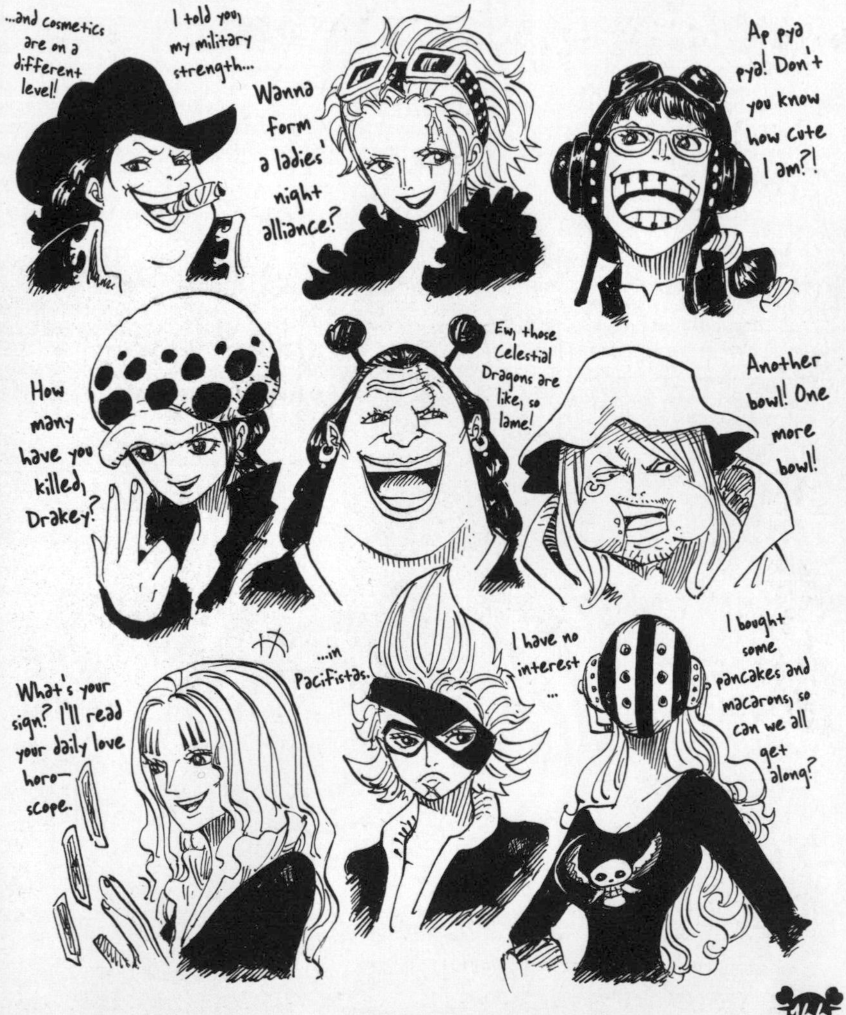
Ap pya pya! Don't you know how cute I am?!
I told you, my military strength...
Wanna form a ladies' night alliance?
...and cosmetics are on a different level!
Another bowl! One more bowl!
Ew, those Celestial Dragons are like, so lame!
How many have you killed, Drakey?
I bought some pancakes and macarons, so can we all get along?
I have no interest ...
...in Pacifistas.
What's your sign? I'll read your daily love horoscope.

(Bokuo Okubo, Kagoshima)

Chapter 720:
PRISONER-GLADIATORS

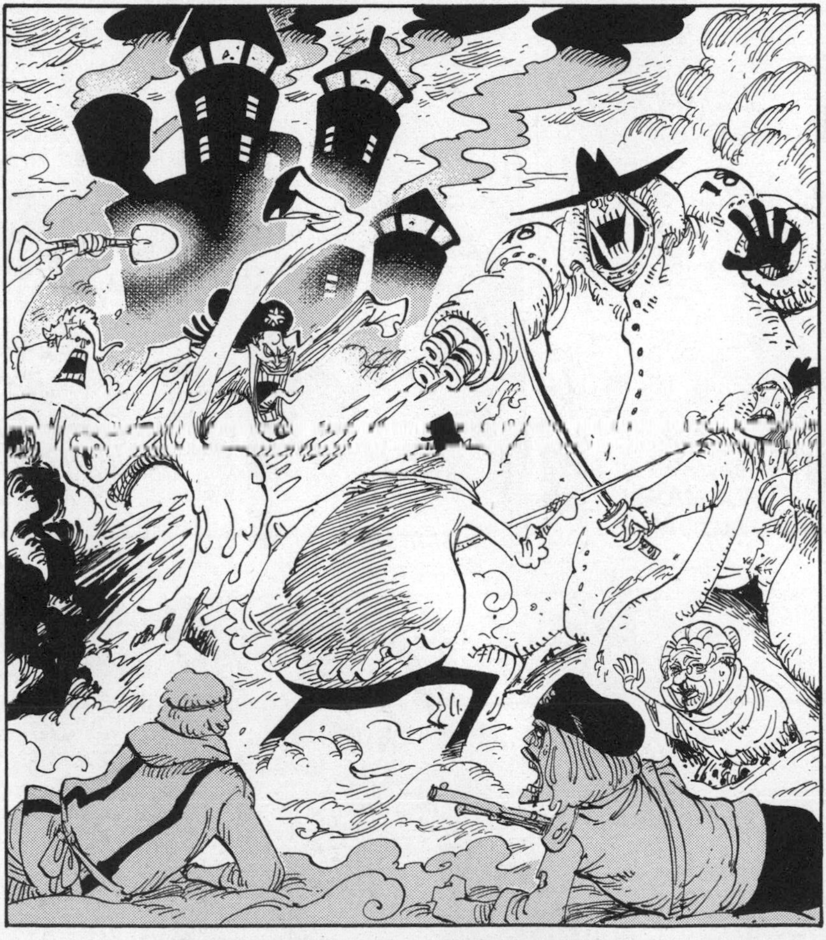

CARIBOU'S NEW WORLD KEE HEE HEE, VOL. 37:
"LIBERATE THE PROLETARIAT!! LIBERATE THE OLD HAG!!"

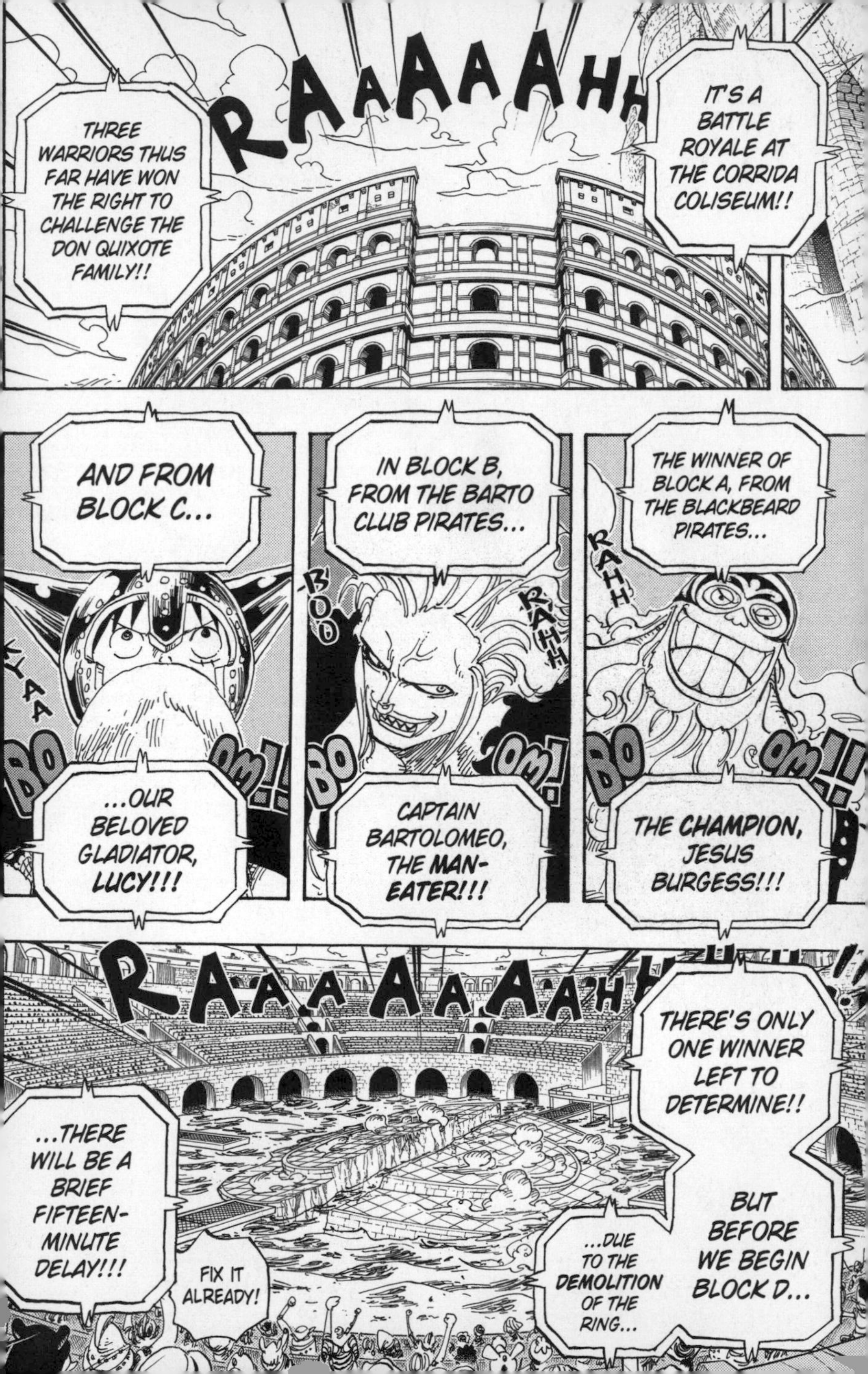

IT'S A BATTLE ROYALE AT THE CORRIDA COLISEUM!!
RAAAAAHH
THREE WARRIORS THUS FAR HAVE WON THE RIGHT TO CHALLENGE THE DON QUIXOTE FAMILY!!
THE WINNER OF BLOCK A, FROM THE BLACKBEARD PIRATES...
RAHH
BOOM!!
THE CHAMPION, JESUS BURGESS!!!
IN BLOCK B, FROM THE BARTO CLUB PIRATES...
BOO
RAHH
BOOM!
CAPTAIN BARTOLOMEO, THE MAN-EATER!!!
AND FROM BLOCK C...
KYAA
BOOM!!
...OUR BELOVED GLADIATOR, LUCY!!!
RAAAAAAAAHH!!
THERE'S ONLY ONE WINNER LEFT TO DETERMINE!!
BUT BEFORE WE BEGIN BLOCK D...
...DUE TO THE DEMOLITION OF THE RING...
...THERE WILL BE A BRIEF FIFTEEN-MINUTE DELAY!!!
FIX IT ALREADY!

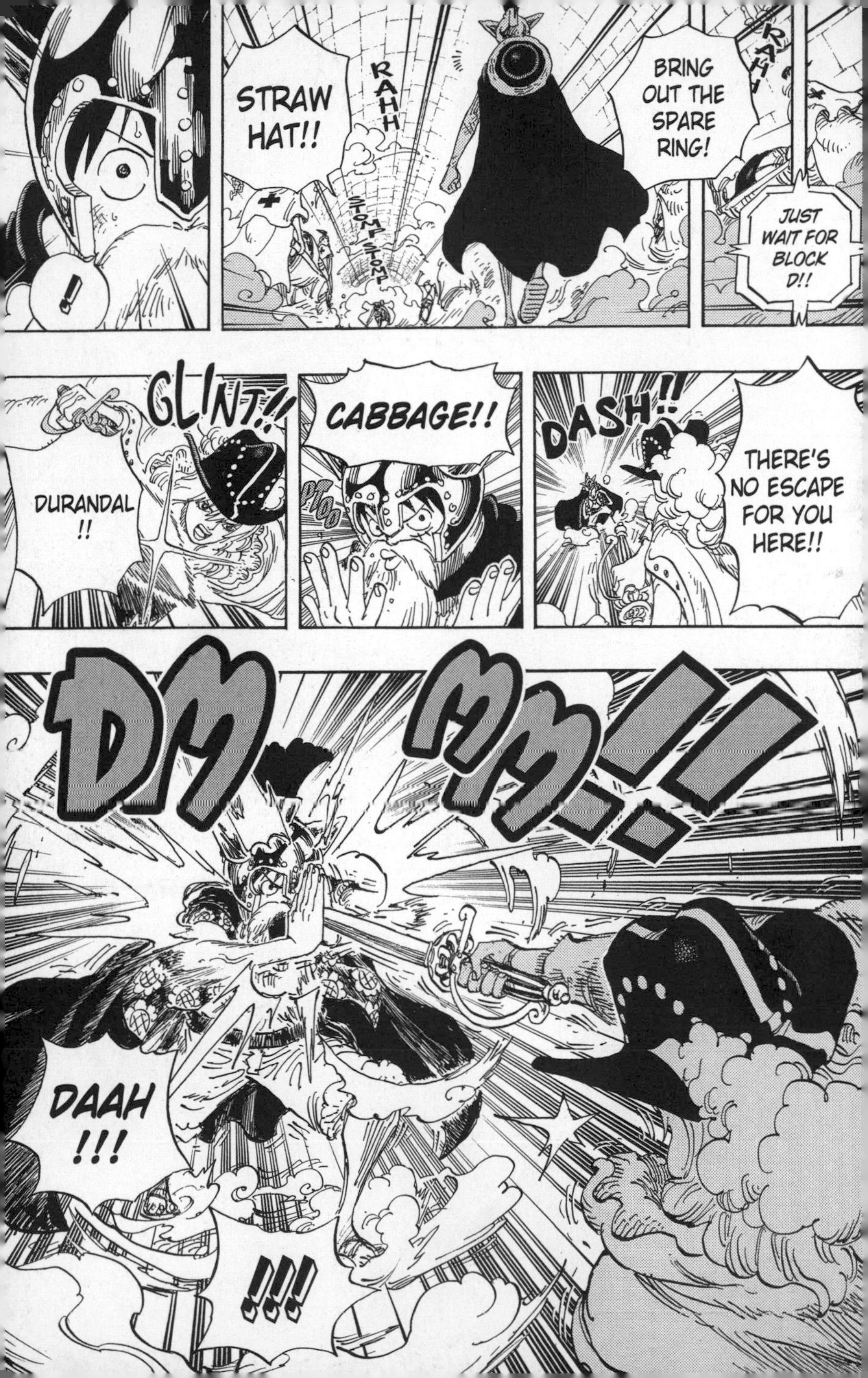

RAHH
BRING OUT THE SPARE RING!
JUST WAIT FOR BLOCK D!!
STRAW HAT!!
RAHH
STOMP STOMP
!
THERE'S NO ESCAPE FOR YOU HERE!!
DASH!!
CABBAGE!!
GLINT!!
DURANDAL !!
DM-MM!!
DAAH !!!
!!!

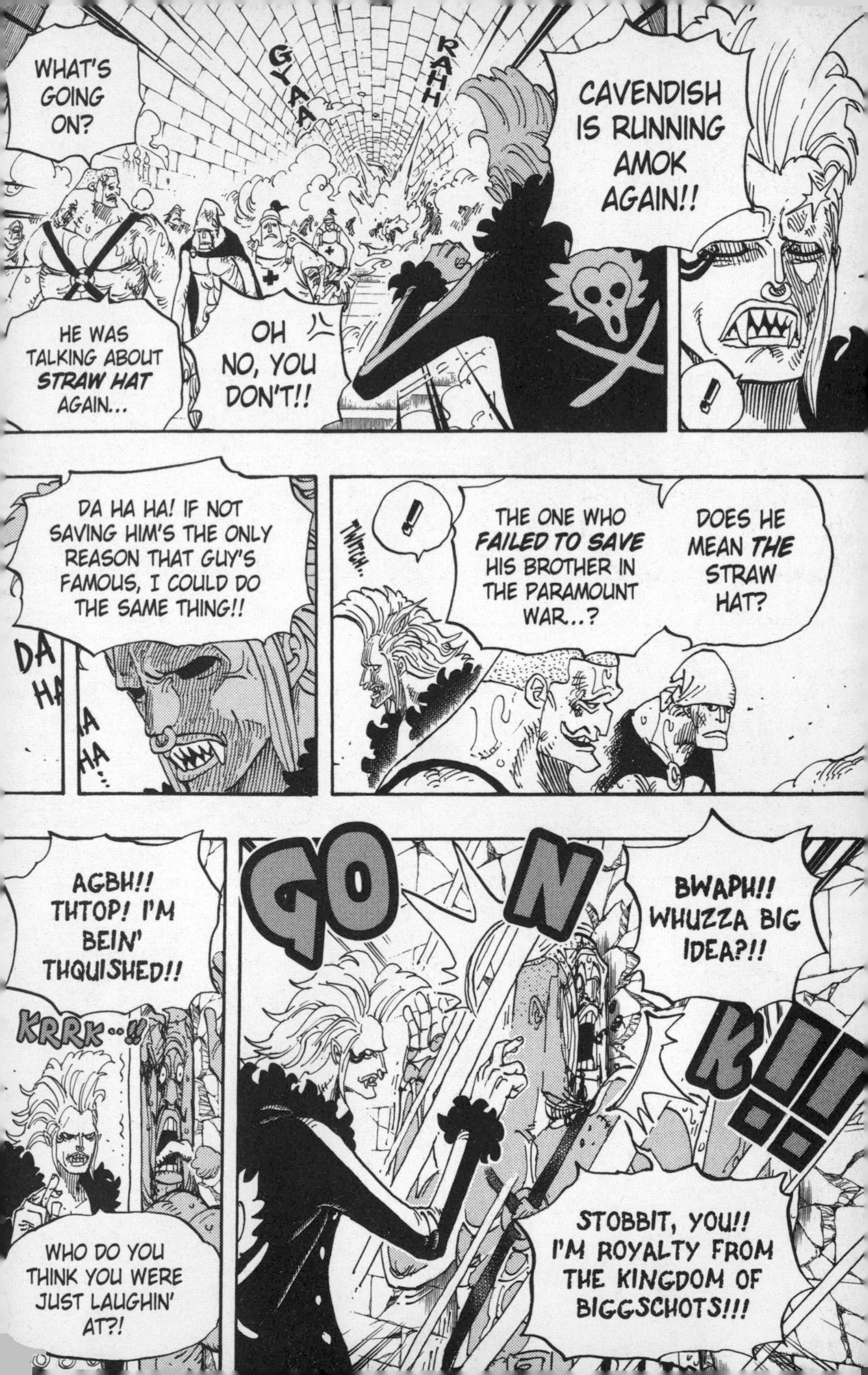
CAVENDISH IS RUNNING AMOK AGAIN!!
!
RAHH
GYAA
WHAT'S GOING ON?
OH NO, YOU DON'T!!
HE WAS TALKING ABOUT STRAW HAT AGAIN...
DOES HE MEAN THE STRAW HAT?
THE ONE WHO FAILED TO SAVE HIS BROTHER IN THE PARAMOUNT WAR...?
!
TWITCH...
DA HA HA! IF NOT SAVING HIM'S THE ONLY REASON THAT GUY'S FAMOUS, I COULD DO THE SAME THING!!
DA HA HA HA...
BWAPH!! WHUZZA BIG IDEA?!!
GONK!!
STOBBIT, YOU!! I'M ROYALTY FROM THE KINGDOM OF BIGGSCHOTS!!!
AGBH!! THTOP! I'M BEIN' THQUISHED!!
KRRK..!!
WHO DO YOU THINK YOU WERE JUST LAUGHIN' AT?!

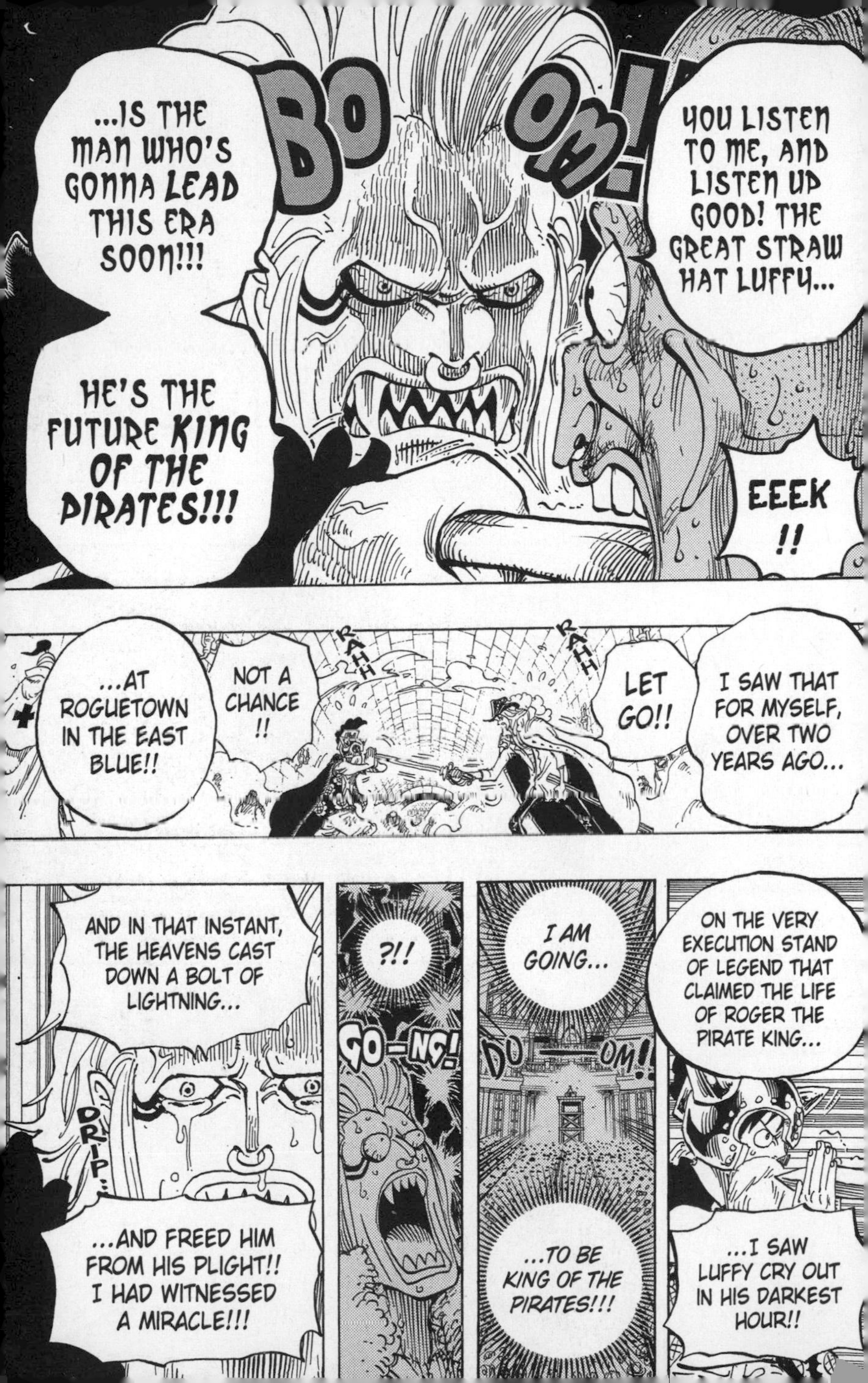
YOU LISTEN TO ME, AND LISTEN UP GOOD! THE GREAT STRAW HAT LUFFY...
BOOM!
...IS THE MAN WHO'S GONNA LEAD THIS ERA SOON!!!
EEEK!!
HE'S THE FUTURE KING OF THE PIRATES!!!
I SAW THAT FOR MYSELF, OVER TWO YEARS AGO...
RAHH
LET GO!!
RAHH
NOT A CHANCE!!
...AT ROGUETOWN IN THE EAST BLUE!!
ON THE VERY EXECUTION STAND OF LEGEND THAT CLAIMED THE LIFE OF ROGER THE PIRATE KING...
...I SAW LUFFY CRY OUT IN HIS DARKEST HOUR!!
I AM GOING...
DO—OM!!
...TO BE KING OF THE PIRATES!!!
?!!
GO—NG!
AND IN THAT INSTANT, THE HEAVENS CAST DOWN A BOLT OF LIGHTNING...
DRIP...
...AND FREED HIM FROM HIS PLIGHT!! I HAD WITNESSED A MIRACLE!!!

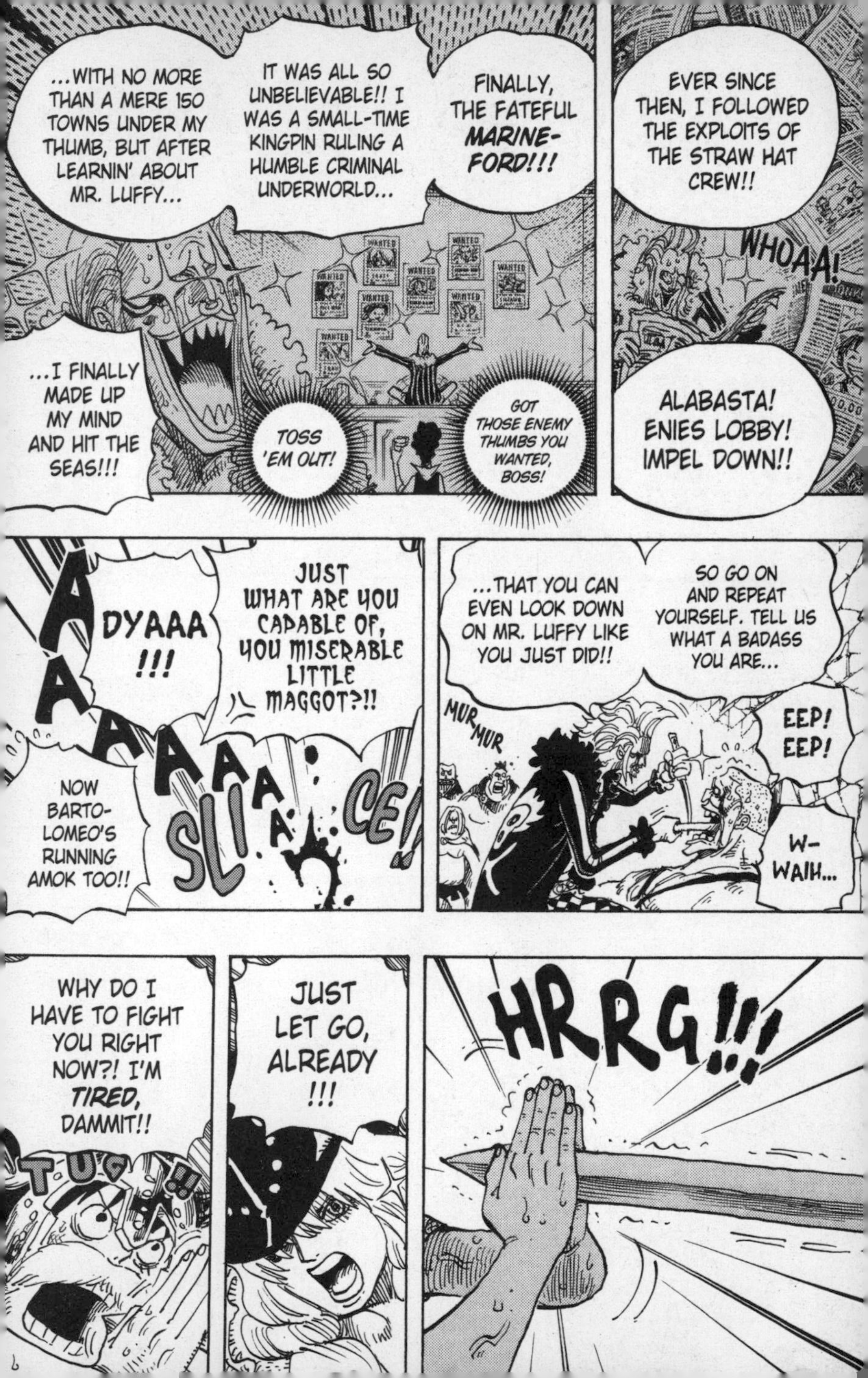
EVER SINCE THEN, I FOLLOWED THE EXPLOITS OF THE STRAW HAT CREW!!
WHOAA!
ALABASTA! ENIES LOBBY! IMPEL DOWN!!
FINALLY, THE FATEFUL *MARINE-FORD!!!*
IT WAS ALL SO UNBELIEVABLE!! I WAS A SMALL-TIME KINGPIN RULING A HUMBLE CRIMINAL UNDERWORLD...
...WITH NO MORE THAN A MERE 150 TOWNS UNDER MY THUMB, BUT AFTER LEARNIN' ABOUT MR. LUFFY...
GOT THOSE ENEMY THUMBS YOU WANTED, BOSS!
TOSS 'EM OUT!
...I FINALLY MADE UP MY MIND AND HIT THE SEAS!!!
SO GO ON AND REPEAT YOURSELF. TELL US WHAT A BADASS YOU ARE...
...THAT YOU CAN EVEN LOOK DOWN ON MR. LUFFY LIKE YOU JUST DID!!
EEP! EEP!
MUR MUR
W-WAIT...
JUST WHAT ARE YOU CAPABLE OF, YOU MISERABLE LITTLE MAGGOT?!!
AADYAAA!!!
AAAAAAA
SLICE!
NOW BARTO-LOMEO'S RUNNING AMOK TOO!!
HRRG!!!
JUST LET GO, ALREADY!!!
WHY DO I HAVE TO FIGHT YOU RIGHT NOW?! I'M *TIRED,* DAMMIT!!
TUG!!

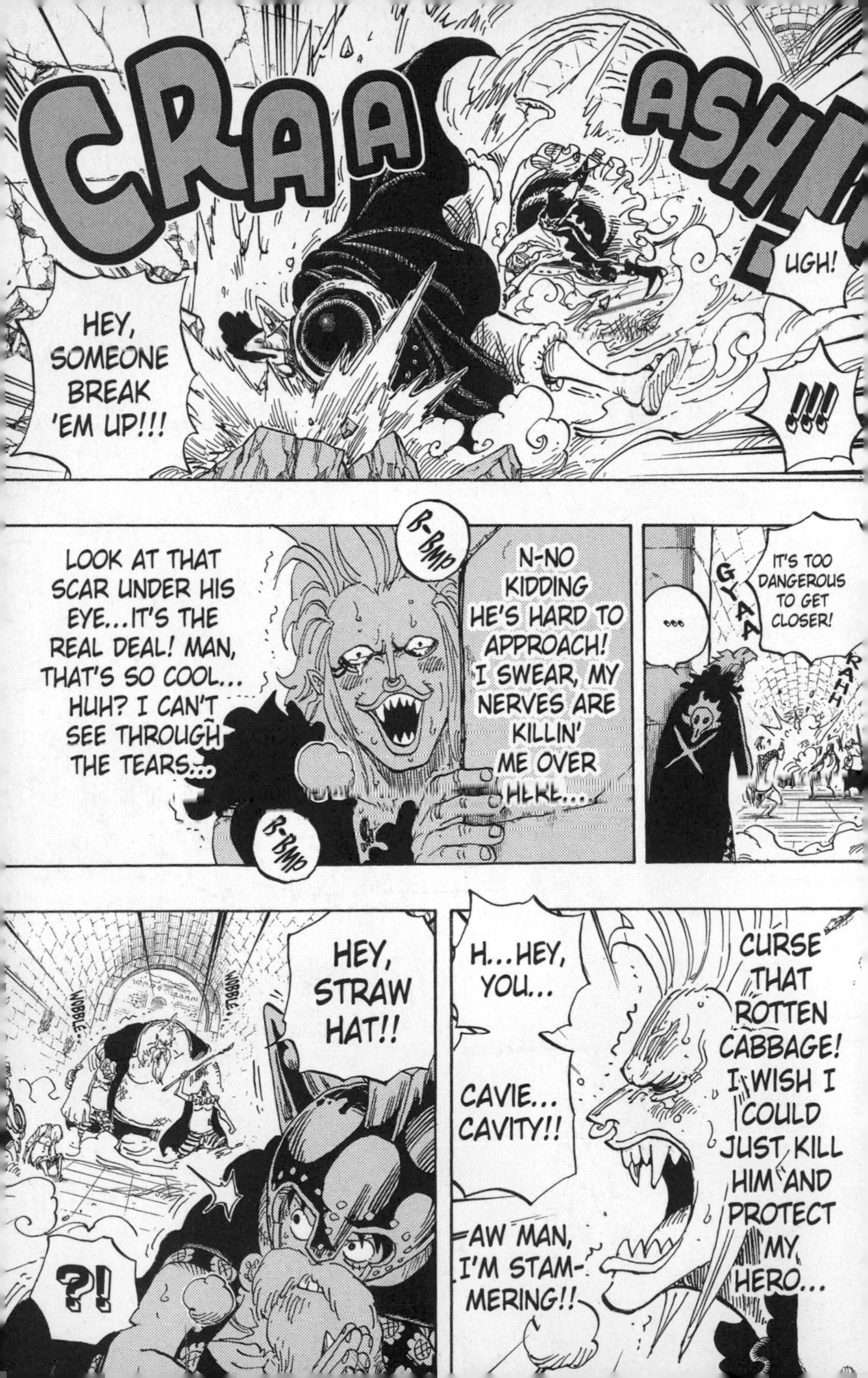
CRAAASH!!
UGH!
!!!
HEY, SOMEONE BREAK 'EM UP!!!
IT'S TOO DANGEROUS TO GET CLOSER!
RAHH
GYAA
...
B-BMP
N-NO KIDDING HE'S HARD TO APPROACH! I SWEAR, MY NERVES ARE KILLIN' ME OVER HERE...
LOOK AT THAT SCAR UNDER HIS EYE...IT'S THE REAL DEAL! MAN, THAT'S SO COOL... HUH? I CAN'T SEE THROUGH THE TEARS...
B-BMP
CURSE THAT ROTTEN CABBAGE! I WISH I COULD JUST KILL HIM AND PROTECT MY HERO...
H...HEY, YOU...
CAVIE... CAVITY!!
AW MAN, I'M STAMMERING!!
HEY, STRAW HAT!!
WOBBLE
WOBBLE
?!

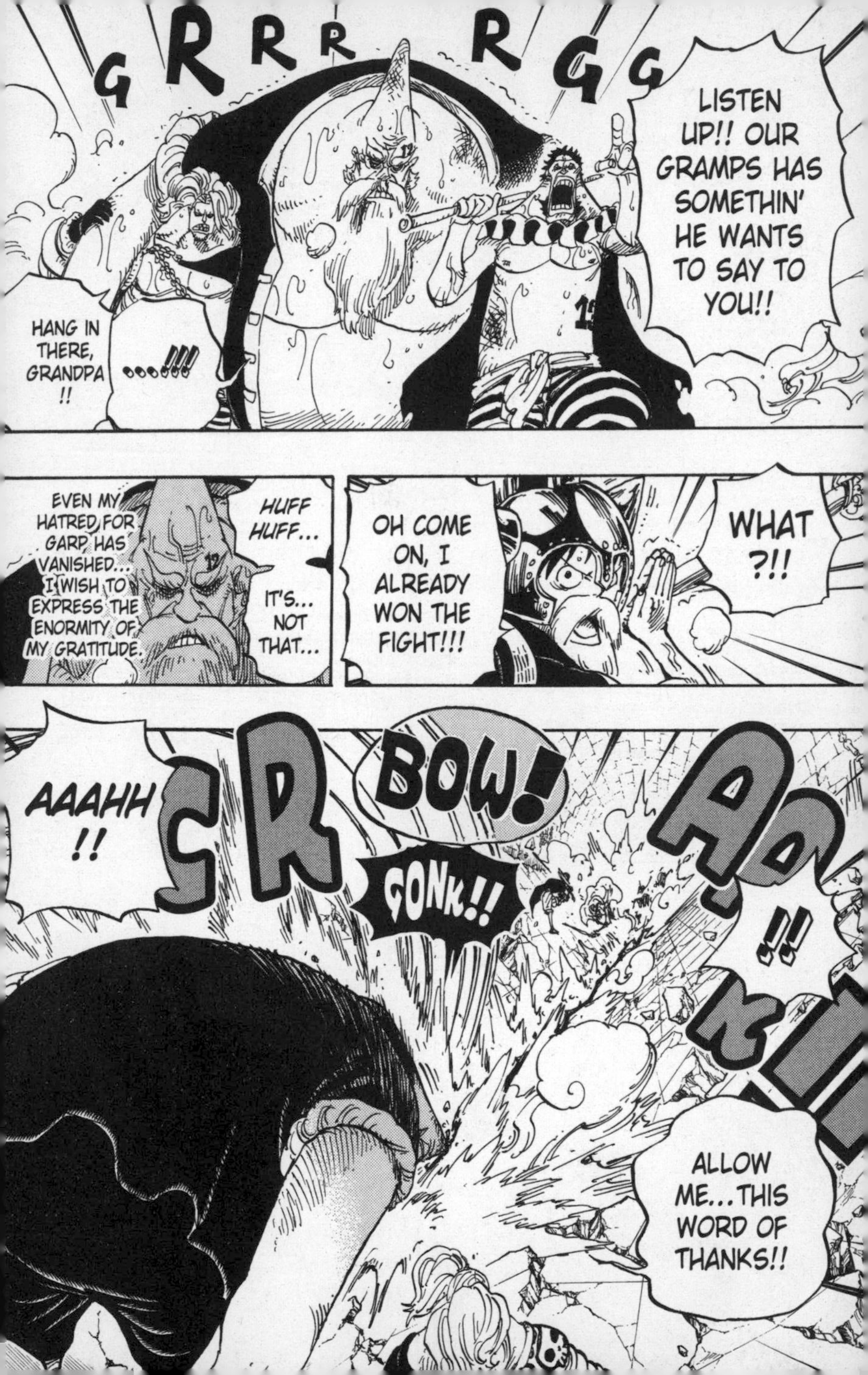
GRRRRRGG
LISTEN UP!! OUR GRAMPS HAS SOMETHIN' HE WANTS TO SAY TO YOU!!
.....!!!
HANG IN THERE, GRANDPA!!
WHAT?!!
OH COME ON, I ALREADY WON THE FIGHT!!!
HUFF HUFF...
IT'S... NOT THAT...
EVEN MY HATRED FOR GARP HAS VANISHED... I WISH TO EXPRESS THE ENORMITY OF MY GRATITUDE.
CRACK!!
BOW!
AAAHH!!
GONK!!
ALLOW ME...THIS WORD OF THANKS!!

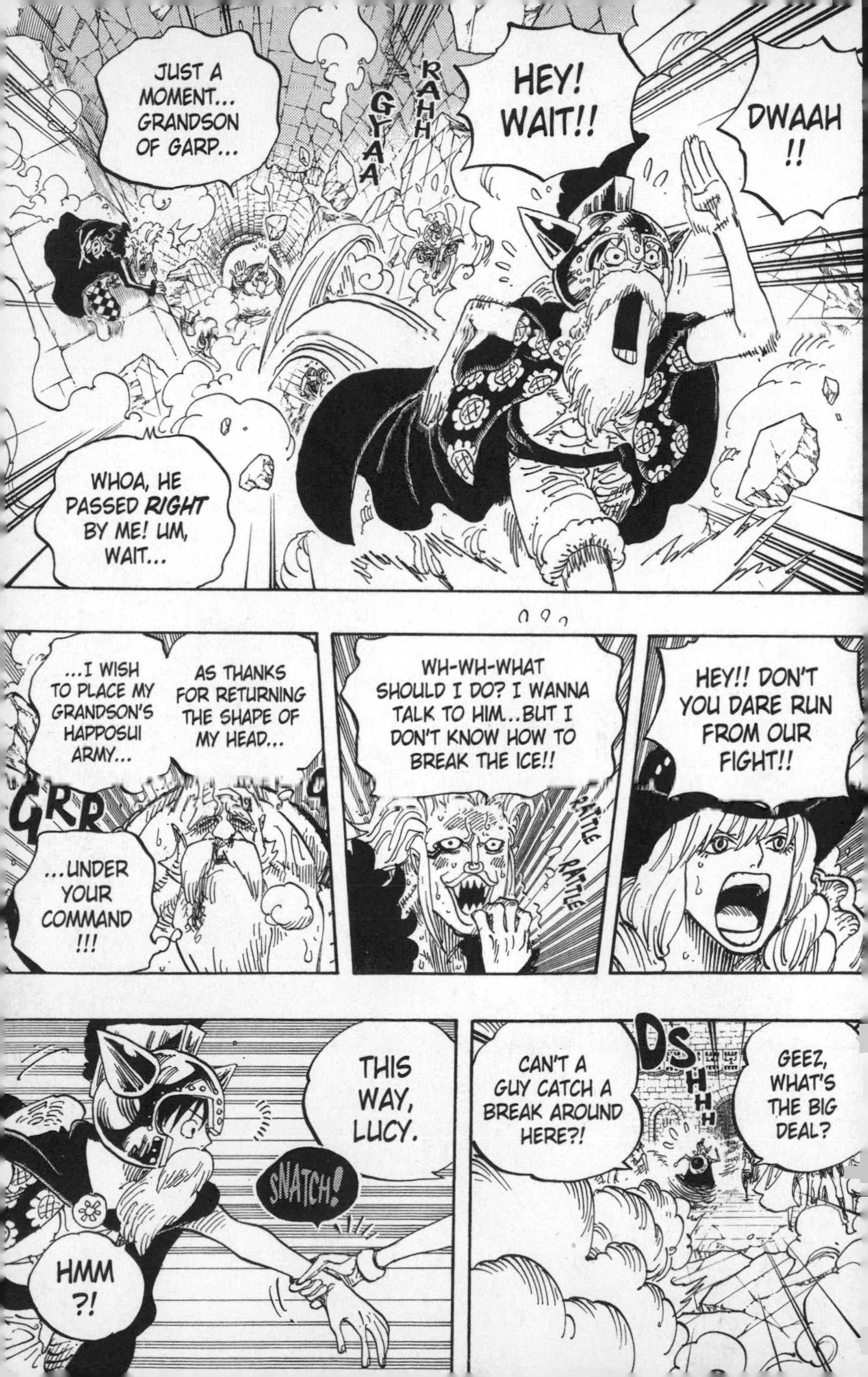

DWAAH !!
HEY! WAIT!!
RAHH
GYAA
JUST A MOMENT... GRANDSON OF GARP...
WHOA, HE PASSED RIGHT BY ME! UM, WAIT...
HEY!! DON'T YOU DARE RUN FROM OUR FIGHT!!
WH-WH-WHAT SHOULD I DO? I WANNA TALK TO HIM...BUT I DON'T KNOW HOW TO BREAK THE ICE!!
RATTLE RATTLE
AS THANKS FOR RETURNING THE SHAPE OF MY HEAD...
...I WISH TO PLACE MY GRANDSON'S HAPPOSUI ARMY...
GRR
...UNDER YOUR COMMAND!!!
GEEZ, WHAT'S THE BIG DEAL?
DSHHH
CAN'T A GUY CATCH A BREAK AROUND HERE?!
THIS WAY, LUCY.
SNATCH!
HMM ?!

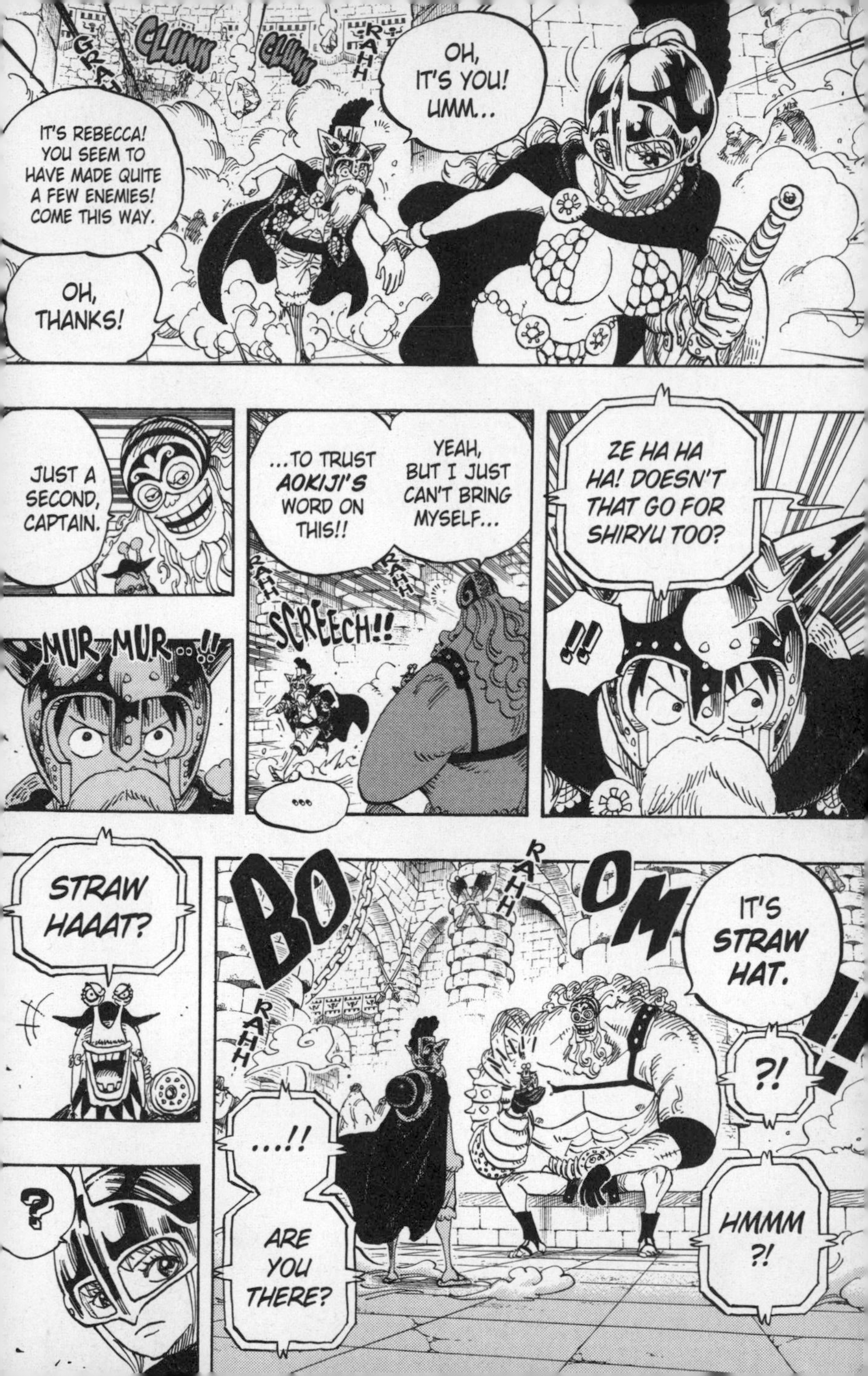
CLUNK
CLUNK
RAHH
GRA
OH, IT'S YOU! UMM...
IT'S REBECCA! YOU SEEM TO HAVE MADE QUITE A FEW ENEMIES! COME THIS WAY.
OH, THANKS!
ZE HA HA HA! DOESN'T THAT GO FOR SHIRYU TOO?
!!
YEAH, BUT I JUST CAN'T BRING MYSELF...
...TO TRUST AOKIJI'S WORD ON THIS!!
RAHH
RAHH
SCREECH!!
...
JUST A SECOND, CAPTAIN.
MUR MUR...!!
IT'S STRAW HAT.
BOOM
RAHH
RAHH
!!
?!
HMMM ?!
...!!
ARE YOU THERE?
STRAW HAAAT?
?

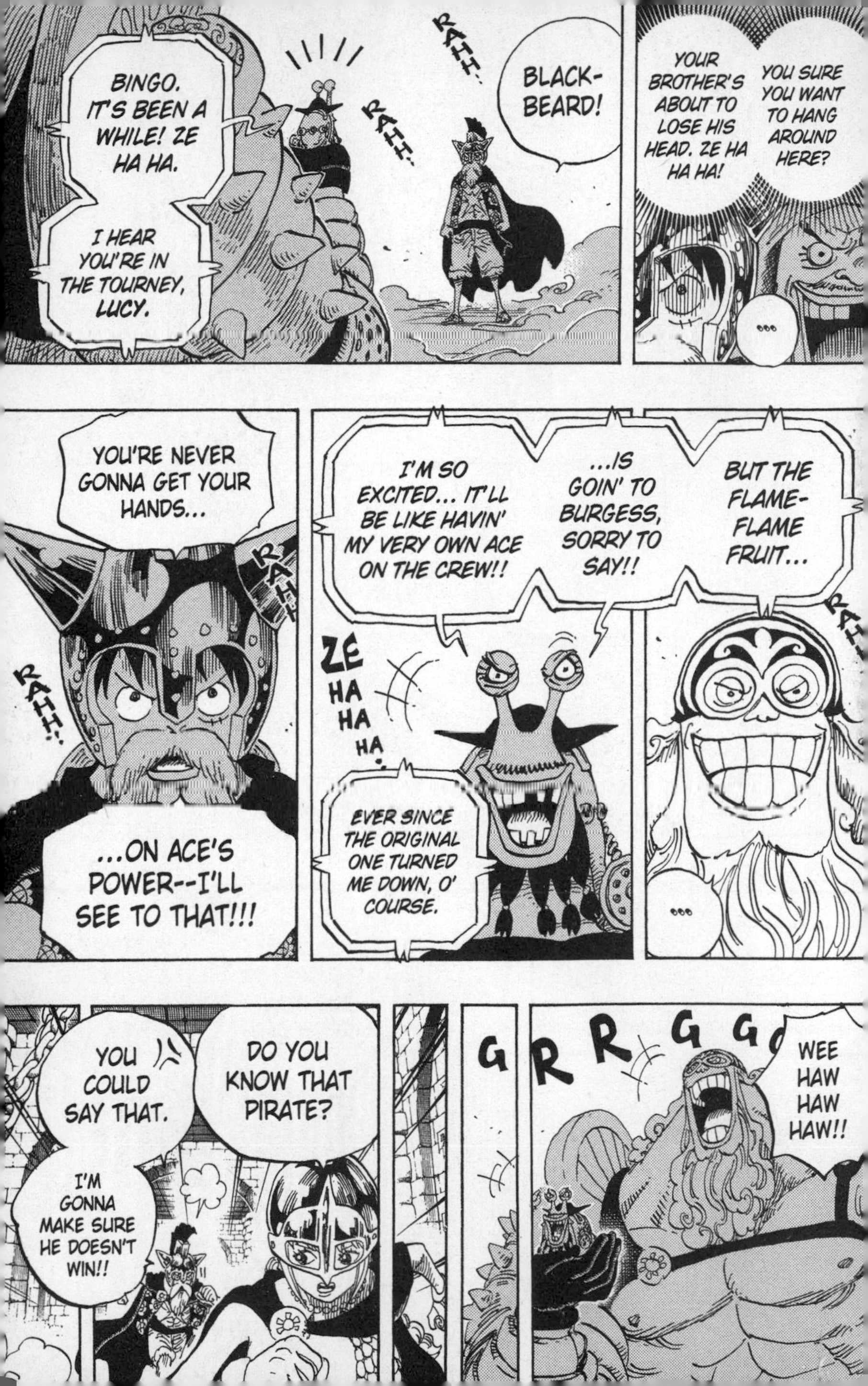
YOU SURE YOU WANT TO HANG AROUND HERE?
YOUR BROTHER'S ABOUT TO LOSE HIS HEAD. ZE HA HA HA!
...
BLACK-BEARD!
RAHH
RAHH
BINGO. IT'S BEEN A WHILE! ZE HA HA.
I HEAR YOU'RE IN THE TOURNEY, LUCY.
BUT THE FLAME-FLAME FRUIT...
RAHH
...
...IS GOIN' TO BURGESS, SORRY TO SAY!!
I'M SO EXCITED... IT'LL BE LIKE HAVIN' MY VERY OWN ACE ON THE CREW!!
ZE HA HA HA
EVER SINCE THE ORIGINAL ONE TURNED ME DOWN, O' COURSE.
YOU'RE NEVER GONNA GET YOUR HANDS...
RAHH
RAHH
...ON ACE'S POWER--I'LL SEE TO THAT!!!
WEE HAW HAW HAW!!
GRRGGG
DO YOU KNOW THAT PIRATE?
YOU COULD SAY THAT.
I'M GONNA MAKE SURE HE DOESN'T WIN!!

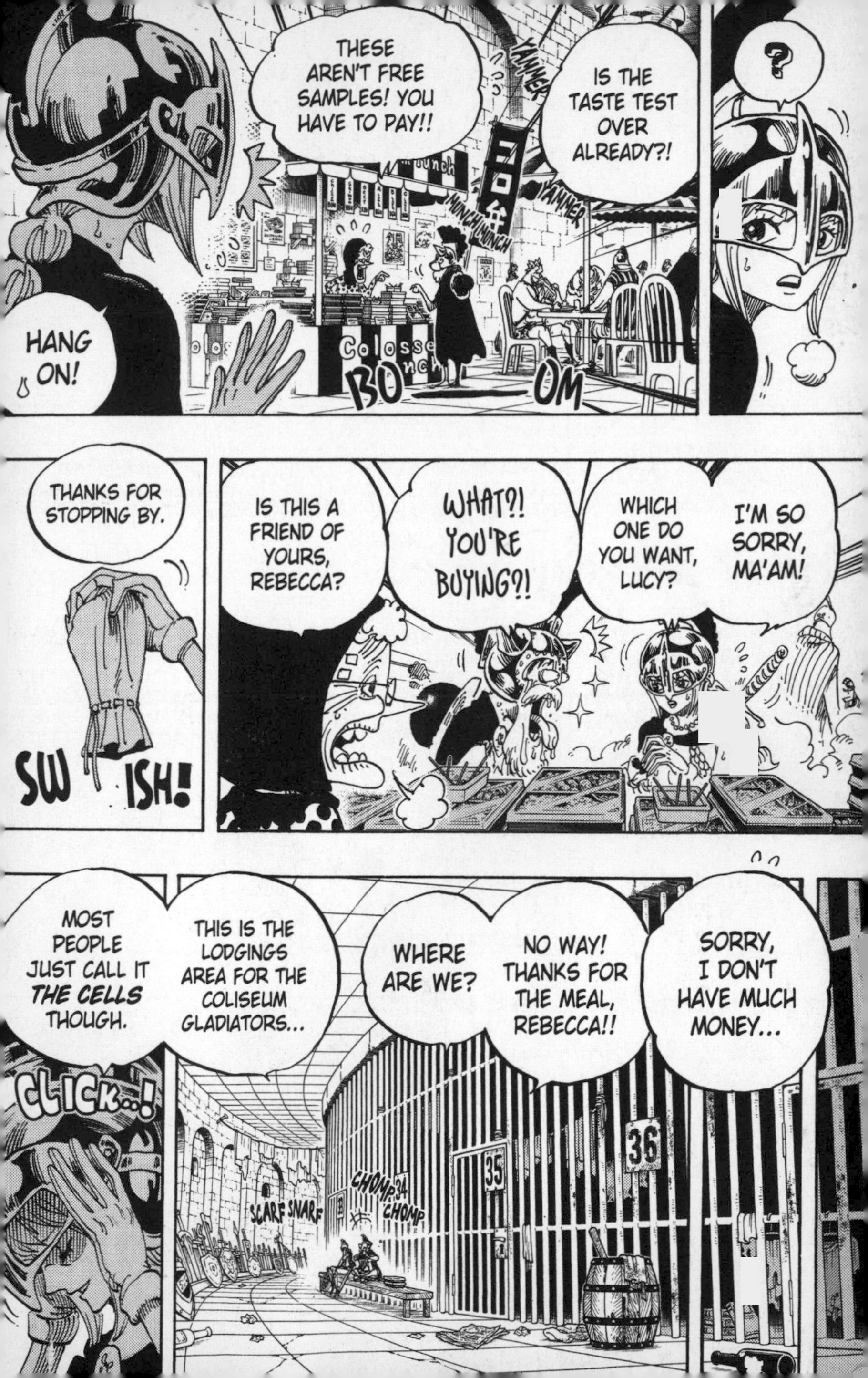
?
IS THE TASTE TEST OVER ALREADY?!
YAMMER
YAMMER
THESE AREN'T FREE SAMPLES! YOU HAVE TO PAY!!
MUNCH MUNCH
BOOM
HANG ON!
I'M SO SORRY, MA'AM!
WHICH ONE DO YOU WANT, LUCY?
WHAT?! YOU'RE BUYING?!
IS THIS A FRIEND OF YOURS, REBECCA?
THANKS FOR STOPPING BY.
SWISH!
SORRY, I DON'T HAVE MUCH MONEY...
NO WAY! THANKS FOR THE MEAL, REBECCA!!
WHERE ARE WE?
THIS IS THE LODGINGS AREA FOR THE COLISEUM GLADIATORS...
MOST PEOPLE JUST CALL IT *THE CELLS* THOUGH.
CLICK..!
36
35
34
CHOMP CHOMP
33
SCARF SNARF

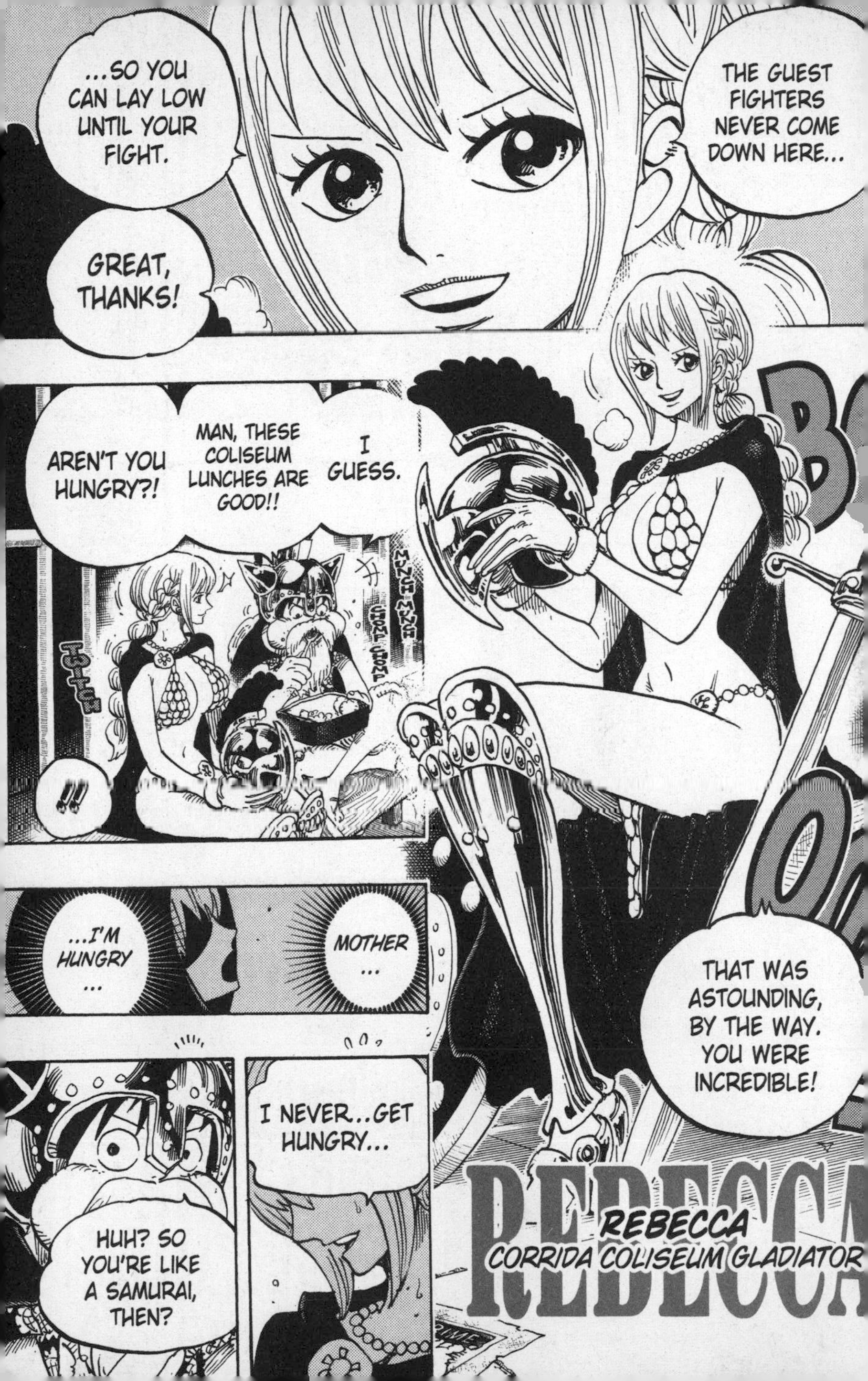
THE GUEST FIGHTERS NEVER COME DOWN HERE...
...SO YOU CAN LAY LOW UNTIL YOUR FIGHT.
GREAT, THANKS!
THAT WAS ASTOUNDING, BY THE WAY. YOU WERE INCREDIBLE!
REBECCA
REBECCA
CORRIDA COLISEUM GLADIATOR
I GUESS.
MAN, THESE COLISEUM LUNCHES ARE GOOD!!
AREN'T YOU HUNGRY?!
MUNCH MUNCH
CHOMP CHOMP
TWITCH
!!
MOTHER ...
...I'M HUNGRY ...
I NEVER...GET HUNGRY...
HUH? SO YOU'RE LIKE A SAMURAI, THEN?

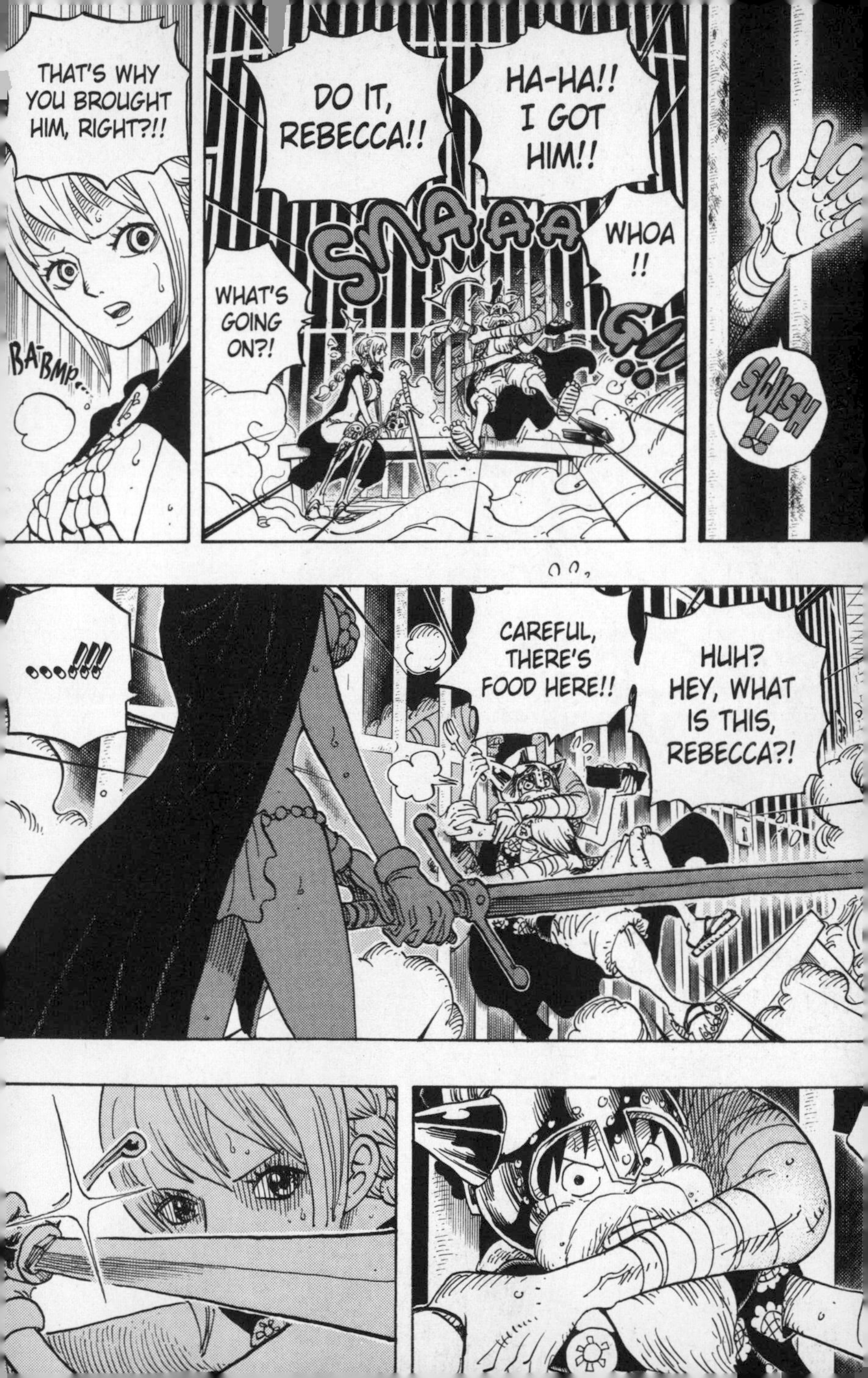
SWISH!!
HA-HA!! I GOT HIM!!
DO IT, REBECCA!!
WHOA!!
SNAAAAG!!
WHAT'S GOING ON?!
THAT'S WHY YOU BROUGHT HIM, RIGHT?!!
BA-BMP...
HUH? HEY, WHAT IS THIS, REBECCA?!
CAREFUL, THERE'S FOOD HERE!!
.....!!!

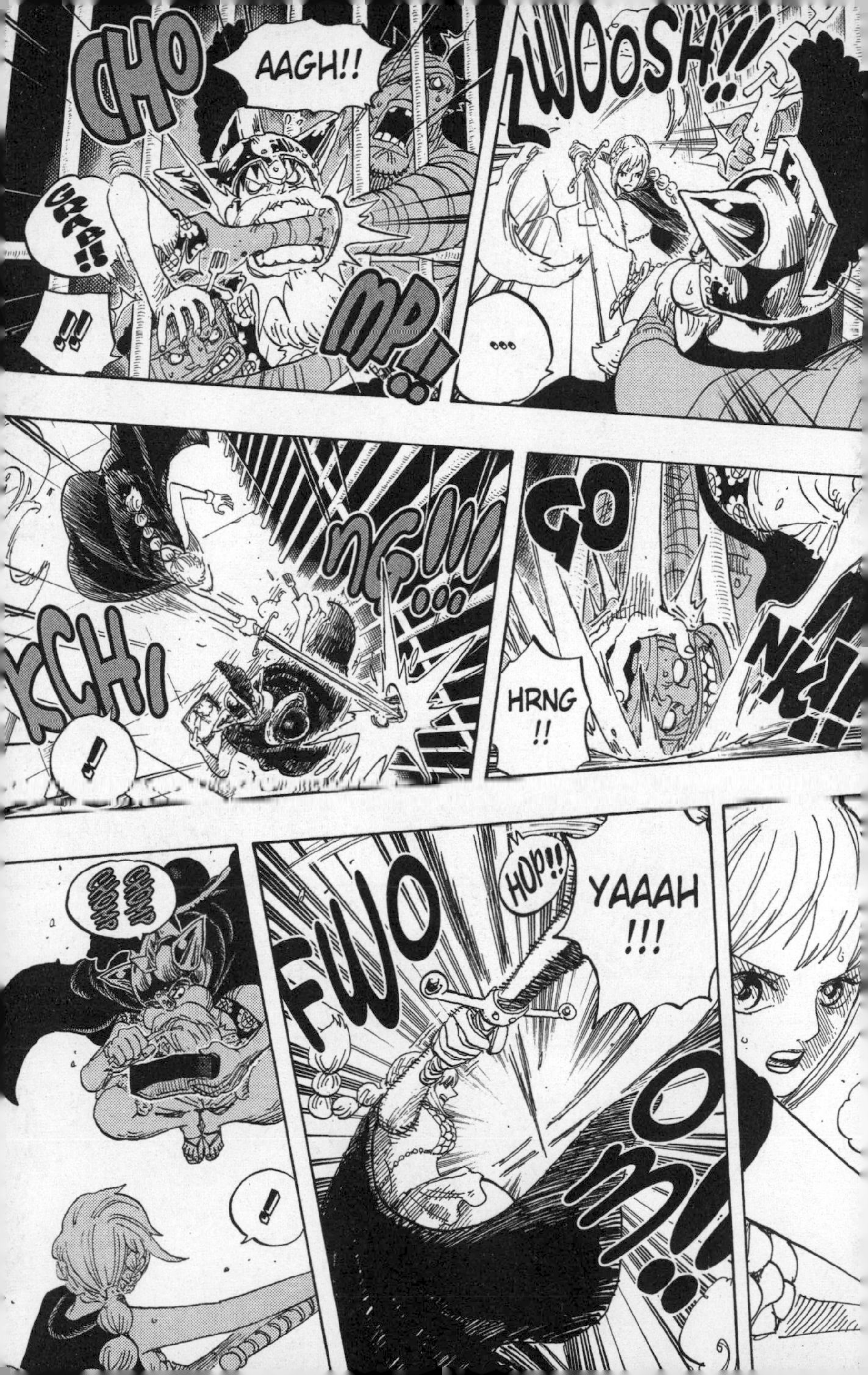
ZWOOSH!!
...
CHO
AAGH!!
GYAAA!!
!!
MP!!
GO
HRNG !!
NK!!
KCHI
NG!!!
!
HOP!!
YAAAH !!!
FWO
OM!!
CHOMP CHOMP
!

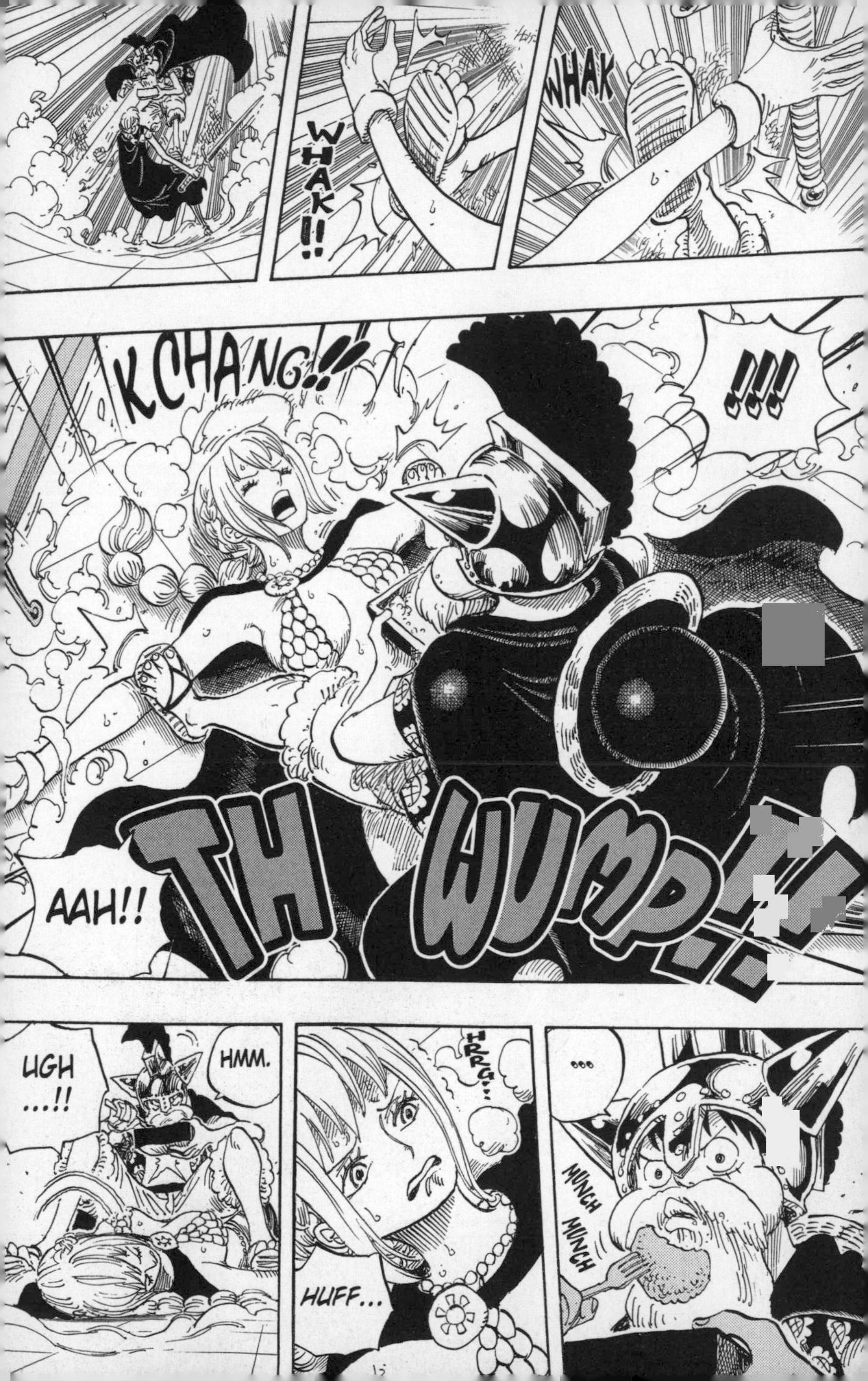
WHAK
WHAK!!
!!!
KCHANG!!
THWUMP!!
AAH!!
...
MUNCH
MUNCH
HRRG...
HUFF...
HMM.
UGH ...!!

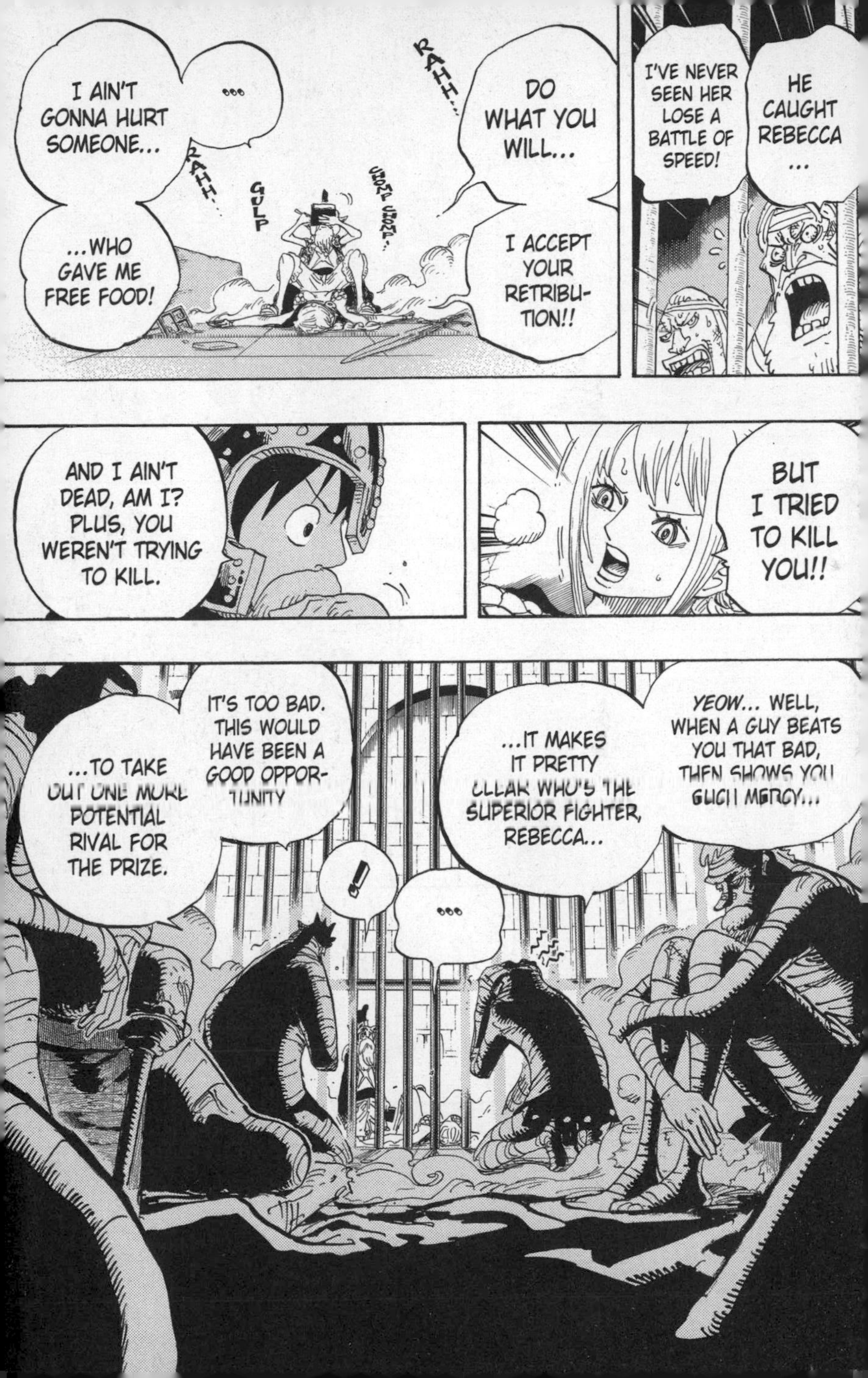
HE CAUGHT REBECCA...
I'VE NEVER SEEN HER LOSE A BATTLE OF SPEED!
DO WHAT YOU WILL...
I ACCEPT YOUR RETRIBU-TION!!
RAHH...
CHOMP CHOMP
GULP
RAHH...
...
I AIN'T GONNA HURT SOMEONE...
...WHO GAVE ME FREE FOOD!
BUT I TRIED TO KILL YOU!!
AND I AIN'T DEAD, AM I? PLUS, YOU WEREN'T TRYING TO KILL.
YEOW... WELL, WHEN A GUY BEATS YOU THAT BAD, THEN SHOWS YOU SUCH MERCY...
...IT MAKES IT PRETTY CLEAR WHO'S THE SUPERIOR FIGHTER, REBECCA...
...
!
IT'S TOO BAD. THIS WOULD HAVE BEEN A GOOD OPPOR-TUNITY
...TO TAKE OUT ONE MORE POTENTIAL RIVAL FOR THE PRIZE.

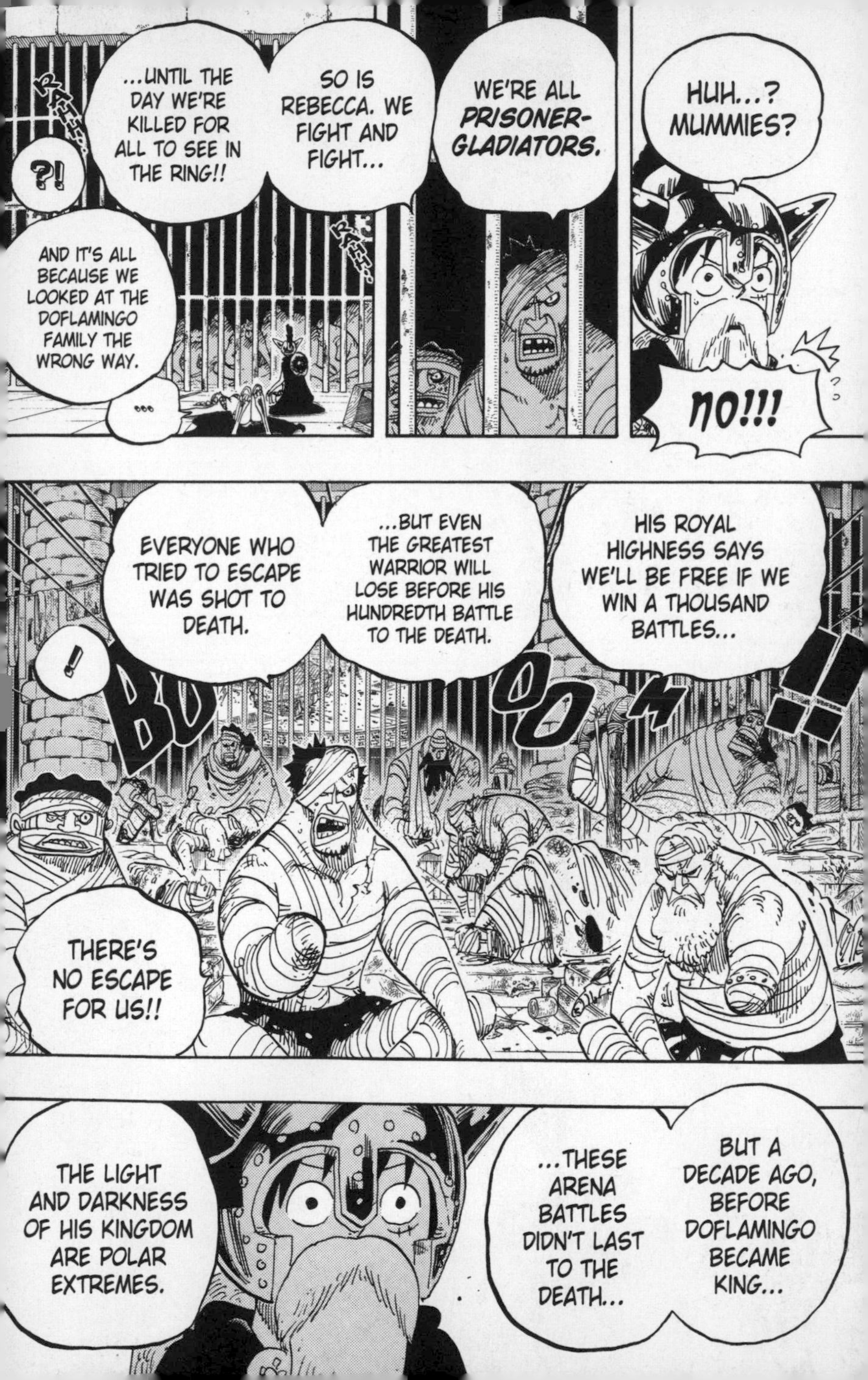
HUH...? MUMMIES?
NO!!!
WE'RE ALL PRISONER-GLADIATORS.
SO IS REBECCA. WE FIGHT AND FIGHT...
...UNTIL THE DAY WE'RE KILLED FOR ALL TO SEE IN THE RING!!
?!
AND IT'S ALL BECAUSE WE LOOKED AT THE DOFLAMINGO FAMILY THE WRONG WAY.
...
HIS ROYAL HIGHNESS SAYS WE'LL BE FREE IF WE WIN A THOUSAND BATTLES...
...BUT EVEN THE GREATEST WARRIOR WILL LOSE BEFORE HIS HUNDREDTH BATTLE TO THE DEATH.
EVERYONE WHO TRIED TO ESCAPE WAS SHOT TO DEATH.
!
BOOOM!!
THERE'S NO ESCAPE FOR US!!
BUT A DECADE AGO, BEFORE DOFLAMINGO BECAME KING...
...THESE ARENA BATTLES DIDN'T LAST TO THE DEATH...
THE LIGHT AND DARKNESS OF HIS KINGDOM ARE POLAR EXTREMES.

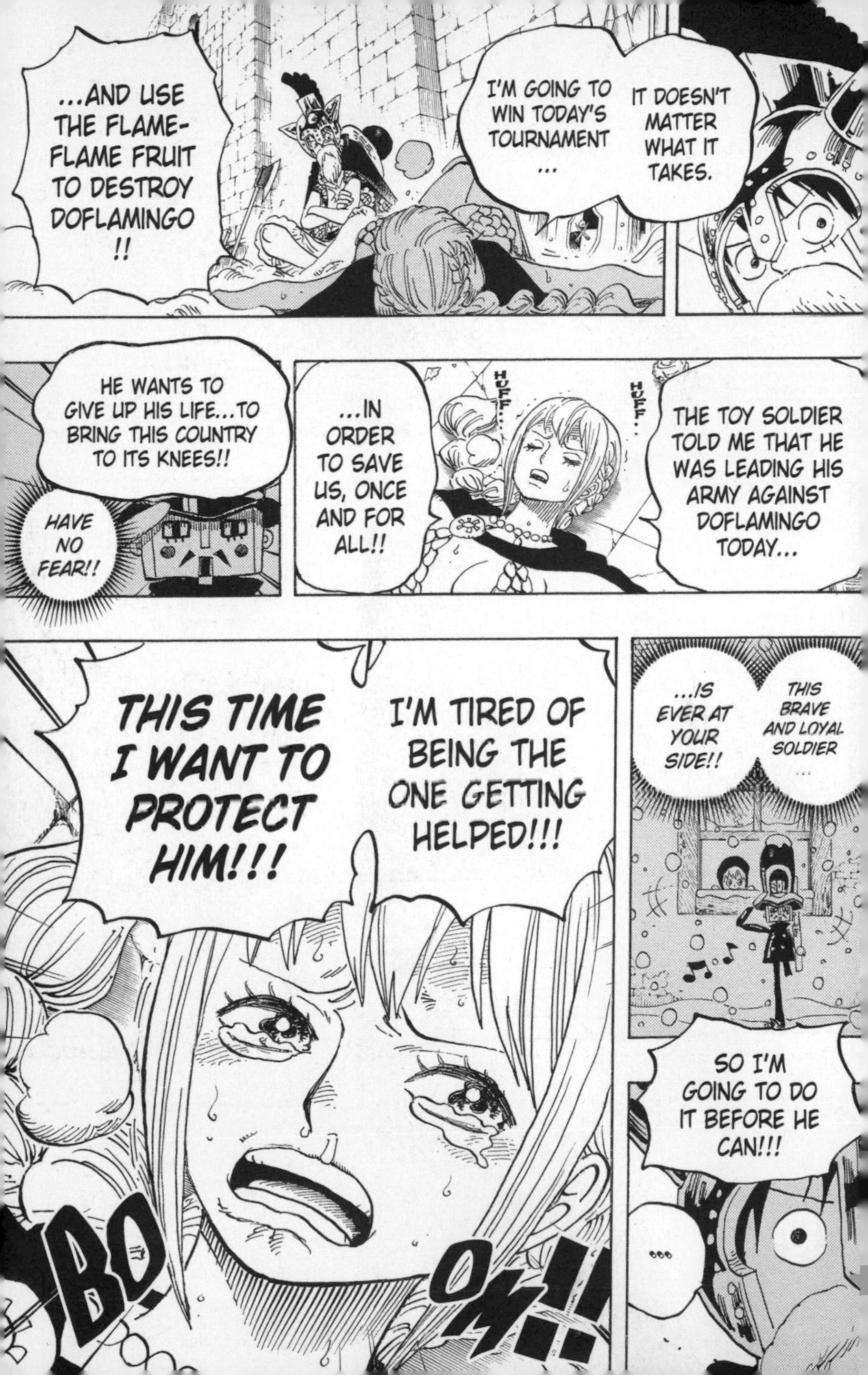
IT DOESN'T MATTER WHAT IT TAKES.
I'M GOING TO WIN TODAY'S TOURNAMENT ...
...AND USE THE FLAME-FLAME FRUIT TO DESTROY DOFLAMINGO !!
HUFF... HUFF...
THE TOY SOLDIER TOLD ME THAT HE WAS LEADING HIS ARMY AGAINST DOFLAMINGO TODAY...
...IN ORDER TO SAVE US, ONCE AND FOR ALL!!
HE WANTS TO GIVE UP HIS LIFE...TO BRING THIS COUNTRY TO ITS KNEES!!
HAVE NO FEAR!!
THIS BRAVE AND LOYAL SOLDIER ...
...IS EVER AT YOUR SIDE!!
SO I'M GOING TO DO IT BEFORE HE CAN!!!
...
I'M TIRED OF BEING THE ONE GETTING HELPED!!!
THIS TIME I WANT TO PROTECT HIM!!!
BO... OM!!

Chapter 721:
REBECCA AND THE SOLDIER

**CARIBOU'S NEW WORLD KEE HEE HEE, VOL. 38:
"TAKE OVER SCOTCH THE OPPRESSOR!!"**

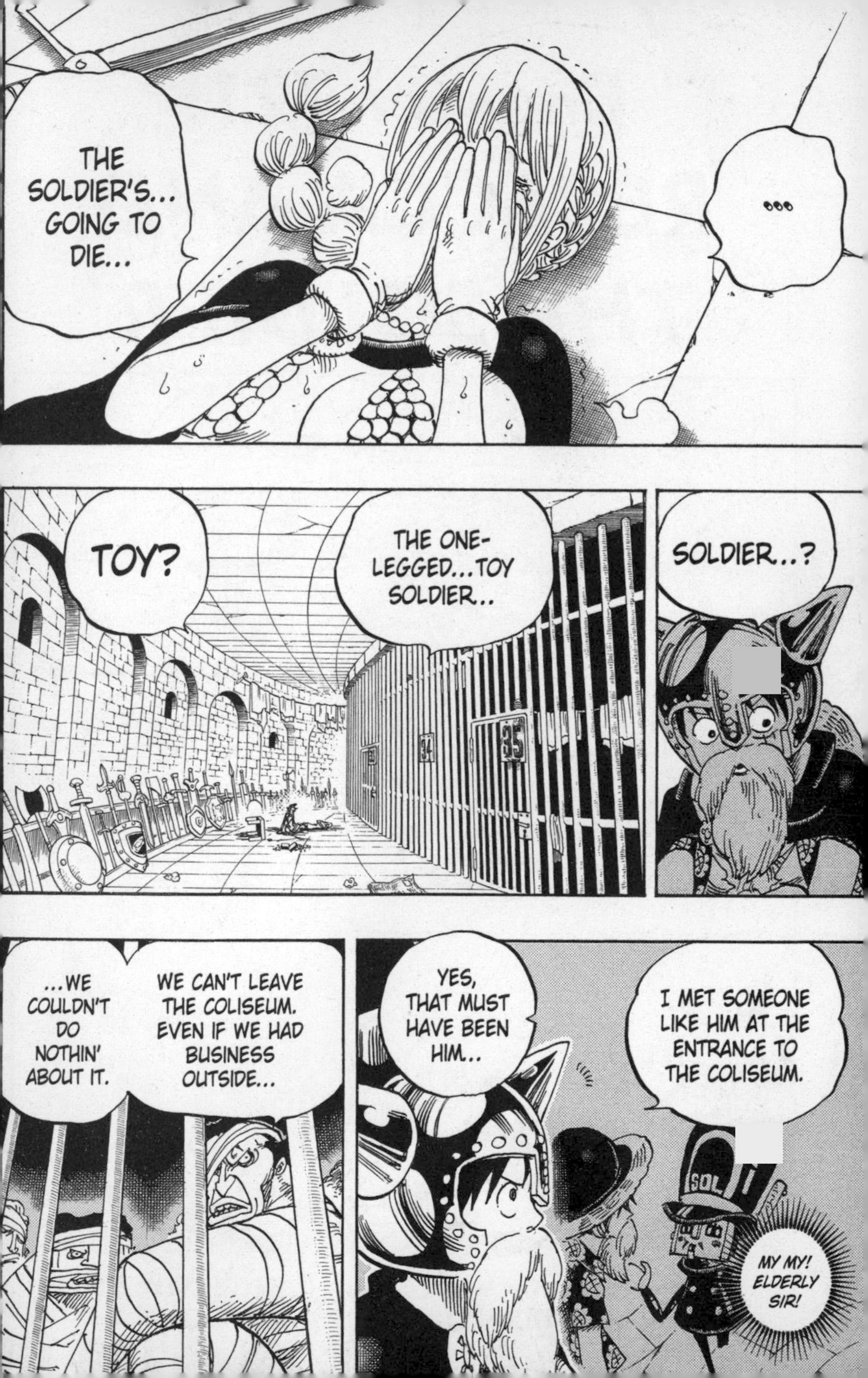
...
THE SOLDIER'S... GOING TO DIE...
SOLDIER...?
THE ONE-LEGGED...TOY SOLDIER...
TOY?
I MET SOMEONE LIKE HIM AT THE ENTRANCE TO THE COLISEUM.
YES, THAT MUST HAVE BEEN HIM...
MY MY! ELDERLY SIR!
WE CAN'T LEAVE THE COLISEUM. EVEN IF WE HAD BUSINESS OUTSIDE...
...WE COULDN'T DO NOTHIN' ABOUT IT.

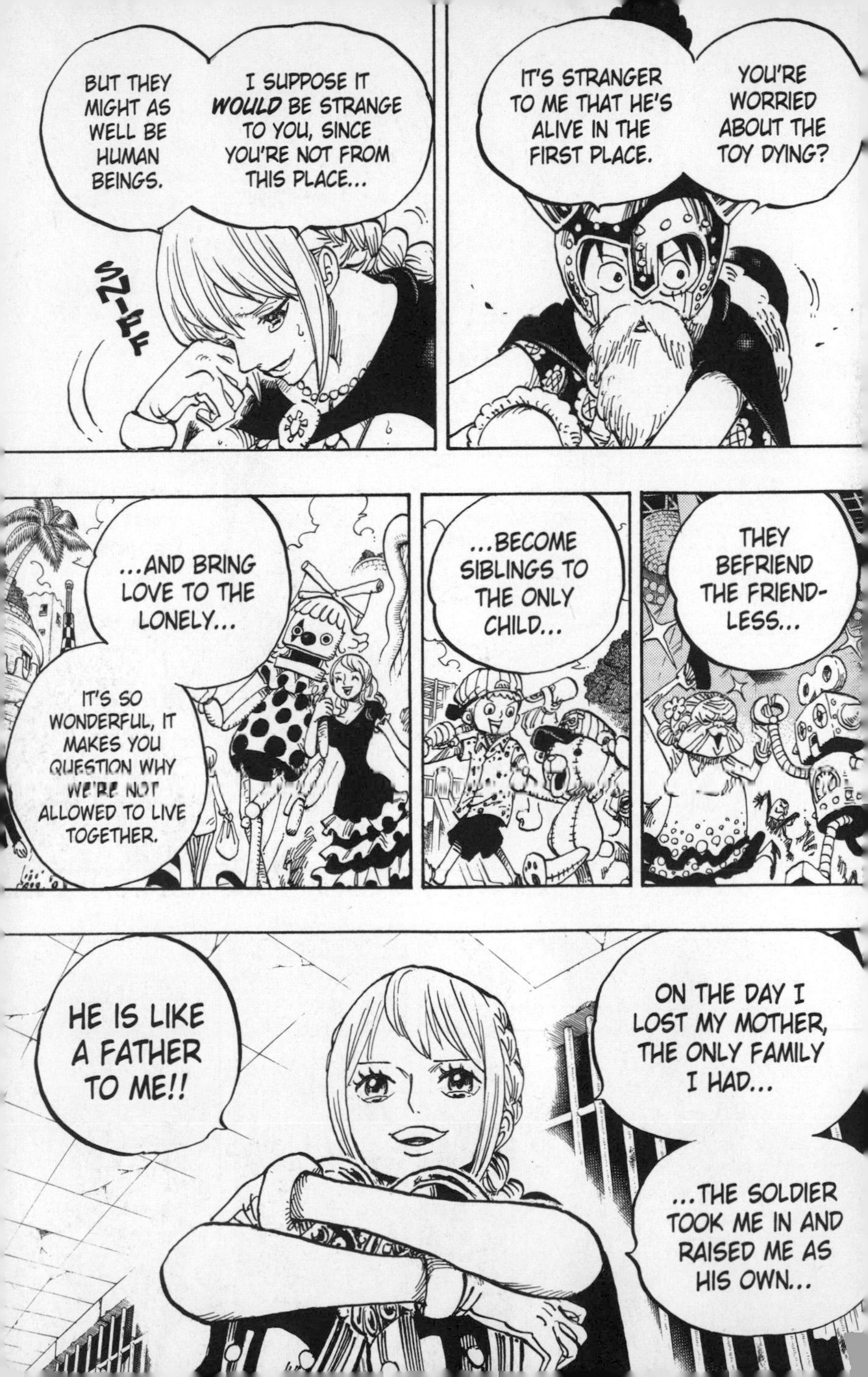
YOU'RE WORRIED ABOUT THE TOY DYING?
IT'S STRANGER TO ME THAT HE'S ALIVE IN THE FIRST PLACE.
I SUPPOSE IT WOULD BE STRANGE TO YOU, SINCE YOU'RE NOT FROM THIS PLACE...
BUT THEY MIGHT AS WELL BE HUMAN BEINGS.
SNIFF
THEY BEFRIEND THE FRIEND-LESS...
...BECOME SIBLINGS TO THE ONLY CHILD...
...AND BRING LOVE TO THE LONELY...
IT'S SO WONDERFUL, IT MAKES YOU QUESTION WHY WE'RE NOT ALLOWED TO LIVE TOGETHER.
ON THE DAY I LOST MY MOTHER, THE ONLY FAMILY I HAD...
...THE SOLDIER TOOK ME IN AND RAISED ME AS HIS OWN...
HE IS LIKE A FATHER TO ME!!

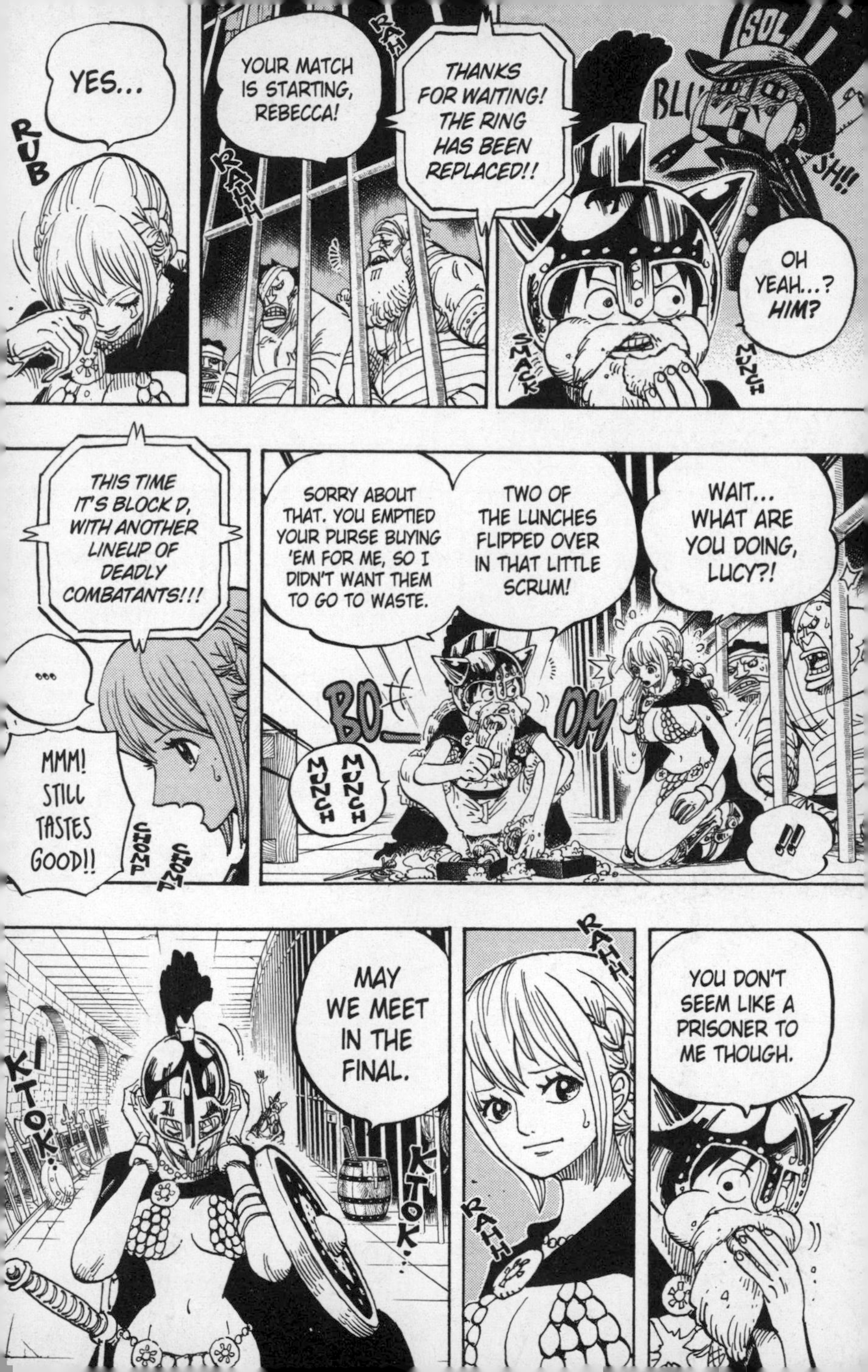

OH YEAH...? HIM?
MUNCH
SMACK
THANKS FOR WAITING! THE RING HAS BEEN REPLACED!!
YOUR MATCH IS STARTING, REBECCA!
RAHH
RAHH
YES...
RUB
WAIT... WHAT ARE YOU DOING, LUCY?!
TWO OF THE LUNCHES FLIPPED OVER IN THAT LITTLE SCRUM!
SORRY ABOUT THAT. YOU EMPTIED YOUR PURSE BUYING 'EM FOR ME, SO I DIDN'T WANT THEM TO GO TO WASTE.
BO— OM
MUNCH MUNCH
!!
THIS TIME IT'S BLOCK D, WITH ANOTHER LINEUP OF DEADLY COMBATANTS!!!
...
MMM! STILL TASTES GOOD!!
CHOMP CHOMP
YOU DON'T SEEM LIKE A PRISONER TO ME THOUGH.
RAHH
RAHH
MAY WE MEET IN THE FINAL.
KTOK
KTOK

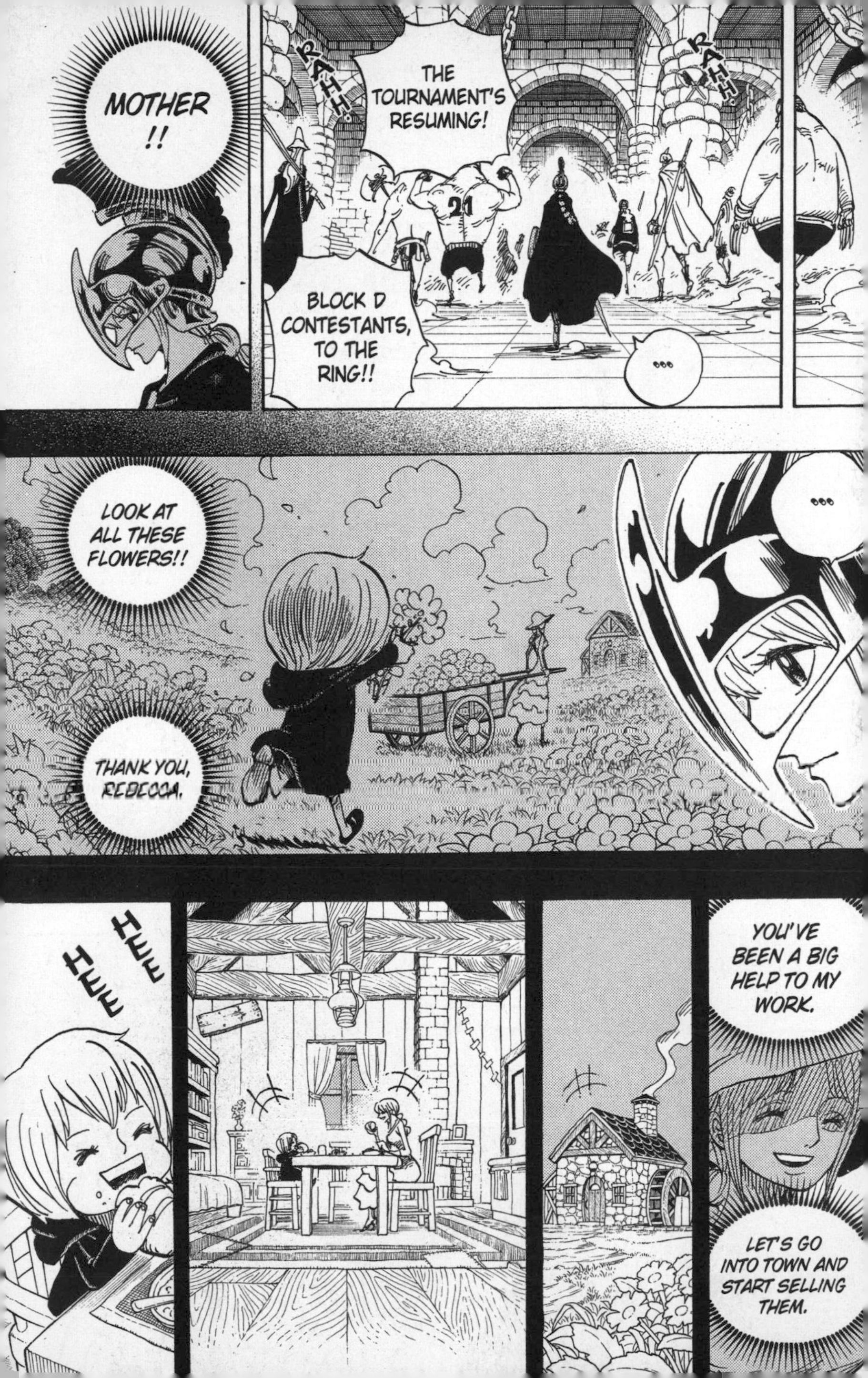
RAHH
THE TOURNAMENT'S RESUMING!
RAHH
BLOCK D CONTESTANTS, TO THE RING!!
...
MOTHER !!
...
LOOK AT ALL THESE FLOWERS!!
THANK YOU, REBECCA.
YOU'VE BEEN A BIG HELP TO MY WORK.
LET'S GO INTO TOWN AND START SELLING THEM.
HEE HEE

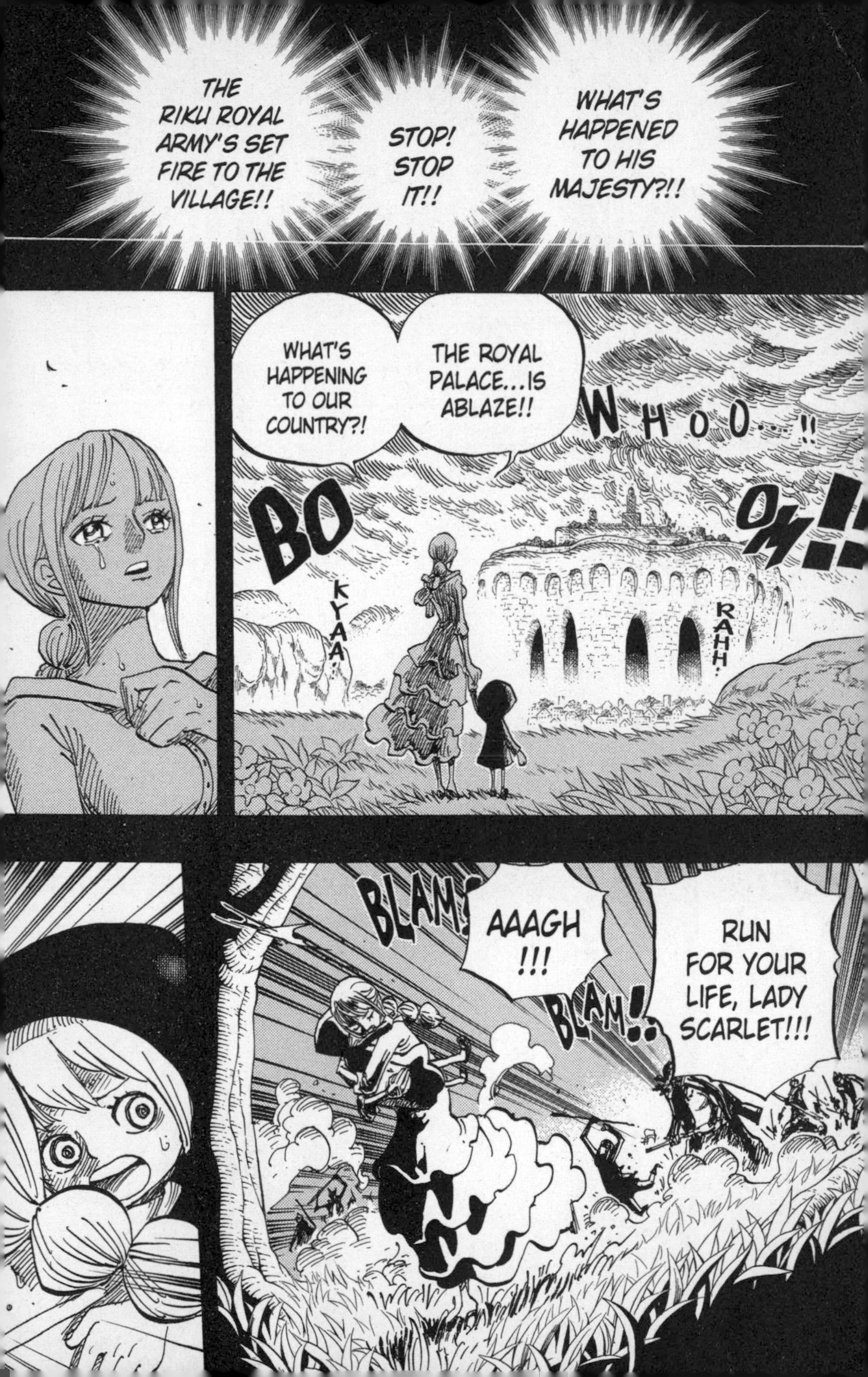
WHAT'S HAPPENED TO HIS MAJESTY?!!
STOP! STOP IT!!
THE RIKU ROYAL ARMY'S SET FIRE TO THE VILLAGE!!
WHOO...!!
THE ROYAL PALACE...IS ABLAZE!!
WHAT'S HAPPENING TO OUR COUNTRY?!
BOOM!!
RAHH!
KYAA!
RUN FOR YOUR LIFE, LADY SCARLET!!!
AAAGH!!!
BLAM!
BLAM!!

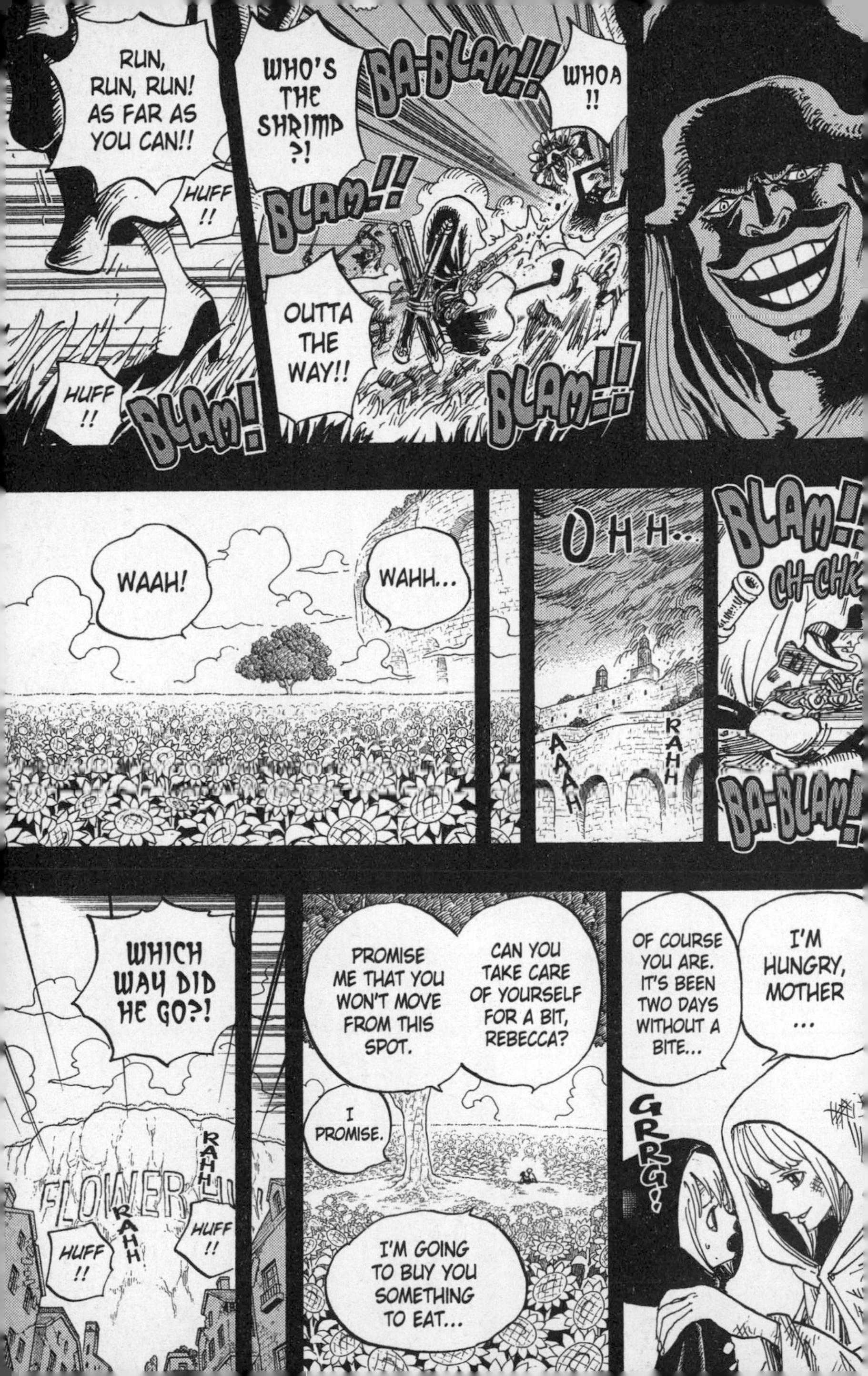
BA-BLAM!!
WHOA!!
WHO'S THE SHRIMP?!
BLAM!!
OUTTA THE WAY!!
BLAM!!
RUN, RUN, RUN! AS FAR AS YOU CAN!!
HUFF!!
HUFF!!
BLAM!
BLAM!!
CH-CHK
BA-BLAM!!
OHH...
RAHH
AAAH
WAHH...
WAAH!
I'M HUNGRY, MOTHER...
OF COURSE YOU ARE. IT'S BEEN TWO DAYS WITHOUT A BITE...
GRRG!
CAN YOU TAKE CARE OF YOURSELF FOR A BIT, REBECCA?
PROMISE ME THAT YOU WON'T MOVE FROM THIS SPOT.
I PROMISE.
I'M GOING TO BUY YOU SOMETHING TO EAT...
WHICH WAY DID HE GO?!
RAHH
HUFF!!
FLOWER
RAHH
HUFF!!

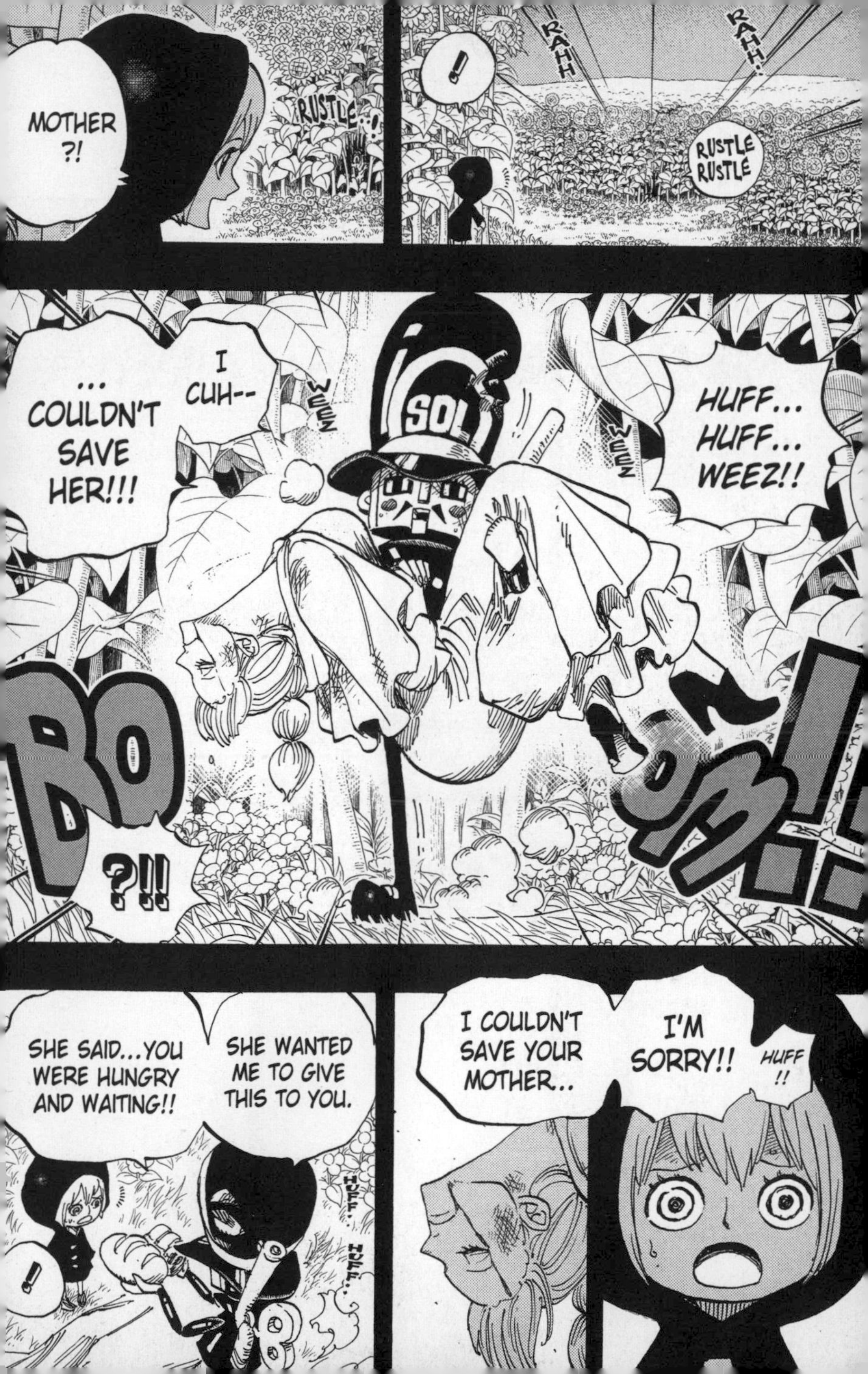
RAHH!
RAHH
!
RUSTLE RUSTLE
RUSTLE...!
MOTHER ?!
HUFF... HUFF... WEEZ!!
WEEZ
SOL
WEEZ
I CUH--
... COULDN'T SAVE HER!!!
BOOM!!
?!!
HUFF !!
I'M SORRY!!
I COULDN'T SAVE YOUR MOTHER...
HUFF.. HUFF..
SHE WANTED ME TO GIVE THIS TO YOU.
SHE SAID...YOU WERE HUNGRY AND WAITING!!
!

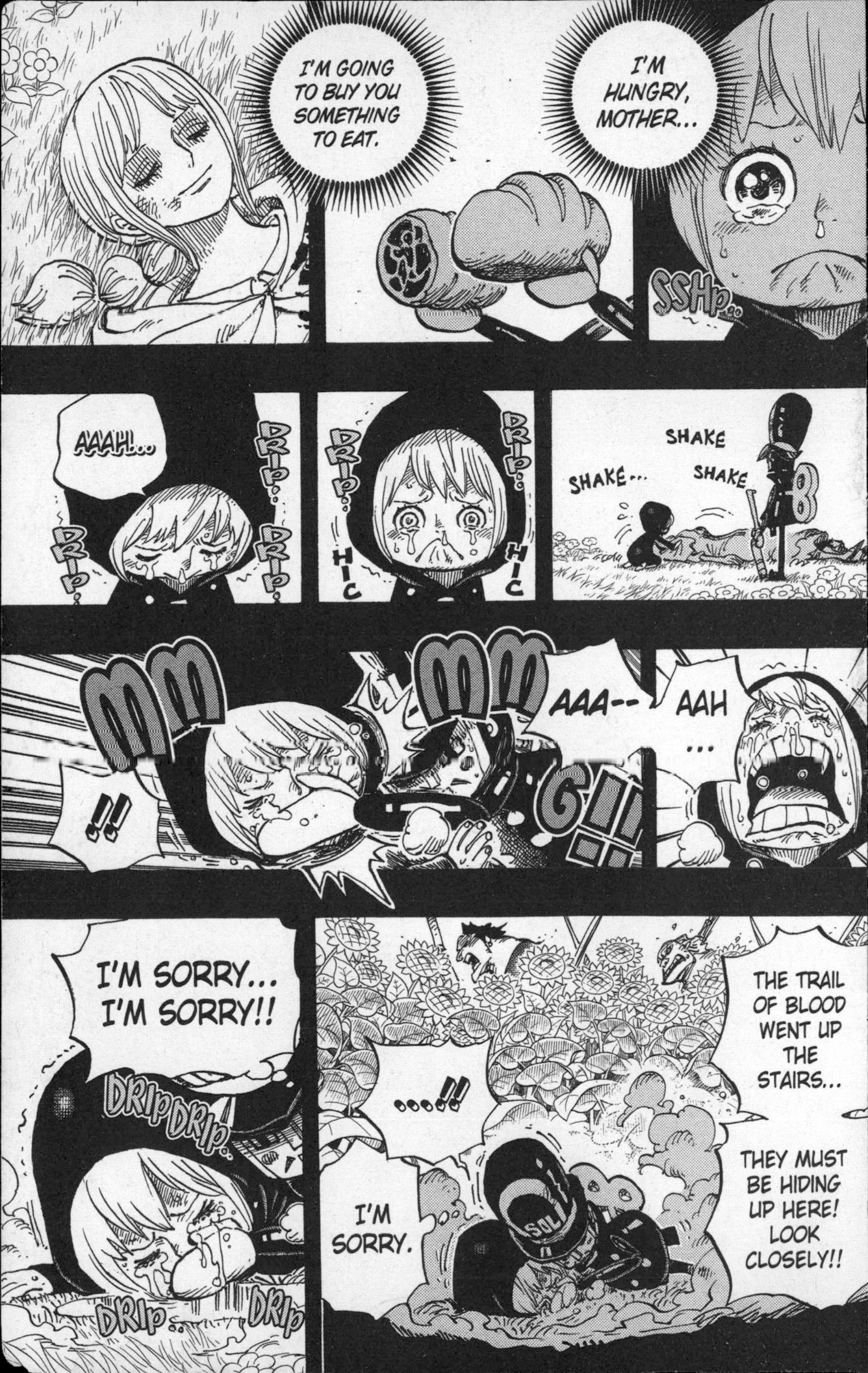
I'M HUNGRY, MOTHER...
SSHP..
I'M GOING TO BUY YOU SOMETHING TO EAT.
SHAKE
SHAKE...
SHAKE
DRIP..
DRIP..
HIC
HIC
AAAH...
DRIP..
DRIP..
DRIP
AAA--
AAH
...
MMMG!!
MM
!!
THE TRAIL OF BLOOD WENT UP THE STAIRS...
THEY MUST BE HIDING UP HERE! LOOK CLOSELY!!
....!!
I'M SORRY.
I'M SORRY... I'M SORRY!!
DRIP DRIP..
DRIP..
DRIP

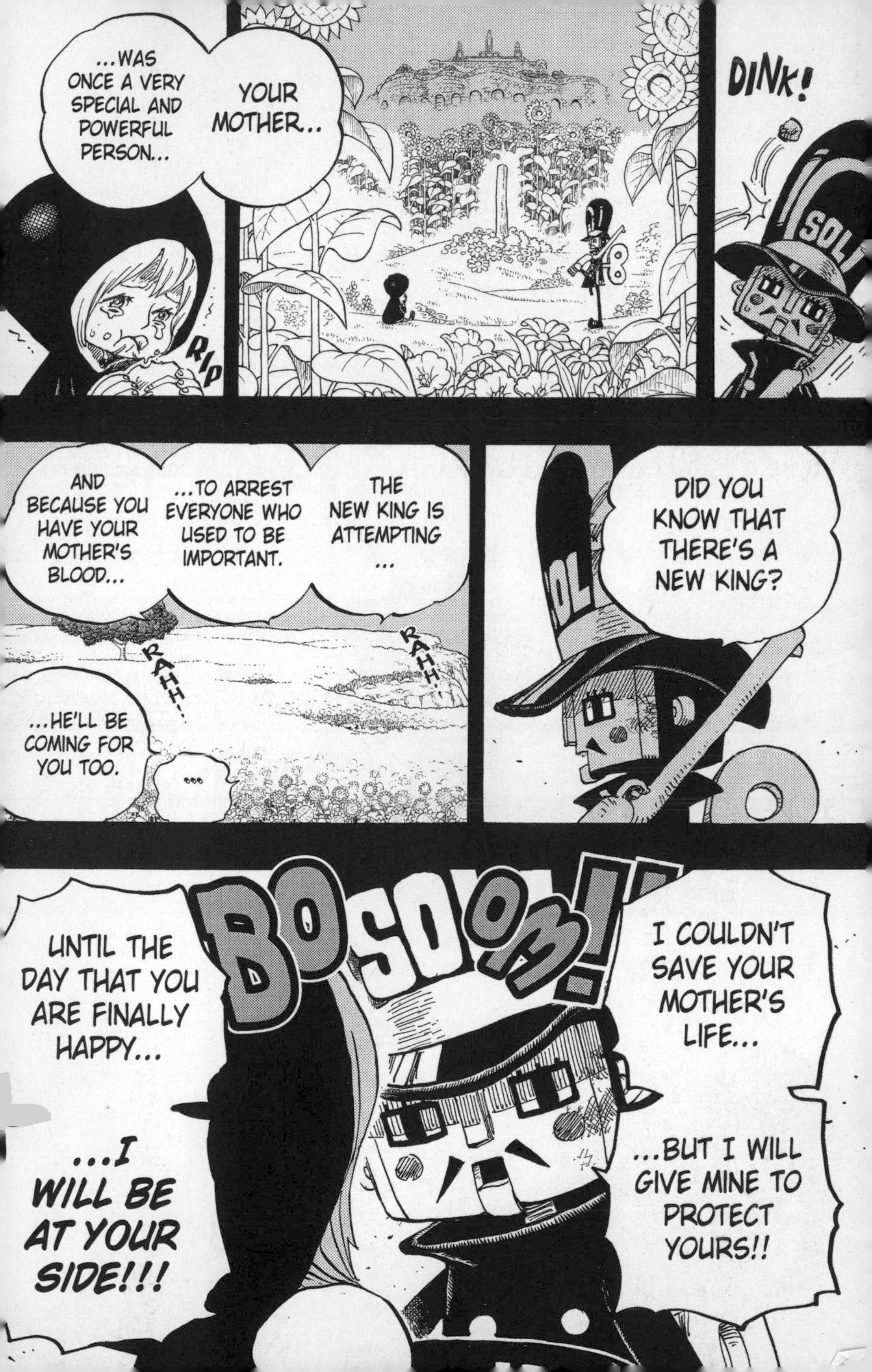
DINK!
YOUR MOTHER...
...WAS ONCE A VERY SPECIAL AND POWERFUL PERSON...
RIP
DID YOU KNOW THAT THERE'S A NEW KING?
THE NEW KING IS ATTEMPTING...
...TO ARREST EVERYONE WHO USED TO BE IMPORTANT.
AND BECAUSE YOU HAVE YOUR MOTHER'S BLOOD...
RAHH!
RAHH!
...HE'LL BE COMING FOR YOU TOO.
...
I COULDN'T SAVE YOUR MOTHER'S LIFE...
BOSOOM!!
...BUT I WILL GIVE MINE TO PROTECT YOURS!!
UNTIL THE DAY THAT YOU ARE FINALLY HAPPY...
...I WILL BE AT YOUR SIDE!!!

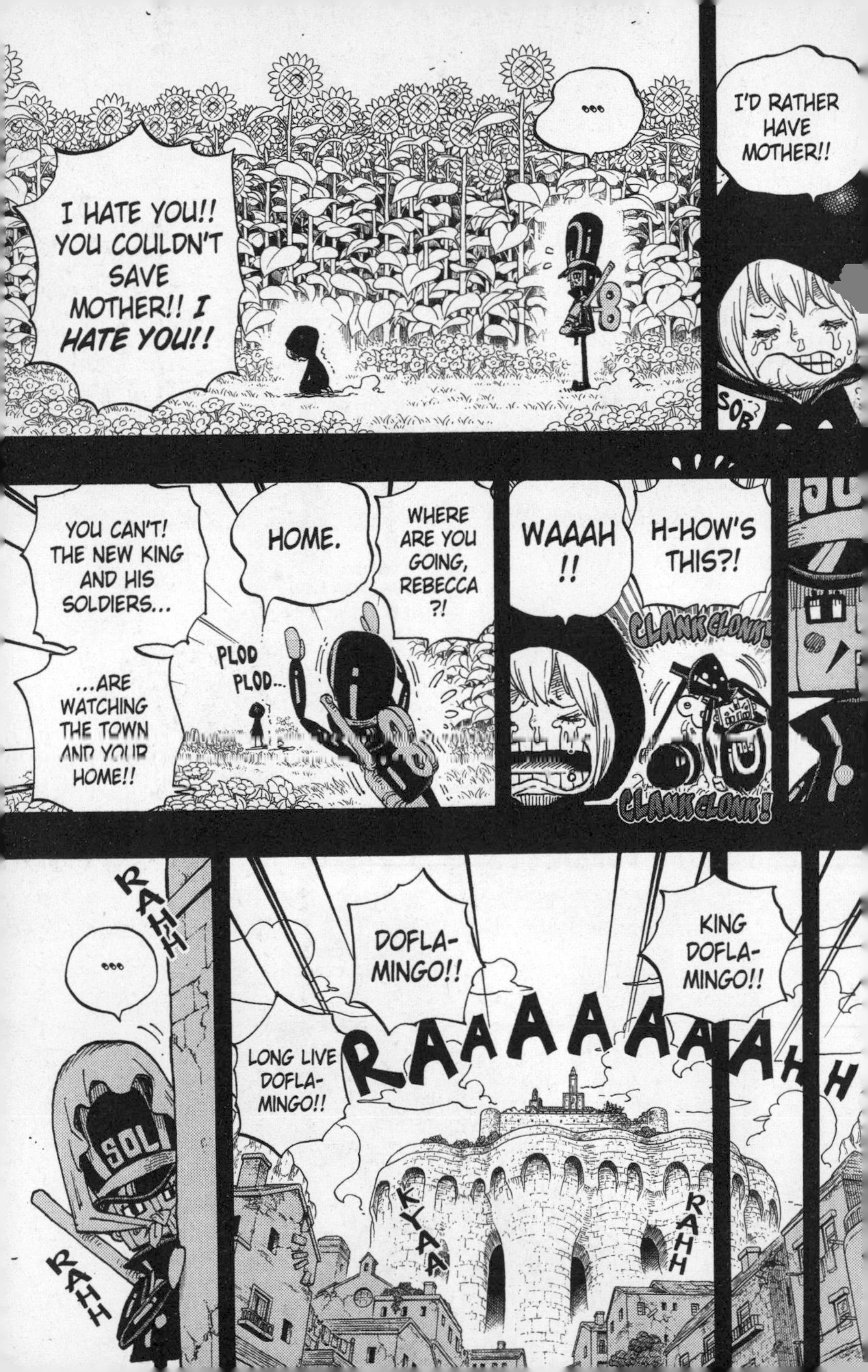
I'D RATHER HAVE MOTHER!!
SOB
...
I HATE YOU!! YOU COULDN'T SAVE MOTHER!! I HATE YOU!!
H-HOW'S THIS?!
WAAAH !!
CLANK CLONK!
CLANK CLONK!
WHERE ARE YOU GOING, REBECCA?!
HOME.
YOU CAN'T! THE NEW KING AND HIS SOLDIERS...
PLOD PLOD...
...ARE WATCHING THE TOWN AND YOUR HOME!!
KING DOFLAMINGO!!
DOFLAMINGO!!
RAAAAAAAHH
LONG LIVE DOFLAMINGO!!
RAHH
KYAA
RAHH
...
SOL
RAHH

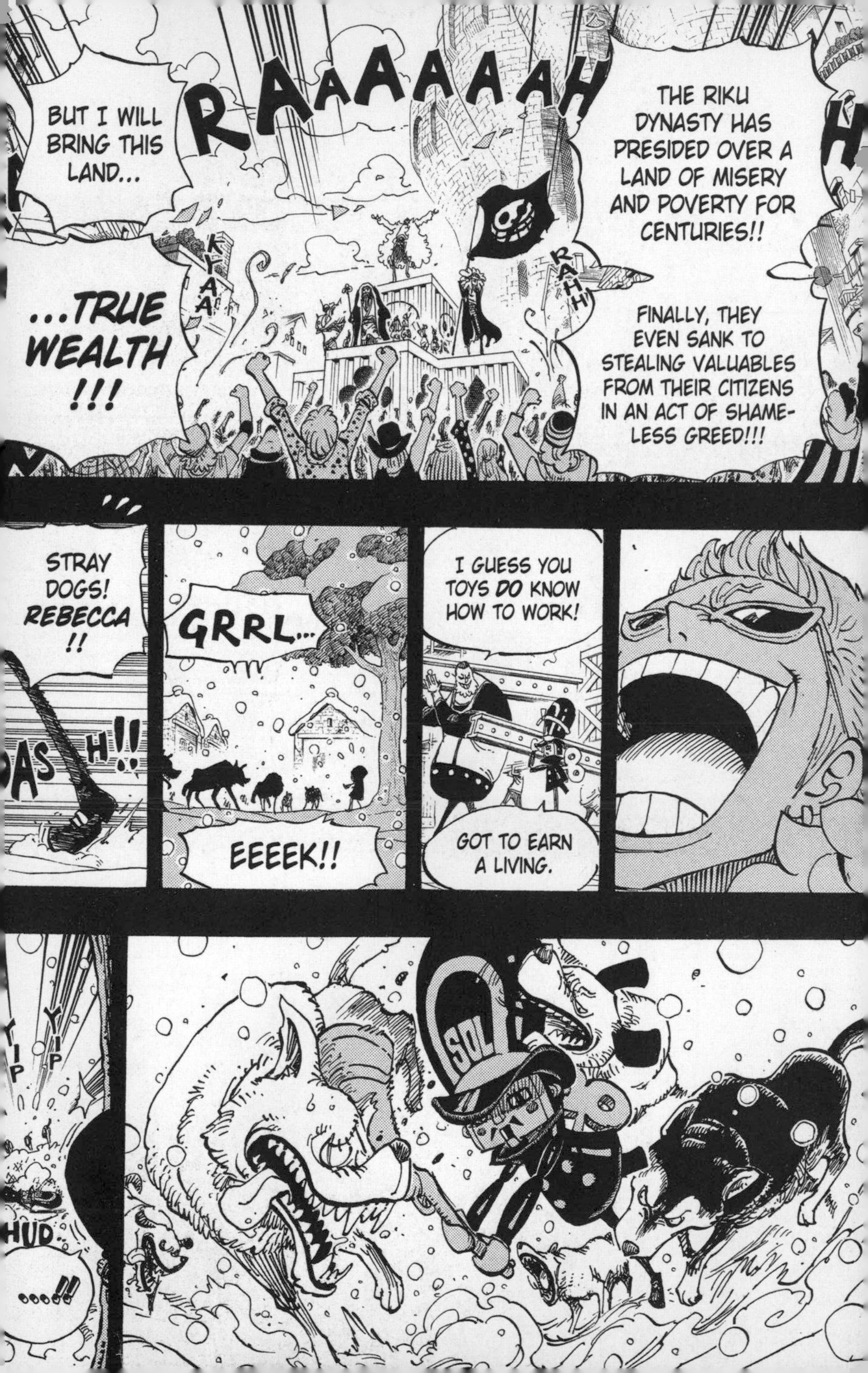
THE RIKU DYNASTY HAS PRESIDED OVER A LAND OF MISERY AND POVERTY FOR CENTURIES!!
FINALLY, THEY EVEN SANK TO STEALING VALUABLES FROM THEIR CITIZENS IN AN ACT OF SHAMELESS GREED!!!
RAAAAAAH
RAHH
KYAA
BUT I WILL BRING THIS LAND...
...TRUE WEALTH!!!
I GUESS YOU TOYS DO KNOW HOW TO WORK!
GOT TO EARN A LIVING.
GRRL...
EEEEK!!
STRAY DOGS! REBECCA!!
YIP
YIP
...!!

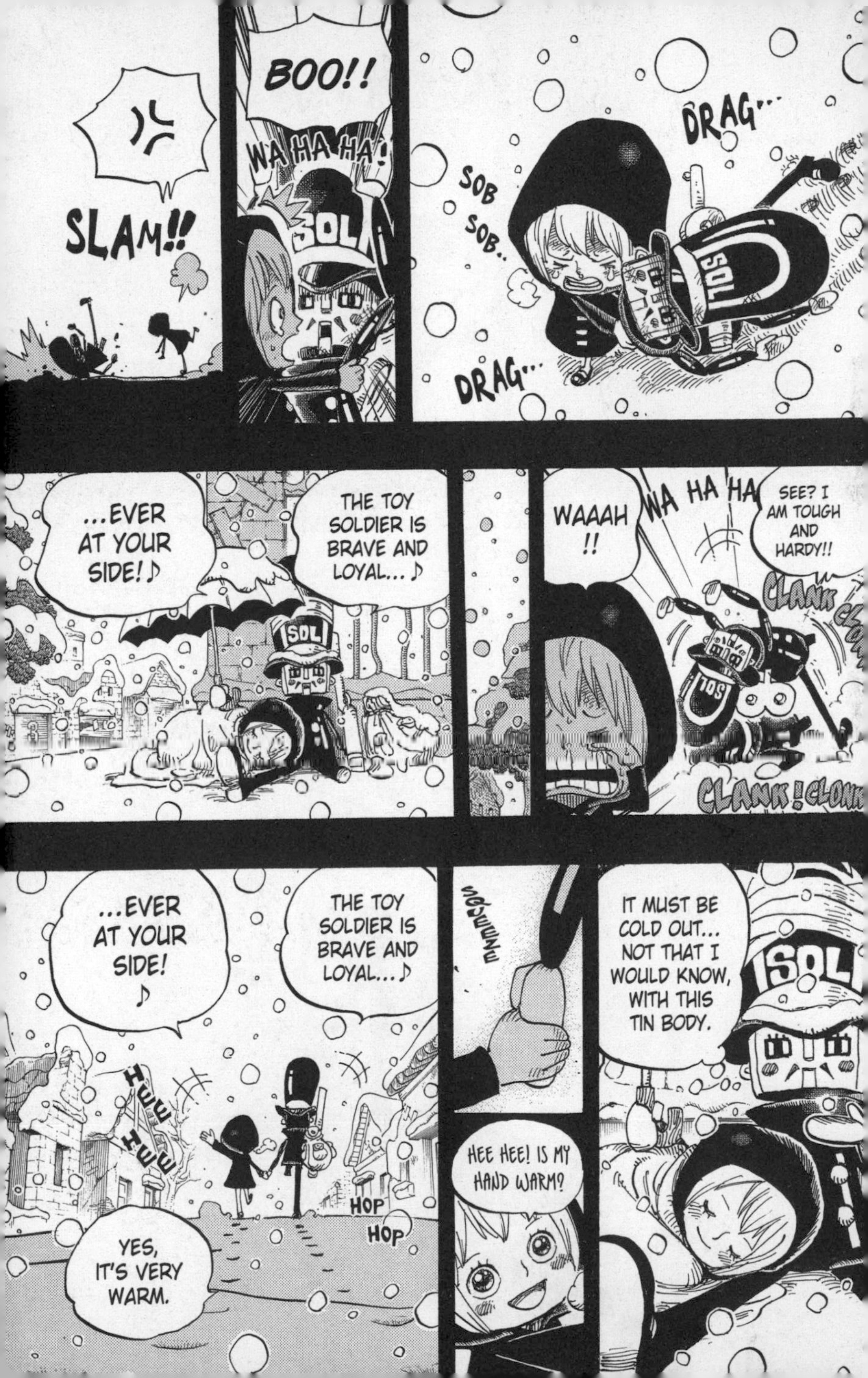
DRAG...
SOB SOB...
DRAG...
BOO!!
WA HA HA!
SLAM!!
SEE? I AM TOUGH AND HARDY!!
WA HA HA
CLANK CLONK
WAAAH!!
CLANK! CLONK
THE TOY SOLDIER IS BRAVE AND LOYAL...♪
...EVER AT YOUR SIDE!♪
IT MUST BE COLD OUT... NOT THAT I WOULD KNOW, WITH THIS TIN BODY.
HEE HEE! IS MY HAND WARM?
THE TOY SOLDIER IS BRAVE AND LOYAL...♪
...EVER AT YOUR SIDE! ♪
HOP
HOP
YES, IT'S VERY WARM.

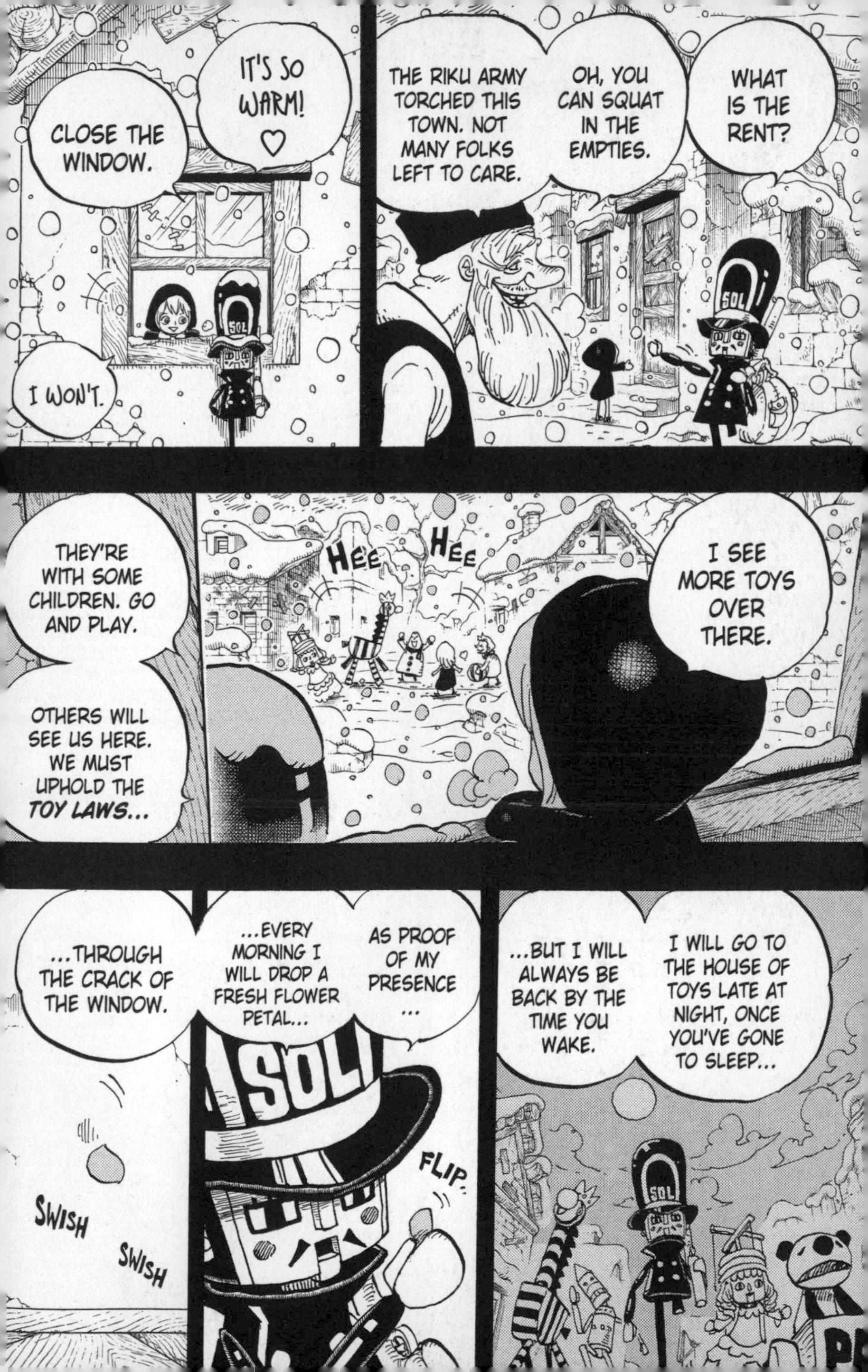
WHAT IS THE RENT?
OH, YOU CAN SQUAT IN THE EMPTIES.
THE RIKU ARMY TORCHED THIS TOWN. NOT MANY FOLKS LEFT TO CARE.
IT'S SO WARM! ♡
CLOSE THE WINDOW.
I WON'T.
I SEE MORE TOYS OVER THERE.
HEE
HEE
THEY'RE WITH SOME CHILDREN. GO AND PLAY.
OTHERS WILL SEE US HERE. WE MUST UPHOLD THE *TOY LAWS*...
I WILL GO TO THE HOUSE OF TOYS LATE AT NIGHT, ONCE YOU'VE GONE TO SLEEP...
...BUT I WILL ALWAYS BE BACK BY THE TIME YOU WAKE.
AS PROOF OF MY PRESENCE ...
...EVERY MORNING I WILL DROP A FRESH FLOWER PETAL...
FLIP
...THROUGH THE CRACK OF THE WINDOW.
SWISH
SWISH

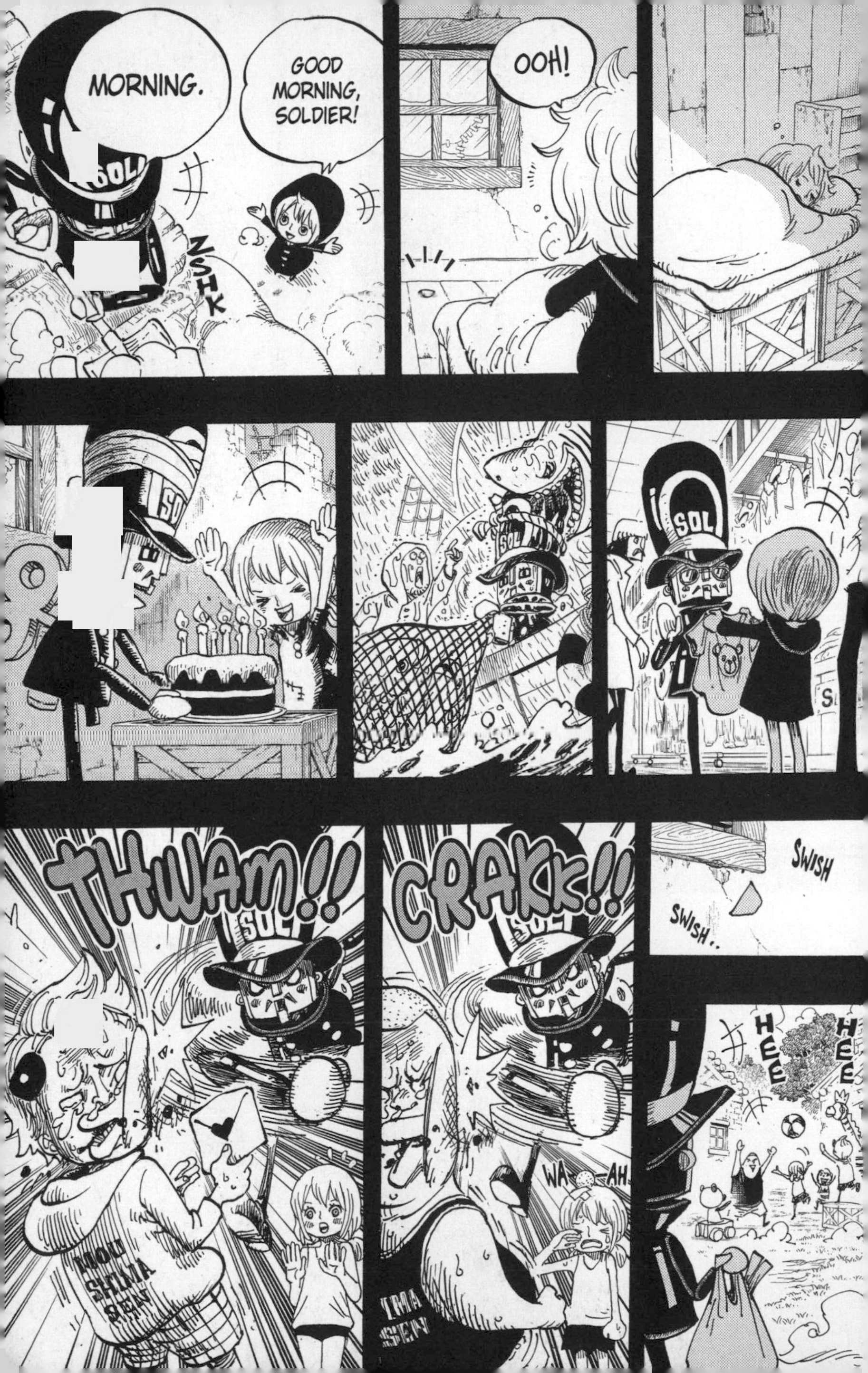
OOH!
GOOD MORNING, SOLDIER!
MORNING.
ZSHK
SWISH
SWISH..
HEE
HEE
CRAKK!!
WA-AH
THWAM!!
MOU SHIMA SEN

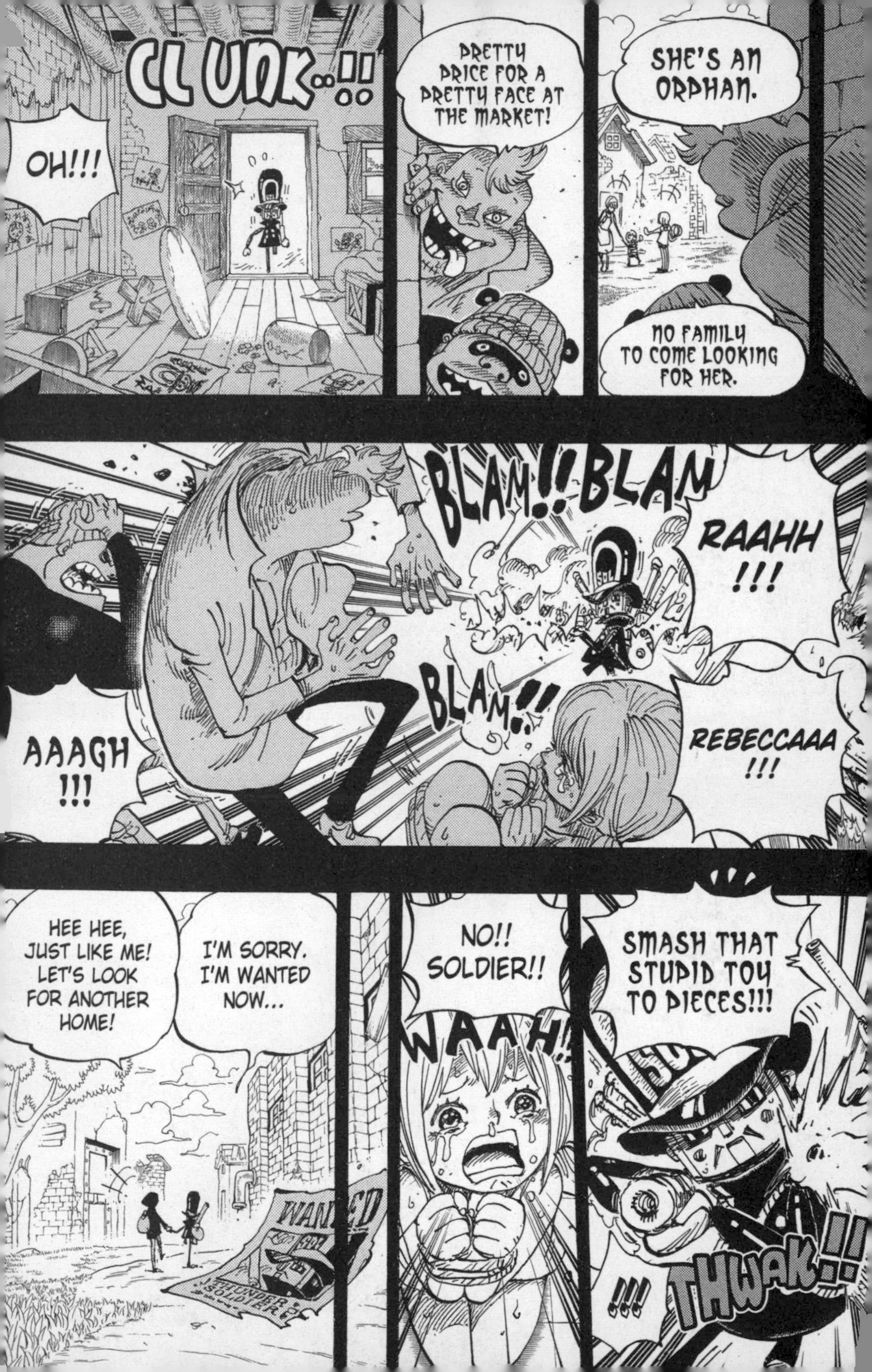
SHE'S AN ORPHAN.
NO FAMILY TO COME LOOKING FOR HER.
PRETTY PRICE FOR A PRETTY FACE AT THE MARKET!
CLUNK..!!
OH!!!
RAAHH!!!
BLAM!! BLAN
REBECCAAA!!!
BLAM!!
AAAGH!!!
SMASH THAT STUPID TOY TO PIECES!!!
THWAK!!
!!!
NO!! SOLDIER!!
WAAH!!
I'M SORRY. I'M WANTED NOW...
HEE HEE, JUST LIKE ME! LET'S LOOK FOR ANOTHER HOME!
WANTED
THUNDER SOLDIER

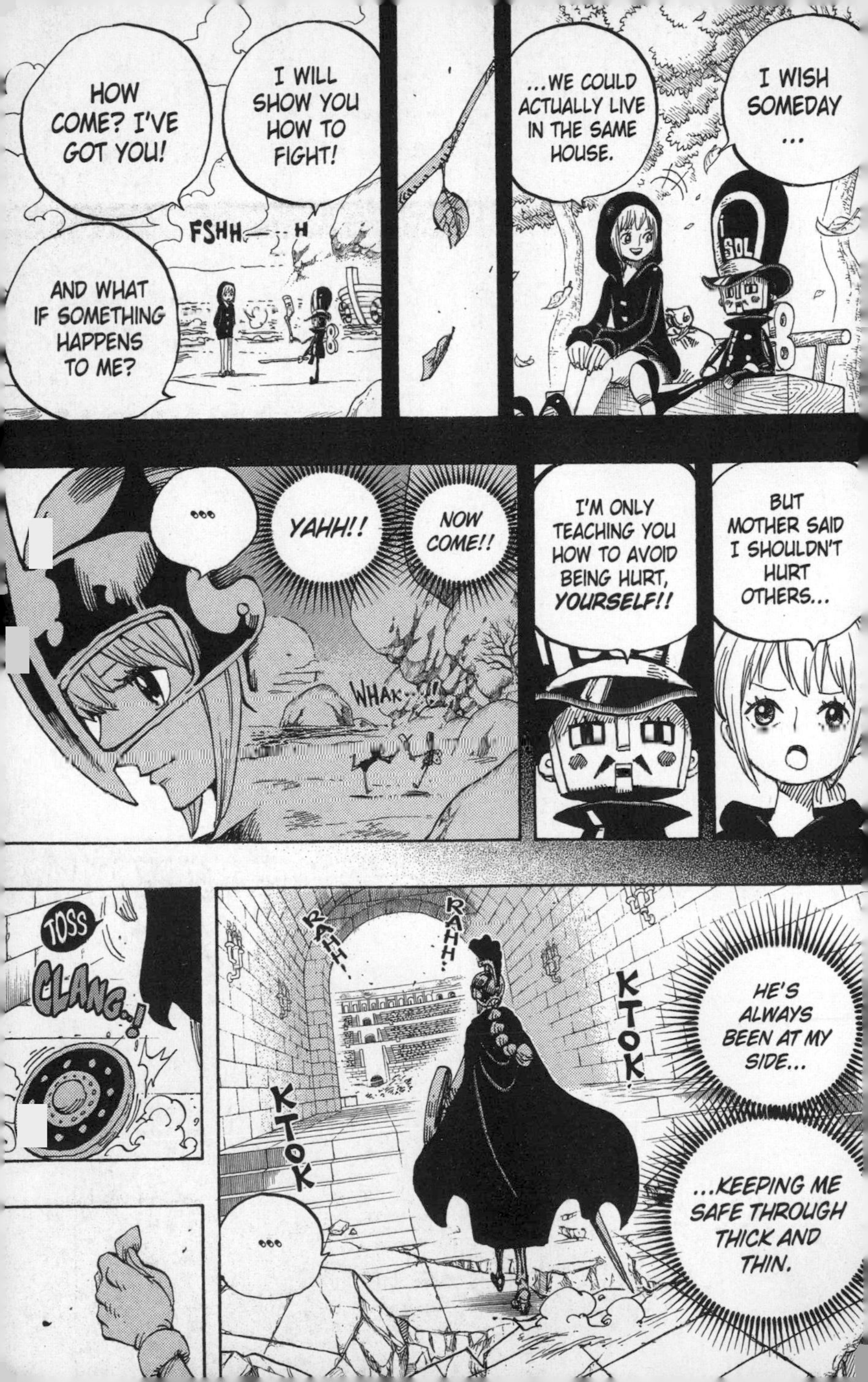
I WISH SOMEDAY ...
...WE COULD ACTUALLY LIVE IN THE SAME HOUSE.
I WILL SHOW YOU HOW TO FIGHT!
HOW COME? I'VE GOT YOU!
FSHH...H
AND WHAT IF SOMETHING HAPPENS TO ME?
BUT MOTHER SAID I SHOULDN'T HURT OTHERS...
I'M ONLY TEACHING YOU HOW TO AVOID BEING HURT, YOURSELF!!
NOW COME!!
YAHH!!
WHAK...!!
...
HE'S ALWAYS BEEN AT MY SIDE...
RAHH!
RAHH!
KTOK!
KTOK
...KEEPING ME SAFE THROUGH THICK AND THIN.
...
TOSS
CLANG..!

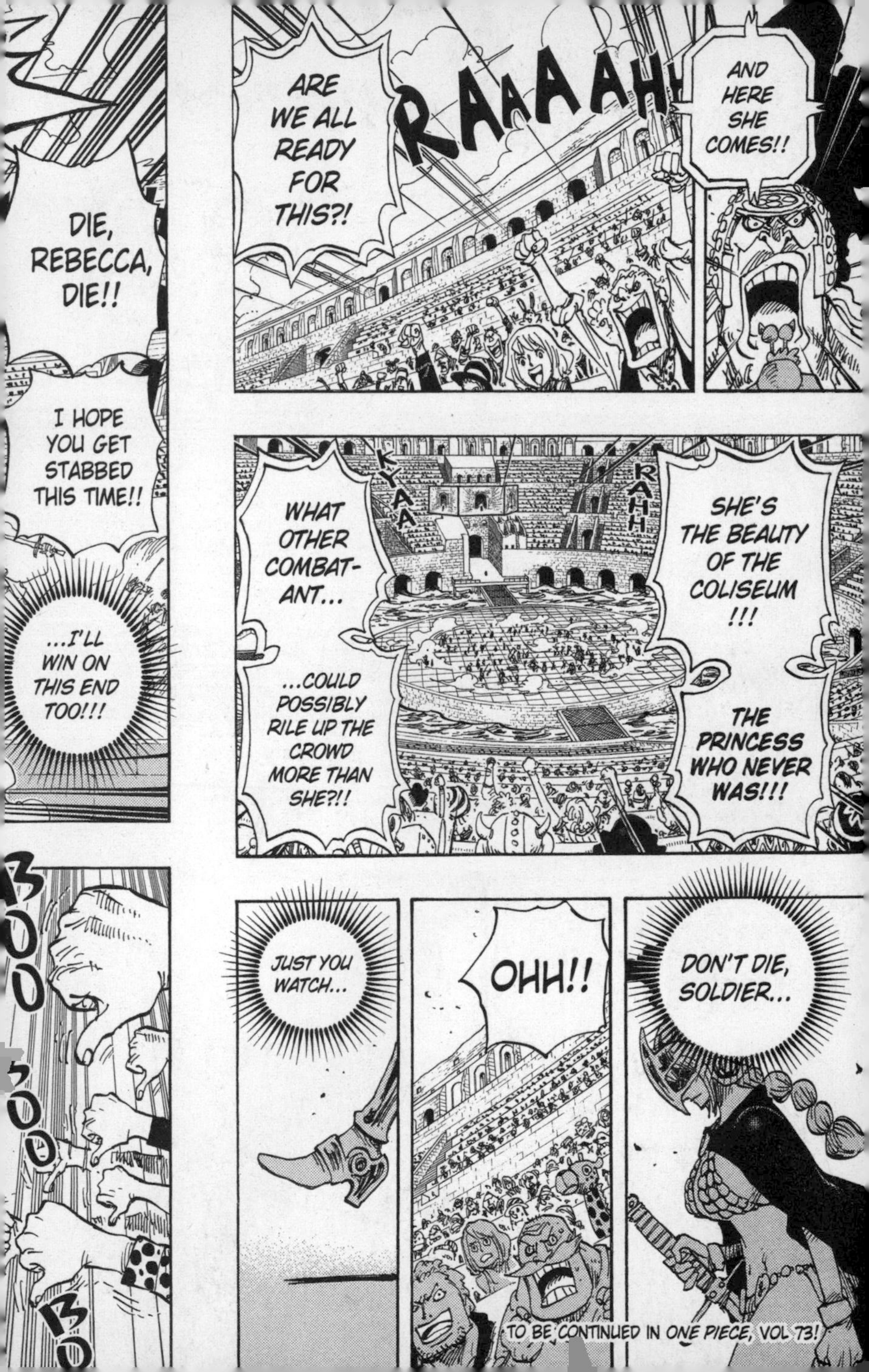
AND HERE SHE COMES!!
RAAAAH
ARE WE ALL READY FOR THIS?!
RAHH
SHE'S THE BEAUTY OF THE COLISEUM!!!
THE PRINCESS WHO NEVER WAS!!!
KYAA
WHAT OTHER COMBAT-ANT...
...COULD POSSIBLY RILE UP THE CROWD MORE THAN SHE?!!
DON'T DIE, SOLDIER...
OHH!!
JUST YOU WATCH...
TO BE CONTINUED IN ONE PIECE, VOL 73!
DIE, REBECCA, DIE!!
I HOPE YOU GET STABBED THIS TIME!!
...I'LL WIN ON THIS END TOO!!!
BOOO

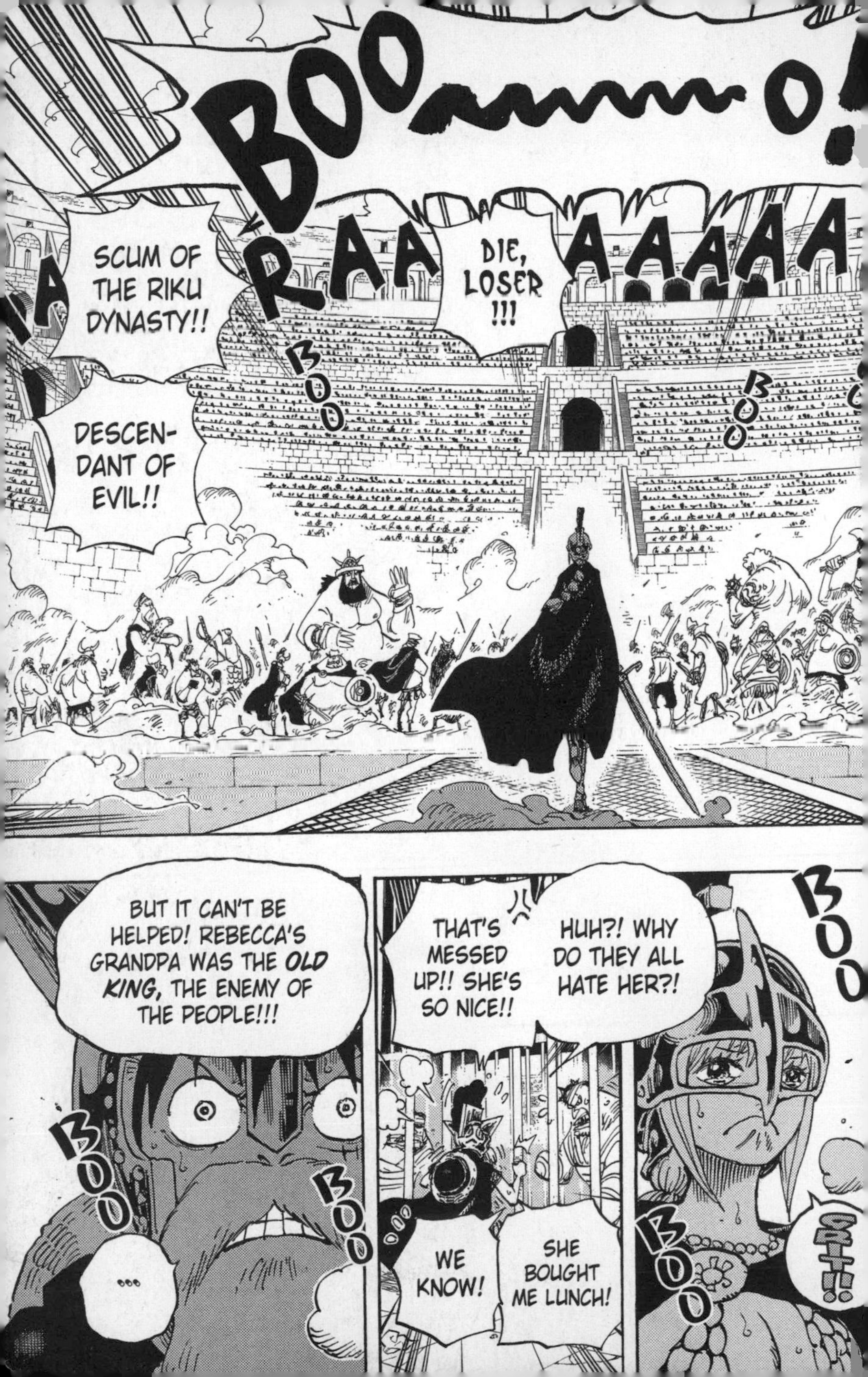
BOOOOO!
RAAAAAA
DIE, LOSER!!!
SCUM OF THE RIKU DYNASTY!!
BOO
BOO
DESCENDANT OF EVIL!!
BOO
GRIT!!
BOO
HUH?! WHY DO THEY ALL HATE HER?!
THAT'S MESSED UP!! SHE'S SO NICE!!
SHE BOUGHT ME LUNCH!
WE KNOW!
BUT IT CAN'T BE HELPED! REBECCA'S GRANDPA WAS THE *OLD KING*, THE ENEMY OF THE PEOPLE!!!
BOO
BOO
...

COMING NEXT VOLUME:

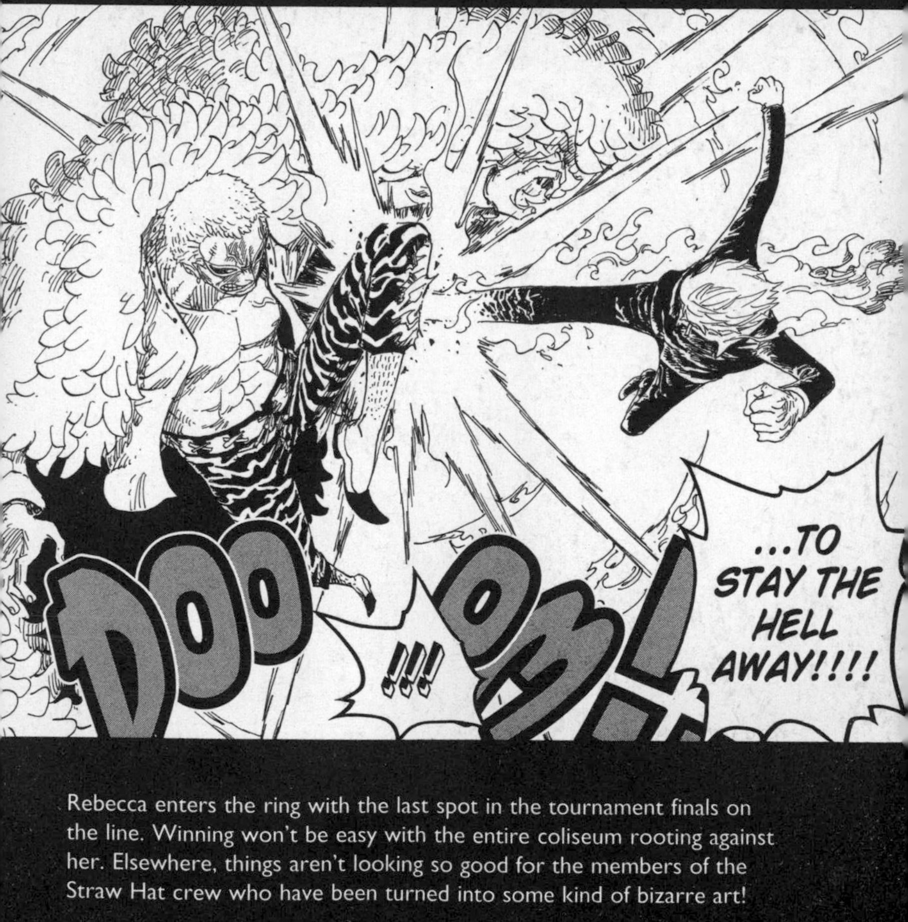
...TO STAY THE HELL AWAY!!!!
DOOOM!!!

Rebecca enters the ring with the last spot in the tournament finals on the line. Winning won't be easy with the entire coliseum rooting against her. Elsewhere, things aren't looking so good for the members of the Straw Hat crew who have been turned into some kind of bizarre art!

ON SALE JANUARY 2015!

FIGHT HELLFIRE WITH HELLFIRE!

Watch the anime on VIZAnime.com!

MANGA PRICE:
$9.99 usa $12.99 can
ISBN-13: 978-1-4215-4032-0

Go to **VIZ.COM** for more
info on **Blue Exorcist** and
other great titles!

Available now at store.viz.com

Also available at your local bookstore or comic store

www.shonenjump.com   www.viz.com

BLUE EXORCIST

Story and Art by Kazue Kato

AO NO EXORCIST © 2009 by Kazue Kato/SHUEISHA Inc.

You're Reading in the Wrong Direction!!

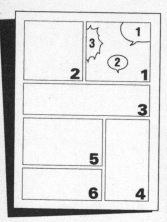

Whoops! Guess what? You're starting at the wrong end of the comic!

...It's true! In keeping with the original Japanese format, **One Piece** is meant to be read from right to left, starting in the upper-right corner.

Unlike English, which is read from left to right, Japanese is read from right to left, meaning that action, sound effects and word-balloon order are completely reversed...something which can make readers unfamiliar with Japanese feel pretty backwards themselves. For this reason, manga or Japanese comics published in the U.S. in English have sometimes been published "flopped"—that is, printed in exact reverse order, as though seen from the other side of a mirror.

By flopping pages, U.S. publishers can avoid confusing readers, but the compromise is not without its downside. For one thing, a character in a flopped manga series who once wore in the original Japanese version a T-shirt emblazoned with "M A Y" (as in "the merry month of") now wears one which reads "Y A M"! Additionally, many manga creators in Japan are themselves unhappy with the process, as some feel the mirror-imaging of their art skews their original intentions.

We are proud to bring you Eiichiro Oda's **One Piece** in the original unflopped format. For now, though, turn to the other side of the book and let the journey begin...!

—Editor

CALGARY PUBLIC LIBRARY
SEP   2014